Scottish Artists in an Age of Radical Change

1945 to the 21st century

interviews and essays by
BILL HARE

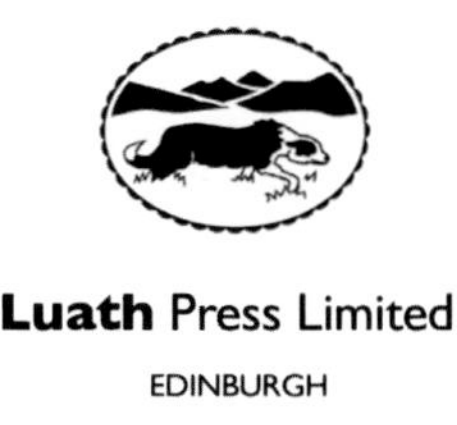

Luath Press Limited

EDINBURGH

www.luath.co.uk

First hardback edition published 2019
First paperback edition published 2022
Reprinted 2023, 2024, 2025

ISBN: 978-1-80425-017-4

The paper used in this book is recyclable. It is made from
low-chlorine pulps produced in a low-energy,
low-emission manner from renewable forests.

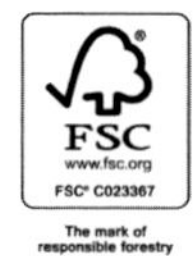

Printed and bound by
Robertson Printers, Forfar

Typeset in 10.5 point Sabon by
Main Point Books, Edinburgh

I would like to dedicate this book to my wife, Margaret Mary

Contents

Preface to the Second Edition

AS AUTHOR OF *Scottish Artists in an Age of Radical Change: 1945 to the 21st Century*, I am delighted that my book is going into a second edition. It is gratifying to find that there are a large number of people – readers and art lovers – who are interested in and admire Scottish modern and contemporary art, and wish to know more about it. I put a great deal of the success of this publication down to the fact that, with the many interviews found throughout the book, the reader appreciates the direct access to the invaluable primary source of the artists themselves. I also hope that my interpretive essays help to enlighten the reader on the nature and significance of Scottish art created since the Second World War.

In terms of content and presentation there is little change from the first to the second edition of this book. It is only with the cover that there is a marked differentiation between the two editions. The second has been brought out in softback and displays a different image from the first. It is on this difference in the choice of cover image that I would like to say a few words.

The cover image for the first edition was taken from Boyle Family's *World Series*; in this case, the only Scottish site from the 1,000 sites created for their epic global project. The reason for the choice of *Barra, Elemental Study (Rippled Sand with Worm Casts)* (1992–3) was based on the idea that when people picked up the book, they should feel that they had a little bit of Scotland in their hands. The cover image for the second edition, although hopefully just as attractive and intriguing as the first – Kevin Harman's *No Man's Land* (2016) – clearly has a different feel to it.

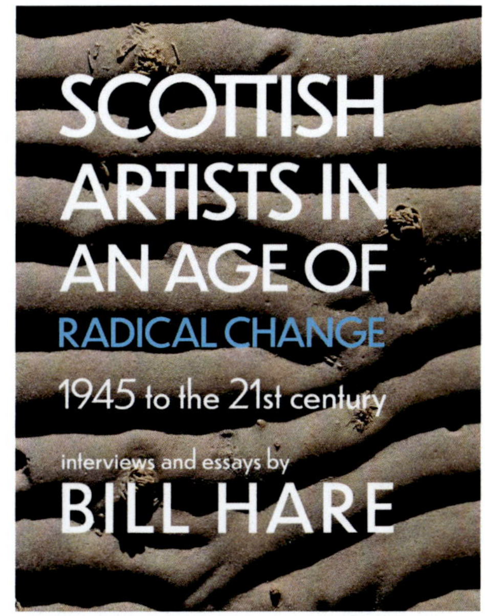

When these two works are compared there are striking differences, but also similarities. Starting with the latter, if you know anything about the work of Boyle Family and Kevin Harman, you will be aware that the role of chance plays a considerable role in both their practice. For instance, the locations of the 1,000 sites in the Boyles' *World Series* were found by inviting a thousand participants to throw a dart at a giant world map blindfolded. Thus it was chance, not premeditated design, which acted as the guiding hand. Kevin Harman's ongoing series of abstract paintings are also produced in a very unorthodox manner. These works are not the conventional paintings on canvas, but are made by a radically different method. Using as his framed support large and extremely heavy double-glazed windows, the artist, with the help of a strong assistant, pours layers of different coloured liquid paint down between the two panes of window glass. Then, again with much assistance, he arduously manipulates the window around into various positions in order to allow the paint inside the glass to find its own colour combinations. Thus, like Boyle Family who start with completely unknown sites, Harman adapts to and improvises with all the unforeseen and unpredictable chance elements in the process of making of his paintings.

There is, on the other hand, a marked difference in the presentation between the works of Boyle Family and Kevin Harman. One of the fundamental aims of Boyle Family's art is to reproduce the physical world as accurately and accessibly as possible. So when viewers stand in front one of their amazingly realistic relief panels it seems as if a small portion of the world's surface is laid bare before them for their direct and uninterrupted scrutiny. In contrast, by the very fact that Harman's paintings are created behind glass, means that there is a transparent barrier between the viewer and the image. In the case of *No Man's Land*, Leonbattista Alberti's analogy of a painting being a window is literally true!

The differences between these works, by two of the most innovative Scottish artists from different post-war generations, do raise the perennial crucial question – should artists strive to eradicate the distinction between reality and art, as with the case the ultra-realism of Boyle Family; or, as with the abstract window paintings of Kevin Harman, should art be autonomous, separate and protected from the world around it? All that being said, hopefully, you will find the appearance of both these works equally attractive and intriguing as cover images.

Bill Hare
August 2022

Foreword

Andrew Patrizio

IT IS A privilege to offer some opening remarks on what is a special and much needed new book, one that brings together in one place many of Bill Hare's writings on Scottish art. The range, vision and quality, exemplified in an extensive set of texts bursting with ideas and passionate intensity, is sure to inspire new generations of writers and curators, as it did me when I had the good fortune to work with Bill at the Talbot Rice Gallery in the 1980s. He was then Exhibitions Organiser at the University of Edinburgh's prestigious gallery and I was an undergraduate, then research student, needing gallery experience and money. What I got though was daily inspiration from Bill, as we mirror-plated paintings, heaved sculptures up the tight stairs, visited artist studios and put together catalogues. As we can read in this collection spanning over four decades, his curiosity is endless, his historical awareness is acute and his enthusiasm is infectious.

Bill Hare cuts a distinctive, not to say unique, profile in Scottish art in the ways he has blended curatorial work, teaching, journalism, art history and visual arts citizenship within Scotland. (He's an example par excellence of how to forge something meaningful over a diverse portfolio career – meeting with gusto the kind of challenge that faces younger generations in today's difficult cultural labour market.) Scotland's art landscape has been populated by some significant characters over the 20th century but I cannot think of anyone who has excelled in these roles in quite this way and kept the loyalty and camaraderie of numerous contemporary Scottish artists. There are some general characteristics and persistent themes that re-emerge in Bill's writing and are worthy of comment. He often uses as a touchstone and starting point the traditional notion of the artistic genre, in order to reflect on how an artistic practice might be understood. Can it be located within portraiture, landscape, history painting or still life? What inherent concepts within each genre might the artist be adopting, honouring, modifying, transforming or subverting. Another characteristic is that in all of his work he ensures that no isolated or essentialist notion of Scotland is offered; instead he explains how Scottish artists admix the specifics of place and nation with transnational urgencies and influences. And finally, it is impossible to miss his modest yet passionate engagement with artistic practice in his home country. I want to reflect on each of these themes here.

Bill is an advocate for Scottish art, in the sense that he champions the work of many artists he believes in and feels inspired and privileged to do so. The conviction in their work drives his writing to its own heights but never in a modish or sycophantic way. I think this is one of the reasons why Bill's writing style has a consistency of tone and language over the decades, although it has been enriched by an ever-expanding range of historical and theoretical sources, as we will see. This consistency, it seems to me, comes from his ability to channel his own appreciation towards such strikingly diverse artists, whose stylistic and ideological positions sometimes have nothing in common. The unity comes from shared levels of integrity, intensity and bravura that Bill identifies in those artists he feels most impelled to write about. That is his project and we are lucky to be able to share it ourselves through this book. For the most part, the writing takes the forms of the catalogue essay, the review article and the interview; and collectively represents what I would call an 'acclamatory journalism' of the highest quality.

Bill is also a natural teacher (as I have witnessed first-hand in the seminar room) not only evidenced through his writing but in his formal work at the University of Edinburgh, the Open University and in front of the great works on display at the National Galleries of Scotland. Many departments dedicated to teaching art history to students young and old and from all social demographics have benefited from his knowledge and commitment. He has numerous ex-students who stay in touch, invite him to write for them in their current positions and look for continued inspiration long after academic study has concluded. This collection of writings will of course also help other teachers to teach and learners to learn, particularly in the area of post-1945 Scottish art. We should all be grateful for that.

There is often a calibration in the texts that follow between the native dimensions of an artist's work, its place within a Scottish context, and the wider international and global histories in which the practice aspires to stand. Bill has written about many non-Scottish artists and is in no sense parochial in his interests. His thinking is entirely and, moreover, instinctively in tune with more recent challenges to local/global, parochial/international dualisms that are all too easily reached for, especially by those who assume a cosmopolitan outlook. Just like many of the Scottish artists Bill engages enthusiastically with, limited forms of nationalism do not inform his work.

Readers will surely appreciate the insights of someone who met and knew most of the key Scottish artists of the post-1945 period first-hand. They may also see that this period, whilst being its own golden age of Scottish visual art, drew on deeper intellectual and artistic foundations from Scotland and further afield. Since working more within the academic sector, particularly since the late 1990s, Bill's range of references has become as wide and inclusive as many of the artists he writes about. Hence the recurrence of the figures of major European theory that punctuate his writing – particular favourites being Freud, Jung and Laing, Lévi-Strauss, Barthes and Nietzsche. Those with a knowledge of such traditions will see, despite the diversity, a shared characteristic in these writers' passion and engagement – they represent the hot, urgent and engaged end of European critical thinking, full of affective resolve rather than cool abstraction and obscurantism.

Living as we do in increasingly globalised cultural landscapes, every writer needs to be assured that they can 'be equal to the moment' of art practice today. Grand visions and bold assertions sweep across Bill's writings in ways that defy standard journalism and reportage. It is certainly not a 'view from nowhere' but rather the view from an Edinburgh outlook tower, firmly founded yet able to look out to far horizons. He shows us what we are missing in art appreciation if we go no further than filling walls of bourgeois living rooms. He is, in other words, as ambitious for art as the artists are themselves.

The role of a writer such as Bill means he receives regular invitations to write journal articles, books and book chapters, exhibition reviews and catalogue introductions. One form that has particular value for Bill is the artist interview. The recorded encounter with an artist is peculiarly intense and complex; a meeting of minds where Bill can explore an individual's vision in all its specificity but can also speculate on wider contexts and interpretations beyond those of the artists themselves. As published records they also have a longer life, where readers can return to them anew over the decades. Some of the interviews Bill has done, for example with William Turnbull and Ken Currie, reveal moments of historical importance and contention in the history of Scottish art since 1945, filtered through one person's standpoint. I would also add that the artist interview is valued by Bill because it offers an almost uniquely respectful space for artists to communicate something of their intentions, beyond or as a supplement to the interpretations that other publics might bring to their work.

It will not be lost on readers just how wide the range of artists is that Bill has written about and/or encountered in person, starting with post-war giants such as Alan Davie, Joan Eardley, Eduardo Paolozzi and William Turnbull.

I have an entirely playful, if problematic, vision of Bill revelling (soft drink in hand, mind you) amongst such individuals in a drinking establishment – some hybrid of New York's Cedar Tavern and Edinburgh's Milne's Bar, with jazz piano weaving around darkened booths, within which Clement Greenberg and Jim Haynes buy in rounds of dry martini and McEwen's Export. He has brought his analytical eye to artists of the counter-culture such as Ian Hamilton Finlay and Boyle Family (the latter I would say inspiring probably his greatest writing). He has felt as engaged and curious regarding modes of figuration and realism as he has with another of his great enthusiasms – abstract art. Concerning the latter, artists such as John McLean, Fred Pollock and Iain Robertson have received concentrated and incisive attention. His time with the Scottish Sculpture Trust and the Federation of Scottish Sculptors left an indelible sensitivity to sculpture, including artists who deserve more recognition and attention than they have thus far received – artists like Bill Scott, John Kirkwood and Matthew Inglis, among others. I have particularly enjoyed reading Bill's writings in which he was able to express early enthusiasm for what became stellar careers, such as those of Steven Campbell and Douglas Gordon, where he skilfully draws out the indigenous reference points that international critics might easily miss or ignore. Finally he has offered critical support to emerging artists when their career trajectories were far from secure (such as Paul Reid, Helen Flockhart, Peter Thomson and Kevin Harman). Whilst this edited collection has only single texts on these artists, it is worth noting that Bill is incredibly loyal to those he respects, returning to reconsider their subsequent work, by invitation, on many occasions. Here again is evidence of his consistent support, earnest appreciation and unassuming camaraderie.

In reading and re-reading the writings contained in this book, more than anything I am struck by the enthusiasm conveyed in every word, expressing a commitment to artists' work that Bill is clearly in awe of. These writings are polemically and emphatically on the side of their subject. The expression of positive enthusiasm in writing is not trendy these days. Suppression of enthusiasm takes the shape of modish coolness and self-conscious positioning in certain sectors of the art establishment. Bill has none of that. But equally, when Bill was starting his life in the visual arts in 1970s Scotland, a more common form of approval was a taciturn nod over a pint after an exhibition opening. Bill is more expressive and less guarded than both those types – more Carlyle than Pater, more Spark than Massie. Certainly more Willie Bauld than Craig Levein. The artists he rates are, to him, larger than life. They grab the world with both hands and spin it on its axis. This mixture of baroque extravagance nuanced within an exacting intellectual lineage characterises how Bill understands the best art of his time.

If Bill's writing teaches me about keeping the heart and soul uppermost in interpreting visual art, he is also a model of respect for the work that artists do and the challenges they face (whether or not they enjoy successful careers in the generally accepted sense). This is reflected in how often that Bill mentions 'privilege' and 'pleasure' in the supporting commentaries and introductions here, when meeting artists in person or writing for them. This meeting in person united with his naturally modest disposition is key, I think, both to how he writes and also how artists welcome his words and insights. In the interviews, we can see that he is never trying to corner them, catch them out or distort their purpose. He is a sympathetic interlocutor, ever respectful of their intentions, helping them reach out to new audiences and interested fans. (Those who he is less intrigued or enthused by, he simply does not write about.) This way of writing has real integrity, as this very welcome and significant book amply proves on every page.

Professor Andrew Patrizio,
The University of Edinburgh,
July 2019

Introduction

Scottish Artists after 1945

I began to make a piece of sculpture to find out what a piece of sculpture should look like.
William Turnbull, 1992

AS THE TITLE indicates, this book is not intended as a history of Scottish art after 1945 – the interested reader can find that well provided elsewhere. Rather, this publication focuses on a number of the actual makers of that history – the creative artists themselves. Through the primary source material of in-depth interviews and supplementary critical commentaries, this book aims to give the reader access and insight into the complex and changing circumstances that these Scottish artists worked under and the artistic ambitions they set themselves during this extremely successful era of Scottish art after World War II.

In 1945, after the unspeakable horrors of yet another 20th century worldwide war, the previously dominant socio-political attitudes and aims of the so-called advanced nations around the globe had to change in intent and direction. This of course included Great Britain, which stood on the brink of one of the most turbulent eras in its history, with each subsequent decade from the 1940s onwards radically shifting in character and experience from that of its predecessor. The highly varied work of the Scottish artists in this book is testament to their response to much of the socio-political, economic, intellectual, technological and artistic changes that continuously occurred throughout the second half of the 20th century and into the 21st century. Thus the Scottish art produced in the 1940s and 1950s is marked by the post-war austerity and Cold War paranoia of the era. The rise of the consumer society and the counter-culture movement made its impact on the art of the 1960s. The cultural rebellion of the 'punk' 1970s and the social disaffection of the Thatcherite 1980s created their own highly critical artistic responses from Scottish artists. Finally, the electronic and digital mass communication age of the 1990s and early 21st century has now transformed the Scottish art scene beyond all recognition compared to its pre-war condition.

Yet despite the undoubted impact of these external socio-economic changes and technological revolutions, I feel that there is still a unifying aim and intent running through the work of the Scottish artists in this book, which is not only socio-political but also philosophical in the area of artistic creativity and aesthetics. By this I mean there is a common commitment to seek out and experimentally search for appropriate and relevant means to represent visually the ontological experience of what it is to be 'thrown' into this protean modern world. Here the artist is as much concerned with the means – the manipulated material selected – as by the critical message and aesthetic effect which is conveyed. To trace this fundamental social and artistic concern shared by these Scottish artists, it is necessary to go back to 1945 and the highly uncertain period after the unimaginable devastation brought about by the World War II.

The young progressive Scottish artists who emerged onto the art scene after the war were highly suspicious, if not downright hostile, to the inherited socio-political shibboleths and institutional dogmas of the pre-war past. On the art scene in Britain, that highly conservative attitude included a deep suspicion, if not hostility, to modern art by the majority of critics and public alike, which permeated through most of the English art colleges. In pre-war Scotland, things were a little different but, on the whole, modernism was mainly seen and eclectically treated as a ready-at-hand way to try out a range of fashionable modern art styles in a picturesque manner. Thus, if young and committed artists who came to the fore after 1945 were to engage seriously with their own experience of modernity in an appropriate representational visual language of modernism, they would have to look elsewhere – and they did. They toured war-torn Europe, lived and worked in Paris, turned to the exciting new art that was coming out of America and constantly sought out for creative examination the relevant art of the past. Full of intellectual inquiry and artistic ambition, they, unlike the older pre-war Scottish artists, did not take a subservient attitude to what was happening on the international modern art scene, but readily drew upon it to make their own individual and distinctive contributions. What distinguished their richly informed approach was the open and speculative nature of their artistic practice which was not intent on producing highly finished, tasteful aesthetic objects; but rather, using their art to present a raw instant of authentic phenomenological experience where the creative process, rather than skilful illusionism, was openly presented to the attentive viewer. To this end these artists drew the physical substance for their art from the vulgar and ready-at-hand material available to them, whether it was wire and cheap plaster, discarded mechanical rubbish, pulp magazine imagery or grass from the fields and sand from the beach. Their challenging, uncompromising work soon marked them out as a fresh and powerful presence on the British and international art scenes for perceptive critics, private patrons and the progressive art-interested public. They would all go on to develop successful careers and establish enduring reputations.

The major Scottish conceptual artists who came to the fore during the 1960s, had little formal art training and were from a literary background before moving to the visual arts. Their approach and engagement with the world was markedly different in manner and intent from the Scottish avant-garde artists of the previous two decades. Yet at the same time they inherited the same open attitude and shared a similar spirit of experimental enquiry in their art practice. In their case this took contrasting approaches, both in the choice and selection of subject-matter, as well as in their methods of creative practice. On the one hand the

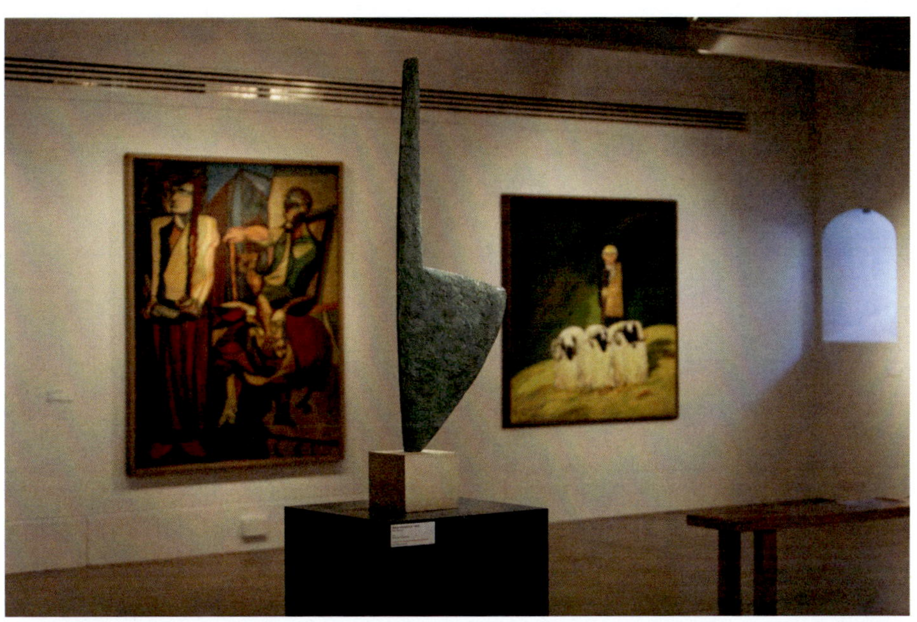

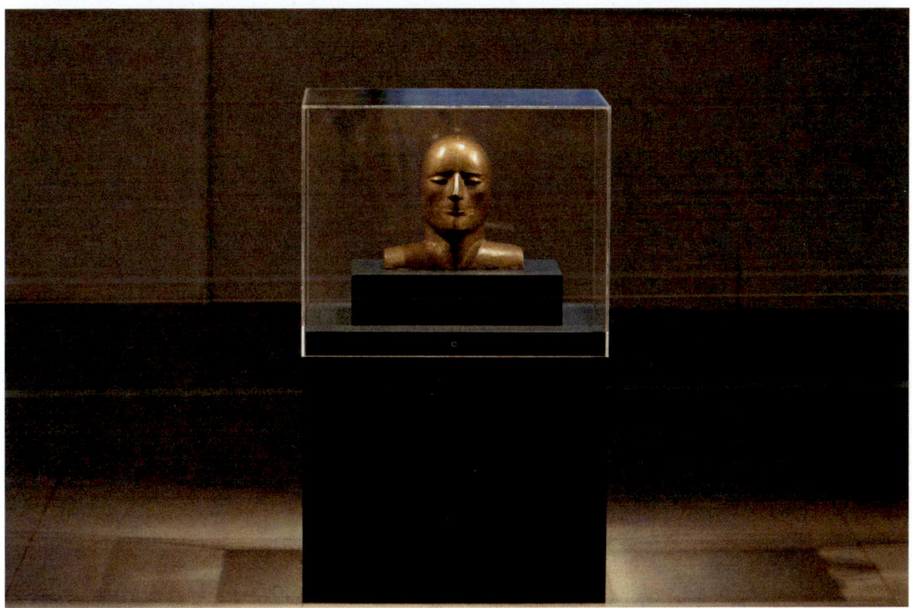

Installation photographs of *The Scottish Endarkenment* exhibition (2016). Top: showing (painting on the right) John Bellany's *The Ettrick Shepherd*, 1967; and William Turnbull's sculpture *Small Blade Venus*, 1989. Bottom: showing Eduardo Paolozzi's *Mr Cruikshank*, 1950.

Reproduced courtesy of Dovecot Studios Photographer: Stuart Armitt

family group wanted to include 'everything' in their art and so developed an all-encompassing strategy which allowed anything on the Earth's surface to become a possible subject for their empirical scientific studies and their highly mimetic replicating process. While the family group were intent on engaging with the whole world out there, the concrete poet, situated and fixed on a bleak Scottish hillside, set out to create his own enclosed world in the form of a landscape garden which he entitled Little Sparta. Furthermore, while the family group wished to keep any political attitudes or personal views and taste out of their completely neutral work, the poet used his classical garden as a visual polemic to discourse critically – and frequently controversially – on a wide range of historical and contemporary issues. In contrast to the family group who took a decidedly hands-on working approach to the shared making of their art, the poet saw himself as the intellectual source and powerhouse of his art and was pleased to delegate the actual physical making of it to skilled collaborators.

To qualify as Scottish for inclusion in this book, the artists should be at least one of three things – either they have been born and bred in Scotland, lived and worked in Scotland for the greater part of their careers and/or were educated at a Scottish art college. On the latter issue, most of the artists who came to the fore after the end of the 1960s did attend art college. This is indicative that art education was now becoming less academic and more liberal – more open and experimental in its approach. Yet up to the 1980s at least, students were still encouraged to develop their optical and graphic skills in the life class. This particular aspect of Scottish art college training consequently fed into figurative painting which has continued to remain a predominant feature of Scottish modern and contemporary art. Back in the 1960s, figurative painting was seen by many to be in crucial competition with abstraction, especially in the form of Abstract Expressionism; and although it survived and subsequently thrived, the best figurative painters drew upon and incorporated into their practice many of the features of abstract painting, from free gestural brushwork to rich colour-field compositional design.

In the hands of a number of Scottish artists, figuration was set the task of visually addressing the socio-economic realities of the politically turbulent decades of the 1970s and 1980s. As can be seen from the artists working during this period, their art could have an overtly critical intent – whether dealing with such issues as economic and physical deprivation, national and communal identity, the threat of nuclear annihilation or, more generally, the collapse of the last remaining vestiges of any kind of stable social infrastructure and community in post-industrial Britain. There were also other dimensions to figurative painting, with its rediscovered potential in expressive power. It could also now address a wide range of different aspects of the human psyche which had long been suppressed; from Calvinist guilt complexes to female oppression under patriarchal domination. On the latter issue, many Scottish women painters shared a common concern by focusing their artistic and critical attention on the inherited representation of the female body in the history of art as their central subject and developing a variety of strategies to deconstruct its cultural and social authority. Scottish modern figurative painting also played an important role in helping to revive and give new vitality and fresh possibilities to the long-time moribund genre of portrait painting.

While figuration has remained the dominant mode of artistic expression in post-war Scottish art, abstraction was not by any means sidelined. During the inter-war years, for instance, Scottish artists pioneered and made important contributions to the early development of abstract art in Britain. After the war, Scottish artists continued to work in an abstract mode but mostly in London, as there was little critical appreciation or public understanding of abstraction north of the border. In the 1960s, an important group of Scottish abstract painters gravitated towards the Stockwell Depot studio complex in London which soon became the main powerhouse for the best contemporary abstract art in Britain. In the initial stages of their work, these Scottish abstract painters were influenced by transatlantic abstraction, which was being heavily promoted in the 1960s, but all of the group subsequently went on to develop their own distinctive mode of abstract painting. They gradually began to create such notable artistic and critical reputations that the highly influential American art critic Clement Greenberg visited their studios and promoted their work through his writings. A number of these Scottish abstract painters are now regarded as notable figures in the canon of British abstract art. In the subsequent decades from the 1970s onwards, younger Scottish abstract painters continued to emerge. On the whole, their work is marked by being more intellectually considered and austere, with intellectual rigour now playing as important a role than that of expressive spontaneity. The immensely important contribution that Scottish artists have made to the history of abstract art has unfortunately still to be duly recognised. A major Scottish abstract art exhibition is long overdue.

It was not only in modern painting that Scottish artists made a conspicuous contribution to post-war British art but also in the area of sculptural practice. This again initially took place in London. North of the border, almost all sculptors, because of the economics involved in making three-dimensional work, had to have a regular income to supplement their art. Thus, most practising Scottish sculptors also taught their craft at one of the four main art colleges. From the 1960s onwards, however, there was a marked increase in the support for sculptural activities, with more outlets for sculptors to display their work in sculpture parks and at sculpture exhibitions, along with more public and private sculpture commissions as new urban schemes came into being and large corporate headquarters were established. Conventional sculpture as practised in the past was seriously challenged throughout the post-war period, especially with the introduction of new kinds of materials and equipment which enterprising sculptors were starting draw upon. Furthermore, the previously traditional figure-dominated subject matter which sculptors were previously obliged to work within was greatly expanded after the 1960s. For instance, Scottish sculptors could now take on a wide array of socio-political themes and issues, which had previously been the almost total prerogative of painters. In fact, the previous clear demarcation line between these two art practices has, over the last few decades, been gradually blurred and almost swept away, particularly with the innovation and wide use of new modes of artistic format, such as installation, performance and time-based practices involving photography and film. In fact, the younger contemporary Scottish artists are just as likely to work in the intangible mediums of time, space, light and sound as in the more traditional solid materials of stone, metal or wood. Again this allows for a much more open, flexible and experimental approach to the making of their art. This I believe has been the predominant characteristic of the most innovative, challenging and stimulating work produced by the best Scottish artists since 1945.

Today, Scottish art still retains a very creative, innovative and ambitious outlook – 'the country is on the move', to quote the late Bob Callender. This healthy condition is much due to the facilities and infrastructure that support art-making in Scotland. These include well-equipped artists' workshops; extensive studio accommodation; artist-run galleries showing exciting new work; much expanded multi-disciplinary courses at Scottish art colleges; a rejuvenated Royal Scottish Academy; an involved and supportive Scottish National Gallery of Modern Art; Scottish universities that have now developed a more comprehensive attitude towards the visual arts in Scotland; and a plethora of art galleries up and down the country exhibiting and selling modern and contemporary art to a much more informed and appreciative public. All of these encouraging developments have proved to be very successful and rewarding investments. As I hope this book shows, thanks to a range of factors – most importantly, the achievements of the artists themselves – the visual arts throughout the post-war era have made an invaluable contribution to the socio-cultural wellbeing of modern and contemporary Scotland. With all our support and encouragement, long may it continue.

Bill Hare
July 2019

Section One
Four Post-War Artists

Alan Davie (1920–2014)
Joan Eardley (1921–63)
William Turnbull (1922–2012)
Eduardo Paolozzi (1924–2005)

AS WITH MILLIONS of others, World War II disrupted and redirected the lives of the four artists in this section. Alan Davie and William Turnbull, respectively, saw service in the Army and Air Force. Eduardo Paolozzi, because of his Italian origins, was interned briefly as an enemy alien in Saughton Prison, Edinburgh and later discharged from the Army on psychological grounds. As an art student, Joan Eardley was evacuated at the outbreak of the Blitz from Goldsmiths Art College, London, to Glasgow School of Art.

After the war, Davie was granted a travelling scholarship by Edinburgh College of Art. He ended up in Venice at the time of the 1948 Biennale and there met the celebrated modern art patron Peggy Guggenheim, and with her encouragement began his career with the renowned Gimpel Fils Gallery, London. His paintings from the 1950s onwards drew great public attention and critical admiration, and secured him an international reputation as one of Britain's outstanding modern painters.

I first came in contact with Alan Davie when I was asked to select and curate a British Council international touring exhibition, *Alan Davie – Works on Paper*, in 1992. As Davie had always been a prolific artist, there was an immense amount of material from which to choose. The exhibition proved a great success in all the many counties it was shown and turned out to be the longest running international touring exhibition that the British Council ever organised. I later kept up my contact with Alan Davie through 108 Fine Art in Harrogate, where I wrote catalogue essays for a couple of large exhibitions that he had there in 2006 and 2015.

At the end of the war, Eduardo Paolozzi was studying at the Ruskin School in Oxford for a year, and in 1945 he moved to the Slade in London. It was there that he first met William Turnbull, who was recently demobbed from the Air Force. Both were dissatisfied with the teaching there and also with the post-war London art scene in general. They decided to further their art education and artistic ambitions by going to Paris, where they visited the studios of such modern masters as Giacometti, Arp and Brâncusi. On returning to London, they found the austere post-war conditions hard, but both managed to secure teaching positions (along with Alan Davie) at the Central School of Art through the support of the Principal, William Johnstone, a fellow Scottish artist. Both Paolozzi and Turnbull were included in Herbert Read's famous 'Geometry of Fear' group of young sculptors who were shown in the British Pavilion at the Venice Biennale of 1952. They also became prominent members of the very influential Independent Group based at the ICA in London and put on radically innovative exhibitions throughout the 1950s. Paolozzi and Turnbull went on to have very successful careers, abroad and in Britain, where, later in their careers, they both had major retrospective exhibitions at the Tate Gallery.

I first met Eduardo Paolozzi when my colleague Andrew Patrizio and I were commissioned by the Scottish art magazine, *Alba*, to interview him to coincide with the Edinburgh Science Festival in 1988. In the following year, for the same festival, Paolozzi had a major exhibition, *Nullius in Verba*, at the Talbot Rice Gallery, the University of Edinburgh, where I worked throughout the 1980s. I later had the privilege of writing the proposal speech on behalf of Paolozzi being awarded an Honorary Degree from Edinburgh College of Art in 2005.

Sadly for me, I never met William Turnbull. Unlike many other London-based Scottish artists, he never tried to build up his reputation north of the border and so there was little opportunity to see his work in Scotland, let alone meet with him. Being a great admirer of Turnbull's art, I did, however, managed to get commissioned by the Fleming Collection magazine, *Scottish Art News*, to do an interview by correspondence with him in 2013. By then, Turnbull was very frail, but with the invaluable help of his son Alex, we managed to put together William Turnbull's last but extremely informative interview.

Joan Eardley's status as a major figure in the Scottish post-war art scene has been growing since her early death in 1963. After leaving Glasgow School of Art, she made the heroic decision, not only to become a full-time artist, but to remain and work in one of the most deprived urban areas in Scotland. Here she developed her own take on modern realism with her Glasgow street painting which distinguished her work from the fashionable 'kitchen sink' realism being promoted on the London art scene in the mid-1950s. About that time, she discovered the small fishing village of Catterline on the Aberdeenshire coast and introduced expressionist landscape and semi-abstract seascapes into her repertoire. My professional contact with her work was through her great champion, Cordelia Oliver, who had known Eardley since their days at Glasgow School of Art in the 1940s. She was preparing a book, the first monograph on Joan Eardley, and so a major retrospective exhibition at the Talbot Rice Gallery was organised for the Edinburgh Festival of 1988. After that exhibition, I wrote an essay on Eardley's work for *Cencrastus* magazine (issue 31) entitled 'Street Kids and Stormy Seas'.

Alan Davie

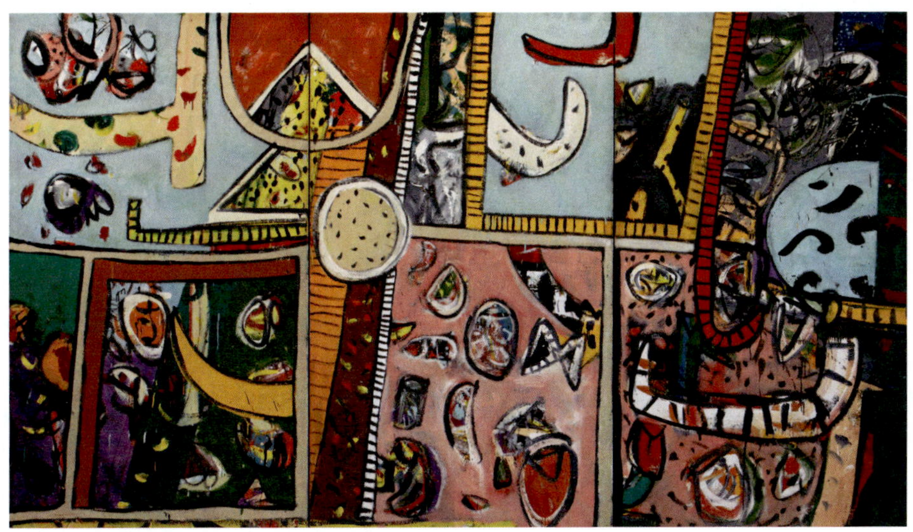

Kaleidoscope for a Parrot
1966
Oil on canvas, 190x300cm

Reproduced courtesy of the artist's estate and The University of Edinburgh Collection

Alan Davie Interview

Could you start by explaining what the particular attractions are for you in painting on paper?
One isn't so self-conscious about working on paper compared with doing a big painting. If a big painting doesn't come off, you're lumbered with the object. You can't just tear it up and put it in the waste paper basket as you can with paper.

But the main reason is that working on paper is more fluid. When working, one's using one's wrist and fingers, whereas on a big canvas one is using the whole body. You see the whole thing much more easily. The medium itself is so mysterious, so inspirational. All you have to do is soak colour on to a piece of paper and all sorts of exciting things happen, which you can never do in oil paint. One can do dozens of small things very quickly and spontaneously.

Has working on paper always been an important aspect of your artistic creativity?
Not really. I started working seriously on paper in 1962. The large-scale work of the 1950s was in oil. The works on paper that I did do in the 1950s were individual works in their own right.

What is your work routine throughout the year now?
For many years I've worked in a regular rhythm – six months working on paper and six months in oils. Almost a kind of seasonal thing. In the same way, especially nowadays, my wife, Bili, and I have a migratory way of life. We follow the sun, going to St Lucia in the winter, then in the spring we come back to England. So there's a seasonal rhythm in the work. I always go back to the West Indies to a completely empty studio and start with works in black gouache. I draw in a very primitive, direct way, making black marks on paper with a brush. Extraordinary things happen, magical things appear seemingly out of nowhere. Obviously one is unlocking all sorts of subconscious images – a really exciting process. Drawing is the most intuitive medium. I think the thing which triggered off my interest in brush drawing was seeing the prehistoric Egyptian pottery decoration in the British Museum – some wonderful designs in black brush. Drawing is one of the oldest, most primitive and dynamic forms of art.

So drawing has become a vitally important part of the way you work?
It's never the case in my work of having an idea first and then putting it on paper. The idea comes out of working. I do a whole series of drawings on an idea which has presented itself. I might do about 20 variations using that idea and developing it. It is very much like improvising on a piano – sitting down and playing, an idea will appear out of putting one note against another, which leads to other notes and, before you know

where you are, a melodic line has appeared, and a harmonic structure presents itself.

Are there other ways in which you generate ideas when working on paper?

Well, for example, sometimes I see something in a book, an image which excites me enormously, and I might incorporate it into a drawing. One finds a kind of imagery which is archetypal, as Jung would say. This is the sort of thing one recognises in primitive art – this archetypal symbol which speaks to different civilisations. I discover the same types of symbols in my own automatic drawings, which is astonishing. For instance, I find myself doing concentric circles and spirals and other signs and symbols which one finds in ancient cultures. So one realises one is getting involved in something timeless, something which has great significance throughout different ages and different cultures.

You've talked about the seasonal rhythm in the way you work, between working on paper and oil. Could you tell us about the relationships between your works on paper and your oil painting?

I develop the ideas in drawings then I decide to try it in colour. So I would go to a bigger scale with gouache. After using the imagery which has appeared through this automatic process, it followed to make colour images, which are often quite different. A black and white drawing creates illusions of space. When you put a black mark on a white surface, you have an object which is floating in space – it has a strange spatial quality. Now, as soon as you fill the white spaces with colours, something else happens. You have extraordinary relationships between one colour and another. Then you get another dimension again when the gouaches are translated into big oils. Quite often it's very close to the image, but the actual scale changes the concept of the work. You've got the quality of oil paint which is very different from watercolour which has a translucent quality. In watercolours, the light is going through the transparent paint on to the paper then coming back to you. In oil paint, the actual bits of opaque pigment catch the light and reflect back the colour. So the whole process is an organic development and an absolutely fantastic adventure. It's beyond oneself, it comes out of something from inside oneself, a setting free of universal imagery, not just purely of me, but having meaning on a human scale which is timeless really.

What one is aiming to do is release some kind of complex image which is going to be charged, exciting and stimulating. So when I discover drawings which have this dynamic quality which interests me, as soon as they are done, I hang them up around my studio walls, so it all becomes a part of my environment. They become exciting things to live with. One of the basic things with me and my work is that I'm making a constantly changing environment. The critical faculty gets developed as I go on working, and the images around me act as a stimulus and as a catalyst for fresh ideas.

What are the deciding factors when you choose to develop paper into an oil? Some of them don't go through that whole process?
When one looks at a small drawing one often can visualise what might happen if you blow it up on a big scale. Others are so complete and final in themselves that they do not suggest this. It's just as simple as that.

Can we turn to one of your major sources of inspiration – why do you think you are so attracted to primitive and non-western art?
It's very difficult to explain. There are certain images in art (it doesn't matter where the art comes from), which are incredibly moving for some unknown reason. The things in art which are most moving for me are the arts of so-called primitive people, art of other cultures and ancient art, right back to the Stone Age. Particularly in the primitive art there seems to be some kind of spiritual intensity, if one can call it that. And it's that kind of intensity which I feel all great art should have, in fact all great art has it. I mean, Picasso, Rembrandt, Uccello, Trecento painting, right back. It always has to have that. Primitive art also has this dynamic quality, intuition and a tremendous intensity.

The word 'primitive' is used and misused quite frequently. What is your definition of it?
Primitive art is anything but primitive. For instance, if you study prehistoric cave art, you see that these people were not all that primitive. They have produced some of the most refined drawings in the whole history of art.

   Of course, all great art, all primitive art is used for spiritual purposes. There is no such thing in primitive art as art-for-art's-sake. The important thing for all these tribal peoples is that art has a spiritual life in the community. This is what I feel. I always maintain that I don't practise art, I don't make art. What I'm involved in is almost a kind of spiritual exercise, really. What comes out of this should have an intense spiritual content.

How do you see the relationship between your paintings and the subject matter and iconography of the primitive art that inspires you?
They're basically the same. The artist in the past or in primitive societies is a kind of shaman, the man who is the spiritual leader, he's the priest, and he's the man who comes between everyday life and spirit life. He links the mysterious elements of the universe with the everyday, conscious living, brings them all together. I feel the artist is still a shaman, able to enter this spiritual realm and produce these fantastic images out of the unconscious, or the spirit world. But in our own civilisation, people have left the artist, although he's still in the same position, he's still in touch with the spirits but on the whole people think he's just a crank. On the other hand, the fact that the art galleries are thronged again means that a lot of people have this need still. I think what people get from art as they go round galleries enthusiastically is this spiritual enlightenment. But, on the whole, people think anything spiritual is just hoo-ha.

Obviously the appearance of your paintings has changed over your career but have your concerns remained the same?
Well, my paintings have an organic life. It's something which happens only gradually. In the last couple of weeks, for example, I've been doing paintings which look as though they've been painted in the 1950s. It's always a matter of stylistic character. It's something which evolves, I don't think one consciously thinks about this sort of thing. Evolution is something purely organic and happens in irrational leaps. It develops along its own lines. Looking at some of my earliest work, the qualities of paint in my first self-portrait are very close to qualities which you find in the work now. It's quite extraordinary. The use of black came from the very start. Very strong black outlines came very quickly, straight away. I didn't have to think about it. These things seemed to be inherent in myself.

The main break which launched me towards thinking about painting was that my father had a whole collection of books, mainly impressionist, in the house. I used to sit and pore over these things. I was absolutely fascinated. I'd never seen any real art at all. I became enthralled by van Gogh and Cézanne and Gauguin. The qualities which these painters had soaked into in my mind, so as soon as I started painting, I was painting these qualities sort of instinctively. So obviously I recognised something in these painters' work; something which was inherent in myself.

Broadly speaking, what is the relationship between the main themes and concerns in your work and the way you paint them?
Well, there's no difference at all really. When the work's going well, the actual style, content and technique have to be completely unified. This is the thing both when you're working and looking at a work of art. One is aware of the technique, quality of paint, subject matter, relationships of colour and the spiritual intensity but it all comes together. Quite often when one is working, certain elements come separate, you become very involved with a certain area where the colour quality isn't right, or a certain area where the drawing of the shapes doesn't quite work. But when the thing's working properly, one's not aware of any difference between the drawing, the quality of the paint and the subject matter.

Have you ever considered yourself as an abstract painter?
No, not really. At one stage I had this vision in my mind – a painting that was completely devoid of form and had no brilliant colour. It was just a very vague notion – an image, a magical thing without any form at all. However, when you make marks on a surface, for me anyway, you can't make a mark without it taking on some kind of significance, some kind of symbolic quality. Even the very movements you make with an arm and a brush automatically make forms like circles, squares or triangles. Now one might think these are abstract but to me there is, even in a circle, a kind of magic about it. So one begins to realise that the circle could be

an ancient symbol, which could mean all sorts of strange things. From earliest times I've felt this, so for that reason I've never felt attracted to pure abstraction. It seemed to me a completely dead art – an arrangement of cold forms on a surface. However, in a painting by Mondrian, for example, I always felt this isn't abstract art, this is sheer magic. How can one explain that? I walk into an art gallery and I see a Mondrian, I say, 'My God!' It takes me into mysterious spaces. In the next room, I see an abstract painting which is just completely dead, just an arrangement of forms on a surface. Mondrian has something else. Perhaps there is no such thing as abstract art.

If you don't consider yourself an abstract painter, what is the relationship between your paintings and the immediate, everyday world?
I'm very involved in the outside world. We do a lot of gardening, swimming, sailing and walking. However, although I get enormously excited about trees and birds and animals, I've never taken it into my head to put all that down in paint. What I get from nature is the same as what I get from art. A kind of revelation of something beyond myself. I get completely saturated by just pure living. For me painting isn't the only thing. There are so many other activities where I'm involved in the same state of pure living. Swimming underwater, when one becomes a fish virtually; it's not a case of being like a fish, but from time to time one really experiences being part of the sea. Life comes from the sea and there is something very magical about being underwater. One suddenly has this contact with the beginning of life itself, in that water – one's taken into that mysterious, fantastical, mystical thing.

Your later work has the appearance of being more considered and controlled than the paintings you were producing in the 1950s and '60s. Does that mean that the role of intuition and improvisation has become less important in your working method?
No, it's not true really. In the early works, improvisation happened in the actual paintings. So many ideas would apply in the one work. Eventually, most of them would be destroyers. I suppose it had a lot to do with youthful exuberance, feeling that, through sheer physical well-being, I could pull the thing off. There was an awful lot of wastage. So when one gets older one gets more patient, so that there still is as much improvisation now but most of it goes on in the drawing stage.

The finished result looks as if it's highly contrived and controlled but it's not the case at all. It's come through a long process of errors, mistakes, struggles, trials and tribulations.

How, then, have the opposites of freedom and control operated in your work over the years?
I think our notions of liberation and being completely free are a kind of dead end. It's like all notions of freedom. In the modern world the

struggle is when nationalities get free, all sorts of chaos sets in and you get many kinds of problems. So freedom isn't the greatest thing in the world really. I often think that the artist is too free. We had the notion in the 1950s and 1960s that complete freedom was the thing. We'd give up all the traditional nonsense and techniques, and we'd work completely free, just from ourselves, just by direct work with paint. To do this many of us worked on the floor – like Jackson Pollock. With liquid paint and a big brush, we'd cover an enormous canvas very quickly. You could get all these qualities coming from liquid paint flowing into each other, just like watercolour. But that kind of freedom, I realised very quickly, was too restricting. I knew Jackson Pollock very intimately just the year before he died. He'd got to that stage where he'd given up painting, he realised that just throwing paint on the canvas was so restricting. In some of the later paintings, he was actually trying to draw – he was drawing heads and things. In order to create new forms and new ideas you had to curb your freedom. By all means you had to use freedom in the gestation of the process but working within restrictions can be so much more productive.

What about your recent use of extended passages from books in foreign languages, as well as English? How is the written word adapted in your paintings?
It's not supposed to have any specific meaning. If I put writing in my work, I am adding another dimension, an element of poetry.

I became very interested in books on primitive art, particularly Indian and Caribbean. I was very interested in the petroglyphs of the Carib Indians, these engravings in stone. I was tremendously excited by these images. So I started making a really extensive study of this art, did a lot of research, and the energy from some of these things crept into my own work. I don't really read Spanish but it seemed to be a very poetic and immediately expressive language. I started writing Spanish quotations from these books on the Caribs into these paintings. There's something very lovely about lettering in a pictorial image. It's something that you find in illuminated manuscripts that I've always loved. It's so very different from just making decorative marks across a painting. If the marks take on the form of actual, readable words it seems to add a poetic dimension: a combination of poetry and painting. Some of the words don't make sense, from the point of view of the actual subject matter of the painting, but this is all to the good because it gives you a sort of complementary other image which contrasts with the image of the painting.

Do you find that texts in the works, for example in the Hopi Studies, make the link more obvious to the source?
The funny thing is that in the *Hopi Studies* these are taken from a 19th century book on Hopi Indian art and ceramics design. The book actually describes what these images were derived from – bird forms or whatever. I actually wrote some quotations of these descriptions in the Hopi paintings. There is a very interesting distinction between writing in the

earlier paintings which is so irrational and not connected to the images I was painting. In the later paintings, there are actual descriptions of the elements in the painting. But apart from the literal meaning, the script conveys a magical quality.

Is this because you want people to be more aware?
No. Painting for me is a purely personal thing. I have no consideration about who's going to look at the picture – it never enters my mind. But it still basically adds up in the end that the lettering in the paintings has a mysterious quality. I mean, after all, the elements of writing are derived from very ancient pictographs. Each letter we use in everyday life in our writing or our printing is derived from a very ancient pictograph. To me, letters in the alphabet are magical things, words are magical. They can unlock all sorts of mysteries.

This interview was conducted by Andrew Patrizio and Bill Hare in 1992 for the British Council's publication *Alan Davie – Works on Paper.*

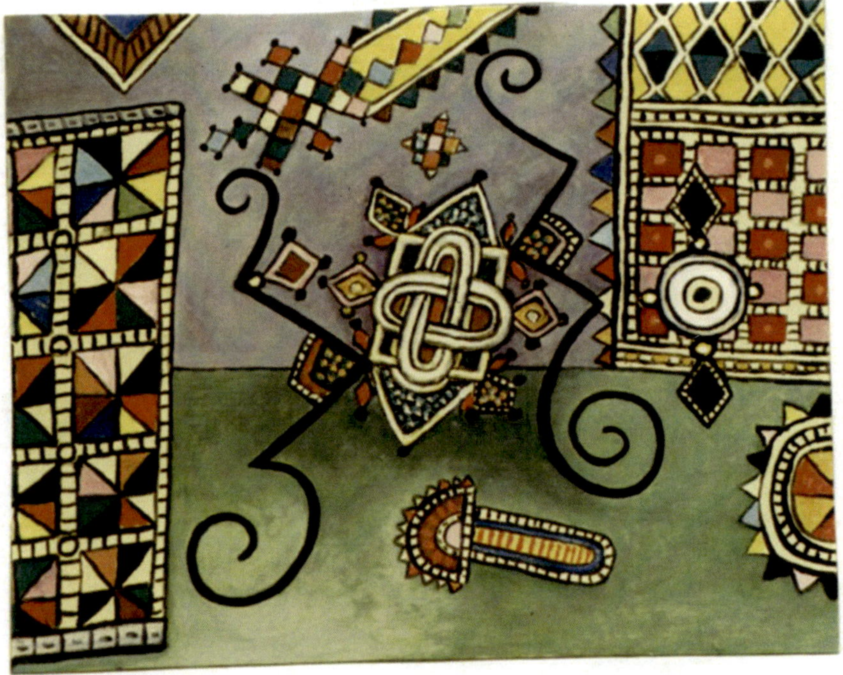

Daidling Dance
1996
Oil on board, 39x48cm
Reproduced courtesy of the artist's estate and 108 Gallery, Harrogate

Disintegrating Targets

Art and Anti-Art in the Work of Alan Davie

The Work of Art seems to be something thrown off – a by-product of the process of being and working. Art just happens…
Alan Davie, *Notes by the Artist* (1958)

I don't practise painting as an Art but a means to enlightenment.
Alan Davie, *Towards a Philosophy of Creativity* (1997)

THE WIDE RANGE of works produced by Alan Davie over the last six decades or so, demonstrates the many different modes and diverse styles of painting which he has practised and produced throughout his long and prodigious career as 'the most remarkable British artist to have emerged in recent years' (*The Times*, 1958). Over the years we can move from Davie's brief engagement with the formal language of cubism in an early work, *Moonlit Tree* (1948), through his own distinctive take on surrealist automatism and gestural abstraction in *Disintegrated Target* (1960), to his later ethnographic pictures, for instance *Study for a Mask, No. 14* (1975). Such a rich and complex stylistic development clearly marks Alan Davie out as one on the most inventive and challenging practitioners of later 20th century painting.

In contrast to the very discernible changes in the constantly evolving stylistic appearance of Davie's painting practice, his own artistic statements – which he regularly produced throughout his career – have a remarkable consistency to them. Not only will Davie express the same ideas and views repeatedly over the years and even decades, but he will regularly use the same phrases and words to do so. This is not, I hasten to add, due in any way to some limitation or inadequacy in his powers of critical expression. It should be remembered that Davie was also a poet – as much a master of words as of paint – and his repetitious mantras were a reinforcement of his unswerving commitment to his own 'philosophy of creativity' which was the firm foundation of not only his art, but also the way he lived his life. That being the case, how then do we reconcile the contrast – some might say the contradiction – between the consistency of what Alan Davie said and wrote about his art and the marked changes in appearance of the art which he created in his studio over more than seven decades?

To address this intriguing question and attempt to resolve this challenging conundrum, it is necessary to examine the central concept of the 'personal' at the heart of Alan Davie's work. On the one hand, he states that 'Painting for me is a purely personal thing' (1992). Yet on the other, in a seemingly contradictory mode, Davie also famously declared four decades earlier in his *Notes by the Artist* (1958) that

'Self-expression is something contrary to art': an idea which most people – through the widely accepted notions of the deeply expressive nature of modern art – would find very surprising, if not truly baffling. In order to accommodate this seeming contradiction, it is necessary to distinguish between the concepts of 'self-expression' and 'self-discovery'. In contrast to this antipathy to 'self-expression', Davie's art is driven by a quest for 'self-discovery' and understanding. He makes this clear with his answer to his self-imposed question, 'Why do I paint? I paint simply to find enlightenment and revelation' (1957), and again in his *Towards a Philosophy of Creativity* (1997) he declares, 'I don't practise painting as an Art but a means to Enlightenment'. Of course, this does not mean that Davie's art has an autobiographical intent in any conventional sense, but rather it records and traces a psychic and spiritual journey involving both personal and archetypal development through a long and deeply involving process of 'becoming what one is'. That phrase is from the writings of the psychologist/mystic, Carl Jung, who had a long-lasting and profound influence on Davie and his art practice.

If Davie's art and career are studied in the light of Jung's transcendental views of the human mind and universal experience, then the seeming contradictions between what he adheres to in his theoretical writings and what flows out of him as he paints begin to form a congenial and organic relationship. This journey of self-discovery – or 'individuation' as Jung termed it – occurs later in a person's life, after all the raw confusions and uncertainties of childhood and youth have been passed through. All evidence indicates that for Davie, after his art college (1937–40) and wartime (1941–5) experiences were over, his life-long journey of self-discovery began during his artistic pilgrimage around Europe in 1948–9.

The first of stages of this spiritual and psychological process of personal enlightenment begins with a great urge to attack and destroy all imposing authorities which stand in the way of a new understanding of self and individual creative freedom. We can see this manifesting itself in Davie's dismissal of orthodox art education – 'At Edinburgh College of Art I learned to hate Art' (1963) – a view which he later reinforced with: 'The real purpose of art teaching for me is the liberation of the human spirit – not the production of artists' (1997). This destructive yet at the same time liberating attitude was also directed at the contemporary post-war art scene in London where he found 'that which I am seeking is not here... what a mass of ugly rubbish is on show here under the name of Art' (1948). Davie's critical eye was, however, not a closed but a highly receptive one, and what was capturing his serious attention in his travels on the continent was a mixture of ancient art – early Christian/Byzantine mosaics, Romanesque church architecture; and modern art – Arp and Klee's biomorphism, surrealist automatism and the abstract expressionists' radically different methods of painting. All these features can be seen to a greater and lesser degree in his early work. At that time Davie wrote to his father from his European journey of discovery, 'I am amazed... my work is becoming something very strange' (1948).

After their return to Britain, the Davies (Alan was accompanied on his tour of Europe by his wife, Bili, whom he had recently married) initially lived and worked in the Abbey Art Centre at New Barnet for about a year or so. As this artistic community was a place that was ideal for his newly discovered creative adventure and interdisciplinary experimentation – including monoprinting, jewellery making and kinetic sculpture – Davie had the opportunity to develop and greatly expand on the innovative possibilities that he had initiated on the continent. Later he was to write:

> At that time I think my work was related to Paul Klee and Arp (rather than abstract expressionists like Pollock) – they had a poetic feeling and a childlike magic which was closest to my own feeling.

That 'childlike' state of pure and intuitive creativity can be linked to a painting like *Baby* (1949), which might also be a celebration of the birth of the Davies' daughter Jane that year. One might argue that at this stage Davie was seeking an imaginative return to a romantic state of pure uncorrupted creative innocence and wonderment, an ideal which he determinately strove to maintain throughout his subsequent career.

At the Abbey Art Centre, Davie also came in contact with Oriental mystical ideas and an ethnographic collection which must have inspired Davie's life-long passion for prehistoric and non-western art. With his newly found enlightened attitudes, he was in total accord with the nature of such esoteric beliefs and human creativity which he described in an interview in 1990:

> All great art, all primitive art is used for spiritual purposes. The artist in the past or in primitive societies is a kind of shaman who links the mysterious elements of the universe with the everyday.

This 'spiritual purpose' became the constant core belief of Davie's concept of art but, to take on the role of artist/shaman, there would need to be a difficult process involving the destruction of the artist's egotistic self. In Jungian terms, this involves coming to terms with, and confronting, one's persona and with its 'shadow'. This is the dark and dangerous side of one's personality that lies deep in the shadowland of personal unconscious.

This struggle and striving for liberation from the controlling powers of inner self and outer secular authority were fought out in Davie's canvases of the 1950s – as exemplified by such works as *Untitled* (1954), where the cursorily drawn silhouetted figure is threatened by all enveloping imprisoning forces, or *Homage to the Black Snake* (1957) which is full of awe and dread for the ever-threatening untamed forces that lurk in the depths of the human mind and history, but must be released and confronted if psychological and spiritual liberty is to be achieved. This destructive/creative dynamic that was the internal driving force for Davie's artistic development reached its climax in the early 1960s, when his output was exceptionally prodigious with up to 200 major canvases in a year. In *Disintegrated Target* (1960), we have a superb example of this astonishing achievement. The title probably makes reference, amongst other things, to Davie's long-standing empathy with Japanese Zen Buddhism's intuitive and anti-intellectual approach to the spiritual life – 'Sell your cleverness and buy bewilderment' as the Zen Master instructs. Davie would frequently exemplify his concept of the loss of self with an analogy from Zen legend, which echoes this painting's title – 'The Zen Buddhist master of Archery does not practise Archery as the perfection of technical skill. Some of the greatest Zen masters were known to frequently hit the bull's eye without aiming at it – it was a kind of shooting of the self – a spiritual exercise' (1997). For Davie, like Zen archery, 'The right Art is purposeless and aimless' (1958).

The straight green arrow in the painting shooting into and disintegrating its target can be read as a sign that the initial part of Davie's all-demanding quest for personal enlightenment had been attained and that the dominance of ego had been finally overthrown and vanquished. This new stage of Davie's quest for personal and spiritual liberty is clearly indicated by the remarkable upsurge in his creative output during this period. It is as though the 'psychic energy' which Jung believed was suppressed by the oppression of the ego had now been released through Davie's exuberant paintings. For instance, colour begins to take on a life of its own in Davie's work and has an essential role to play in his art and philosophy; as he was later to say in 1990, 'colour is the veritable stuff of life' and *Magnetic Orange* (1960) would be a perfect example of such colouristic vitality.

Davie's views on colour echo those of his fellow mystic/abstractionist Kandinsky, with their musical analogy: 'The colours must sing together very much like the notes in music' (1990). This synaesthetic interconnection between painting and music was always something important to Davie who was also a very fine practising classical musician and a professional jazz player in his earlier career. Unsurprisingly, jazz was particularly influential on the development of his later painting technique where, through intuitive improvisation, the painter could completely lose himself and allow the painting to create its own self – as Davie writes in 1958, the artist 'must contrive to pay as little attention as possible to the end to which he is moving – allowing the end to come when it comes.' A superb example of this jazzy, improvised approach to painting is *Tonight's the Night* (1964), with a title that seems to come straight from a Blue Note jazz label.

The decade of the 1960s was probably when Davie's critical reputation and international art world standing was at its zenith and he was particularly fortunate to have such a supportive gallery in Gimpel Fils, who always encouraged him to develop his painting in whichever direction it led him. Unlike many artists who were more concerned with the advancement of their careers than the integrity of their art, Davie took little interest in the machinations of the London art world which John Berger curtly dismissed in the mid-1960s as 'extremely parochial.' Davie, now with his own accommodating studio space and domestic dwelling well outside the distracting metropolis in semi-rural Hertfordshire, was able move on to a new stage in his personal and artistic development. At this point, he was psychologically and creatively in a position to extend the power of his art and transcend his own previous psychic struggles by linking up to and developing a creative dialogue with the universal source of Jung's concept of the 'Collective Unconscious'. This is shown by the way the predominantly inchoate gestural technique of his earlier practice as exemplified by *The Red Joy* (1958) is now replaced with a more clearly articulated iconography of archetypal signs and symbols as seen in such work as *Flying Machine* (1965–8) and *Sweet Flapper* (1968); both of which are animated and infused with a double dose of élan vital and jouissance. The great works of this period of the later 1960s are both the final triumphant outcome of all the preceding struggles and innovations in Davie's earlier work; and at the same time, the inviting open gateway to the richly creative developments to follow.

From the 1970s, there was a notable stylistic shift in the appearance of Davie's work as can be seen if we compare, say, *Crazy Dog in a Rocking Chair* of 1963 with *Daidling Dance* from 1996. Both works are involved with visually depicting the appearance and sensation of movement but, while the early painting expresses frantic animation through the power of the impulsive brush strokes the artist intuitively makes, the later picture is much more controlled and uses a proscenium type compositional arrangement, with highly decorative signs acting out their much more formal choreographed movements within the stage-like pictorial space.

A range of various factors brought about this marked change in Davie's work. From an iconographical point of view, Davie began to see a clear link between the content of the outpouring of his own automaticism and the imagery to be found in a wide range of non-western and ancient cultures – 'this archetypal symbolism which speaks to different civilisations I discovered the same type of symbols in my own automatic drawings' (1992). With the discovery of this shamanistic power to make contact with Jung's Collective Unconscious through the transcendental mystic power of his art, Davie travelled extensively in order to seek out numerous non-western cultures in all their visual manifestations, from Carib petroglyphs to Jain cosmology. Thus, he transformed his art from a psychic journey of personal discovery into one which, through the loss of self, embraced all of humankind and the universe of eternal symbolism. In order to achieve this within the practice of his painting as a modern western artist, Davie had to radically re-adapt his studio practice. He ceased working horizontally from all four edges of the canvas, with his pictures laid on the floor as previously, and now employed a more conventional method of upright easel painting. Furthermore, the crucial role of improvisation no longer took place immediately and directly on the canvas, but rather on the paper of his innumerable pen and ink sketches and gouaches which he produced in preparation for his large complex oil paintings. Yet what these later paintings may lose in immediate and dramatic expressive intensity, they make up for in their richly decorative and rhythmic patterning as demonstrated by the wonderful life-affirming *Homage to the Earth Spirits No20* (1984).

In an interview I had the privilege to conduct with Alan Davie on behalf of the British Council in 1992, he adamantly maintained, 'I don't practise art. I don't make art.' Yet for all his consistent anti-art (or non-art) rhetoric, Davie was never an arch rebel – such as a bohemian poseur or an iconoclastic Dadaist. In fact, it would be more correct to describe him as a self-appointed outsider – but I would argue a keenly observing and critically aware outsider – who was still responsive to the art world from which he, at the same time, distanced himself. If you study Davie's career in the wider context of that art world to which he was linked, whether or not he liked it, then you begin to see that it cannot merely be by chance that the internal stylistic changes which take place throughout Davie's work are broadly in line with the development of progressive modern art in the second half of the 20th century.

For instance, the dark tragic nature of his painting in the 1940s and '50s echoes similar qualities in the angst-ridden existentialist art of post-war Europe, and also with the beat generation's avant-garde culture in the America of abstract expressionism. Furthermore, Davie's artistic credo that 'you can't see life if you are in it' (1962) is also very close in commitment to the 1960s counter-culture's aim to merge art and life so that they become indistinguishable from each other; while the kaleidoscopic, sensual joie de vivre of Davie's painting of that decade is very much in tune with the bright colourful exuberance of both post-painterly abstraction and even some aspects of Pop Art painting. Finally, Davie's work of the 1970s onwards is very much in tune with the decline of high modernism and the rise of postmodernism, especially with his particular contribution to the emerging post-colonial multicultural transnationalism of the late 20th century. Finally, to return to Davie's theoretical writings, what are we to make of the follow-up statement Davie made after his claim that 'I have no consideration about who's going to look at the picture – it never enters my mind' (1992)? If that is the true attitude of the artist, may we then ask, if Davie is indifferent to the viewer's critical response, is it equally legitimate for the viewer to ignore Davie's writings and respond to his painting in whatever way they wish? If that is so, then can all of Davie's writings on the spiritual intent behind his art be put to one side so that the critical evaluation of his painting only concerns itself with aesthetic quality and art historical judgement? The purely visual attraction and the fascinating pictorial interest as found in the paintings of Davie are undoubtedly – and rightly so – wonderful pleasures in their own right. For what is most important, and will continue to be so as long as the art of modern painting is treated with the appreciative response and critical respect it deserves, is the arresting visual power and superb technical and inventive character of Davie's work. Yet at the same time, I would also hold that the attraction which we have for Alan Davie's art should not be solely dependent on its immediate impact but, as I hope this essay has demonstrated, is founded on and sustained by a multi-layered creative process of complex – sometimes even contradictory attitudes – concerning the artist's spiritual beliefs and the viewer's aesthetic response.

This essay was written by Bill Hare in 2015 and published by 108 Fine Art, Harrogate. See also: 'Alan Davie's Jiggling Spaces' by Bill Hare and Andrew Patrizio in *The Journal of the Scottish Society of Art History*, Volume 15.

Joan Eardley

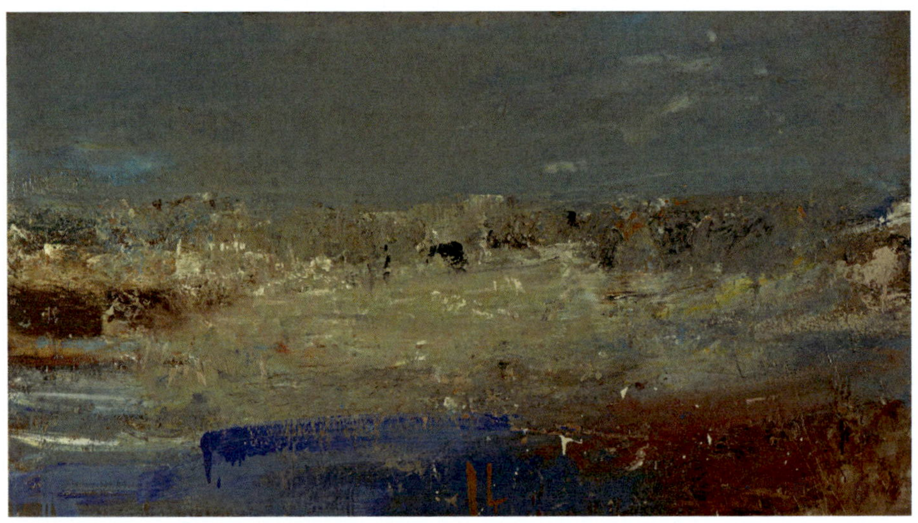

Seascape (Foam and Blue Sky)
1962
Oil on board, 94x167cm

More than Meets the Eye

Sight and Vision in the Art of Joan Eardley

I suppose that painting is only a visual reaction to things, in a way – but to me it must be more.
Joan Eardley, 1948

LET'S START WITH the obvious – everyone would agree that the most important thing for a visual artist is their optical faculties – the way they use their eyes. Yet in the act of artistic creativity this involves both their visual powers of perception and the imaginative depths of their vision. This may appear to be relatively straightforward; however, it is crucially important that we understand what we mean by this because seeing/looking is a highly complex affair which involves an infinite variety of intuitive and conscious optical actions and subsequent affected experiences. As the great visionary artist William Blake famously observed, every eye sees differently; and of course, even on a mundane level, this is the case. For example, an artist studying a bowl of fruit in order to paint a still life picture will look on the ripe sight in a very different manner from a person who is starving – or for that matter, compared with someone else who has a fetish about the erotic shape of a peach for instance. Another important aspect of this issue that also needs to be taken into consideration concerning the wide spectrum of differing points of views is that each individual's perceptions are constantly evolving throughout their life cycle. This phenomenon of continuing change in visual action and reaction is particularly important in our understanding of the way the work of an artist develops and evolves over their whole career.

Human sight is both a biologically innate and a culturally conditioned faculty. This duality is best demonstrated by the distinction between the reflex action of seeing anything and the conscious act of looking for something. Within the work of Eardley, this fundamental visual dialectic is the dynamic tension which motivated the course of her career as a modern painter. On the one hand, throughout her artistic development, she continued to retain a direct and unmediated view of the world – to see her subject as 'funny bits of colour.' Yet, on the other hand, as an ambitious artist she also needed to look and study her subject in a highly informed and visually articulated manner. Thus, not surprisingly she was a most conscientious student at Glasgow School of Art in the 1940s, learning by attentively working from the model and closely examining the art of the past. Furthermore, the young Eardley also travelled to the great cultural centres of Europe to be in direct touch with the canonical works of art history. Throughout her hectic and highly prolific career she always found time to make regular trips to visit the London galleries in order to

be fully aware of what was going on in the contemporary cosmopolitan
art scene. All this enabled her to express herself visually through her
painting in a richly informed and sophisticatedly experimental manner.

The essential difference between innate seeing and informed looking
in the work of Eardley is most exemplified by a comparison between her
only self-portrait – a student piece from 1943 and her most controversial
picture, *Sleeping Nude* (1955). In the first work, Eardley almost turns the
conventional ritual and assumed purpose of self-portraiture on its head by
seeming to eliminate rather than promote her own distinctive individuality
and objective presence. Through an act of subtle self-effacement,
she appears to be reverting to Lacan's pre-mirror stage of awareness
development where her subject-self and immediate surroundings have not
yet become consciously separated and clearly distinguished from each
other. In this painting, it's as if the artist as her own subject is trying to
convey an almost childlike visual experience of her veiled self, enwrapped
in the world around her. Interestingly, Eardley's subsequent choice of
children as her preferred human subject matter may be a strong indication
of her creative desire to retain, and personally identify with their non-
objective, unselfconscious, spontaneous 'visual reaction to things.'

By the middle of the next decade, however, Eardley, through a
dedicated process of historical and contemporary art study, had greatly
enriched her painting to a high level of technical and intellectual potential.
This is clearly demonstrated in *Sleeping Nude*. With this picture,
Eardley turned seeing into looking by producing a carefully considered
concentrated image, redolent with informed references and allusions to
a range of cultural and historical sources-from western figure painting,
both ancient and modern – to the terrible assault on European humanism
in the nightmare form of the Holocaust victim. Unfortunately at that
time, through a deadly combination of philistine ignorance and gender
prejudice, this challenging work provoked such a hostile reaction that
Eardley must have felt she needed to re-direct the purpose and practice of
her future painting.

The most conspicuous outcome of Eardley's shift in attitude and
approach to the subsequent development of her art was her treatment of
the human presence in her later painting. She began to evolve an elaborate
strategy of presence and absence with the human content in her pictures.
For instance, from the mid-1950s, the Catterline land/seascapes quickly
became a major source of additional inspiration for her work. Yet what
is so striking about Eardley's portrayal of this small fishing village is the
almost total absence of any human community.

Furthermore, although Eardley continued to pay equal time and
attention to her beloved Glasgow street scenes, her treatment of the
children there radically changed. In a manner similar to her early self-
portrait, the figures of these street kids begin to become more and more
isolated and lose their former clear delineation and visual articulation
as they start to disintegrate into ghostly presences and echoing traces

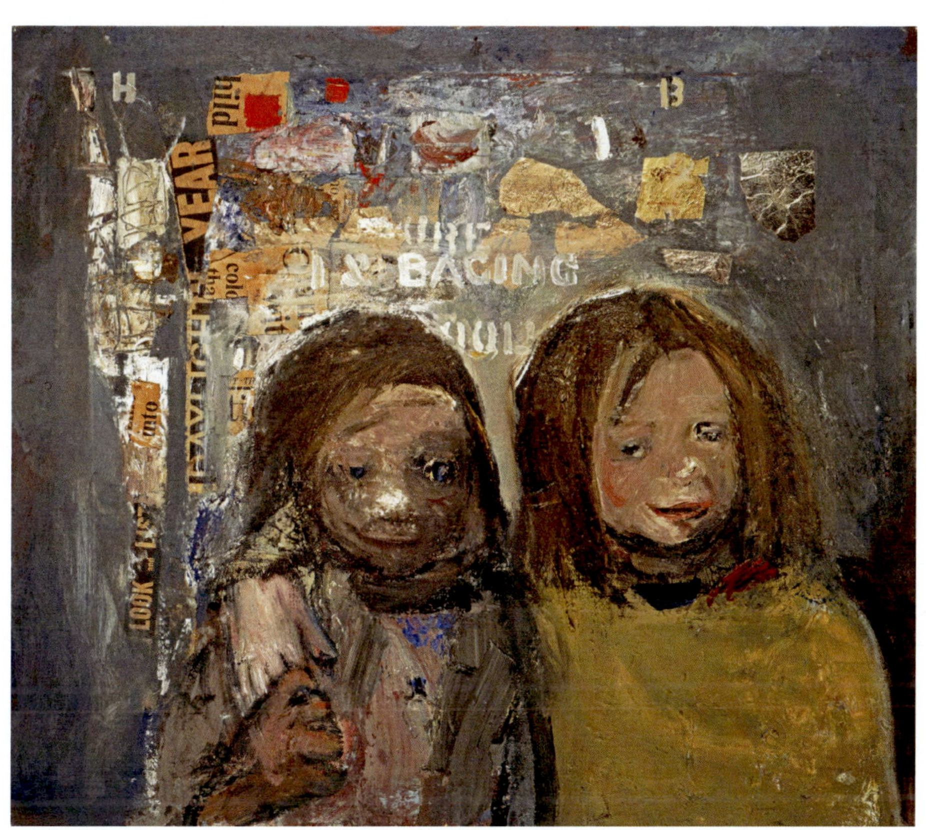

Children and Chalked Wall 3
1962–3, oil, newspaper, metal foil on canvas
61x69cm

which merge into the crumbling urban decay of the graffiti scrawled walls of their vanishing childhood. Notably in her final presentation of the deteriorating condition of childhood as evocatively depicted in such works as *Children and Chalked Wall No. 2* and *No. 3*, Eardley places much focus and great emphasis on the children's eyes. As the kids seem to gradually disappear along with their vanishing world, their haunting gaze becomes more and more riveting. It's as though the artist wishes to preserve the innocence of their uncontaminated sight from the inevitable process of human corruption and ever-threatening historical social change.

With the last great triumph of her heroic career, in the form of her epic series of seascapes, such as *The Sea* (1959) or *Seascape (Foam and Blue Sky* (1962), Eardley seeks to challenge this entropic state of civic and visual decline and restore to the power of her own sight a regenerated childlike intuitive vitality infused with visionary intensity. Through the long years of sustained out-door painting practice, her highly responsive technique enables Eardley to confront directly her turbulent subject and physically and creatively lose herself in the awesome sublime of the raw forces of the sea. Physical reality is miraculously transformed into transcendental metaphysical experience through the intuitive gestural brushstrokes of the transfixed painter. All opposites between existence and essence are finally resolved and everything finally merges with each other – land and sea, sky and earth, dark and light, near and far, stillness and movement, the painter and her subject, the objective look of world and the subjective vision of the experience of that world. All are now seen and felt as at one with each other on the all-revealing surface of Eardley's painting.

This essay was written by Bill Hare in 2008 and published in *Scottish Art News*, issue 10.

William Turnbull

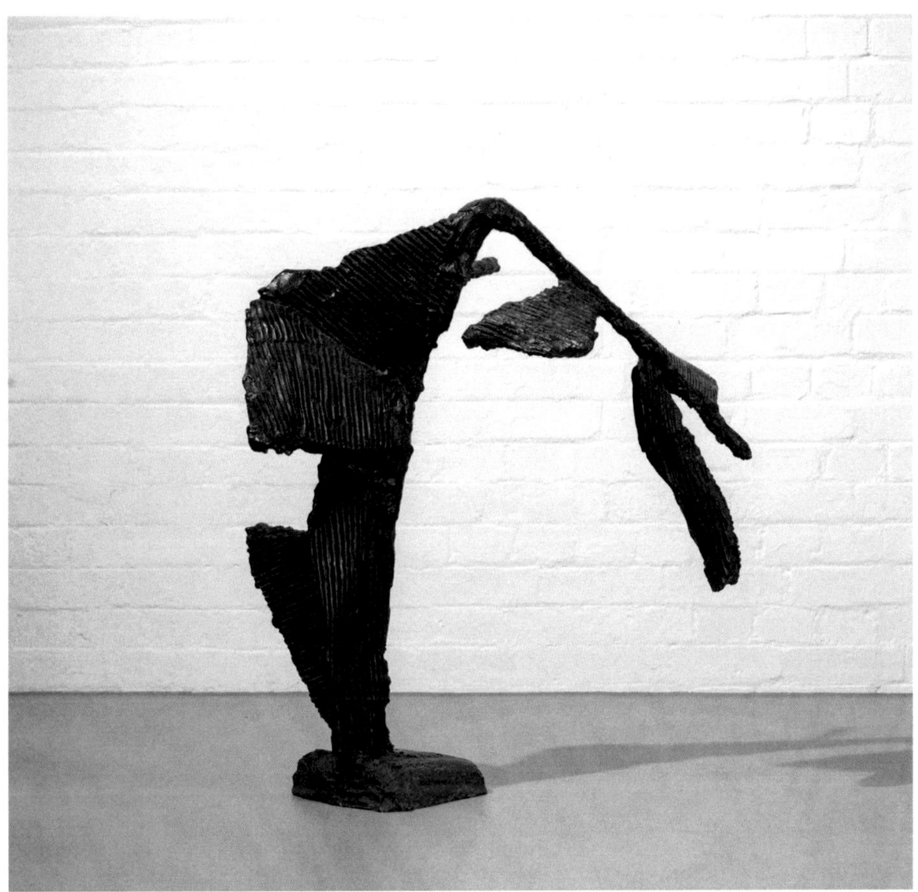

Pegasus
1954
Bronze, 89x46x74cm

Reproduced courtesy of the artist's estate

William Turnbull Interview

*I am sure many people who know and admire your work will still be
unaware of your Scottish background. You were born and brought up in
Dundee and worked in the illustration department of DC Thomson, the
popular periodical company, before you were called up for war service.
Looking back on these early years are there any experiences from that time
which might have played a part in the development of your later work as an
artist?*

I grew up in Springhill in Dundee, which overlooked the Caledon shipyard
where my father worked as an iron turner. Everyone worked there till the
yards closed down during the Depression. I had always been fascinated by
drawing. Our relatives in America would send these women's magazines
to my mother. They were full colour illustrations, quite unlike anything
in Scotland at the time, where the print was black or black and red only.
I was completely struck by the colours and would copy them furiously. I
had enrolled in an evening class when I was 15 and was spotted by one
of the senior illustrators at DC Thomson who happened to be teaching
the course. They asked if I wanted a job and that was that. At this time
during the early '30s, everyone was being laid off from the shipyards, so it
was quite a surprise to everyone that I managed to get a relatively well-
paid job drawing and illustrating. I had always been passionate about
drawing, so I considered myself extremely fortunate.

There was something really interesting about illustrating magazines
especially as I'd spent my whole childhood looking at them. The
illustrators at DC Thomson were tremendously skilled at what they did
and they did it so well and so quickly. I mean the skill these illustrators
had wasn't to be sniffed at just because they weren't painting pictures
that were going into the museums. They were very skilled at what they
did and I learned an enormous amount about drawing and other things
from them. Most of them had been to art school, which was something
I knew very little about. It opened up a whole new world to me. Most
of them lived across the River Tay and I remember being invited to their
houses on a number of occasions. They introduced me to van Gogh and
a number of other impressionist painters. It was like another world, quite
unlike anything I had been exposed to or experienced and obviously
had a profound impact on me. It's actually an incredibly random set
of events, without which my entire life would have been very different.
Certainly this introduction to European art gave me a more international
perspective than I might have had. It also made it very clear to me what I
liked and what I didn't like.

*After you left the RAF in 1946, you decided that you wanted to be an
artist. In order to achieve this, you first went to the Slade School in*

London (1946–8) then moved to Paris (1948–50). How useful did you find these two periods in your artistic education?
I joined the raf when I was 17. I did my flight training in Leuchars and in Canada and ended up flying Catalinas in India and Sri Lanka (or Ceylon as it was known then). I loved the experience of flying and being up there 'by yourself' without anything else. You felt as if you were in the middle of nowhere. It was absolutely beautiful. I think these spatial sensations were so different from what you got in a motorcar. It certainly did have an effect on the way you thought about 'space' – as almost being an object. When the war finished, they wanted me to become a peacetime pilot and flying instructor but I always knew that I wanted to become an artist. It was quite a change of lifestyle, flying and eating in the officer's mess, then going back to art school and becoming a penniless artist.

When I got demobbed, I got a small ex-service grant which I used to enrol at the Slade. It was one of the biggest let downs I had experienced so far. The view of art was so provincial and narrow minded that I realised that this wasn't where I wanted to be. Having been through what I'd just experienced, it was very difficult being in this small, sheltered environment. I think, in the end, I only ended up going to the life drawing classes, to draw from the model. The rest of the time I was never there. Luckily the guy that ran the place, who was Scottish and whose name I unfortunately can't remember, helped me get my grant transferred to Paris where I feel my art education really began.

I went to Paris because I wasn't really interested in the art scene in London or the artists in London and I was interested in the artists in Paris and what had been going on there for quite some time. I got on really well with the people I met there. I liked the art. I always had done. I felt I was in the place I really belonged.

There were two other British artists who were in Paris at that time, Raymond Mason and Eduardo Paolozzi. It was interesting to meet artists like Braque and Brâncuşi, to see what the person was like aside from their work. I was invited to Picasso's studio. That was quite unlike any studio I'd ever been in. I also had a very strange experience at Brâncuşi's studio where he let me in (after I put my foot in the door) and he left me alone for half an hour before asking me to leave. But it was really Alberto (Giacometti) that I was closest to. He was a very friendly man to me and we got on extremely well and I admired him enormously.

There was a rule where if you bought a coffee, you could sit for four hours in the cafés so everyone would meet there. I had no money and became an authority on French cinema because this was the only place you could keep warm in the winter. The only time I ate properly was when friends would come to town and take you out for dinner. Eventually I ran out of money completely and was forced to return to London but by this time the art scene had shifted away from Paris and the emphasis was shifting to London and New York.

When you returned to London, you taught at the Central School of Arts and Crafts (1952–61) under William Johnstone, along with other fellow Scots, Eduardo Paolozzi and Alan Davie. Did you feel there was any particular bond between you and these other Scottish artists?
When I got back to London, I was completely broke and ended up working the night shift at a Lyons Maid ice cream factory with writers and an odd assortment of people. On the first night, I got so fed up I just walked away from the conveyor belt and the ice cream ended up everywhere. In fact, I was still working there when my work was selected for the British Pavilion at the Venice Biennale in 1952. I remember how frustrating it was not being able to go because I couldn't afford it. Teaching at the Central provided a much needed lifeline. I never really wanted to teach but am grateful that it allowed me to at least earn a living doing something I enjoyed.

I never got on with Alan Davie. He had a very high opinion of himself which I didn't share. With regards to Eduardo, I think that if there was a bond, it was more to do with the fact we had shared certain experiences and were interested in the same things rather than it being particularly because we were Scottish.

Initially Eduardo and I were very close. He was actually the best man at my marriage to my first wife, Katharina, and we shared a studio in Paris. One day, Eduardo came into the studio (which we shared with an Irish artist called O'Leary) and announced he had a show. When we turned up at the opening, the owner came over to me and asked why I didn't want to exhibit my work. When I asked him what he meant, he told me he had wanted to do a show of my work but that Eduardo had told him that I didn't like showing my work. That was pretty typical of Eduardo.

In the 1950s, you were also one of the young radical British artists who formed the Independent Group at the ICA. I have always felt, however, that your work was different and 'independent' from that of other members of the Group, such as Richard Hamilton, Nigel Henderson and Eduardo Paolozzi. Do you agree with this, and if so, in what ways?
The Independent Group formed out of discussion groups we had at the ICA in the early 1950s when it was in Dover Street. At first, the discussions were open to the public but eventually we made them invitational as this seemed to raise the level of the discussions.

It was probably the first time, certainly in Britain, that artists, writers and architects shared a forum for the exchange of ideas. Within the group itself, there were big differences of opinion. Britain was still very 'post-war' and depressed and everyone was looking to America as the future. American culture, films, music and art were beginning to have a big impact. I had always loved the gangster films like Howard Hawks's *Scarface*. I liked the clothes, the look. I've never really understood artists wanting to look scruffy. This was one of the reasons I got on with Francis (Bacon) who was always well turned out.

As for the connections between us, there are, I guess you could say, links between my work and Eduardo's, as there are links between his and Hamilton's. Having said that, my work is pretty different from Richard's, though we both used collage. Eduardo and Richard incorporated the American imagery into their work whereas I never felt that was what I wanted to do with my work.

Your early work of the late 1940s and 1950s is characterised as highly experimental and inventive. You famously said: 'I began to make a piece of sculpture to find out what a piece of sculpture should be like.' Why did you have such an open approach?
I was, during this period, learning about being an artist and how to make the art I wanted to make. Besides my drawing experience at DC Thomson, I had very little formal training, which I think was a good thing. Everything in Britain was so old fashioned and neo-Romantic. I see my art as the opposite of Baroque.

I think it was in Paris that I began to serve my apprenticeship among artists like Giacometti and Jean Hélion, who was also a good friend of mine. It was through Hélion – he was married to Pegeen Guggenheim – that I got to meet a lot of these guys.

One of the reasons I enjoy working in plaster is that it's a very organic process. It starts as nothing, a bag of dust, and becomes something. I've never really believed in planning what you're going to make. The only period where I had to actually plan was when I worked with steel as you can't just start improvising with big sheets of metal. That was the nearest art ever came to being conceptual and that was simply due to the process and the logistics involved. I've always been interested in how little you can have of an object and it still be recognisable.

In 1956, you made the statement for the Independent Group's This Is Tomorrow exhibition at the Whitechapel Art Gallery that 'a great deal of modern sculpture and painting [is] the sum total of a number of possible permutations… the observer or user is one of the units.' How big a part does the consideration of the spectator's reaction play in the making of your work?
I've never allowed considerations about other people to interfere with the making of my work. It's always nice if someone says they like your work but – and here's the difference – it's never changed what I do if they don't like it. I think initially people wrestled with my paintings more than my sculpture. No one was really making these types of pictures back then, certainly not in Britain, and it ran very counter to what most people thought of as painting to the point that the works were frequently being physically attacked. There was a large orange painting in the Tate in the 1970s and someone sprayed IRA all over it.

I've never set out to shock with my work but my paintings, especially earlier on, did often provoke people. This quote probably refers to this rather than my being influenced by others in the creation of my work, though it is such a long time ago I can't remember making it.

In British art at least, you are that rare phenomenon – both a sculptor and a painter. Within your own practice, what is the relationship between your painting and your sculpture?

I've always regarded the two as equally important. In some respects, they are both dealing with the same things but using different materials. I think you can see that in the patinas and the surfaces of the sculptures and the paintings. The surface of the sculpture is as important as the shape of the piece itself. When I first started casting in bronze, the range of colour available for a patina was very limited to black and a green if you were lucky. I'd spent a great deal of time when I first came to London in the British Museum. After looking at ancient bronzes and seeing the colour and variation they were able to achieve, I began experimenting with acids and various chemical processes to develop or 'reintroduce' many of the colours they now use at the foundry. There is a lot of time spent and a lot of attention given to finishing my sculptures.

Do you see your art within the context of any particular movement in modern painting?

I've always tried to avoid being part of groups. I've often found myself in the unusual position where I've often felt a far greater connection to artists from other countries than to other artists in Britain. You could say my painting was influenced by the artists I met in New York much in the same way my sculpture was influenced by the artists I met in Paris but this was actually far more to do with these individuals themselves rather than any movement they may or may not have been part of. I have never felt any great desire to be part of any group or movement. In fact, I can't really think of anything worse.

You have said that you regard your paintings as 'objects' and would prefer them to stand on the floor rather than hang on the wall. Does that mean that you wish them to be regarded in the same manner as your sculptures?

I think what I meant by that was that I've never regarded my paintings as two-dimensional objects. My paintings, certainly post-1957, don't refer to anything, only to themselves. Even with the earlier heads and figures, which Alex, my son, is intending to show at Chatsworth House, I've always tried to think of my paintings as three-dimensional. I don't have a problem with them hanging on the wall but just feel that I like them to have their own space and be regarded as objects rather than pieces of two-dimensional decorative ornamentation.

Have you ever had an exhibition consisting solely of your paintings? If not, how would you feel about that?

Waddington Galleries had a show of paintings in 2007 which sold out. I've been cataloguing the works on paper with my sons Alex and Johnny, as well as the paintings, and it's very interesting to see things that I made over 50 years ago. I'm happy with how my paintings look. When I look back at them now, I feel pleased with what I've created. They look good. Hopefully people will get over their ideas about sculptors not being able to paint and painters not being able to sculpt and judge the works on their individual merits. Both Rothko and Newman liked and were very supportive of my paintings. That was always enough for me.

This interview was conducted by Bill Hare in 2013 for *Scottish Art News*, issues 19 and 20.

A Matter of Love and Death

Eros and Thanatos in the Work of William Turnbull

IN STARK CONTRAST TO the past, since 1945 the representation of the human body in Scottish art has become a central area of critical focus, some might also say even a polemic battleground, for much discourse and fierce debate. This discourse has ranged over political, psychological, sexual and gender issues in an ongoing debate concerning shifting identities within modern and post-modern society. In the immediate post-war years, there was a great deal of rethinking and experimentation in figurative art in the light of the terrifying way the human body had been targeted and terrorised by the Holocaust and the devastating military attacks on civilian communities – from the aerial attack on Guernica to the dropping of the Atomic Bomb on Hiroshima and Nagasaki. Two Scottish artists, William Turnbull and Eduardo Paolozzi, were very much a part of this radically new development in post-war figurative art. This initially took place in the late 1940s and 1950s in Paris and London where they both worked in close contact with each other and within the leading avant-garde circles of that time. In these two cultural centres of modernism they had access to a wide range of artistic and ethnographical sources to guide them in their particular approach to the reformulation of modern figuration.

William Turnbull and Eduardo Paolozzi both rejected the moribund academic conventions and romantic nostalgia that still prevailed in much of the British art world in the immediate post-war period and set out to radicalise the practise of sculpture within an emerging contemporary context of imminent social revolution – as Muriel Spark wrote of this time 'everyone began to consider where they personally stood in the new order of things.'

The highly challenging ambition which these two young sculptors set themselves required them to seek a much more appropriate artistically stimulating and creative environment. So in 1948 Turnbull moved to Paris and set up his studio there. This move gave him the opportunity to pursue an open and experimental approach to the making of new kinds of sculptural objects. These included mobiles such as, *Hanging Sculpture* (1949), his 'base' pieces like *Playground* (1949) and raw crude constructions of subjects which would continue to hold his creative attention throughout his subsequent career such as *Horse* (1950), *Head* (1950) and *Pegasus* (1954). In Paris he could also visit the museums of ancient and non-western artefacts, and also the studios of the most progressive modern artists, such as Giacometti, Dubuffet and Brâncuși. Furthermore, in the French capital Turnbull was also greatly stimulated by the intellectual atmosphere generated by the presence of such figures as Jean-Paul Sartre and the challenging implications that his 'very important'

philosophy of existentialism had on artistic practice. The crucial
existential attitude of not following *a priori* rules within artistic practice is
very much echoed in Turnbull intriguing statement that he 'began to make
a piece of sculpture to find out what a piece of sculpture should be like.'

Turnbull continued his speculative investigative approach to his
practice and career even after he was financially forced to come back to
London in 1952. There he soon became involved with the revolutionising
cultural activities of the circle of young innovators who formed the
Independent Group at the Institute of Contemporary Art. He later also
joined the teaching staff of the most progressive art educational institution
in the country at that time – the Central School of Arts and Craft. There
he taught along with his fellow Scots – William Johnstone, Alan Davie
and again Eduardo Paolozzi, as well as the likes of Richard Hamilton
and Victor Pasmore. In 1952, he and Paolozzi were included in Herbert
Read's group exhibition, *New Aspects of British Sculpture* which showed
at the Venice Biennale of that year. The work in this exhibition, which
became famously known as the modern sculpture of 'The Geometry
of Fear', after Read's catalogue essay, did help to bring the challenging
work of a new generation of young radical sculptors to the notice of
a wider international public. Their raw brutal art which Read saw as
an 'iconography of despair' struck a chord with the pervasive mood of
apprehension and anxiety in the immediate post-war British society. This
was a period of bleak economic and cultural austerity in heavily rationed
Britain which was still living with the devastating aftermath of world wide
conflict. At the same time, Britain – along with the rest of the world – was
also having to come to terms with the awesome consequences of the very
real likelihood of the imminent outbreak of atomic warfare in the early
years of the Cold War. This mood of anxiety and austerity is well captured
in a 1950s photograph of Turnbull in his London studio at Hamilton
Gardens. Although the bare studio has a makeshift stove it appears unlit
as the artist is still heavily wrapped up against the cold in his heavy duffel
coat and scarf. Examples of Turnbull's work in this Spartan setting are
two lacerated oval egg-shaped plaster objects lying on their sides on
ledges above the stove. These seemingly simple, but powerfully emotive
and evocative, pieces were from an important generic series entitled *Head*
which Turnbull was developing in the early 1950s, and which he would
show in the ICA exhibition *Wonder and Horror of the Human Head*
(1953).

As was to be the case with all of his future practice, the thematic
content in Turnbull's early work was distilled down to a few 'consistent
subjects in sculpture'. These were the totemic standing figure, the horse
and the head motives – all of which were also conceived as independent
'objects' in their own right. Turnbull was adamant that 'sculpture can be a
fragment of something as a subject, but not a fragment as something as an
object.' Furthermore, with his quest for essential lucidity and simplicity,
Turnbull realised with his *Head* series 'how little will suggest a head.'

An important factor in directing Turnbull towards this realisation must have been his earlier Paris visit to Brâncuşi's studio. Over his career the Romanian master had produced a number of detached head sculptures such as *The Sleeping Muse* (1910) and *New Born* (1920) which Turnbull might have actually seen. Brâncuşi's works make a striking comparison with Turnbull's later *Head* series. The smooth and highly polished heads of Brâncuşi are reflective, not only of the futuristic utopianism of early 20th-century modernism, but also fashionable Parisian art décor chic. Turnbull's heads by contrast, are the product of a very different modern world where those earlier utopian dreams have turned into contemporary dystopian nightmares – as Patrick Elliott has observed:

> Whereas Brâncuşi's heads have the appearance of newly laid eggs, Turnbull's, though calm and compact, look as though they have been to hell and back.

These heads of Turnbull are however, not just pitiful, battle-scarred survivors of modern history's unrelenting assault on the human body. They are also sinister and disturbing presences, something like Giacometti's *Disagreeable Objects*. Their bomb-like appearance ominously suggests that they might also be the very source of that destructive violence (Roland Penrose's young son immediately saw Turnbull's *Head* as a grenade). With his *Head* series Turnbull demonstrated one of his most effective strategies in his sculptural practice: his ability to condense two opposing forces within the same work of art – victim and victimised. With Turnbull's *Head* there can be found on the one hand, the same tender sense of budding potential and fragile vulnerability that is echoed by the life-giving eroticism in Brâncuşi's sculpture. On the other hand, however, there is also a disconcerting sinister dimension to these uncanny objects. They may look 'calm and compact' but that sense of controlled compression can also fearfully threaten to release an explosive blast of destructive power from their grenade-like form. Thus, through this visual duality and conceptual ambiguity, Turnbull's art is able to focus our attention on the great paradox of our existence that life and death, creation and destruction – Eros and Thanatos – are not separate entities, but are in fact an interconnected and an unbroken continuum from the egg in the womb to the headstone over the grave.

In the later 1950s and early 1960s, Turnbull was also making a series of totemic figures to which he gave the generic title *Idols*. Originally formed in plaster Turnbull had these figures later cast in bronze at a foundry where he liked to work alongside the labour force. By chance, out of this collaboration a number of works were produced from the plaster moulds originally made for the casting process of Turnbull's other bronzes. To the first one of this 'recycled' group of sculptures Turnbull gave the appropriate title *Source* (1958).This potent figure, still bearing all the marks and air holes of its intended destruction through the casting procedures, now rises and swells like a resurrected goddess of fertility in whom the recurring cycle of growth, decay and regeneration are embodied.

Turning now to Turnbull's early paintings of the 1950s, they also focused on the human body in the form of the head motif which was treated in a highly simplified and direct manner, such as *Head (calligraphic)* (1956) and *Mask* (1955–6). Such schematic imagery certainly again bears out Turnbull's observation 'how little will suggest a head'. In these paintings Turnbull treated his subject in a similar raw and intuitive way as he did with his sculptural *Heads* and *Masks* of the same period. By the 1960s, however, Turnbull had eliminated any mimetic figurative reference in his painting and also began to work on a monumental scale. This seismic shift almost certainly had a good deal to do with Turnbull's contact, and 'dialogue', with American abstraction, and particularly with the work of Barnett Newman. Turnbull, however, rejected the concomitant mystic symbolism associated with much of such abstract expressionist work. He even denied that they were abstract paintings despite showing them in the important *British Abstract* exhibition of the Situation Group in 1960. Consistent with his sculptural outlook, Turnbull has always regarded these later paintings of his, not as symbolic abstractions, but independent 'objects' which, through their enveloping scale and expansive colour, create a very physiological and environmental effect on the spectator. These great walls of 'saturated fields of colour', which are not to be seen as 'hermetic abstract works, but non-figurative works that are a result of a powerful subjective response to things seen' are intended then to have a reciprocal impact on the spectator's awakening and responsive physical sensibilities. The visual dialectics between Eros and Thanatos which are built into Turnbull's earlier sculpture such as the *Head* series appears to be resolved in these later non-figurative paintings, and it is the pleasure-giving Eros alone, which seems to be the all-prevailing sensual presence.

Turnbull's sculpture and painting of the 1960s and early 1970s were predominately abstract in manner if not mystical in meaning, but by the 1980s his sculpture, if not his painting, had returned to figuration with the same essential subjects of head, horse and female figure. On the other hand, however, the visceral tragic mood of the earlier sculpture had now been abandoned. By the 1980s Turnbull was creating much more pared down stream-lined objects whose patinated surfaces were engraved, rather than indented, with esoteric 'signs' as seen for instance in such work as *Ancestral Figure* (1988). With his wife Kim Lim, Turnbull had regularly visited the Far East and was drawn, not surprisingly, considering his long standing fascination with ancient and non-western artefacts, to many of the distinctive ceremonial objects used in oriental cultures – such as masks and weapons – for instance, samurai swords. Through these contacts Turnbull was inspired to return to, and rework with fresh insight, an earlier theme in his sculpture the standing female idol. He produced over the decade a number of totemic figures such as *Large Siren, Leaf Venus* and *Blade Venus.*

Large Blade Venus (1990) shows how enduring the influence of Surrealism has been on the development of Turnbull's sculpture. That surrealist dimension in Turnbull's art, however, has always had more to do with George Bataille than André Breton. This can be gauged by the fact that it is Giacometti's sculpture of his surrealist period in the early 1930s to which Turnbull's work is closest in spirit – and as Colin Rhodes suggests '[Giacometti was] the artist who comes closest to the concerns of Bataille.' Furthermore, this can be particularly seen in the way these two sculptors have treated the female form with the same inner duality between alluring sexuality and threating violence which is also the recurring theme at the core of Bataille's writings on human relationships. This constant fluctuation between Eros and Thanatos can equally be appreciated for instance in works such as Giacometti's *Woman with her Throat Cut* (1932) and Turnbull's *Large Blade Venus,* where in both cases the female presence simultaneously entices and endangers through erotic attraction and threatened retribution. Yet even if their thematic concerns are similar their stylistic interpretations are very different. While Giacometti employs a highly theatrical baroque treatment to the overtly sexualised body of the female form recalling in a perverse way Bernini's *The Ecstasy of St Teresa*, Turnbull, on the other hand, distils the figure down to a single concentrated silhouetted image of awesome hieratical authority. Not that this in any way denies *Large Blade Venus* the same dramatic tension; on the contrary, Turnbull's sculpture seems to vibrate which inner tension between erotic and ominous forces. This is due to the fact that everything within this arresting object is balanced literally on a knife edge.

Motion and stasis have always been of crucial concern to Turnbull, going back to his mobiles of the late 1940s, and in *Large Blade Venus* he demonstrates his profound belief that 'ultimate motion is ultimate rest'. As with the perfect balance between motion and rest as aimed for in Japanese haiku poetry within Turnbull's sculpture, eros and thanatos are held in absolute equilibrium with each other. There is on the one hand, the sexual allure of the sensual upward curve of the blade rising to the erect phallic handle; while, at the same time, this upward movement is held in perfect poise by the downward curve of the deadly weapon towards the execution block below. As with the ever-recurring sacrifice and regeneration ritual at the heart of the archetypal fertility myth of Frazier's *The Golden Bough*, *Large Blade Venus* must also forever draw blood from her sacrificial victims in order that her natural counterpart, *Leaf Venus,* can regenerate again.

This previously unpublished essay was written by Bill Hare in 2016 for *The Scottish Endarkenment* exhibition, which Andrew Patrizio and Bill Hare curated at the Dovecot Studios for the Edinburgh Festival.

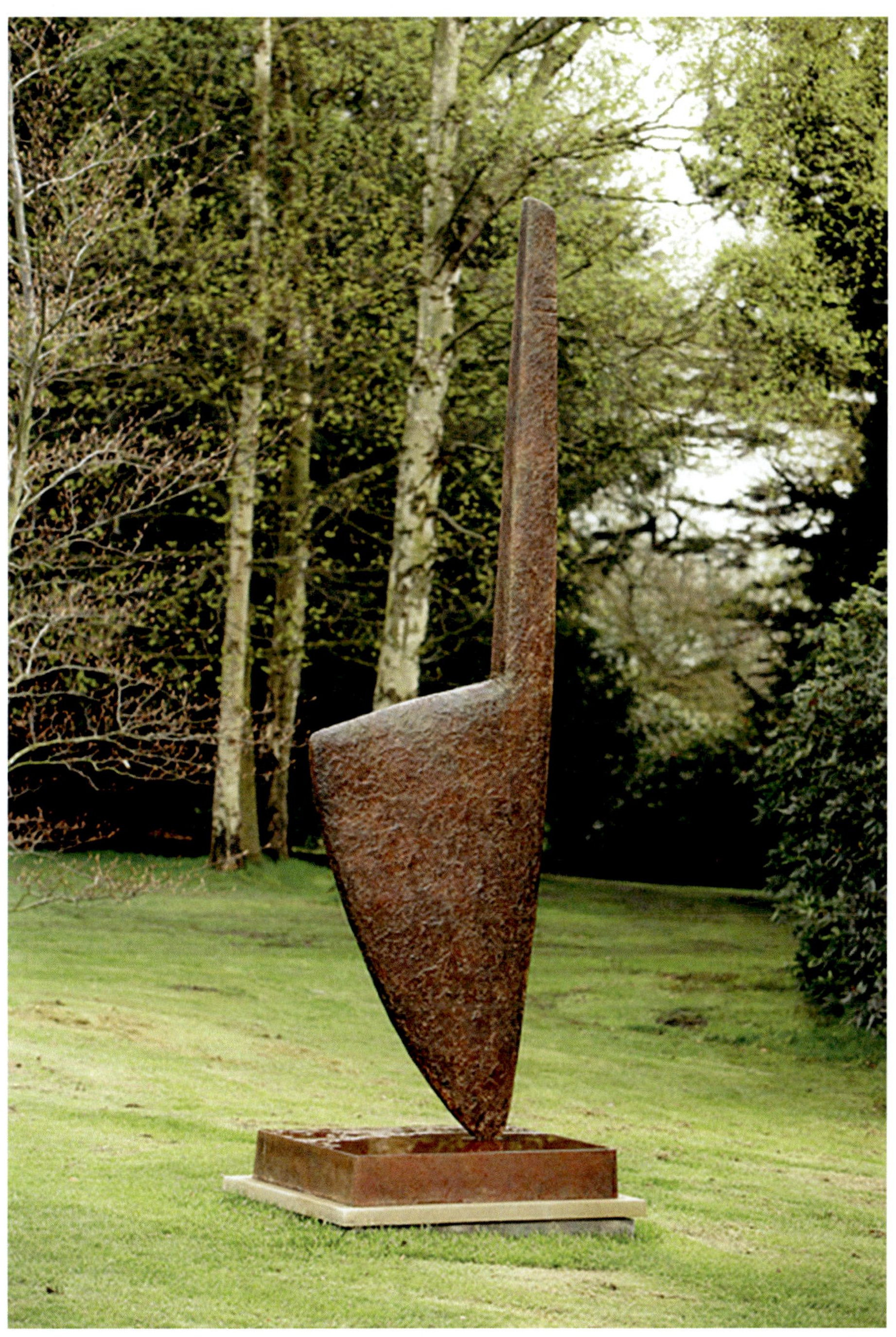

Large Blade Venus
1990
Bronze, 317x99x68cm

Reproduced courtesy of the artist's estate

Eduardo Paolozzi

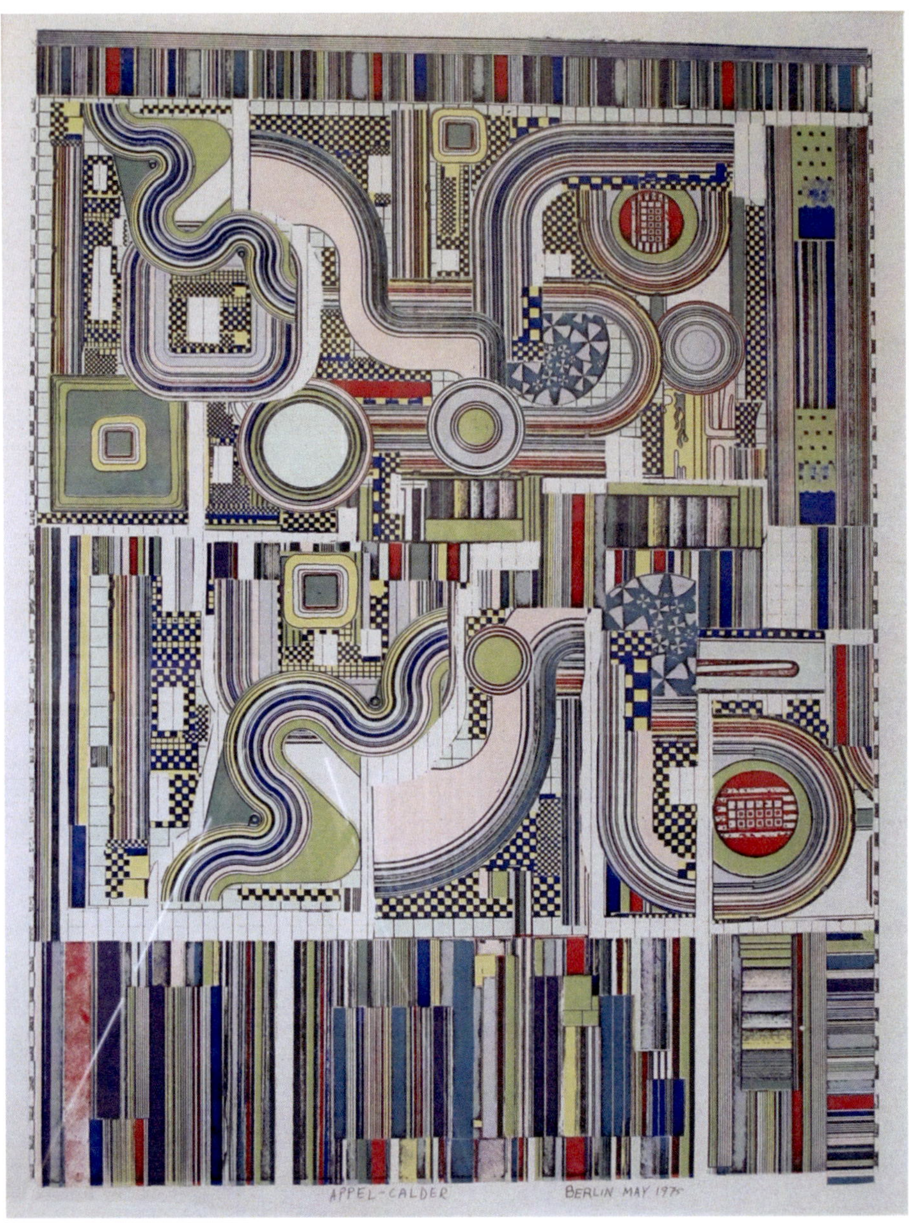

Appel–Calder
1975
Screen print, 72x54cm
Reproduced courtesy of the Paolozzi Foundation

Eduardo Paolozzi Interview

Your project for a sculpture in Leith Walk, Edinburgh (The Manuscript of Monte Cassino), is your first public commission for your native city. Were your approach and ideas for this sculpture affected in any way by its proximity to this area where you were born and brought up?
First of all, you've got to deal with the particular area where you are shown. In this case, it was an area I'd known as a child, a homogeneous world. The Leith I knew is long since gone: the Leith of the tram cars and the flea-pit cinemas. I think the house I was born in has been demolished. I don't know who was responsible but they made a mess there, a ghastly urban mess. But it was the same kind of mess that was repeated in a lot of cities in England where they've ripped out this heart and they've put in the speculators and people who don't have too much sensitivity about people's needs. They've destroyed and they've created a kind of area which is made up of bizarre parking areas and underground passes that are totally without soul. The people who have created this have got no involvement other than profit. They don't actually live there. They might be just speculators from the south, who are like carpet-baggers, just pillaging towns. You're inheriting a mess. That makes the problem doubly difficult. And there's no other examples to draw upon in Scotland which could give you a kind of model or a guide to improving that area. It's an area that has a lot of room for development and there's not much movement. There's always this myopicism where people don't look at other models, other activities, in other parts of the world. They seem to be oblivious to what other places are able to do. For example, in my Rhinegarden project, I made a number of big bronze abstracts but also included stones from a nearby bridge that was demolished. It's certainly an area which has been humanised by very simple sculptures. But whether in that particular area in Leith Walk, it's not only a question of money and budget. You need a support system, enthusiasm and a group of people who are enthusiastic about the development of an area. Not just an exercise in tidying up. What I've tried to touch on, in the beginning, about the ambiance of Scotland is you've got to get vibrations from all these bodies. These bodies have to come together as a cluster. On the edge of the cluster, or in the middle of the cluster is the artist himself. But he's not the cosmos. One's made a lot of suggestions about the area but one's not necessarily had a lot of feedback. From that particular point of view, where you see Calton Hill, a good landscape gardener without any help from a fine artist could just extend the Calton Hill idea with rocks and stones. It would be quite feasible. But we're talking about imagery and vision and I'm still looking for it.

Was Scottish art's apparent reluctance to concern itself with industry, technology and its effect on human society one of the factors which made you decide to look elsewhere for stimuli to develop your ideas?

I'm wondering about that. Not quite. I would have thought there's a strange paradox about Edinburgh College of Art that instead of it embracing technology and design, as an historical moment and more or less rejecting classicism, they could have gone the other way. In New York, they've just started a new academy which works to the precepts of the École des Beaux-Arts. The irony is that Edinburgh College of Art was well equipped to have gone the same way instead of trying to keep up with modernism. That to me is a bigger question. The question of struggling with art and technology seems to be a kind of secondary one.

It is relatively easy to locate themes concerning anxiety and pessimism about the industrial and technological world in your work of the 1950s, for instance your St Sebastian, yet your sculptures of the 1960s, for example Poem for the Trio MRT, *seem forged, like the society Harold Wilson also envisaged, in the 'white heat of a technological revolution'. Is your work of the more optimistic 1960s less critical than the previous decade?*
The 1950s of course was the beginning of the Cold War. The nice guy business was over. Society has changed radically since the '60s. I think in general there was a kind of optimism about that time. The *Poem for the Trio MRT* was trying to make a statement about working in a factory environment. I don't know how one uses the word pessimism. I mean, a newspaper report has warned that even a glass of tap water might be dangerous. It's almost impossible to take a realistic view and not be depressed about the way, whatever the reason is, technology is at an accelerated pace destroying everything. Nothing could be more human and natural than a glass of tap water. But to think that people now view that with suspicion must be the apotheosis of pessimism about future life.

From the early 1960s you showed and continue to show a willingness to bridge fine art with engineering practice and commercial print processes, ie by using and designing industrial components assembled by skilled craftsmen and collaborating with silkscreen printers. Was this interdisciplinary approach a response to the debate which had been initiated by people like CP Snow who, in his influential lecture The Two Cultures (1959), urged for more interaction between the fields of art, science and technology?
When you say art and technology, I wonder what art you mean and what technology you mean. I don't see why one has to put this in its own little cubby-hole. The artist might theorise endlessly about art and technology and there's a long history of dead corpses who've been dogmatic about that. They've all disappeared. One's so familiar with the knowledge in architecture that you have to use a good team or your project will never be built. It's also not very new. There's the famous Moholy-Nagy story of him telephoning and having his art made by someone else. A lot of great art would be impossible. If you're able to include, when you talk about technology, the building of a classic airliner, these things are absolutely impossible without whole teams and a whole tradition. But I

can't understand why you have to make two categories: hand-made art and great art that's made by teams of anonymous people. So when you're talking very generally about art and technology, you break it down in one way and I break it down in another. I see all kinds of ironies. You can commission a young artist to do a mural in an electronics factory – it could only fetch hostility. It doesn't necessarily guarantee illumination, nor is it closing this imaginary gap between art and technology. You've described two opposing forces whereas I see the opposing forces in a completely different way. I gave a lecture at King's College and I saw two thrusts of thought: the lecture was called 'Jesus and the Volkswagen'.

Is this a conscious interdisciplinary approach, bridging gaps between the areas of industry and the hand of the artist?
It just seemed very natural at the time. Not every sculptor who has bronze sculptures has his own foundry so you grow up with that notion. It's different for a painter who can buy enough canvasses to do abstract art *ad infinitum*. It's much more difficult if you're going to do a lot of sculptures.

In an interview with Richard Hamilton in 1965 you emphasise directness as being of prime importance in your work and that can certainly be seen in the organic bronze sculptures and raw collages of the '50s. Did you have to sacrifice this desire for directness when you moved into a more collaborative working method?
Well it's just a different kind of directness, I suppose. And of course we're talking of something nearly 40 years ago. I find every situation changes. It's totally different. So if you have any dogma, you've got to throw that overboard. I don't even know if there's such a thing called collaboration. I can't see why one should wrestle with this idea. I mean it depends on the social structure, about the magnificence of the object and as I was saying, a lot of that vibration comes from controls beyond the artist.

Various aspects of your work – the diversity of imagery, the obsession with the importance of detail and your much-quoted desire not to be 'morally edifying' – seem to suggest a similar approach to the analytical method of the scientist. Is there a conscious intention on your part, like the objective scientist, to discover an underlying order to experience?
Discovery is quite a good word. The World Service has a programme called *Discovery*, I don't know if it's still running. But science has got so complex now. Even the language, trying to describe it to the layman, is so complex that it's almost incomprehensible I would have thought. And there's evidence of this. I've used a lot of images from *Scientific American* for collage but a lot of the language is quite incomprehensible unless you've got a knowledge of physics or of mathematics. But they always sugar the pill by having wonderful archaeological articles which are quite comprehensible. I don't know if that's deliberate, but we know, for example, that archaeology or micropalaeontology are very attractive

things to read about. But also I would suggest that if explanation of technology is getting complex, so is explanation of modern art.

Do you as an artist feel obliged to try to come to terms with this difficult language of technology?
There's always hope that you will catch up with it later on and that there's always hope that one will reach another form of enlightenment, that you can fit parts of it together. I think fitting the parts together is part of the process of enlightenment.

The diversity of experience is very much reflected in your renowned use of collage and assemblage. Free association is very much a feature of the 20th century, in art, ie Surrealism and in science, ie psycho-analysis. However, there is also the more structured use of association. I am referring to Eisenstein's theories and use of montage in film. Here the film-maker brings images A and B together not only to create something new, meaning C, but also to urge the viewer to some kind of political thought and action. Do you see your work, in any way, serving such a purpose?
Not that much but I'm getting very much into writing, which was the raw material of Eisenstein, where his projects came from. But of course he drew quite a lot. What you haven't mentioned is that when Eisenstein did a film about the knights sinking in the ice that was all done in midsummer. In a way, cinema is sometimes closer to the theatre, which is a sort of cabinet of illusion. Making an object in a way you have the kind of opposite thing – it depends on its setting for it to be noticeable. It's very interesting to see how part of creating is often having an instinct for the right discipline to conceive the object.

If you are now considering the written as opposed to the visual medium, does this then mean the 'object' has changed?
Mm. There's a tradition. The written work of Leonardo da Vinci is colossal. The *Hammer Codex* is almost entirely text, with very few illustrations. Also Michelangelo was a great writer and wrote a lot of poetry. It's only if you're thinking in terms of art as conceived by Henry Moore that the whole idea of writing seems rather unnecessary somehow. But I think one has to redefine all these emotions and the disciplines you are able to manipulate.

From the 1970s, there seems to be an increasing emphasis on the destructive dimensions of science and technology on human society, in your thinking. There is even an echo of Thomas Carlyle in the statement, 'modernism is the acceptance of the concrete landscape and the destruction of the human soul', from your essay 'Junk and the New Arts and Crafts Movement' (1979). Does this, aligned with the ecological concerns of recent work, represent a shift in your attitude to the uses of science and technology?
I think that when I wrote that text it was really mild compared with what's happening now. I think that the race towards destruction is

colossal. That was all written before Chernobyl. Post-Chernobyl, they slaughtered 100,000 reindeer, all radioactive and buried in a deep pit. They can't even use the land now. Things have got worse. Probably the most moving metaphor, the most real metaphor is in the work of Francis Bacon who shows the whole dilemma. He's finalised it into the human figure. I myself think he's a very great artist and I think he's much greater to me than, say, Giacometti and even more impressive than late Picasso. It may be something to do with the way Bacon lives: a very simple, straightforward way. Also is the idea of dying. As you've suggested, I think the Arcadian thing is over. Pinter has used the phrase that we're all spiralling remorselessly toward self-destruction. You can either use art as a kind of mirror to your own soul, but you can also use it as a kind of shield. As a device for Arcadia I think David Hockney does that. I see a totally different California: he sees it as a kind of Eden, the Englishman's Eden. I see it as a hellish plateau of a thousand souls dying every day.

You said in the press before the last election that you did not intend to vote. The reason for this was your lack of faith in politicians' will and ability to deal with the mounting problems of the late 20th century. Does your recent The Artist as Hephaestus figure – the Greek Vulcan – in the role of teacher as well as maker seem to suggest that concerned artists and scientists now have the onus of responsibility on them?
One of the atmospheres that I've tried to pick up is that there's a certain feeling evoked by the figure holding symbols between the two hands, some might have called it a criticism or confusion. I like the idea that the artist is confused – what I was saying about discovery. No longer, like in the age of Enlightenment, do the universe and people's minds work like mechanisms. There's so many, one might say, broken wheels. On the figure, my instinct tells me that, as we've all got hands and feet and eyes, when people see a figure, they're able to make these immediate connections between 'I am' and 'That is.' There's another reason. If you do choose to make a figure you can't just make it homogeneous. You have to include your own notion of modernism. You've also got to show that it's constructed, which is the 20th century condition. You've got to see that it's all built up of different pieces. Sometimes the pieces don't fit. And that again becomes a projection of 'If the world doesn't fit any more, how does man?' In the art school, the figure is still important. It's not necessarily a disadvantage if you have Greek Mythology on the school syllabus.

There is the opening shot of you in the film EP Sculptor, shown on Channel 4, drawing from the classical sculptures in the Glyptothek, Munich…
That's the same thread. One is trying to disturb, which I think Bacon does very successfully, people's pre-judged ideas of how the modern artist functions in modern society. One of the things I wanted to wipe out right away at the beginning of the film is that it's not a man in a welding mask grinding away at a bit of old junk. You can get this incredible recharging

from the history of the subject. It's not all over. The door isn't closed. I thought it was an important statement to make in what I call the post-Beuys era. There is a mass of fundamentals and if you close the doors on that and open other doors… Maybe that's part of creativity – opening and closing doors. In the past, it was very homogeneous how you studied sculpture but now it's absolutely wide open. Everything's possible. And yet there's a paradox to that or an irony. Everything's possible and yet nothing is really successfully realised.

This interview was conducted by Andrew Patrizio and Bill Hare in 1998 for *Alba*, issue 11.

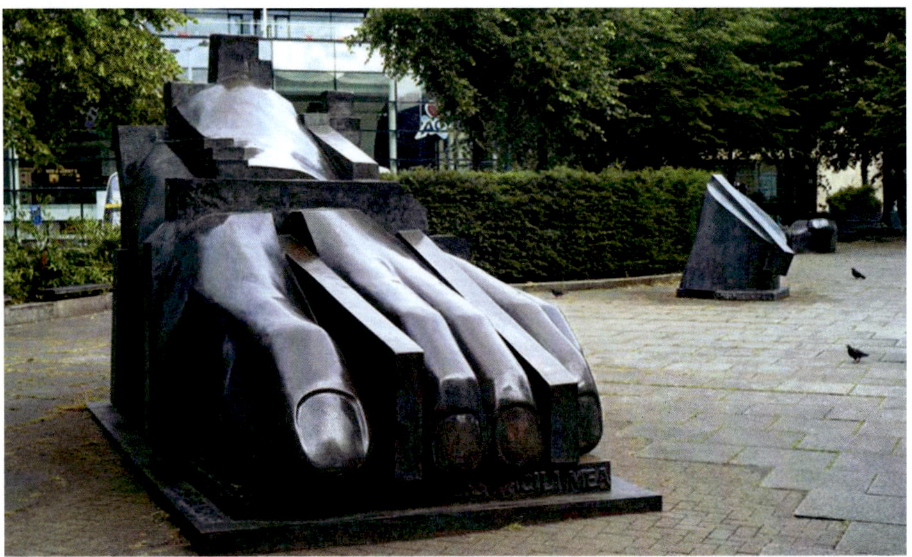

The Manuscript of Monte Cassino
1991
Bronze, 2.89x5.32x2.46m
Photograph © Luigi Giannetti

Five Counterculture Artists

Ian Hamilton Finlay (1925–2013)
Boyle Family:
Mark (1934–2005)
Joan Hills (1931–)
Sebastian (1962–)
Georgia (1963–)

IAN HAMILTON FINLAY and Boyle Family were without doubt two of the most important Scottish conceptual artists to emerge during the upheavals of the radical 1960s – the third would be Bruce McLean.

After leaving the Army, Finlay initially turned his artistic attention to writing both prose and poetry and, during the 1950s and early 1960s, he was part of the international movement of concrete poets. In the mid-1960s he and his wife, Sue, acquired a farm on the Southern Uplands at Stonypath and began to turn it into a landscape sculpture garden which later became the world-renowned Little Sparta. From this base, working with an array of highly skilled collaborators, Finlay engaged artistically and critically with the world-wide art and literary scene. Through a range of strategies, he gained both international fame and controversial notoriety with his particular interpretations and polemics on such sensitive issues as military power and revolutionary history, as well as art and politics. While Finlay was alive, I visited Little Sparta on a couple of occasions in connection with work for *Alba* magazine and also for an important Finlay exhibition, curated by Duncan Macmillan at the Talbot Rice Gallery, entitled *The Poor Fisherman* after Pierre Puvis de Chavannes (1991).

Boyle Family, initially known as Mark Boyle, came into being in the late 1950s when Mark Boyle and Joan Hills met in Harrogate, where Mark was in the Army and Joan was running a hairdressing business. Mark had previously studied law at University of Glasgow while Joan had attended Heriot-Watt University, Edinburgh. Both were ambitious, creative individuals and wanted to collaborate on a range of innovative artistic projects. They soon decided to make for London and quickly gravitated towards the then centre of British artistic radicalism, the ICA. They soon involved themselves in a number of avant-garde experimental practices such as installations and happenings and became prominent figures in the London counter-culture and pop music scene. Out of all their different and disparate activities, their major ongoing project emerged in the form of their *World Series* which aimed to seek out 1,000 randomly selected sites around the globe and then to study and reproduce the terrain of these sites as mimetically accurate as possible. Even though their two children joined and doubled the manpower of Boyle Family, there are, not surprisingly, hundreds of the World Series sites still to be visited in this sublimely epic project. I first made contact with Boyle Family when, in the late 1990s, they were typically having an out-of-the-way exhibition in a small flat in Leith. I had my baby son Jackson with me and Joan instantly fell into raptures over him. From this auspicious first encounter, I was invited to the Boyles' wonderful house in Greenwich in order to write about their work. Later I had the privilege to write a catalogue essay for their spectacular retrospective exhibition, *Boyle Family*, at the Scottish National Gallery of Modern Art in 2002.

Ian Hamilton Finlay

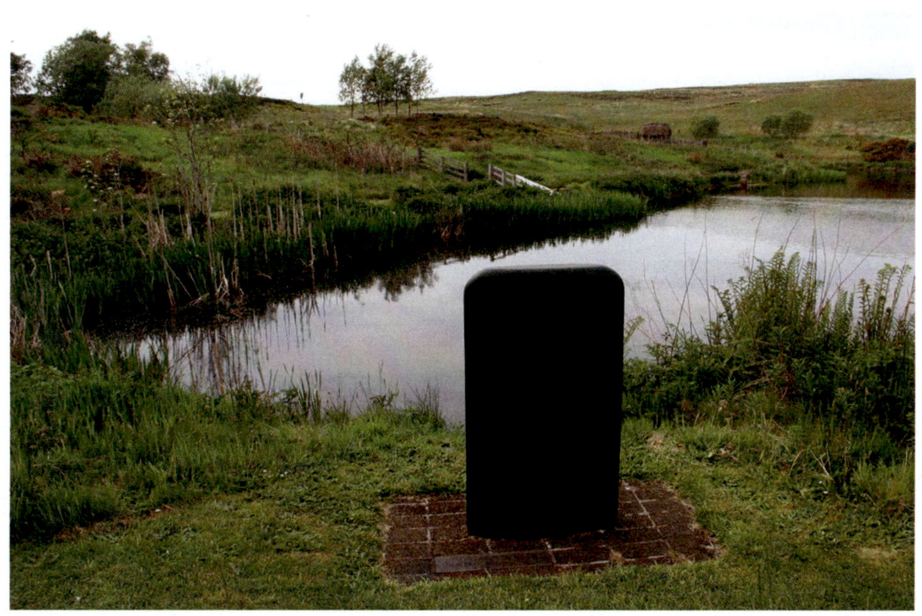

Nuclear Sail

1974

Slate (with John Andrew)

Reproduced courtesy of the Estate of Ian Hamilton Finlay

Minedscapes

Militarism and Modernism in the work of Ian Hamilton Finlay

Certain gardens are described as retreats when they are really attacks.
Ian Hamilton Finlay – *Detached Sentences*

AFTER BRIEFLY ATTENDING Glasgow School of Art, Ian Hamilton
Finlay entered Army service in 1942 and became a sergeant in the rasc
while seeing military action in Germany. After the War, he left the
Army, travelling around Scotland to pursue a variety of occupations
and artistic activities, such as writing short stories and poems, some of
which were included in his first important publication, *The Dancers
Inherit the Party* (1960). In 1961, Finlay, along with Jessie McGuffie,
set up Wild Hawthorn Press, which was to become an important outlet
for his later writings and artworks on paper. This was followed in
1962 by Finlay's periodical *Poor. Old. Tired. Horse.*, which was the
launching forum for much of the initial experimentation in his work
with visual and textual modernism, resulting in Finlay's involvement
with the emerging international concrete poetry movement. Although
geographically peripheral to the great cultural centres like London and
Paris, the radical and multi-disciplinary artistic activities of Finlay linked
him to the burgeoning counter-culture movement. Always the maverick
and jealous of his artistic integrity and personal independence, with his
wife Sue, Finlay moved to a remote and abandoned hillside farm on the
Southern Uplands called Stonypath. There they committed themselves to
a very Spartan existence, yet one which proved to be an enriching and
profoundly rewarding one for Finlay's artistic creativity and later critical
reputation. With great determination and imagination, together they
succeeded in transforming their original patch of bleak moorland in to
one of the most celebrated modern landscape gardens in the world, when
Stonypath became Little Sparta. It was here in this horticultural arcadian
setting of picturesque shady groves and hand-built miniature water ways
that Finlay had the opportunity to begin his strategy to engage with the
forms and iconography of military weaponry.

At the heart of Finlay's artistic attitudes and creativity is his alignment
with the pre-Socratic philosopher Heraclitus' view that flux, with its
never-ending ebb and flow between order and chaos, is the essential
nature of our existence. This attitude is implicit in Finlay's *Heroic
Emblems* prints, such as *Thunderbolt Steers All* and *Et in Arcadia Ego*
where military destruction, human mortality and the natural cycle of
things are played off against each other in an epic and tragic dialectic.
Furthermore, at the outer limits of Little Sparta, where the constructed
garden meets the natural wilderness of moor land beyond, there is carved
out on broken tablets of marble St Just's ominous epigram, 'The Present

Order is the Disorder of the Future'.

It should not take Shelley's 'Ozymandias' to make us realise that all civilisations come and go. We see this for instance by the fragmentary nature of the remains that have come down to us from the glorious achievements of the classical world. This is exemplified by the meagre scraps of writing from the early philosophers which have so inspired the poetic art of Ian Hamilton Finlay. Those fragments of Heraclitus' volatile philosophy are again echoed in Marx's prophetic warning that 'all that appears solid melts into air.' These words from *The Communist Manifesto* were written in the middle of the 19th century when much of Europe, particularly France, were experiencing yet another period of revolutionary fervour. For many, including Marx, all this transforming upheaval was ultimately due to the fact that a new modern epoch was coming into being. As the earlier Heraclitus and St Just might have foreseen, the old order was giving way to a new one in an unprecedented disruptive and disorderly manner with great social upheaval and mass violence continually breaking out throughout society. This was a period described by Marx as one of

> constant revolutionising of production, uninterrupted disturbance of all social conditions, everlasting uncertainty and agitation (which) distinguished the bourgeois epoch from the earlier ones.

Yet despite all the change and uncertainty, this was also a time of great anticipation, with many looking forward to unprecedented beneficial progress for all mankind.

This optimistic attitude was shared by the radically progressive artists of the time. Not only was the modern world now coming into existence, but with it, also a new kind of art which was appropriate for that brave new world of constant change and seemingly endless progress. In a time of such turmoil and violent conflict it is not surprising that progressive artists should take on a provocatively inspiring name which was looted from the military lexicon. For the first time such radical socially concerned artists became identified as the 'avant-garde'. Finlay would be an important heir to the ideals and aims of the original spirit of the avant-garde as can be seem in the way he has sought out, and reworked in his own individual manner, the methods and visual languages of modernism to engaged with the pressing forces of history that assail and threaten the very existence of our present world.

To understand this inheritance from modernism which Finlay has had to deal with in his art it is necessary to go back and briefly examine its troubled and disputed history since the mid-19th century. The early avant-gardists such as Courbet and Baudelaire very much saw themselves and their work as being in the vanguard of socio-political change through their strident opposition to existing inherited artistic conventions as well as their radical new approaches to representing the experiences of modernity. As with Marx, Baudelaire also regarded the dominant characteristic of modernity as 'transitory, fugitive and contingent' and thus the artist of modern life must address this constant changeability in contemporary society or be in danger of 'tumbling into the void of an abstract and indefinable beauty'. For a number of reasons however, that initial revolutionary spirit of social engagement as exemplified by the art of Courbet began to dissipate throughout the subsequent decades of the 19th century with the establishment of a dominant bourgeois society and its capitalist ideology. With the passing of those earlier revolutionary socio-political ideals for modern art the avant-garde gradually 'succeeded in detaching itself from society' in the words of Clement Greenberg which he wrote in his profoundly influential essay *Avant-garde and Kitsch* published just before the outbreak of World War II. Unlike Courbet, who was dismissive of 'the trivial goal of art for art sake', Greenberg argued that modernism should aim to free itself from all social connections and aim 'to the level of an Absolute... where subject matter or content becomes something to be avoided like the plague.' After America's great military successes and its post-war economic and military world domination, Greenberg's version of high modernism triumphed. Avant-garde practice turned self-critically inward-looking towards its own internal formal autonomy. Consequently, for the vast majority of people in western society modern art had become not only irrelevant to, and independent from, the socio-political dynamics of their lives; but also as invisible as the military weapons of mass destruction which were concealed behind the rhetoric of Cold War politics.

None of this has been lost on Ian Hamilton Finlay. He has used the different strategies of his art practice to draw our attention to the interconnectedness between modernism and modern militarism. For instance, 'absence of presence' has become a notable strategical feature in much of contemporary art practice. Ian Hamilton Finlay has given his own particular take on this phenomenon, particularly in dealing with the theme of militarism in his work. This aspect of his art practice involves the concept and utilisation of camouflage for instance. The artist has even provided a number of definitions in his witty *Camouflage Sentences* series. In one example, Finlay quotes Heraclitus yet again with 'Nature loves to hide', while in a more humorous view he observes that 'Camoufleurs are Monday painters'. In the end, however, he shows his deadly seriousness about this issue when he points out that, 'afv crews who applied camouflage colours to their vehicles, staked their lives on their art.' It is this dialectic of dual purpose in camouflage that attracts Finlay for it is used both to threaten as well as protect. This duality runs through the use of camouflage in various works found in the garden at Little Sparta. For Finlay, camouflage is inextricably linked to the transforming power of metamorphosis, which is the central message of his admired pre-Socratic philosophers. This transformation can take a fairly light-hearted form when the shell of a sculptured tortoise is labelled as *Panzer Leader*, or the when the 18th-century garden folly practice of placing carved stone pineapples over gateway entrances is replaced at Little Sparta by sculptured hand grenades – which, of course, have been given the nickname of 'pineapples' by the soldiers who actually use these weapons in action. Probably, however, Finlay's most celebrated transforming use of camouflage practice is his miniature stone aircraft carriers, which also double up as bird-tables and bird-baths. In such works Finlay, with masterly wit and cunning intelligence, condenses within a single object a whole range of dialectical concepts such as man and nature, the sublime and the beautiful, terror and power. In a truly uncanny fashion, what at first glance might appear to be a familiar piece of kitsch garden furniture turns out to be an unexpected and unsettling presence in such a seemingly peaceful setting.

These challenges to normal appearances and expectations can also take other forms at Little Sparta. Not only are works concealed behind a veil of horticultural camouflage but some are placed in the remoter outposts of Finlay's Apollonian territory. For instance, on the isolated banks of Lochan Eck with the bleak Southern Uplands as a backdrop, there is to be seen a diminutive slate monolith which has written on its brick base the inscription 'Nuclear Sail' (1974). Perspective and scale are crucially important strategies in the display and understanding of Finlay's work at Little Sparta. Thus, from a distance, and being ignorant of the work's title, the approaching viewer could be forgiven for initially mistaking this work as yet another piece of modernist sculpture in the Moore/Hepworth or Richard Serra mode – very much favoured by private corporations and public institutes as a way of displaying their economic and cultural power. On the other hand, the bleak rural setting for this work should eventually undermine such identification. Such Scottish landscapes are home to indigenous memorial monuments and standing stones and so Finlay's monolith from a distance could also be mistaken for one. Thus, even before a valid identification has taken place, Finlay has set up a dialectical interplay of the ancient and modern in the mind of the viewer, which will be exploited when the identity and true significance of the work can be fully meditated upon.

As with all of Finlay's visual works and poetic texts, *Nuclear Sail* – despite its stark simplicity of compact form – is bursting with conflicting allusions and possible meanings. The first and most pressing contradiction is of course embedded in the title itself. The word 'nuclear' immediately brings to mind missiles that can be launched at any time by Polaris nuclear submarines which are based at the Holy Loch. Thus, we have here yet another piece of Finlay's petrified modern armoury, this time in the form of what appears to be a conning tower. This possible identification is, however, challenged by the other title word, 'sail'. To appreciate the significance of this apparent contradiction, it has to be remembered that at the heart of Finlay's aesthetics there is a constant dialogue between the ancient and modern worlds. Thus, *Nuclear Sail* condenses and encapsulates the history of naval warfare from the earliest sighting of the

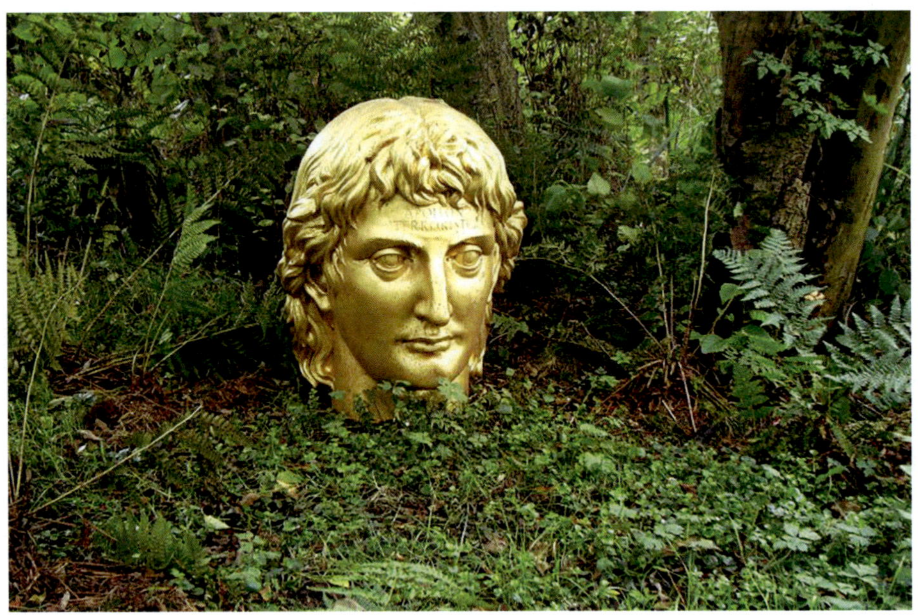

Apollon Terroriste
1989
Inscribed gilded epoxy resin (with Alexander Stoddart)
Photograph: Wikimedia Commons

sailing warships in the ancient world to our own times with its hidden nuclear-powered vessels of ultimate destruction. Furthermore, it is not only through time that we are encouraged to travel imaginatively but also through space. This takes in another intriguing feature of *Nuclear Sail*, for it is placed on the bank – rather than in the water – of Lochan Eck. This placement might be explained in two ways, one poetic, the other political. Firstly, Finlay has always been fascinated by boats and, even though Little Sparta is land based, being roughly equidistant from Scotland's eastern and western seaboards, the garden is full of poetic references to the natural and human bond between land and sea. Finlay, for instance, sometimes referred to Little Sparta as 'An Inland Garden'. Secondly, the Cold War political and military implications of *Nuclear Sail* take us back to the issue of camouflage (conning tower/dorsal fin) and invisibility. Therefore, although we may not be able to see these nuclear submarines as they hide far away on their deadly journeys in the depths of the world oceans, we on the land – wherever we may go or hide – are always within their sights and range, forever under their constant threat of annihilation.

On the opposite bank of Lochan Eck to *Nuclear Sail*, Finlay has placed in contrast *Inscribed Column*, which is a dedication to that most revolutionary figure, St Just. On it is written St Just's words, 'The world has been empty since the Romans', which could be imagined as an ironic comment on the anonymous blankness of *Nuclear Sail*. Finlay articulated his feelings about this crucial difference between the ancient and modern world with regards to their attitude to militarism in a letter to Yves Abrioux (1984). There he wrote:

> Democracies are not at ease with their weaponry, or their art, since both involve (take their stand on) other values – those of the 'Southland'. Classicism was at home with power; the modern democracies (whole secularism has produced extraordinary power) are not. The warship is an unrecognised, necessary temple.

Finlay is correct. For instance, in ancient times an erected military monument would have openly celebrated the triumphs of the victors – whether on a Roman distance slab from the Antonine Wall or, for that matter, on a Pictish standing stone as found at Aberlemno. In our time, however, we prefer to live in a condition of voluntary blind unawareness to the military threat of self-annihilation and only watch conventional local conflicts at a safe televised distance. Not wishing to be confronted with the truly frightening reality of our own precarious situation, the ultimate sin that a critic like Noam Chomsky or an artist such as Finlay can commit is to draw our attention and warn us of the dangers which will result from this state of our false consciousness and denial. As Cleo McNelly Kearns perceptively points out in her essay, 'Armis et Litteris':

> Finlay deploys the explosive shocks of this visual minefield he has planted to masterly effect... Here are the ultimate blasphemies, idols peculiar to our time, which, unlike more 'primitive' ages, will not even recognise what they serve.

The treatment of militarism in Finlay's Apollonian and neo-classical work has a pronounced Nietzschean will to power dimension to it as he philosophises with 'a hammer'. Nietzsche, in his early work, *The Birth of Tragedy*, presents Apollo and Dionysus as the twin deities of the creative arts, yet each also possessed their own awesome destructive powers. With such contradictions in mind, Finlay announces this disturbing duality of the divine, with the inscribed Temple dedication, 'To Apollo, His Music, His Missiles, His Muses'. The Apollo of Little Sparta, however, is not that of Nietzsche but is rather the Hyperborean Apollo of the ancient Greeks. As Stephen Bann has pointed out, from his northern outpost, Apollo is 'a displaced deity' forever seeking throughout history human agencies to carry out his will – be it an ultra-revolutionary St Just or a nuclear missile for instance. At Little Sparta, Apollo is regularly given the idealised portrait head of the French revolutionary, as exemplified in *Apollon*

Terroriste or is armed with weapons of modern warfare – for instance, a Kalashnikov rifle – as seen in *Apollo on George Street*. (The austerely committed Little Sparta is of course the inveterate enemy of the indulgent and decadent 'Athens of the North'.)

Finlay's art is highly complex and has a dual ancient and modern outlook, with militarism and modernism the intertwined twin themes in his work. For instance, these two features of Finlay's work come together again in *Luftwaffe – after Mondrian* (1974) which is part of a series created as 'Homages' to the founding fathers and movements of modernism, including the other two pioneers of abstraction, Malevich and Kandinsky. Mondrian, however, must have had a particular appeal to Finlay, as both he and the Dutch mystic were obsessed with the concept and nature of social and artistic order and the ideal of the Absolute. Yet while Mondrian continuously strove to attain such a perfect state – not only in his art but also within his working, living environment and ultimately through his philosophical writings on modern society – Finlay, in contrast, had complex attitudes towards all forms of Utopianism within the history of human affairs. In *Luftwaffe – after Mondrian*, the absolute ideals of modernism and the threat of militarism collide. In Finlay's work, the compositional format clearly references Mondrian's World War I proto-abstract work, *Jetty and Ocean*, which was painted at the time when the Dutch artist had fled back to Holland to avoid the military slaughter of the time. *Luftwaffe – after Mondrian*, as the punning titles implies, again deals with modernism on the run from yet another military threat. This time, Mondrian's mystical crosses are now turned into the militarist symbol of the Luftwaffe, creating a conflation of those two extreme ideals of modern romanticism – Mondrian's transcendental mysticism on the one hand and the Nazis' will to power on the other. Interestingly, Finlay here points out that both the Nazis and Mondrian were, in their very different ways and for very different reasons, committed to the Absolutist idea of finally putting an end to art.

Finlay always prefers to keep an objective distance from the actual making of his multi-medium work through his use of skilled collaborators. This practice must add to the marked tension in much of his work between a strong sense of intellectual detachment and a powerful feeling of passionate commitment. Thus, Finlay's art is always open to multiple, even contradictory, interpretations through his creative strategy of layering his work with contingent references, tangential quotations and polemic debates. At the heart of Finlay's artistic purpose is to set up a meaningful dialogue between our present situation and our inherited histories, in order that we might realise the burdens of our past choices and the vital importance our future options and ultimate survival.

This previously unpublished essay was written by Bill Hare in 2016 for *The Scottish Endarkenment* exhibition, which Andrew Patrizio and Bill Hare curated at the Dovecot Studios for the Edinburgh Festival.

Boyle Family

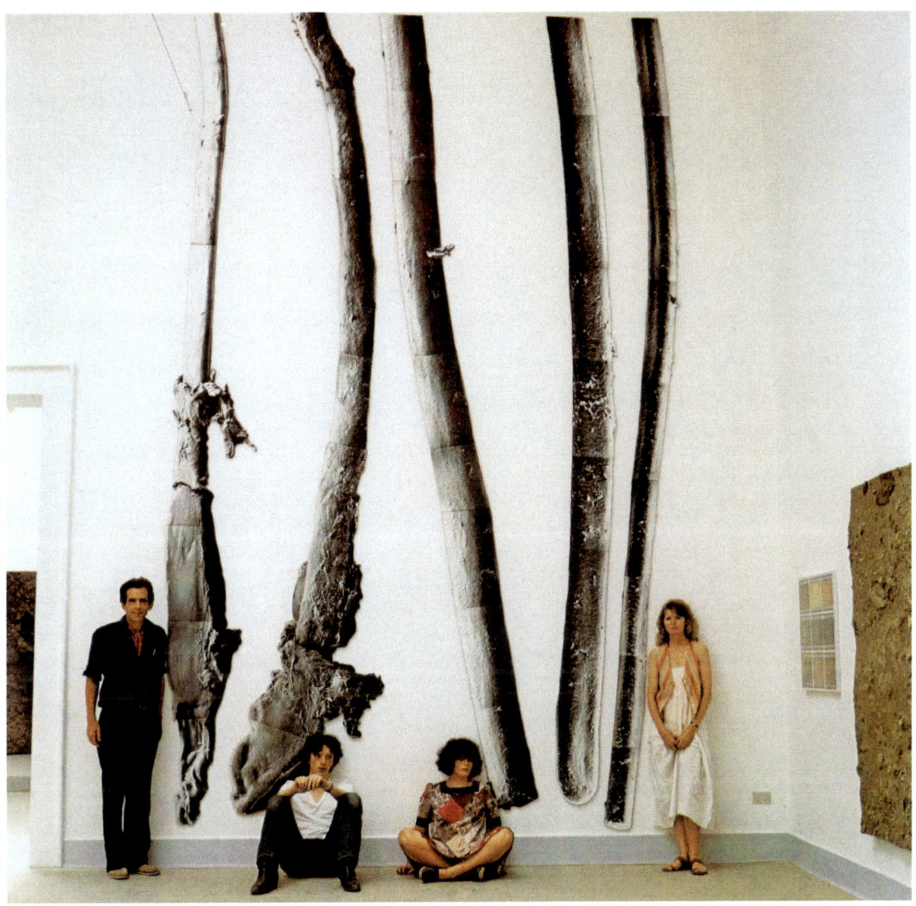

Boyle Family with mosaic of electron microscope photographs of
human hair
Venice Biennale, 1978
Reproduced courtesy of the artist and Fleming-Wyford Foundation

Boyle Family Interview

The particular occasion for this interview is the acquisition and display of your Tidal Series at the Scottish National Gallery of Modern Art (currently on display in New Acquisitions at the SNGMA). Maybe we could begin by you giving an account of the making of this important work?

SEBASTIAN BOYLE: We all first went to Camber Sands in 1966, which is a very important trip in our work as that was when Mark and Joan made the first resin and fibreglass studies of the surface of the Earth. They had already moved on from making their assemblages to making the first Earth pieces using a grid system to transfer real material onto boards covered with resin. In the demolition sites in west London they were working in, they would find a board, cover it in resin and then transfer the real material from the site – whether that was bricks, stones, twigs, bottles, newspaper, dust, etc – to the appropriate place on the board.

But these transfer pieces were very heavy and had to be flat and Mark and Joan wanted to make larger pieces that presented the details and shape of the surface of the Earth, not just the detritus lying on top. They'd heard about resins and fibreglass and they wanted to experiment with these new materials. They needed somewhere where they would be relatively undisturbed and so a beach close to London seemed a good idea.

So we went there around Easter 1966 and the first *Beach Studies* were made. We then went back in 1969 when Mark and Joan wanted to make a series of works that included time as being an element in the work. Questions of time and change had been present in the 1960s projection works but the *Earth Studies* seemed fixed and permanent and they wanted to show this isn't the case. So *Tidal Series* is a critical series for us. It introduces time into the *Earth Studies* and provides a link to the wider Boyle Family project. The series comprises 14 studies made on the same square of the beach after each tide, two tides a day, for a week, showing the constantly changing tide and ripple patterns created by the sand, the wind and the tide.

I would now like to turn to the broader aspect of Boyle Family as an artistic phenomenon. Unlike other artists, you have operated under a number of different names, such as Mark Boyle, Boyle and Hills, the Institute of Contemporary Archaeology, the Sensual Laboratory, through to Boyle Family. What were the reasons for all these name changes?

SB: Initially works were exhibited under Mark's name, which was partly because when Mark and Joan started out, they didn't expect to be making a living as artists. They and all their artist friends were sure they would always have to have second jobs to get by. When they started to exhibit in the early '60s, most art dealers thought it was easier to sell work by a single male artist and, for Mark and Joan, the possibility they could actually make a living out of making art seemed so amazing that it was a battle which they felt they didn't need to fight. All their friends knew that Mark and Joan were working together as a team. Mark's name was almost a *nom de plume* for the two of them. Later in the 1960s, they created the Institute of Contemporary Archaeology and the Sensual Laboratory almost as front organisations to interact with 'officialdom' in some way, whether that was to help get permission to work at a site or deal with the police, a film lab or a hire company. Companies didn't like dealing with scruffy looking artists. So the Institute of Contemporary Archaeology sounded appropriately official for doing the *Earth Studies*, and Sensual Laboratory was their production company for the projection pieces and later for their interactions with the music business. Then, over time, we shed those cover names and it just came down to the four of us working together and to give a public face to that fact we adopted the name 'Boyle Family'.

Can I now go back to the beginnings of what eventually would become Boyle Family? Although both of you were originally from Scotland – Joan, Edinburgh, and Mark, Glasgow – you met by chance, or fate, in Harrogate in 1957. Neither of you had much, if any, formal art training, yet you wanted to make art together. What was it that made you feel you could form a creative partnership?
JOAN HILLS: Passion. I think it was just a sum total of wanting to be together, and working together, and bashing ideas around in the same space for a number of years and this is what came out of it. From the very first meeting we knew that we would be creating something together. He was writing poetry, I was painting, and we were interested in music, jazz, theatre and performance.
SB: You thought you were going to do something creative together but you weren't thinking that would be necessarily as visual artists. It was a whole spectrum of possibility. Over the next few years you experimented with different art forms and techniques, such as happenings, projections, film, photography and sculpture because you were not sure which techniques and abilities you might need.
JH: Exactly. We wanted to experiment, try things out and see where they might lead. We still don't know if what we do is art. That issue seems superfluous.

Joan, you and Mark moved to London at the beginning of what would later be known as the 'swinging '60s'. What was it like for you trying to break into the London art scene then and how did you establish your credentials as radical and innovative artists so quickly?
JH: When you were in it, how did you know when it was starting to swing? You didn't. You were just leading an everyday life and still interested in the things that you were interested in, like going to galleries, listening to plays on the radio. If anything like the *Theatre of the Absurd* plays came to the Royal Court, we would go and try to see them. We were

extremely interested in Beckett and seeing everything that was possible. There weren't hierarchies that you had to get through. The old ICA on Dover Street was a place that people went to and hung around in because they were interested in pictures or writing or communication. We went to some of the shows and talks and met a few people.

SB: It was a small scene – I remember that you and Mark would say that when you were putting on an event, slightly later, in 1963–4, that you would call up 20 or 30 contacts and friends who were interested in what you were doing and who would come and support you – and vice versa. Whether it was at Better Books bookshop, the ICA, Signals, or, what did you say, Gallery One or Gustav Metzger's event with the acid at the South Bank?

JH: That's right.

SB: You weren't really looking to establish yourselves as radical and innovative artists, were you? You were just trying to make work?

JH: No, we were just trying to get on with our lives.

SB: I think 1963 was really quite a turning point. Somehow you got the show at Woodstock Gallery under Mark's name. You also went up to Edinburgh to visit your parents, taking slides of the assemblages with you and went round to see Jim Haynes who had started his paperback bookshop. He had a gallery in the basement, didn't he?

JH: He wanted very much to get the things down into the basement gallery but some of them were just too large to go down the staircase. It was his suggestion that I take the slides round to the Traverse Theatre, which was in a tenement on the Royal Mile and when I got there, they were preparing for their first production at the festival. That's when I first met Ricky Demarco. They didn't have a gallery but he was very enthusiastic about what they were going to be doing and thought it would be great to put on our show at the same time in a room upstairs. So that was the beginning of the Traverse Gallery.

SB: It was in doing the exhibition during the festival that you met the artist Ken Dewey who'd been asked by John Calder to put on a 'happening' as one of the events at the international drama conference at the McEwan Hall.

JH: Yes. It was a very conflicting period for drama because many people thought that British theatre and drama in London were pretty superb but we felt that more exciting things could happen. Ken Dewey brought that out in all of us.

SB: Calder had asked two American artists, Alan Kaprow and Ken Dewey, to come over and do events to mark the end of the conference. Dewey worked collaboratively, particularly with local artists, and he must have thought that you and Mark were good people to get involved with his 'happening' or event. The event they put on, *In Memory of Big Ed*, was really the first British performance art event that went out into the wider public consciousness. It caused a huge furore because it had involved a nude model being taken across the balcony and was on the front page of most of the national papers. Questions were asked in Parliament and the police prosecuted Calder and the model. It caused a major scandal, but one unexpected consequence was that you were then the artists who'd put on 'that' event in Edinburgh. It wasn't planned but it gave you a bit of a name and meant you were able to put on more events in London and get more people to come and see them.

JH: It didn't feel as rapid as that at the time, but I'm sure these things counted. That's absolutely true.

During that period of great social and cultural upheaval in post-war Britain, you were regarded as a vital force within the British Counterculture movement. How did you see what you were doing in relation to all the other changes that were taking place at the time?

SB: I have the sense that Mark and Joan were beginning to find a kind of identity among a group of people at the ICA who were trying to do something different, whether in music, theatre, film or art. It was a group of people who believed in experimentation, aware that they were part of a new generation trying to do something alternative to abstract expressionism or Pop art. They wanted to be grounded in the real world and real experience. Joan had done a bit of work with her film colleagues, working for the Labour party of Harold Wilson.

JH: Inserts for the election of 1964. We never saw Pop art as our thing, we saw it as fantasy somehow.

sb: You felt, though, that it was an exciting time, with Kennedy as President and Wilson talking about the white heat of technological change – the world was changing and Britain was changing.

JH: There's no doubt that we were aware things were developing in different directions. Society was just breaking down a bit, as far as new ideas were concerned. It was a stimulating time.

Your wide-ranging activities during the 1960s such as your initiatives in the area of happenings and light projections have had a profound impact on the development of both British art and popular musical entertainment. Looking back, are you surprised that this aspect of your work has been so influential?

JH: No, because in the days of going to dances and things in the 1950s and early '60s, ballrooms had glitter balls, music, perhaps a colour wash on a wall and that was it. Suddenly, we were able to create something that came from another background altogether, slightly scientific. In our projection events we were setting up little scientific experiments, which we watched as they developed and then we'd start another one and that would go on top of the first, then we'd fade one out, start another and so on. When we went to the States with Hendrix and Soft Machine, we found the big New York and Californian light show teams were doing something very different. In some ways more commercial.

SB: You weren't thinking of it as being popular entertainment but an art event. You did some experiments with the projections on your own terms at home, for us, and for friends, then you started doing it on a wider scale, developing projection events such as *Son et Lumière for Earth, Air, Fire and Water* in art spaces, before you were asked to do a projection event, at the first night of the London underground club, UFO. I think it is important to say that UFO wasn't only a great club and it wasn't just about the music. It was a great art club. It was a place where theatre and dance groups performed, poets came and read and avant-garde films were shown. It was a meeting place for all sorts of alternative artists from all over the world and, while it became famous for the music and the projections that Mark and Joan were doing, I think that it was also very important as a creative hub. Their projections became the main visual element of the club and the bands who played there wanted these kinds of visuals for their gigs. The psychedelic light show has been credited with being the beginning of the big rock gig stage show with amazing projections and special effects – and Mark and Joan were there at the beginning.

Throughout the 1960s, in your monumental ambition to include 'everything' in your work, you took a multimedia, collaborative approach involving theatre, film, sound, music, archaeology and scientific research. Yet, by the beginning of the next decade you were cutting back on this highly varied approach and focusing mainly on what was to become the epic World Series. What brought about this change in artistic strategy?
SB: It wasn't so much a change in artistic strategy as a change of scale. Up until 1971, Mark and Joan hoped that it might be possible to put on quite large-scale multimedia performances using projections, film and sound and at the same time make progress with the *World Series* and other *Earth Studies* projects. Indeed, the idea was that these events could be put on at museums to coincide with our exhibitions and that it would be an interesting way of showing the range of our interests, combining exhibitions maybe with our concerts with Soft Machine and contemporary theatre or dancers such as Graziella Martinez.

So the exhibition that launched *World Series* at the ICA in 1969 was billed as being by Mark Boyle, the Sensual Laboratory and the Institute of Contemporary Archaeology, bringing together the *Earth Studies*, projections, events, body works and sound pieces. And Soft Machine did a gig with Boyle Family projections during the show and during the following exhibitions at the Gemeentemuseum in The Hague and the Henie Onstad Kunstsenter near Oslo. The combination of the exhibitions and the concerts was great for us, the museums and I think for Soft Machine, whose members liked playing in venues that weren't the usual rock venues and festivals. It would have been great to have kept it going. Unfortunately, we then had a bad experience in Berlin in 1971 at an alternative culture festival, where we were putting on an exhibition, Soft Machine gig and a performance piece Mark and Joan had been developing called *Requiem for an Unknown Citizen*. This was an event piece studying society at large using theatre, random films, sounds and projections. The festival turned out to be a bit of a fiasco and we hastily performed *Requiem* instead at the De Lantaren Theatre in Rotterdam.

This experience, coupled with the problems of having a theatre group and the financial problems it posed, led to the realisation that it wasn't going to be possible to have a large team without major funding. Mark and Joan were still interested in making multimedia, multi-sensual work but the team was limited to us as a family and the presentations were kept on a smaller scale within the exhibitions, showing film installations before video became widely available to artists. There was a shift to the *Earth Studies* and the *World Series* in particular but we have always thought that the projections, films, sound works and happenings are part of our continuing overall body of work.

Maybe we should now concentrate on the work with which Boyle Family is most identified, the World Series. Could you tell us something about the circumstances that brought this mammoth project into being?
SB: After making the first *Earth Studies* in Camber Sands and then working on sites in the area around our flat in Holland Park, Mark and Joan wanted to do a *London Series* but, as they couldn't drive, this was approximately a two square mile area of west London, which we could all walk to. Then we had to leave that flat as it was being knocked down to clear space for Shepherd's Bush roundabout and Mark and Joan realised they couldn't start a new *London Series* each time we moved and that, rather than do a *British* or *European Series*, they could expand the *Earth Studies* project to be a survey of the whole of planet Earth. The Americans and Russians might have been racing to get man to the moon but we could undertake our own study of the Earth. For the *World Series*, it was decided that 1,000 sites should be selected by using the biggest map of the world that we could find, blindfolding people, and then asking them to throw or fire darts at this map. We would then go to these sites and study them.

You must have realised that 1,000 sites randomly scattered far and wide across 'the surface of the Earth' would never be completed in any of your lifetimes. Thus you would have to be selective as to what you could accomplish. On what basis is the selection of sites made?
SB: No, Mark and Joan really did think that they were going to be able to do it in their lifetimes! They wrote in the catalogue for the ICA show that it was a 25-year project and that they could do 40 sites a year. We realised pretty quickly that it wasn't going to be possible, probably when we went to The Hague in 1970 to do the first site and realised how much work was going to be involved. I think we've undertaken and completed approximately 20 of the 1,000 sites. Each one is a bit like making a short film – it's a major undertaking. Of course, all the other works we've done have in a sense been helping us fund and make the *World Series* project. Quite often, the selection of which site we will do ties in with an exhibition. For example, while we were having a show in Oslo we went and made works in Norway and we made the Sardinian one for the Venice Biennale in 1978.

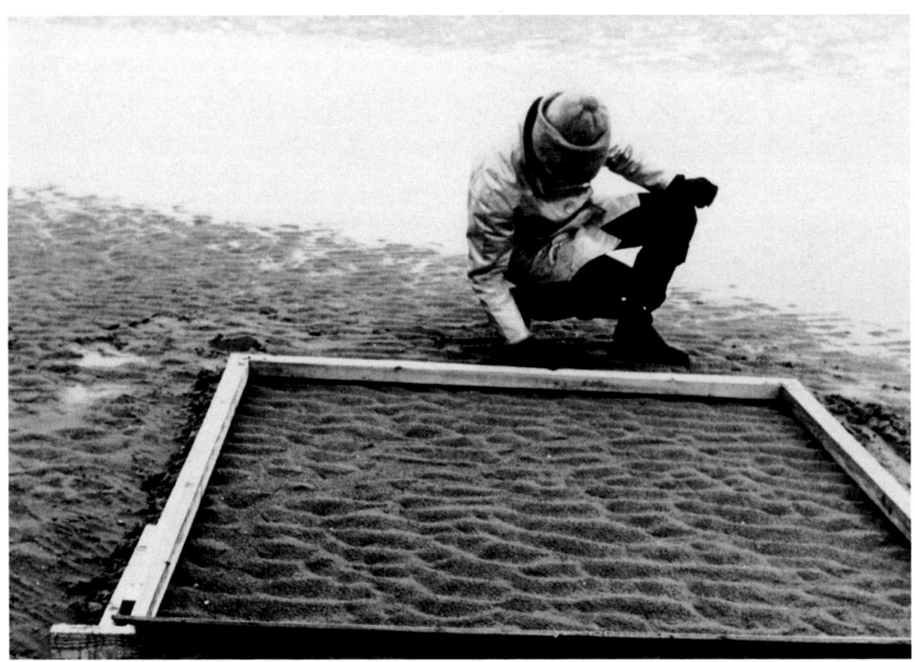

Joan Hills at Camber Sands
1966

Reproduced courtesy of the artist

Your aim is to replicate these various sites as accurately as possible without 'any hint of originality, style, superimposed design, wit or significance'. When you're in the process of making a World Series piece, what are the factors that allow you all to feel that you have fulfilled this demanding aim of absolute exactitude and objectivity?
JH: We use larger and larger maps to 'zoom' in to a site. Eventually, we throw a metal right angle in the air and where that falls is the first corner of the piece. We extend that six feet and work on that, and there's never any question of saying, 'it would be better over here or over there'. You couldn't improve on what you get in a random selection.
SB: We know that it's not possible to be absolutely exact and objective but we're trying to be as objective as we can. The main thing is to take ourselves out of the site selection process. We then try and figure out how we are going to do it, whether it's going to be one of our resin *Earth Studies*, or a film or video work that we're going to make, or if there is some other way of doing it. I am not sure we ever feel we have fulfilled the aim of absolute exactitude and objectivity. Mark and Joan made a list of possible studies we were going to make at each site. We try to complete

as many things on this list as possible, which includes making the actual study of the six-foot square, studying examples of animal and plant life on the site, the weather and what we call 'elemental studies' of the major types of rock and earth in the area. We include studies of ourselves in the project because we have to acknowledge that we are not neutral observers – just by being there we are having an effect on the site, so we include ourselves as active agents. We've never managed to complete the whole list.

Boyle Family had a major retrospective exhibition at the Scottish National Gallery of Modern Art in 2003. That must have given you the opportunity to see the body of your work as an organic unity. From your point of view, what holds such highly complex and varied work together under the name of Boyle Family?

SB: That was a very important exhibition for us as it gave the British art world a chance to see the range and variety of the work and how it works together. There are all sorts of ideas and concepts that underpin our work. One of the key questions for us is how to look at anything objectively, to see it for itself. Not to look at it to tell a story or fit an agenda or even to make an artwork but simply to see, bear witness, record and maybe begin to understand. Mark and Joan came up with a number of frameworks for how to do this. One is 'contemporary archaeology' that we would study the contemporary world as if one were an archaeologist looking at evidence of a past society. Another key to understanding our work is the idea you have to 'isolate in order to examine'. The question is how are you going to choose what to examine? Are you going to impose your value system, your value judgements, on that process? And how did you come by those values? Our random selection techniques are a way of trying to open up that process. They are far from ideal but they help. It's not just the surface of the Earth we're interested in, but everything – human beings, plants, animals, societies, physical and chemical reactions, bodily fluids and so on. We use random selection techniques to try and take ourselves out of the equation, to help us choose and focus on just a minute selection of the infinite number of possible subjects for study.

As artists who, although London based have their roots in Scotland, and over a long career have frequently exhibited north of the border, do you think of yourselves in any way as Scottish artists?

JH: You bet. This sounds parochial but because we have a *World Series*, that interest takes us everywhere.

SB: We certainly think of ourselves as Scottish artists and if there's one trait which we see holding Scottish artists together – and maybe all Scottish people – it's a certain bloody-minded determination to actually just get on with things. Maybe we needed that bloody determination in order to keep on going for 50 years.

This interview was conducted by Bill Hare in 2014 for *Scottish Art News*, issue 21.

Unmapping the World

The Cartographic Art of Boyle Family

We don't want images – we want transparency.
Mark Boyle

UNLIKE MANY OF their 21st-century postmodern contemporaries who feel they now inhabit a virtual world of Baudrillardian hyper-reality, Boyle Family still firmly hold to the belief that there is 'something out there'. Through the many voyages that make up their epic quest for unmitigated contact with the direct physical and sensual experience of the world, they have become modern-day adventure explorers, bringing back, like their mythic and ancient predecessors, fabulous, eye-opening, mind-bending wonders from *terra incognita*.

Boyle Family have always been dedicated to challenging the constrictive and life-denying forces of establishment authority, whether in the area of social decorum, intellectual and moral prejudice or artistic orthodoxy. Interested in the liberating role that chance can play, Boyle Family first turned to participation 'performance' as a means of pursuing a direct and unrestricted involvement with the reality of the world. From this their *World Series* was launched at the ICA in 1967 and again in 1969. There, a thousand locations were fixed by blind-folded participants throwing darts at an unseen target, which turned out to be a huge world map. In this way, the selection of *what* was to be the subject of the Boyles' art was left to blind providence, not subjective aesthetic choice. Conversely, *how* the work was to be made would be dealt with in a highly controlled and precise fashion. Once one of the sites was located, a member of Boyle Family would throw a metal right-angle and its landing position would mark one of the corners of the panel area to be replicated. Then, not unlike a medieval family workshop, the Boyles would all involve themselves in a set of problem-solving, labour-intensive procedures. This would include collecting a wide range of environmental data, all of which would feed into their endeavour to reproduce in three dimensions – as exactly as possible and on a one-to-one scale – the unique nature and distinctive appearance of one minute area of on the Earth's surface.

Boyle Family, which originally consisted of Mark Boyle and Joan Hills, and now includes their grown-up children Sebastian and Georgia, has been consistently committed to breaking down the barriers of conventional representation in order that we, as sentient beings, might experience the world through their art, as directly and accurately as possible. In the catalogue accompanying Boyle Family's 1986 Hayward Gallery exhibition, *Beyond Image*, Mark Boyle stated that they were simply 'trying to remove the prejudices that the conditioning of our upbringing and culture impose. Trying to make the best visual description, our senses and minds can achieve from a random sample of the reality that surrounds us'.

Greenwich – their home – is base camp for their worldwide artistic experiment, *Journey to the Surface of the Earth*, launched in 1964. This is a huge documentary project encompassing the *World Series* and its many off-shoot mini-series in which particular sites – tidal beaches, ploughed fields, urban pavements etc. – are recorded and reproduced under a range of changing environmental conditions. Greenwich, of course, is the centre point of the cartographic world. It is that central marker on the Earth's surface to which all other global points, including the 1,000 randomly selected sites in the *World Series*, can be related within any modern mapping system. The notion of centre and periphery is the dominant feature of all human map-making since time immemorial – for instance, the earliest Babylonian maps of 10,000BC show the Earth as a disk surrounded by water and Babylon at its centre and in the work of the greatest map-maker of the ancient world, Ptolemy, his *Geographia* sited the Mediterranean as the hub of human civilisation. Thus maps are as much concerned with affirming where you are than with showing you how to get somewhere else. This can also involve confirming a sense of superiority over those in the rest of the outside world – those whom the Greeks and Romans called Barbarians, the 19th-century Imperialists dismissed as Natives and we patronise as the 'Other'.

Since the 1960s – and the gradual overthrow of centralised metropolitan modernism – two significant artistic strategies have been used to undermine the restrictive authority of conventional cartography. On the one hand, Robert Smithson followed what might be regarded as a Lewis Carroll *Hunting-the-Snark* approach in his site/non-site land art practice. Like Carroll's 'Brave Captain' whose map was 'a perfect and absolute blank', Smithson sought out remote, unmappable terrains such as Mono Lake in northern California. As he observed, 'if you look at the map, you'll see that it is in the shape of a margin – it has no centre… In a sense, the non-site is the centre of the system and the site itself is the fringe at the edge'. Thus, Smithson wished to 'de-centre' his public, to project us out to those terrains ungraspable by maps. Conversely on the other hand, Boyle Family takes a Pascalian approach, for, like the 17th-century French philosopher, the Boyles believe that the centre is everywhere and the circumference nowhere. Their method of pinpointing each of their chance-located sites by means of increasingly enlarged and focused maps means that any point of the globe's surface might and can be the centre of their artistic and scientific attention. These maps, however, are only a means to an end; Boyle Family eventually aim to break through the layers of conventional cartographic representation and return to the actual physical reality beyond the veil of cartographic signage.

Clearly Boyle Family work touches on a wide range of modern and contemporary art practices, including process art, performance, installation and land art, as well as utilising the readymade. Furthermore, their panels challenge a number of conventions, not only concerning what we choose to call art and our attitude towards the kind of 'reality' put on a gallery wall but also how that reality should be represented in our contemporary world of synthesised, electronically generated imagery. Furthermore, the older conventions of the picturesque and the *belle pictorial* are also held up to scrutiny, while the accepted notions of artistic creativity which today are almost exclusively styled as individualistic, if not downright egotistic, are challenged by their family group anonymous unity. Finally, as with the best modern art, their work creates all kinds of ambiguities and contradictions between content and presentation – landscape becomes still life, the mimetic realism attains all the visual characteristics associated with abstraction and their initial map-dependent art in the end refutes the cartographic process.

Maps, by their very abstracting nature, take us away from the physical factuality of the world. Navigation began with travellers' selective remembrance of distinctive landmarks but, inevitably, within more complex human societies, a system of signs and symbols was devised to turn the natural features of the Earth into a fixed, conventional language of symbolic/semiotic representation. As Nelson Goodman forcefully put it, maps are 'schematic, selective, succinct, conventional, condensed and uniform'. Goodman's short but accurate description of the purpose and practice of cartography is the very antithesis of the socio-philosophic and artistic vision behind the art of Boyle Family.

For instance, Mark Boyle has lamented the fact that 'from the beginning we are taught to choose, to select, to separate'. His desire to heighten our sensual experience of the world is indicated not only by *Journey to the Surface of the Earth* but also by the various pseudo-scientific names the Boyles went under during the 1960s, such as *The Institute of Contemporary Archaeology* and *The Sensual Laboratory*. The need to make direct contact with the public led to a series of what might loosely be termed 'happenings'. In 1964, for instance, Boyle Family staged an event entitled *Street* where an invited audience was ushered into vacant shop premises marked 'Theatre'. When the expectant audience was seated and prepared for a play to begin, the proscenium stage curtain was pulled back, only to reveal the shop window through which could be observed the raw, unmitigated reality of the street life passing outside. *Street* was a clear indication that the fundamental purpose of the Boyles' art was to remove and erase the physical, social, psychological, aesthetic and semiotic barriers that separate us from the direct experience of the rest of the world. All their works can be viewed as attempts to break down these barriers but, because of the impossibility of engaging with the totality of the physical world, they have to be granted the concession that 'to study everything, we may isolate anything'. Yet it should always be remembered that despite the dialectic tension in the work between chance and unpredictability on the one hand and a dedicated commitment to high-precision mimetic description on the other, the finished product – the relief panel itself – is not intended to close down our attention to mere aesthetic contemplation. Rather, it should free us up to activate our now heightened sensual awareness of the physical world. We have to see through and beyond the 'art' on the wall; we have to be able to say, like the artist, that 'we don't want images – we want transparency'.

In our multimedia world of constant signage, it would seem iconoclastic madness to say 'we don't want images'. This is especially alarming coming from a contemporary artist who *should*, according to Hal Foster, be 'a manipulator of signs more than a producer of art objects'. Unarguably the Boyles, as has been their wont throughout their independently minded career, are still out of step with a contemporary art world which has become so self-regarding that 'to see something as art requires something the eye cannot descry – an atmosphere of artistic theory, a knowledge of the history of art: an art world' according to Arthur C Danto. The work of Boyle Family has been a consistent and persistent critique of all systems of representation – from cartography to Baudrillardian hyper-realism. A *World Series* panel and the concept of the simulacrum are worlds apart. The simulacrum, by its very being and purpose, takes us further and further away from the physical, sensual reality of the world which it discards; while a Boyle Family work is able, if we have the correct receptive attitude, to put us back in contact with our own being and our place in the physical world. In fact, the art of Boyle Family authenticates the factuality of the world and where we stand in it. Ironically, this is achieved by the transforming power of highly detailed mimetic description. Yet there is no illusionistic or *trompe l'oeil* trickery involved here; such truthful beauty surpasses and goes infinitely beyond mere verisimilitude.

This essay was written by Bill Hare in 2000 and published in *Contemporary Visual Art*, issue 31. See also: *Old Habits of Looking, New Ways of Seeing: The Paintings of Boyle Family* by Bill Hare in *Boyle Family* edited by Patrick Elliot (National Galleries of Scotland, 2002).

Two Figurative Painters

Alexander Moffat (1943-)
Jock McFadyen (1950-)

THE TWO ARTISTS in this section were born within touching distance of the end of World War II. Being from a later date, they therefore had different concerns to those of the previous generation. It was the 1960–70s that saw their art education and the beginnings of their artistic careers. They were both determined to uphold the inheritance of modern figurative painting against the then more fashionable modes of contemporary art such as abstraction, pop art, minimalism and conceptualism. Moffat was a contemporary of John Bellany. They met and teamed up as students at Edinburgh College of Art in the early 1960s and formed a rebellious partnership against what they both regarded as the moribund art establishment and art scene in Scotland at that time. This most publicly manifested itself in the audacious Edinburgh Festival exhibitions of their work on the rails outside the Royal Scottish Academy and the National Gallery of Scotland in the mid-1960s. Both were passionately committed to modern figurative painting – for instance, Bellany was strongly influenced by German expressionism and Moffat, who had more political intent in his work, was more inclined to Léger's utopian socialism. Unlike Bellany, Moffat chose to remain in Scotland and, in the 1970s, began to make his reputation as a modern portrait painter; firstly of his personal acquaintances and then notable literary and artistic Scots. In the 1980s, as head of drawing and painting at Glasgow School of Art, he was one of the main driving forces behind the return to figurative painting in the 1980s, with many of the successful young Scottish painters of the decade being his former students.

McFadyen, by contrast, has spent his whole artistic career working in London. Educated at Chelsea Art School in the 1970s, he first came to prominence with his keenly observed and cuttingly satirical depiction of the social underclass of London's East End which was stylistically presented through a mixture of influences from Hogarth to George Grosz. He went on to be artist-in-residence at the National Gallery (1981) and stage designer at Covent Garden (1991). After that from the 1990s onwards, the figurative element in his work began to disappear and his subjects became predominantly landscapes and cityscapes usually painted on an impressively cinematic large scale.

Moffat was a very influential figure on the Scottish and British art scene and wider afield for decades before I got to know him personally

when I began working with him on our book, *Facing the Nation: The Portraiture of*
Alexander Moffat (Luath Press, 2018). Although I knew of McFadyen
through his distinctive work, because he was a London artist, I did
not have any dealings with him until 2012 when we did an interview
for *Scottish Art News*, which was also used in the catalogue for his
Edinburgh Festival exhibition at Bourne Fine Art, *The Ability to Cling*,
in 2012. Later I requested his stunning painting *Calton Hill* for inclusion
and as the publicity image of the exhibition *The Scottish Endarkenment*,
in 2016. I was delighted that that painting was subsequently acquired for
the Scottish National Gallery of Modern Art's collection.

Alexander Moffat

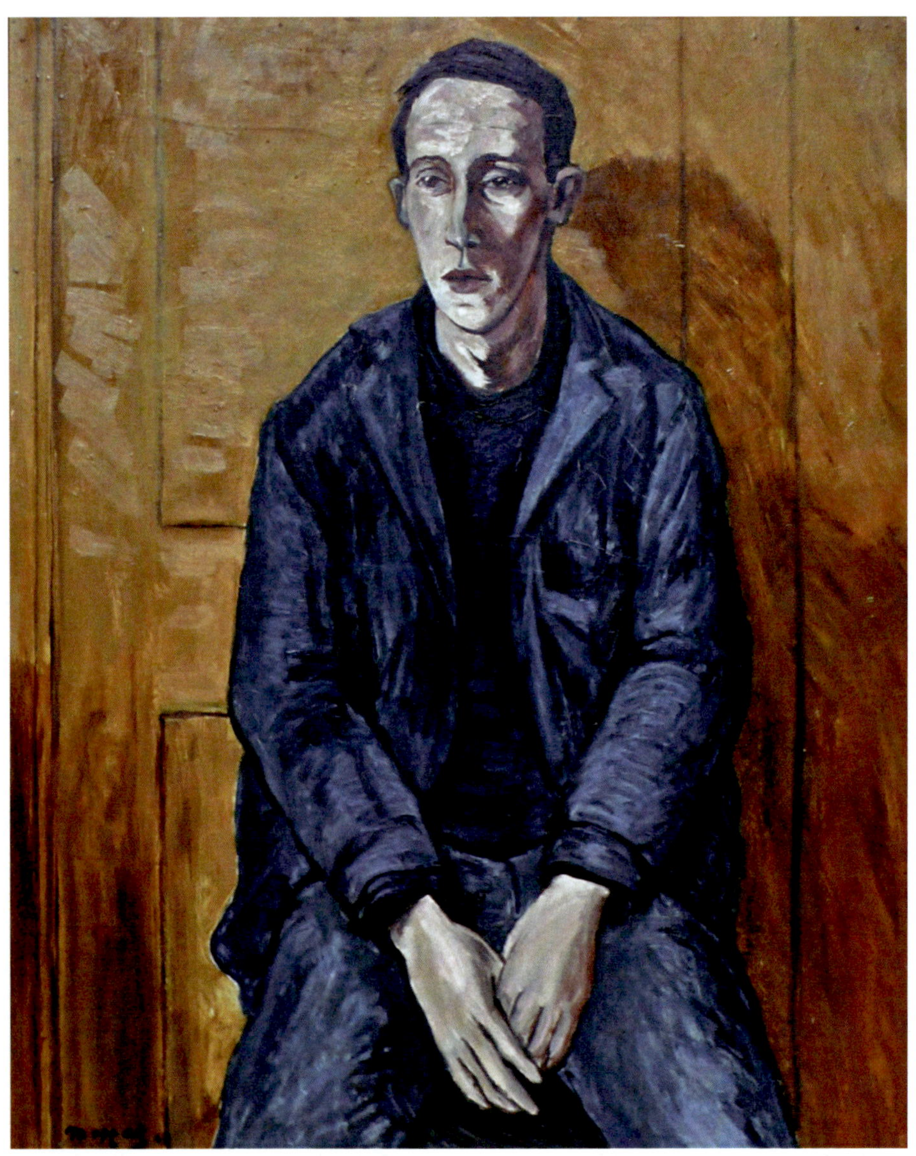

Ken Harrold
1963
Oil on board, 81x61cm
Reproduced courtesy of the artist

Alexander (Sandy) Moffat Interview

Do you think of yourself as a portrait painter or as a painter who sometimes paints portraits, along with other types of subjects such as landscapes? What position does portraiture hold within your work as a whole?
A painter who often paints portraits, with portraiture occupying a central position within my work.

Could you explain the relationship between portrait painting and the rest of your work?
Most of my paintings include the human figure and painting a portrait is closely related to that main activity. I was once asked if I thought everything was really there in the face. I do think it is. When Braque was asked if he believed painting was enough, his reply was simply 'Yes'.

I've recently come across an essay by Siri Hustvedt where she's discussing Picasso's *Weeping Woman*. She writes:

> the face is the focus of identity – the place on the body to which we give our attention. We do not recognise people by their hands or feet, even those intimate to us.

And she elaborates:

> To some degree at least, while we are looking at someone in life, in a photograph, or in a painting, we have her face. The face we perceive supplants our own.

What drew you to making portraits in the first place?
As a human-centred figurative painter, I guess it was inevitable that I would be drawn to the individual portrait in one way or another. It all began during my student years when, along with John Bellany, it became necessary to move on from an experimental abstract period towards a language of figuration that would take on board the modernist viewpoint developed in the early years of the 20th century. The catalyst for what was a momentous decision was both political and aesthetic – a combination of hearing Hugh MacDiarmid speak at the Edinburgh International Festival's Writer's Conference and seeing a large Kokoschka exhibition at the Tate, both in the summer of 1962. Kokoschka's humanism struck a chord and his youthful portraits of Adolf Loos and Herwarth Walden, painted in Vienna in that special era before 1914, were the works that first convinced me that painting portraits was consistent with my desire to be a modern artist.

So you see the genre of portraiture having a significant relationship with modernism?
I do, but the relationship needs careful explanation. To simplify,

modernism took many different directions in the first half of the 20th century in all of the arts. In music, the main directions stemmed from national traditions… Stravinsky and Prokofiev/Russia, Bartok and Kodály/Hungary, Debussy and Ravel/France, Schoenberg and Webern/Austria, Vaughan Williams in England and Erik Chisholm in Scotland. In the visual arts, there was a huge difference in what happened in Paris as opposed to Berlin but portraiture was never neglected by any of the main modern movements wherever they were. Within the various arenas of cubism, futurism, surrealism, German expressionism, Neue Sachlichkeit and so forth, portraits of distinction emerged. Scotland's pioneering abstractionist, William Johnstone, painted portraits of his friends and fellow borderers Hugh MacDiarmid and Francis George Scott. Of course, there were other groups of artists who rejected figuration, most famously centred on the Bauhaus, in their desire to create an art that was independent of history and tradition. With the arrival of Walter Gropius in America in the mid-1930s, these views gained the high ground. During the Cold War, art became politicised with figuration strongly associated with Stalinist socialist realism. Clement Greenberg announced that 'Abstraction is the major mode of expression in our time' and a hard-line dogma emerged intent on projecting a 'proper modernist style' that discarded the work of many of the most creative and individual artists of the century. Modernism became 'Americanised' with the autonomous 'art object' its main goal. Ideology, tradition and history, all fundamental to European culture, were ignored and rejected. By the mid-1960s, art schools had caved in and promoted this version of modernism but for better or worse there was resistance in Scotland. This was the situation I found myself dealing with as I began to make my way as an artist.

It has taken time but we now seem to have moved on from that kind of narrow inclusiveness, while gaining a greater awareness of the importance of local circumstances and tradition. The work of many of the great modern painters from Picasso onwards has been re-assessed with portraiture rightly regarded as a key component of their oeuvre. We no longer consider Modigliani or Balthus less modern because they painted portraits. Above all, we now clearly understand that never again should one single version of history be accepted as the truth.

Let's move on to a more general question – what do you think is the status of portraiture today? Recently there have been several major portrait exhibitions in London, with Picasso and Cézanne at the National Portrait Gallery and Hockney at the Royal Academy. Do you see this as a revival in the critical and public interest in portraiture as a distinct art form in its own right? If so, what do you think has brought this about? Cézanne is rightly regarded as the 'father' of modern portraiture and both Picasso and Hockney painted wonderful portraits but I'm not sure if they actually reflect the status of portraiture right now, although I wish they did! There has always been a popular interest in portraiture but critical opinion, on the other hand, is much more divided. In the 1960s when I made my first portraits, portraiture was critically suspect, regarded as a deeply flawed genre. This state of affairs was largely historical in origin. In the 18th and 19th centuries, the fashionable priorities of gentility throughout Europe generated unquantified numbers of portraits of rich people, the nobility, dukes and duchesses, flattering representations of the utmost banality. I saw portraits like that in the RSA during my student period, hack work with no relevance to modern life or painting. At the time, a critical voice such as John Berger questioned the very nature of portraiture: 'it seems unlikely that any important portraits will ever be painted again', arguing that after Géricault portraiture degenerated into servile and crass flattery. He qualified this by making reference to 'those sincere artists' – Corot, Courbet, Degas, Cézanne and van Gogh who made intimate portraits of their friends. It was this aspect of portraiture that had an immediate appeal for me.

We might take up Berger's infamous death sentence on portraiture later but can I ask you – what do we mean by portraiture now, compared with the past? How would you define what constitutes a portrait in the 21st century?
I'm unsure as to what's meant by portraiture now. A lot of what I see has nothing to do with painting but is more concerned with copying the surface information of a photograph. It all appears quite reactionary and academic. Putting current fashions to one side, defining what a painted portrait is in the 21st century shouldn't be too problematic. After all, we humans haven't changed much over the past thousand years in terms of visual identity, nor in other ways as well. It seems we were much more equal in the middle years of the 20th century in the aftermath of two terrible World Wars but now we are much more unequal again. Portraits should tell us about all of these things. Indeed, most of the great portraits of the past century do precisely that with time and place right there in the portraits of Beckmann and Dix, as well as in the portraits of very different artists such as Klimt, Spencer or Andy Warhol.

You just mentioned the allure of the photographic image and, of course, photography has dogged portraiture since its invention. Does photography play any part, either directly or indirectly, in your attitude and approach to making portraits?
I worked as a photographer for several years after leaving art college and I continue to take lots of photographs but for me painting and photography are quite separate activities. Of course, there's been a continuing and fascinating dialogue between them from Delacroix and Degas onwards and we mustn't forget the influence of painting on photography. There are a number of photographers I particularly admire – Paul Strand, Edward Weston, Walker Evans, August Sander and Manuel Álvarez Bravo are particular favourites and I've more than likely been influenced by specific aspects of their work. The photographs of a painter like Edvard Munch interest me greatly too. His experiments with double exposures, hand-

held self-portraits etc fed into his painting but when asked to explain the difference between painting and photography his reply was straight to the point: 'The camera cannot compete with painting as it cannot be used in heaven or hell'. We live in an age obsessed by the photographic image and I agree with Wim Wenders when he says the task of the artist is to retrieve the image from its present degraded condition. According to Wenders, there are so many images circulating the globe with ever-increasing speed that we look at all the time but we no longer appear to have the means or the skills to see. He regards the 'recovery' of the image as an ethical and moral task essential for the future of all visual art.

Despite the loosening of firm generic categorisation and the ubiquity of the photographic image, most people still seem to feel that the painted portrait should involve the depiction of visual resemblance of another person. How important to you is individual 'likeness' in your practice of portraiture? For instance, it seems to me that a mimetic correspondence is more of a concern in your preparatory drawings than in the finished painted portraits.
Likeness is important – there's no point in denying that simple fact. All of the great portrait painters from Titian and Velázquez, to Manet and Degas and even Picasso insisted upon likeness and that was why they were so admired. I'm always conscious of the need to capture a likeness but this has to be balanced against the desire to make a good painting. I usually feel I can't really get to grips with the painting aspect until the sitter has gone.

Of course 'likeness' is not a very stable concept. So what other aspects – over and above resemblance – should the portraitist be seeking out in the sitter?
I agree that likeness is an elusive concept but the painter seeks permanence. I'm with John Berger on this when he says:

> Painting is, first, an affirmation of the visible which surrounds us and which continually appears and disappears. Without the disappearing, there would perhaps be no impulse to paint, for the visible itself would possess the surety (the permanence) which painting strives to find. More directly than any other art, painting is an affirmation of the existent, of the physical world into which mankind has been thrown.

So in a sense, a portrait is an affirmation of an individual human being.

Of course, these two central concerns of portraiture – individual likeness and general type – are not mutually exclusive; in the best portraits, they are successfully integrated by the artist. In your own practice, how do you accommodate the twin demands of likeness and type? Which of them do you prefer to emphasise?
I always concentrate on the individual in front of me. That for me is the most important part of portraiture. It's about attempting to capture the

humanity of my sitters. If one can make a good painting on that basis then the twin demands you speak about should take care of themselves. I keep on coming back to the idea that a portrait must work as a painting, not simply as a likeness of some type or other.

Do you ever use symbolic meaning in your portraiture, say through the use of colour or the placement of significant objects as clues to the sitter's character, for example?
In my earliest portraits, there's only the sitter, nothing more, as nothing more was needed. Colour became increasingly important but I'm not sure I used it symbolically at that stage. Then in 1976, I painted a portrait of Neal Ascherson, incorporating quotations from George Grosz and setting Neal in Berlin where he had worked as *The Observer*'s East European correspondent throughout the 1960s. I further developed this idea in a series of three large group portraits entitled 'Berliners' with Neal placed amidst a collage of images of Berlin in the 1920s as well as the 1960s. It was this concept of the 'expanded portrait' that provided a starting point for the *Seven Poets* series I embarked upon in 1978. In the portrait of Hugh MacDiarmid, subtitled 'Hymn to Lenin', I used imagery from the Russian Revolution of 1917, a crucial event for MacDiarmid with Mayakovsky and Tatlin's Tower in the foreground. I placed John Maclean, the Scottish socialist leader, at MacDiarmid's side while the landscape element that symbolises Scotland moves from the Borders where MacDiarmid was born to the Shetlands where he lived in the 1930s. In the portrait of Sorley MacLean, the mighty Cuillin perhaps becomes a symbol for all Gaelic history and culture. So colour as well as imagery becomes increasingly symbolic in those works.

This brings us to the question as to the selection of the sitters for your portraits. How do you decide who you want to portray and what portrait commissions you are willing to accept?
There were few commissions in my early days but I accepted them willingly as I had to make a living. My first major commission came in 1973 when Edinburgh University asked me to paint their Principal and Vice Chancellor, Sir Michael Swann, on his retirement. Swann was a scientist and we both agreed there should be no gowns or mace, none of the traditional trappings of high office. This would be a modern portrait. Many years later I was delighted to read in *The University Portraits* (Second Series 1986) that my painting was considered 'the most important portrait the Court has commissioned in recent years…'

Whom do you feel you are painting your portraits for – yourself (surely first and foremost it should be readily recognised as a 'Moffat portrait'), the sitter, or whoever commissions the portrait or the viewer? Who has priority? Whose judgement is most crucial in deciding the merits of your portraits?

All of them in a way. That's what makes painting a portrait different from my other works where I do, first and foremost, paint for myself and I have priority. With a portrait, other factors come into play but of course my judgement is crucial during the painting of the portrait.

Ultimately what do you feel is the purpose and role of your portraits?
I hope they will be seen as human documents. In an age obsessed by triviality and celebrity, perhaps it's essential to think differently about power and prestige. It's a matter of solidarity too. I very much hope the abilities of the individuals I've portrayed will be taken seriously and that they have in their own particular ways made a difference in the world. What I'm saying is that all people are equal.

Undoubtedly your most renowned portraits are of celebrated literary figures. Does that type of sitter set you a particular challenge? How do you go about conveying their creative power, their intellectual personality and their celebrity status?
There was a sense of responsibility involved in portraying people like the poets who shaped and contributed in such an important way to the art and culture of modern Scotland. Had it not been for them, I probably wouldn't be painting or believing art to be important. MacDiarmid's status as the poetic peer of Eliot, Pound and Yeats was initially intimidating. How does one put that into a painting? George Davie, an equally formidable character, posed a different set of problems. How does one deal with the fragility of extreme old age? Throughout the many sessions I spent drawing him, I was aware of Giacometti's comments on drawing the old and ill Matisse: 'I was drawing, and at the same time observing what cannot be captured by drawing'. But there was fun too… When I began my portrait of MacDiarmid in the summer of 1978, I knew he was battling cancer and hadn't long to live. Once the bottle of whisky was opened, however, there was a stream of good-natured banter about the other poets I intended to paint and whether or not they might prove suitable subjects for a portrait when suddenly Valda came in and scolded him for not having his false teeth in. He laughed and said there was no need for that as the artist would simply see to it with the stroke of a brush.

How much does the gender of your sitter affect your approach to painting a portrait? Do you try to bring out different qualities in a female sitter than that of a male one?
So what kind of qualities would I try to bring out in a female sitter? Certainly painting Muriel Spark was a very different experience from painting the group of male poets. Although she shared many similarities with her male counterparts – much the same age, intellectually formidable and with an uncompromising seriousness about art and the role of the artist, what was immediately different was her elegance, her feminine allure. When I asked if she wanted me to include additional imagery in

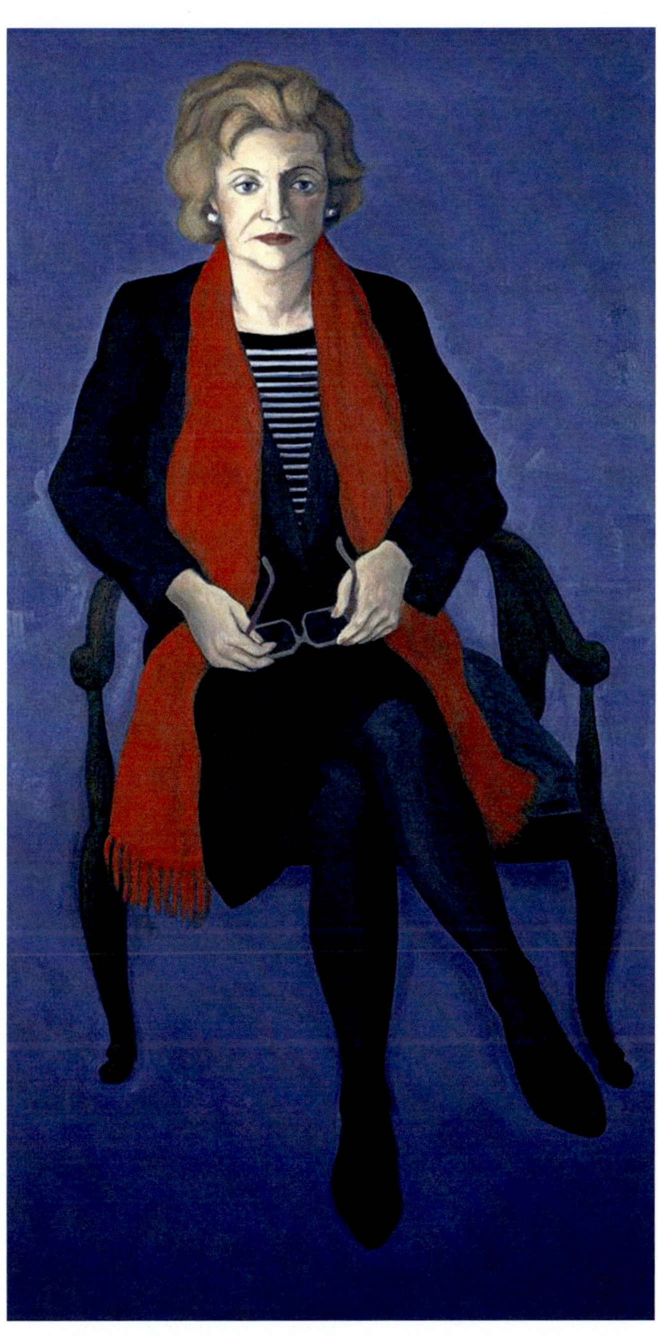

Muriel Spark
1984
Oil on canvas, 183x91cm
Reproduced courtesy of the artist

the background, 'No, no, I only want me' was her reply. I do, however, think of the blue background space as a homage to the Venetian painters, alluding to Italy where she spent the final years of her life. There was a problem of sorts, though, in that every time she arrived at the studio she had a different hair style – she would visit the hairdressers before each sitting. That's something I never had to contend with any of my male subjects!

Can we now turn to the stylistic aspect of your portraiture? You have said that your 'favourite portraits all come from the first half of the 20th century'. That would seem to indicate that you see your work within the distinctive tradition of modern portraiture. Would that be correct and, if so, what are the stylistic qualities of modern portraiture that particularly appeal to you as a portrait painter yourself?

It's true that in my younger days my favourite painters and paintings, writers, composers etc., all came from the first half of the 20th century. In terms of portraiture, the works of Picasso and Matisse were readily available in books and exhibitions when I was a student but the German artists associated with the Weimar Republic were mostly under the radar. Grosz, Dix and Beckmann only became visible after a visit to Berlin, Dresden and Leipzig in 1967. What really appealed to me in their portraits was their ability to place the individual within a social context and an unflinching mission to reveal the truth, no matter how ugly or awful it was.

The stylistic properties all of these artists seem to have in common is the emphasis they placed on drawing, creating new idioms for the expression of modern life. As a result, drawing, especially in relation to the portrait, has always been crucial for me. I consider my portrait drawings to be just as important as my paintings.

The Scottish moderns, too, have been influential. That's the tradition I hope to have contributed to after all. James Cowie, Edward Baird and William McCance all made significant contributions with their portraits. The double portrait of *Robert Colquhoun and Robert MacBryde* (1937–8) by Ian Fleming that hung on a wall in the east corridor of the Mackintosh Building was a painting I would look at it every day during my Glasgow years. Perhaps it's not a truly great painting but it has a special resonance in terms of the story of modernism in Scotland. There are, however, two remarkable portraits by one of my predecessors as head of the painting department in Glasgow, David Forrester Wilson... *The Young Shepherd* (1929) and *An Islay Woman* (1931) that stand apart from anything else in Scotland at the time and there's a self-portrait by Gillies from 1941 I greatly admire. It's a pity he didn't paint more portraits or self-portraits. One of the criticisms of Scottish modernism was that we didn't produce any female artists of the calibre of Frida Kahlo or Paula Modersohn-Becker but new light has recently been shed on a number of outstanding women artists – who all painted portraits – such as Bessie McNicol, Agnes Miller Parker and Dorothy Carleton Smyth, who, had she not been struck down with a brain haemorrhage, would have become the first female Director of Glasgow School of Art in 1933. Just think about that…

In your answer, you touch on the subject of Scottish portrait painting. Do you feel that Scottish portraiture has a distinctive character? If so, what are the features of that distinction and who in your opinion most exemplifies the 'Scottish' approach to portraiture?
Without doubt. There are of course many who deny there are national differences and distinctiveness with regard to the arts. They claim that art is 'universal' and there's no need for any further explanation. That's fine but it conveniently sidesteps the complexities that surround cultural identity and fails to address essentials like the profoundly Russian nature of Stravinsky's music. *The Rite of Spring* may be a high-culture text, the paradigm of modernism in music, internationally significant way beyond any concerns of 'narrow nationalism'. And yet Stravinsky chose to give it a subtitle, emphatically present in its universal interpretation: 'Pictures of Pagan Russia'. Artists and composers cannot simply be described as 'international' modernists who came from nowhere in particular. There's no need to apologise or deny that one is a Scottish artist.

The prevailing view is that Scottish painting is mainly French influenced and to a great extent that is true and, like French or German painting, there is no one defining style – there are only individual artists working at different times across the centuries. I've just talked about some of the moderns who eschewed what we might call the 'French' influence – Baird and Cowie or example – and I should name a few more such as Steven Campbell, Adrian Wiszniewski and Ken Currie, bringing the story right up to date.

JD Fergusson wrote at great length about the distinctive character of Scottish painting. Talking about the Glasgow School, he had this to say:

> The whole school at their best had the Scots characteristic of independence, and vigour, colour and particularly quality of paint, which means paint that is living and not merely a coat of paint placed between containing lines like a map.

That's quite a statement and could certainly be applied to those artists – Ramsay, Raeburn and Wilkie and onwards via McTaggart to Fergusson and Bellany, who for me exemplify a Scottish approach to portraiture.

You have acknowledged the influence of other portrait painters on your own work, but nevertheless, you quickly managed to formulate a very distinctive style which makes your portraits readily recognisable. Looking over your career as a portrait painter – which goes way back to the 1960s

– do you see your portraits as a coherent and consistent body of work?
What do you feel holds them all together?
All I can say is that after 50 years of painting portraits, I do recognise
a certain consistency of approach. There are probably distinct periods
– early, middle and later – but overall I agree that there is a coherent
body of work. Sometimes, however, I've wished that this wasn't the case,
that there could have been a few minor eruptions. That might have been
useful, perhaps leading to more experimental pictures or simply taking
me in a different direction. There was a period, too, during my 50s when I
didn't paint many portraits. I thought I had nothing new to say, that I was
simply repeating things I'd done before. I believe a lot of artists experience
similar feelings but eventually we all get going again and find there are
new discoveries to be made, new territory to explore. What holds them
together? It may well be that my belief in humanity still holds, despite the
dark times we have lived through.

This is an abridged version of the interview conducted by Bill Hare for *Facing the
Nation: The Portraiture of Alexander Moffat* published in 2018 by Luath Press.

Jock McFadyen

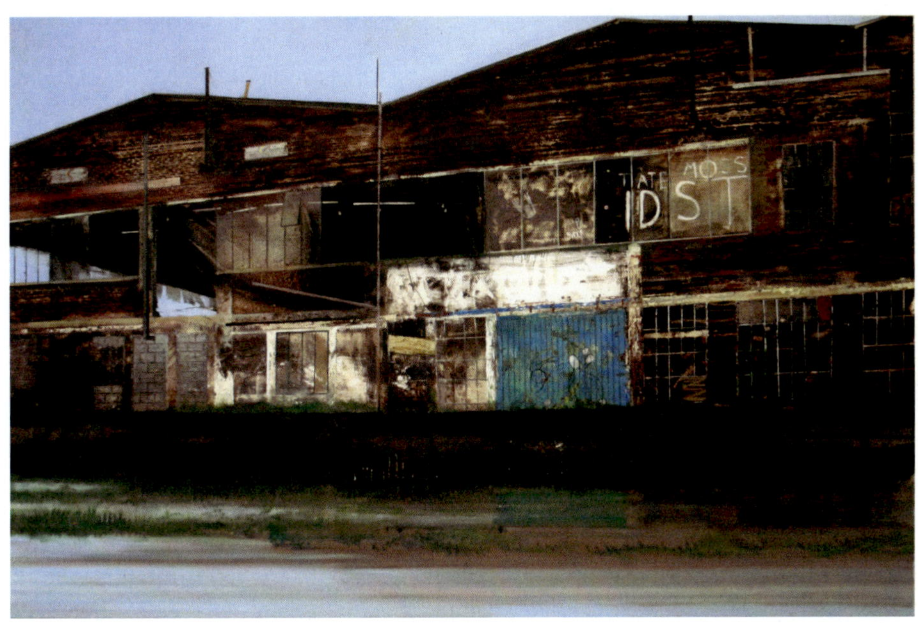

Tate Moss
2008
Oil on canvas, 200x300cm

Reproduced courtesy of the artist and Fleming-Wyford Foundation

Jock McFadyen Interview

*I think you are the second living artist to have a one person show at
The Fleming Collection after Will Maclean. As you know, The Fleming
Collection has always been very much committed to showing the best
of Scottish historical and contemporary art in London. How do you see
yourself and your work within that national context?*
I am in a queer position with Scottish art. I was born in 1950 and brought
up on the outskirts of Glasgow. The McFadyens are from Tiree but
generations were drawn to the mainland for work. All the men in my
family worked in the shipyards and that was the world I knew but, when
I was 16, my father got a job in England so, in 1966, we came south.
My family moved back to Scotland after a few years but I stayed on in
England, got married, had a child, went to art school, got divorced, left
art school, got a studio and started exhibiting my work using the difficult-
to-shed nickname 'Jock'. It must have been a good 20 years before my
mother began to call me Jock instead of Jimmy (same difference to the
English).

Having gone to art school in Chelsea, Scottish art wasn't on my
radar. It didn't figure in any of the books I had swotted up on for college
and, like any other student, I was steeped in the art of the time: Bruce
Nauman (Scottish first name...), Gilbert & George, RB Kitaj and Jasper
Johns. In 1974, I sold my first painting to Allen Jones, an artist whose
entire generation seemed to have an international reputation. Mark Boyle
was one of my heroes and I was vaguely aware that he was Glaswegian,
Craigie Aitchison was one of the tutors at Chelsea, but their Scottishness
was an accident of birth and peripheral to their art.

I met John Bellany when we were both exhibiting at the Acme Gallery
in the late 1970s and also got to know Bruce McLean around that
time. It was when I had my first Scottish show at the New 57 Gallery in
Edinburgh in 1979 that I became aware of a domestic Scottish art scene
which was totally unfamiliar to me. I only had a hazy awareness of the
Colourists until I started exhibiting with Bill Jackson at the Scottish
Gallery in London in the mid- to late-'80s. By that time, the so-called
New Glasgow Boys had emerged but the 1980s was a decade-long love
affair with figuration and the main protagonists included Schnabel,
Clemente, Kiefer, Salle *et al* and they were from all over the place. I am
still not sure that I know what Scottish art is but I think my favourite
must be McTaggart if I can't have Whistler...

*Like you, after nearly 50 years in the business, I still don't know what
constitutes Scottish art. I think that has a lot to do with this amorphous
concept called 'Britishness'. My students sometimes challenge my choice
of Scottish artists by pointing out that many of them – like your good self
– have worked for most of their careers in London. Does not that make*

them English artists? My argument is that London is the capital of Britain and artists from all over the UK come to the great metropolis to further their careers but that does not necessarily compromise their geographical and ethnic origins. Picasso never became a French artist, even if he became a French citizen, and for all his travelling around, David Hockney is still a Yorkshire man – even more so now. As you say in your case, and this is true for most artists, this is not a big concern. They have much more pressing challenges to face each day in their studio, wherever that is located. Let's turn to something that is much more important – your own work. I recently reread David Cohen's book, Jock McFadyen: A Book about a Painter and I noticed that the opening chapter is entitled A Painter's Progress, which seemed to place your earlier work within a Hogarthian tradition of British social realist art. Would that be the case?

Yes, I am with you on all of that and where you go to college is important too. Art school is a big influence on painters because your job is to find out who you really are as an artist. It is a process of closing down options (abstract, figurative, conceptual, painterly, hard, soft, schematic, international, provincial, still life, portrait, landscape etc). You have to crack an egg to make an omelette and, halfway through the omelette, you can't change your mind and go for a boiled egg. You close a lot of doors and what you are left with is what you are. It is very different from being Canaletto and inheriting the family firm...

Nationality seems irrelevant while all this is going on. The big elephant in the room is modernism, that great cliff-face of a 19th century idea about the 20th century which is still going strong today. Nowadays we are in the 21st century and art has gone completely to the market for its validation and the big players are Chinese, Indian or Arabic and where that leaves Scotland I haven't got a clue... Despite all this, I am from Glasgow and I have turned out to be a painter rather than an artist. Painting has a comfortably tangible history which is full of excitement and, yes, there was a Hogarthian element to my work in the 1970s but it was a commentary on the undoing of painting, using pictorial form to comment on art as a comedy of manners. But in the end, it all became too knowing and, in 1982, I emerged from my studio below 2,000 old master paintings in Trafalgar Square as a painter who was much more interested in contemplating what lay beyond his front door than art's dialogue with its own history. I began to look at things and wonder if I could make a picture of what I saw. I dumped the idea of art as a strategy and started to look painting squarely in the eye. It was the most exciting stage of my career.

I'd like to pick up on this point you make about seeing yourself as a painter rather than an artist. Modern painting has been driven by the ebb and flow between figuration and abstraction. I realise I am taking you back to 'art as a strategy', and maybe spoiling your painterly pleasures, but how do you see the development of your work throughout your career in relation to this central dialectic in modern painting?

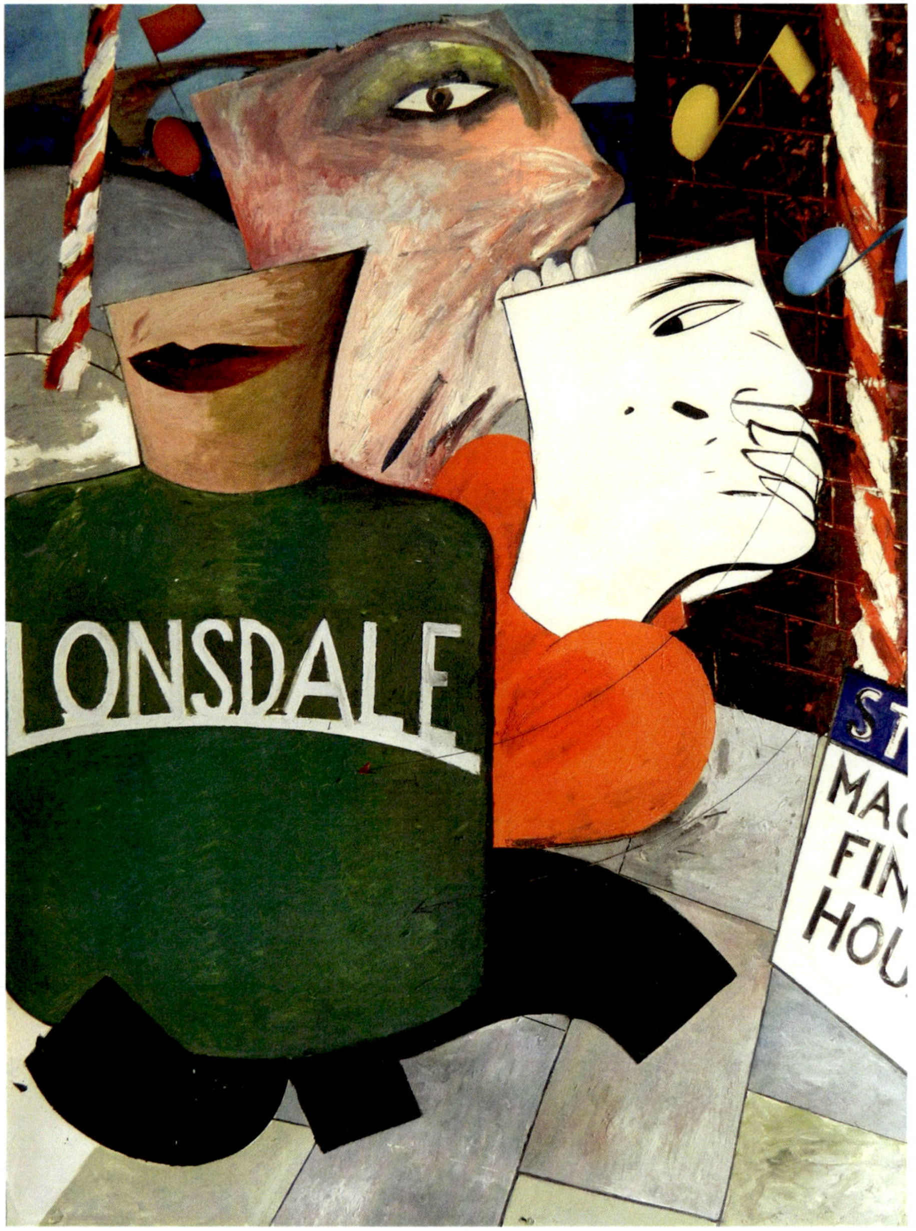

Maggie's Finest Hour

1983

Oil on canvas, 137x101cm

Reproduced courtesy of the artist and Fleming–Wyford Foundation

Yes, painting or art... I think in painting these days it is not just figurative versus abstract but a three-way thing between figuration, abstraction and 'conceptual' painting. Painting which is harnessed to a conceptual strategy might be figurative or abstract (Richter possibly?). My early work fitted that bill but I began to see painting as a credible and organic way of describing the world. Issues of style or the painter's hand were not as compromising as might once have been imagined. Painting – because of its surface, capacity for scale, depth of field and focus as well as its century of pictorial experiment – is more sophisticated than photography or cinema (both of which I love) in very particular ways.

I have to confess that I look at a lot of current art with the same indifference as ragtime jazz, golf, fishing or motor cars. I find the audience thing irritating too – all the careful unpicking, decoding and deconstructing doesn't thrill me in the slightest. And it isn't because I don't speak the language. If, for instance, I find a pile of crappy old paintings leaning in a dusty corner of a junk shop, it's impossible to resist the urge to pick them up and pore over them to try and work out how the ground might have been applied or whether it inflects the surface and where the painter struggled with this or succeeded with that.

In the end I don't know that much about painting. All the great museums not seen and chapels and caves not visited ensure that I will die in ignorance of most of the paintings in the world. I'm ignorant of most of painting but I feel that the other stuff (art) is like an unfinished crossword where I haven't solved all the clues but I know that I could if I could be bothered. I don't feel that about painting because painting is so much bigger and more complex, it precedes us and yawns before us.

I find your comments on 'the condition of painting' really interesting as you come from a personal and professional position rather than an academic, theoretical one.

Could we finally turn to the actual content of your paintings? There seems to be a marked difference between the subject matter of your early work and what we find in your paintings now. What brought about these changes?
In my people paintings, the figure would often come quickly because of working fast to capture the essence of someone I had seen. The real work would be the structure and all the painterly stuff which ensues from that: form, rhythm, surface, resonance and whether the paint blooms or not all the preoccupations of abstraction in fact.

The shift away from the figure towards landscape was helped in 1990 when I designed the sets and costumes for Kenneth MacMillan's last ballet, *The Judas Tree*, at the Royal Opera House. I think MacMillan was the Francis Bacon of ballet and it was fantastic to work with him but, during the project, it became clear to me that something was missing. That thing was the figure. There was no figure to invent because there were real people – the dancers. I found myself contemplating the set and began to feel that perhaps I had always been a painter of places. I turned this revelation over in my mind like a new toy and set forth to paint the world. And it is worth saying that landscape and portrait have quite different psychological and emotional positions. Ask any advertiser...

When I was young, I was enthralled by the work of other painters and lifted what I could to put my pictures together. But by the time I was a student at Chelsea in the 1970s, my ambition for painting had become closer to that of the contemporary novel, photography or the cinema. I see my pictures as being closer to road movies or even songs about the landscape than having much to do with current painting. Exceptions might include late Michael Andrews but Sickert, Hopper, Whistler and Lowry are hardly contemporary. Maybe that applies to me too. I think in the end I am just a fairly intuitive painter who loves movies and novels.

This interview was conducted by Bill Hare in 2012 for *Scottish Art News*, issue 18.

Four Abstract Painters

Fred Pollock (1937-)
John McLean (1939-2019)
Russell Colombo (1947-)
Iain Robertson (1955-)

SCOTTISH ARTISTS, SINCE the 1920s, have played a significant role in pioneering and developing abstract painting in Britain. Unfortunately, much of that important work was carried out south of the border, mainly in London. This certainly would apply to the first generation of Scottish abstractionists such as William Johnstone, William Turnbull, Alan Davie, Wilhelmina Barns-Graham and William Gear.

The next group of Scottish abstract painters who emerged in the 1960s, including John McLean and Fred Pollock, were also based in London around the studio complex at Stockwell Depot. Both these two artists were, not surprisingly at that time, influenced by transatlantic painting but, by the late 1970s, they had developed their own distinctive take on abstract painting, so much so that the highly regarded American critic Clement Greenberg would visit their studios and promote their work in his writings. Since the 1980s, McLean in particular has had a very successful career, including designing stained glass windows for Norwich Cathedral, and is now regarded by many as having been one of the most important and innovative practitioners of abstraction in Britain. Russell Colombo and Iain Robertson are from a more recent generation of abstract painters who chose to remain in Scotland, although in the 1990s Robertson moved to the home of English abstraction in Cornwall. These two younger painters have continued to follow the example of McLean and Pollock and work in an expressive mode of gestural painting but with their own personal stylistic touch.

While I was working at the Talbot Rice Gallery in the 1980s, I helped to curate solo exhibitions for each of these four artists. More recently, I included them in a group show of Scottish abstraction, *Mark of Beauty*, which I curated for the Union Gallery in Edinburgh in 2012.

Fred Pollock

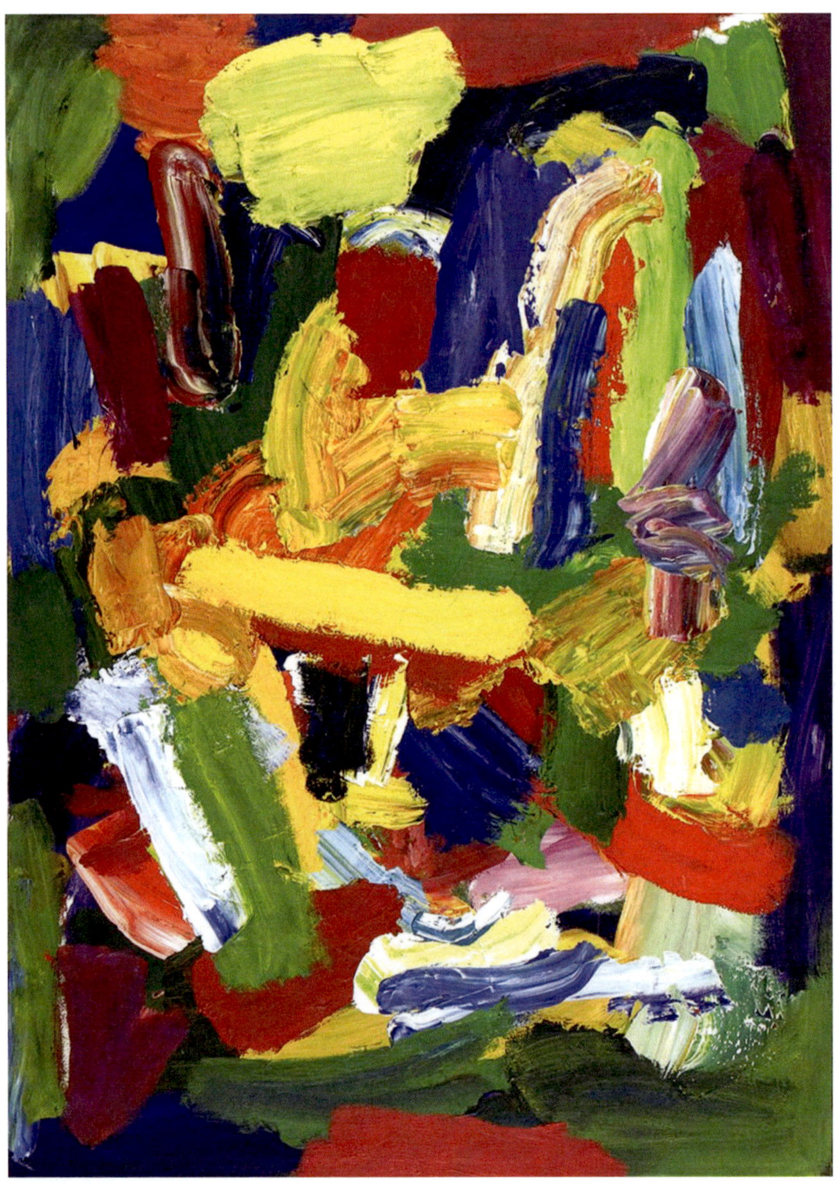

The Painter's Song
1993
Acrylic on canvas, 214x150cm
Reproduced courtesy of the artist

Whaur Extremes Meet

Seeing as Painting / Painting as Looking

I cannot therefore entertain the hope of being intelligible to those who have not, by pains and practice, acquired the habit of distinguishing the appearance of objects to the eye, from the judgment which they form by sight of their colour, distance, magnitude and figure. The only profession in life wherein it is necessary to make this distinction is that of painting. The painter hath occasion for an abstraction, with regard to visible objects, somewhat similar to that which we here require; and this is the most difficult part of his art.
Thomas Reid, *The Craft of Painting* (1764)

'IT'S "THE LOOK of the thing" that counts'. This was the clear and concise statement of priority and intent that opened the first exhibition, *Poussin=Abstract*, which the Poussin Gallery mounted back in 2005. Furthermore, their declared connection with the great 17th-century French classical painter revealed that the Poussin Gallery was deadly serious in their belief that the 'look' in visual art is anything but 'superficial'. If such is the case – and I am the last to argue with such an observation – then I would contend the work of Fred Pollock, conscientiously and rigorously developed on the principle of the 'look' over a long and sustained career, is in complete and harmonious accord with the optical intent at the heart of high quality abstract art.

With such proclaimed artistic and aesthetic attitudes, it is not surprising that the presence (as opposed to the ghost) of Clement Greenberg is keenly sensed here. Pollock, in fact, came into direct contact with the 'Grand Master of modernism' when Greenberg curated an exhibition, *Four Abstract Artists,* at the Fruitmarket Gallery, Edinburgh, in 1977. (Interestingly, all four Scottish painters who were involved – Abercrombie, Gouk, McLean as well as Pollock – are now closely connected with the Poussin Gallery.) At the end of his catalogue essay to that exhibition Greenberg wrote:

> These young artists may take their directions from North American influences, but they don't submit to these. They're not defined by them. They are their own. And being on their own, they'll have their up and downs. That's when their character will show.

That was written over 30 years ago yet Pollock's painting still demonstrates that, despite necessary shifts in mode and technique, his underlying 'character' and approach to his artistic practice has remained consistently focused on the visual power of colour to create pure and unmediated sensations of form and space. Refuting the accusation of formalism, as with all true modernist artists, Pollock never operates in his studio to a prescribed formula of intention, but openly approaches each work with as a receptive response as possible – one mark linking with the next, one chromatic chord responding to another, one composition formulating into a picture which relates back to its pictorial heir and then forward to its successors... Thus the modern artist or poet, in the ringing words of the great Hugh MacDiarmid, who provides the title for this essay, must 'dodge the curst conceit o' being richt/ That damns the vast majority o' men.' The thing that requires being 'richt' of course is the look of painting itself or to use another of Greenberg's critical colloquialisms, 'it has to sit right'.

Greenberg always traced his aesthetic philosophy and analytical method back to the 18th century Enlightenment and was adamantly Kantian in his disinterested approach to critical judgement. He also held that, despite the predominant critical narrative, there was never 'a break with the past' in the history of art. Presumably the same could also be said of the history of philosophy and, if that is so, then it might be appropriate to trace Greenberg's Kantian attitudes and ideas back to the major figures of the Scottish Enlightenment – Thomas Reid and David Hume, the latter of whom 'awakened Kant from his philosophical slumbers'. Significantly, both of these Scots philosophers had a keen passion for the visual arts and were also on personal acquaintance with the two most eminent Scottish painters of their day, Allan Ramsay and Henry Raeburn, and had their portraits painted by them.

Yet, despite their shared interest in visual culture, Hume and Reid's analytical writings on tactile, aural and visual experience were fundamentally at odds. In a very small nutshell, Hume came out of the Idealist/Nominalist School of Cartesian thinkers, which was deeply sceptical that we could rely on our senses to verify the external world. For Hume, our belief in the world's existence is, in fact, ultimately due to the internal ideas that we formulate through experience and memory in the human mind. On the other hand, as a modern Realist, Reid strenuously challenged this notion. In Reid's Common Sense view, if we are fully aware, through the direct agency of our immediate senses, there is no need of mediating ideas and concepts in order for us to experience external reality. It is therefore gratifying from our point of view that Reid chose to use the unique optical skills of the painter to demonstrate his contentions.

Anticipating many of the now accepted concepts of contemporary post-structuralism theory, Reid lamented the nature of our socially conditioned, quotidian attitude to the visual world as being like a veil of conceptually constructed signs:

> To us it is a language perfectly familiar; and, therefore, we take no notice of the signs, but attend only to the thing signified by them. Thus, to our great loss, we don't really see the world; rather we immediately fall into our habitual reading of it. We pass from the sign to the signified, with ease, and by natural impulse; but to go backward from the thing signified to the sign, is a work of labour and difficulty.

Such 'a work of labour' is the chosen lot of painters in general but acutely so for pure abstract artists like Fred Pollock.

In the work of Pollock, the central role of seeing/looking is of fundamental and crucial importance. Reid draws our attention to the fact that seeing/looking is not only an experienced act on our part but also a medium by which we engage with the visual world and, like the modernist artist, we all need to be readily aware of its specific characteristics. With great dedication, Pollock, through his essential painterly practice, successfully manages to attend to both the somatic and the artistic qualities of his specific medium of expression. On the heavily worked surface of his pictures, the intuitive action of seeing and the creative process of painting meet and interconnect in the most direct and free encounter. It is only through years of intense observation and painterly experimentation that Pollock has managed 'to go backward from the thing signified to the sign'. In these richly sensuous paintings of Pollock's, not only is colour revealed to us as the most fundamental feature of our visual world but the very experience of seeing is re-constructed for us – not in light as with nature, but through the highly articulated artifice of colour placement and arrangement.

Thus, with Fred Pollock, we have a very unusual situation. Normally with the presentation of pictures in a painting show we, as viewers, move immediately and unconsciously from our involuntary action of seeing to the conventionally rehearsed act of looking at something that holds our attention for aesthetic and cultural reasons. In marked contrast, however, Pollock's intently optical paintings manage to turn the tables on us by making us intensely aware of the physiological process of seeing through the aegis of the constructivist medium of pure painting in tactile colour pigment. Of course, even with Pollock's painting, we will go on to the self-conscious act of looking and recognition, but the original impact of the initial experience of spontaneous seeing should also remain with us.

What might seem to be implied here – a return to a sort of Ruskinian 'innocent eye' – would certainly be anathema to everything that is being preached by contemporary theories on post-structuralism. This seeming lapse into romantic yearning for our mythical original and uncontaminated being, however, is definitely not the case on my part. Not for a moment am I denying that painting, including Pollock's, is a language of communication. Even abstraction is a distinct part of that system and Fred Pollock's pictures should never be regarded as spontaneous outbursts of raw instinctive expression. On the contrary, they are carefully considered and constructed semantic entities; thus, they are as much conceptual as perceptual in their nature and in their making. These paintings are there not only to be seen and looked at but also to stimulate enriching dialogue through their visual articulation.

As with all highly sophisticated communication systems, the language of painting is multi-layered. Firstly, there is what might be termed the subliminal level of visual language, which Lacan for instance calls the 'real' and Kristeva the 'semiotic'. This is an innate and pre-symbolic mode of expression and the early abstractionists staked their faith on the transcendental power of this language to inspire spiritual enlightenment. In the early stages of abstraction, many believed that abstract art, operating at this level of visual communication, could have infinitely greater universal significance than mimetic art. Secondly, although abstract art does appear to operate to a greater degree at a subliminal level than other kinds of painting, it has also developed its own particular conventional systems of communication through its distinctive internal historical progress. Thirdly, the mode of expression that painters develop is also dependent on the artistic company they keep and the influences they fall under in the development of their art. Thus, painters are drawn towards particular languages of painting through the traditions they inherit, the influences they seek and the community of fellow practitioners with whom they keep company. Fourthly, the final level is the most particular and subtle to discern. This is the artist's own individual manner of visual communication. This is what might be termed the personal rhetorical style of display and delivery which allows us to distinguish and appreciate the crucial differences in means of expression and technique between one painter, in this instance, Fred Pollock, and another. Needless to say, the multi-layer structure of painterly language is closely interlinked and any crude attempt at separation through heavy-handed analysis of specific examples can have detrimental effect on the overall aesthetic effect. At our own peril, 'we murder to dissect' as Alexander Pope succinctly put it in his *An Essay on Criticism*.

The ever-perceptive Reid realised much more than most that perceptual seeing and the conceptual discernment involved in the act of looking were always closely interconnected. Both modes could, however, with proper practice – as found in the attentive focus and technical skill of the dedicated painter – remain distinct from each other. Pollock's paintings reveal and exemplify this amazing achievement. His paintings are immediately wondrous but also go on to encourage and sustain absorbing aesthetic meditation. This is because their unmediated openness operates at the multi-levels of visual communication as previously discussed. Consequently, this causes at least a dual reaction in the attentive and absorbed viewer. Through the initial optical contact with Pollock's pictures, we intuitively see their polychromatic brilliance and instantly bask in the sensual delights they offer. The first encounter operates at the subliminal level of visual communication where seeing and painting are at one with each other. Following the involuntary impulse of our initial attraction, we then move from the original action of seeing the painting into the subsequent act of looking at it. Now our awareness and experience of the different levels of painterly language comes into action. Instinctive seeing is now succeeded by sophisticated looking and informed recognition, but hopefully, however, never to be subsumed or eradicated by them. These tangibly real and visually vibrant pictures simultaneously make us realise that seeing is the innate existential pleasure of simply

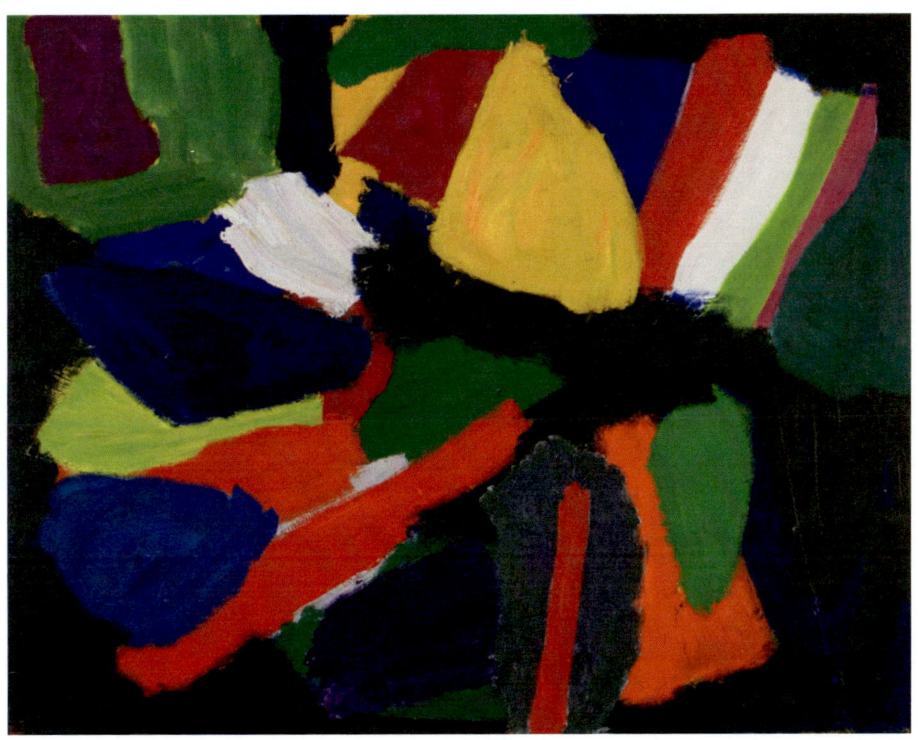

Delta Sound
1988/1996
Acrylic on canvas, 173x214cm

Reproduced courtesy of the artist

being alive; while, at the same time, they also offer us the freedom to look and critically read and assess the distinctive signs of highly sophisticated modern painting and contemplate their aesthetic significance.

One of Fred Pollock's long-term admirers, the master of English modernist sculpture, Anthony Caro, got it precisely and concisely right when he commented on the work of this outstanding Scottish modern painter: 'these paintings don't only look good at first acquaintance; they stay good.' They still do because, as Greenberg observed back in 1977, 'Pollock's paintings not only stay good, they stay their own'.

This essay was written by Bill Hare in 2008 and published by the Poussin Gallery, London.

John McLean

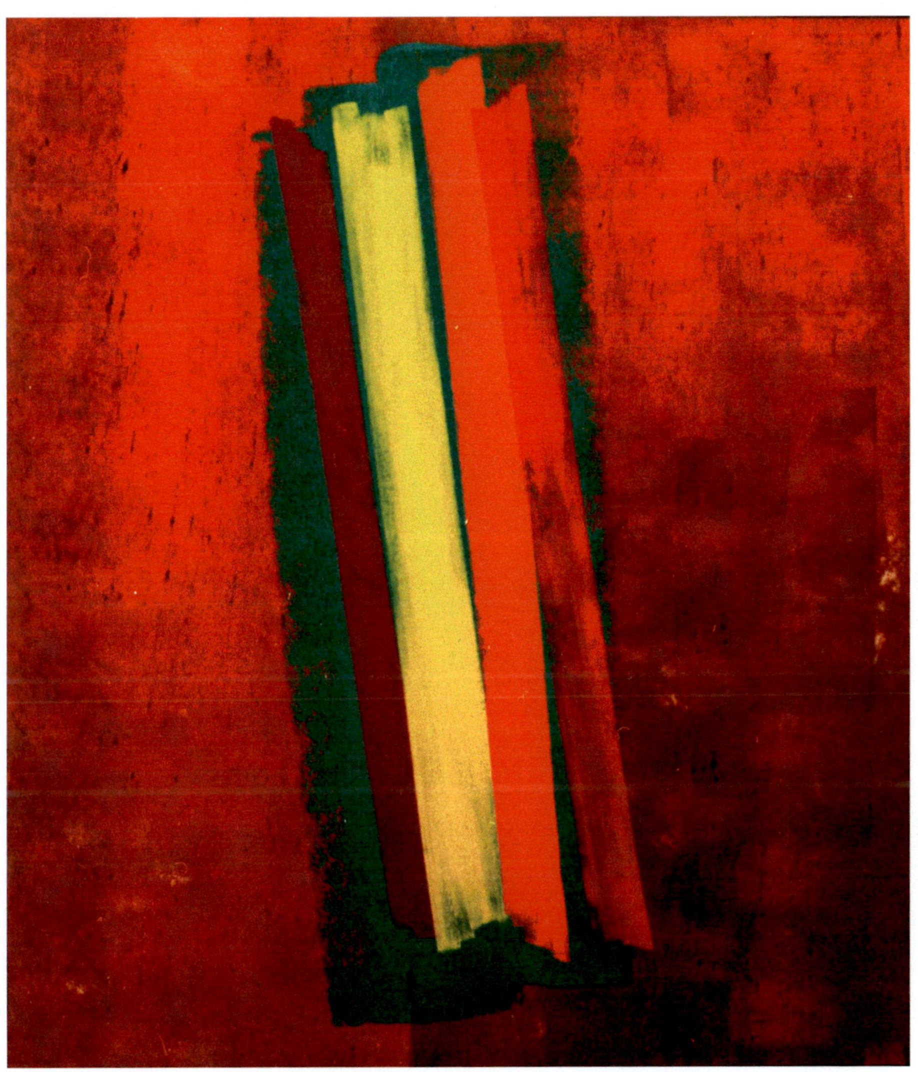

Lagoon
1987
Acrylic on canvas, 127x110cm
Reproduced courtesy of the artist's estate

John McLean Interview

Constable said it was his childhood experience of growing up in Dedham Vale which made him a painter. What about you, what made you a painter?
If Constable was expressing more than the depth of his feelings for his motifs, his remark is pretty vague when you think of his mature paintings. It tells you nothing of how he evolved his means of expressing himself. Similarly, it doesn't tell you much about my work if I tell you I spent my adolescence on the north-east coast of Scotland and think it very beautiful. I am not repudiating my background. It's just that its relation to my work is too nebulous to talk about. The only thing worth mentioning is that when I left for London in 1963, nearly everything I had painted had been figurative.

Which artists have influenced the development of your work? And what other influences have there been?
Let's skip the early figurative work. The Americans Louis and Noland were shown in London in the early '60s and, for me, the directness of their painting seemed to open up the future. But it took me a while to get rid of what, looking back on it, was an unnecessary intricacy in my own work. A painter who helped me beyond this was the Washington artist Sam Gilliam, who worked wet into wet. I saw his painting in the late '60s. It was only when I worked as loosely as he that I really came to terms with the directness and scale of Louis and Noland, not to mention Pollock who influenced all three. But happy as I was with this new work of mine, it began to dissatisfy me because of its all-overness and limited colour. It was at that juncture I saw Jack Bush's 1972 show at Emmerich's in New York. I loved seeing his chunks of colour floating. You get a similar feeling in some of Miró's paintings. The latter is an unsung revolutionary when it comes to freeing colour and space. Those are my main debts. Other than artistic influences, they are too indefinite and complex to put into words.

Many might feel your method of painting is unconventional…
My touch is directly related to the scale I'm working on. I've found a good way of putting a ground onto, say, a 6ft x 4ft canvas with a squeegee mop. The sponge is a reservoir for paint. It even holds thick stuff. And it's sensitive to pressure. Not being a precision instrument, accidents happen that open up possibilities. All the interesting abstract painters I know finding themselves having to improvise ways of getting the paint on. My methods are unconventional only when compared with, say, Rowney's fine art accoutrements. The squeegee will probably outlive its usefulness. How I put the paint on is dictated by the way the paintings are going. I have a plan of campaign when I start. In the exigencies of work, that plan gets adapted or abandoned. I play my hunches and I keep on the look-out. If and when the painting comes alive, it's always in a surprising way.

Certainly I cajole it or bludgeon it but it's still a surprise – the final form. I realise planning and surprise might seem contradictory but there it is.

Turning to the content of your paintings, you are one of the 'purest' abstract painters I know. By that I mean you are not like some abstract painters who are inspired by the natural world and are basically landscape artists.
You're right. Any feeling of landscape in my work is incidental. But purity isn't my aim. It's only an impression resulting from comparison with other less abstract painters' work. Also, painting abstractly doesn't mean independence of the natural world. The most obvious aspect of the natural world that affects my work is light. Spirit, mind and energy go into it too. Is there any underlying mystical dimension to your work? I'm not a mystic and I don't want to take anything from the simple direct fact of the painting there on the wall. But nevertheless, 'spiritual' maybe describes the effort in art, the nurturing as opposed to faking like Frankenstein and his monsters. Abstract painting didn't appear from nowhere. Its roots are in Cézanne, the impressionists and so on, right back. It grew. It is unavoidable. You can't concoct real art. Most art you see is concocted, fake. That includes a lot of abstract art.

You praised Miró for 'freeing colour and space'. Is that the ultimate aim in your own painting?
I know it sounds evasive but since I don't work to a theory, my ultimate aim is a matter of hindsight. And because I'm always learning, I'm always adjusting my immediate aim. I have a horror of trying to pin it down in words. It really exists only in its embodiment in paint in each successful picture. Certainly colour is very important. When the colour's right, the space is right. But then it's the light of the painting that makes the colour right.

I know that you have a great deal of respect for Clement Greenberg. However, his concept of modern art is very much under attack in our present post-modernist era. Do you take much interest in this kind of thing and has the shift in the taste for painting affected your work in any way?
What shift in taste for painting? In the important commercial centres for contemporary art (so that excludes the uk), dealers are busy sacking their neo-expressionists and taking neo-geo, neue-stille – call it what you will. From time to time, the market place needs these stimuli. Art journalists thrive on them too. I can't get worked up about it and it has no effect on my work.

Is that because you feel abstract art and postmodernism are fundamentally antithetical?
Abstract painting is antithetical only to the inability to look at art. I can't take the term 'postmodernism' seriously. It's just an intellectual fad. You mentioned Greenberg. Certainly I respect him. No one since Roger Fry has written so clearly and intelligently about contemporary art. No critic

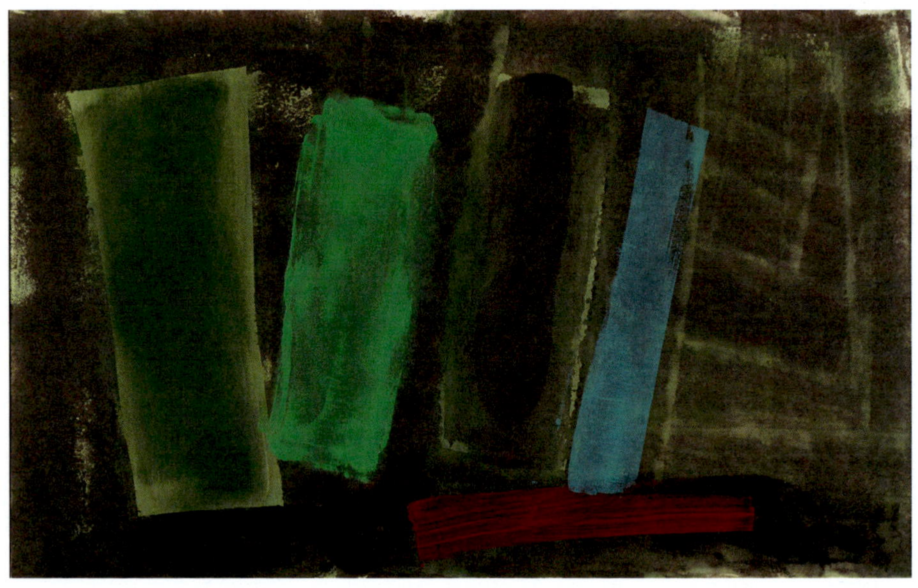

Pitcundrum

1985

Acrylic on canvas, 127x110cm

Reproduced courtesy of the artist's estate
and the Fine Art Society, Edinburgh

has either his energy for getting round studios or his eye for good work. He is the best of the very few critics I listen to on a level with those few artists whose comments I take seriously and that's the end of it. There is an idea that, if you respect Greenberg, you therefore follow him but that's propaganda.

In parenthesis let me mention the latest from the anti-Greenberg industry: Professor TJ Clark of Harvard's *ad hominem* argument that Greenberg's judgement is vitiated by its being somehow a function of early Marxist influence. That's shoddy thinking. It doesn't matter what Greenberg in his youth read or didn't read, whom he talked with or didn't talk with, his eye is his eye. He hasn't got a 'concept of modern art', as you put it. Clark won't realise his argument is phony because, like a lot of art world academics, he has scant idea of the subtlety and no idea of the independence of visual judgement.

Do you think there is any critical mileage to be gained in the arguments between figurative and non-figurative painting?
No. I enjoy both. Most of the best art of the last 40 years has been abstract. That's unarguable. I personally think this kind of debate is pretty futile.

However, the relationship between image and imagery interests me. For example, have you consciously striven towards creating an 'image' for your painting? I mean, an abstract painting has an image even more than a 'representational' work, doesn't it?
By image I assume you mean something like signature – as far as my work goes – a 'McLean look'. If my work seems homogeneous in that sense, I don't wilfully bring that about. It's the feeling, not the 'look' of a painting that concerns me. Each successful work has a unique feeling. I can't foretell that feeling as I work on a painting. As I said before, it's always a surprise. Abstract and representational painting equally have an image, which for me is the feeling of the whole painting.

This interview was conducted by Bill Hare in 1987 and published in *Alba*, issue 6.

A New Kind of Space

Colour and Light in the Painting of John McLean

JOHN MCLEAN IS far from being a great painter, so unequivocally judges the reviewer in the recent spring issue of *Modern Painters*. However, on closer inspection we find that this is not the informed verdict of an experienced art critic but of an academic philosopher. Just imagine how much he would welcome outsiders declaiming such categorical verdicts on issues in his own profession!

Being a mere art critic myself, I would tentatively suggest a rather contrary view and propose that if John McLean is not yet a great painter – after 40-odd years of dedication to the practice of his craft – he has gone a long way to become a very good one. My disagreement with John Haldane is not, however, just a matter of personal taste and judgement. I have to say that I consider the grounds on which he came to his conclusions, as laid out in his review of McLean's small retrospective exhibition at the Crawford Arts Centre, University of St Andrews, last March were ill-informed and unconvincingly argued.

Central to Haldane's view of the painter's work was this damning statement: 'McLean is consistent in his preoccupations and uneven in his realisation of them.' Firstly, taking the seemingly complimentary side of this judgement, what does the reviewer consider as the consistency in McLean's art? It seems that the whole thrust of Haldane's thesis is that the finest aspect of Scottish modern painting is colourism; almost every significant figure of the last 75 years in Scottish painting has been a colourist according to Haldane. Yet McLean patently fails to join Haldane's illustrious colourist company, which includes Robert Motherwell, Alan Davie and even Bruce McLean – an odd assortment of Scottish Colourists if ever there was one!

In response let me say that in my opinion, and many of those with much more critical experience and refined taste than mine, such as practising artists and perceptive critics, one of the most distinguished and admired qualities of McLean's painting is his highly sensitive response to colour, light, subtle tonal values and their role within the complex relationship between pictorial composition and framing format. All that being said, however, I am personally of the opinion that colour, crucial though it is to the distinctive character of McLean's painting, is not ultimately his most consistent preoccupation. That I would suggest is his obsessive attention to the construction of pictorial space. As McLean stated a few years ago in *Art Review* (February 1994), 'the best abstract paintings do not just deal with their own actual surface but with a new kind of space'. Unfortunately those like Haldane, who mainly see abstract paintings as a kind of magic, in that pigment can be spread across a surface in a fashion that makes no attempt to mimic the appearance of solid objects, but yet catches the attention and stimulates the imagination, are always in danger of merely responding to the most obvious superficial qualities of abstraction. As McLean himself pointed out again in the *Art Review* article, 'I think folk who write off abstract art like that must see pictures like the top of an iced cake'.

As with all great painting – from Titian to Motherwell and McLean – what is on the surface has to be securely founded on the way the artist manipulates what Hans Hofmann termed the 'push and pull', ie the optics of pictorial space created by the placement of colour marks. I feel that McLean is as much a pictorial constructivist as a colourist but not in any Russian ruler and compass fashion. He is crucially concerned to make sure that the order, balance and structure of his composition is absolutely right, where every component contributes to a perfect pictorial unity. For instance, if Haldane had looked a bit more closely at the actual surface of McLean's canvases, he might have been more appreciative of the carefully balanced process involved rather than dismissing it as he put it of one work – 'three daubs on an elongated unprimed canvas'.

Turning now to the question of the 'uneven' nature of McLean's painterly performance. The insulting use of the word 'daubs' reveals the common notion that a painter like McLean must be an abstract expressionist, and as we all know, such artist's work is pure intuition and uncontrollable adrenaline. Thus, they must be hit or miss 'action' merchants. Of course, like all serious artists, McLean wishes to express his feelings through his art, yet what is far more important for this painter is that in the end the picture itself feels right and can speak for itself. That means that the artist does not impose his will, but rather sets up the conditions for dialogue between himself and his work in a process which leads on from one painting to the next in an ongoing evolutionary scenario.

Finally, the reason why I think some inattentive viewers might read the marks on McLean's canvases as 'daubs' is that they confuse the grace and elegant ease which the artist brings to the final outcome of his pictorial negotiations, with a lack of Victorian earnestness and expressionist angst. Unlike many lesser artists, McLean is not prepared to fake this, for as he pointed out, 'My paintings may look easy, but that is only because all the hard work takes place elsewhere.'

This essay was written by Bill Hare in 1996 and published in *Contemporary Visual Art*, issue 24.

Russell Colombo

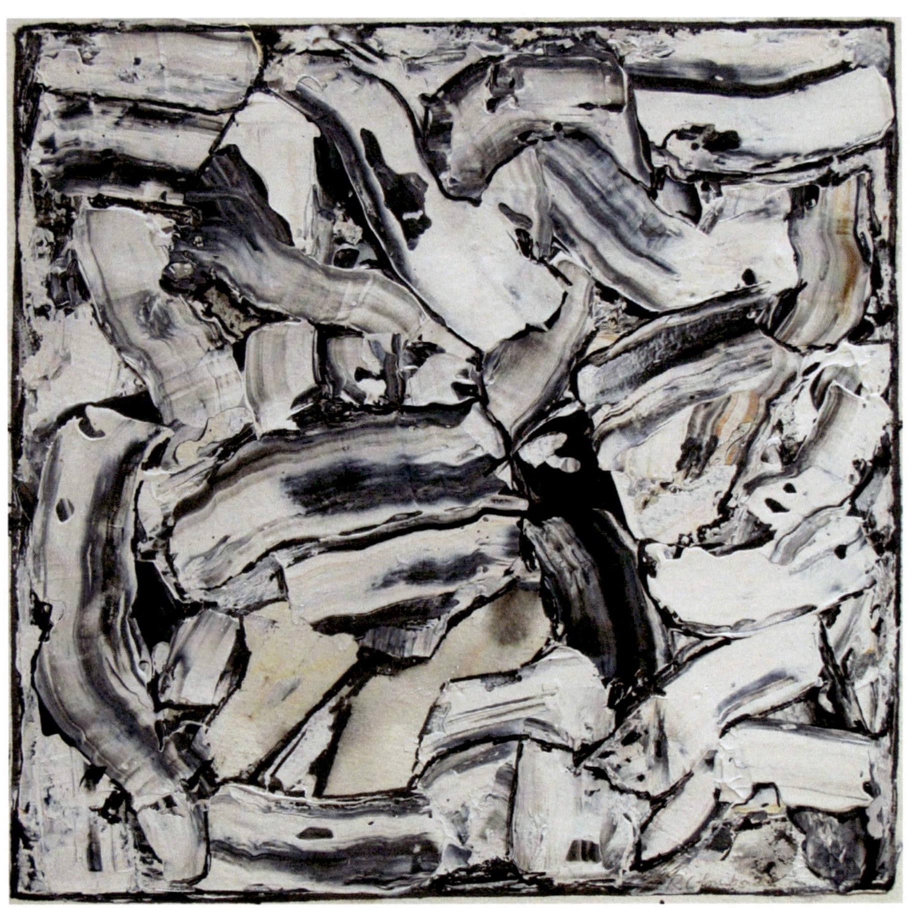

Untitled

1988

Acrylic on paper, 23x25cm

Reproduced courtesy of the artist

The Painting of Russell Colombo

TO THE PEOPLE who still find modern art difficult to come to terms with, abstraction is usually treated with the most suspicion. The famous put-down that 'a child of three could do that' is still reserved, with relish, for this particular example of modern art. Other more considered reactions might acknowledge the artist's skill but express the opinion that abstract art seems relevant to nothing else but itself. Self-indulgent, inhuman, inaccessible, are some of the more common accusations levelled against it.

Some types of highly formal abstract painting might merit some of the hostility and indifference of the public. Yet I hope that anyone who has an eye 'which watches and receives' can clearly discern that the work of Russell Colombo flies in the face of these criticisms. The reason for this, I would suggest, is that Russell Colombo continues within a tradition of abstract painting in which, broadly speaking, the human desire for uncovering the underlying order of things and revealing it through direct visual communication remains the paramount concern of the artist.

Of course, someone could retort that the qualities that I have attributed to the best abstract painting are the hallmarks of great art long before modernism came along. This may be so. There is, however, a fundamental difference between modern art and that of the past, which, amongst other things, lies with our changed relationship with nature.

It may be a little surprising to point out to those coming to Russell Colombo's work for the first time that he is first and foremost a painter of nature; not however, that any of his paintings present the conventional topographical single view of the outside world – that is now much better achieved by photography than painting. In fact, it was around the middle of the 19th century, when photography first began to alter people's view of the world, that the illusionistic role of painting – transcribing the continually changing appearances of real forms and space into a fixed image on a flat surface – began to be seriously questioned. Not only did the static illusionistic painted image appear to be inadequate, but also undesirable in the rapidly changing modern world.

Nineteenth century philosophy and scientific investigation, particularly in the form of Darwinian evolution, began to undermine the biblical humanist view of man's separate elevated position in the natural world. He (she was never allowed to) could no longer claim to be 'the measure of all things'. Thus, it became increasingly untenable for artists who wished to accommodate these new modern ideas and experiences to continue to follow the Renaissance tradition of using painting to present the external world solely according to human scale and values. As you might have expected, there was an initial crisis of confidence in the future of art. 'Painting is dead!' the cry went up. Yet, in fact, the opposite occurred. Painting began to realise its distinctive authority in its power to engage

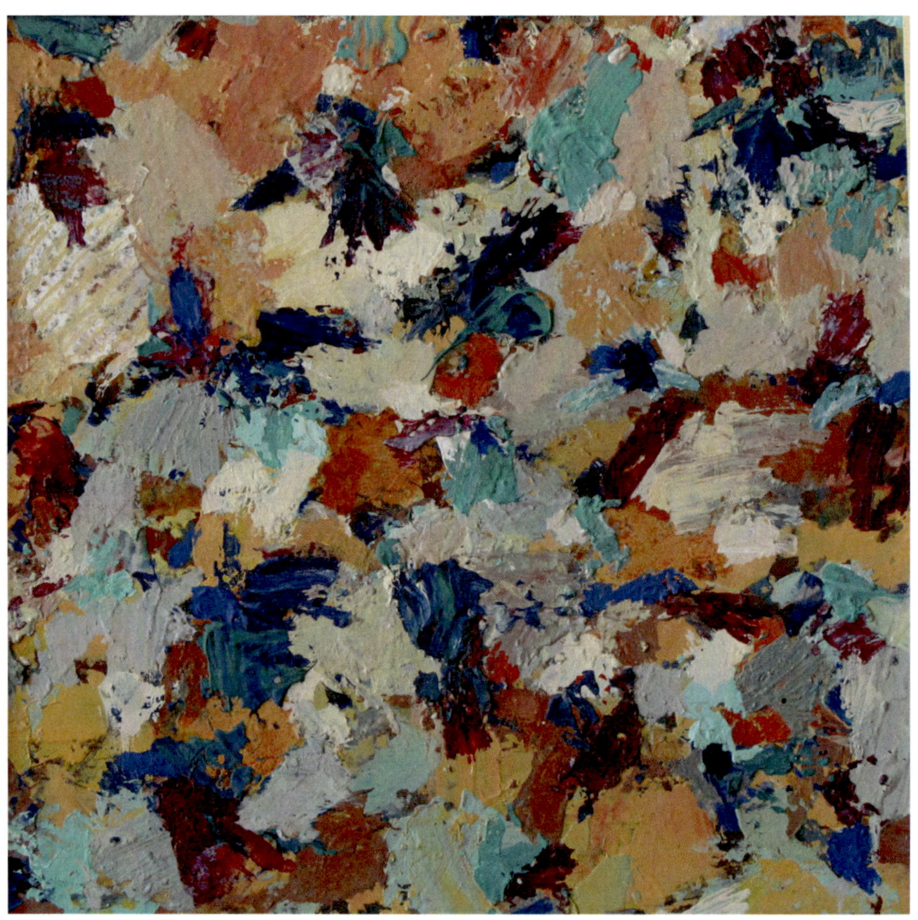

Untitled
1990
Acrylic on board, 25x25cm
Reproduced courtesy of the artist

with and visually express Man's evolving position within the historical and natural scheme of things. Instead of being like Alberti's 'window onto the world', framing, but also dividing, the artist/spectator from the nature, modern painting now began to develop its own surface-orientated, all-over arrangemen of flexible forms which paralleled the principal characteristic of modern man's relationship with nature – the continuum of reality.

From the Impressionists onwards, this balance between the commitment to the integrity of the language of painting and the need to develop pictorial equivalents through colour, gesture, texture, for the perceived qualities of nature have been the motivating force behind the best of abstract art. As Hugh MacDiarmid wrote:

Our task is not to reproduce nature but to create and enrich it.

Russell Colombo's paintings do not 'reproduce nature'. He does, however, work from observed aspects of reality, whether it be distanced landscape views or close-up microscopic details. The artist then works to transform his initial source of inspiration into a pictorial composition which expresses, through interlocking and overlapping areas of related colour, the suggested structures and rhythms which lie beneath superficial appearances. Ultimately, the paintings, with their overall immediacy of vibrant surface colour, celebrate the integrated relationship between the perceptive powers of our senses and the underlying forces of nature.

Bad abstract painting, whether it is pretentiously esoteric or vacuously decorative, deserves all it gets from the public. But it would be a great loss, both for the artist and those seriously looking to art for deeper insights into human experience, if all abstract art was equally dismissed. Abstract art is not 'easy'. In our brave new mechanised world where almost all experiences come second-hand, media-packaged, the paintings of Russell Colombo may initially appear difficult. Abstract art is not intended, unless it is mere commercial design, for transient mass consumption.

As MacDiarmid observed about the paintings of the great Scottish abstract painter, William Johnstone, who once said 'Painting taught me to look beyond the object, the visual world, into the inner world which was me':

His work of course is not 'simple' in any way.
Any more than life is itself.

Russell Colombo's paintings grow out of a delicate, but complex relationship between art and nature, which is not over even with the last brush stroke. Those who wish to continue extending the rich possibilities of his paintings for themselves will, I can assure them, be rewarded a hundred-fold.

This essay was written by Bill Hare in 1988 and published by Hawick Museum.

Iain Robertson

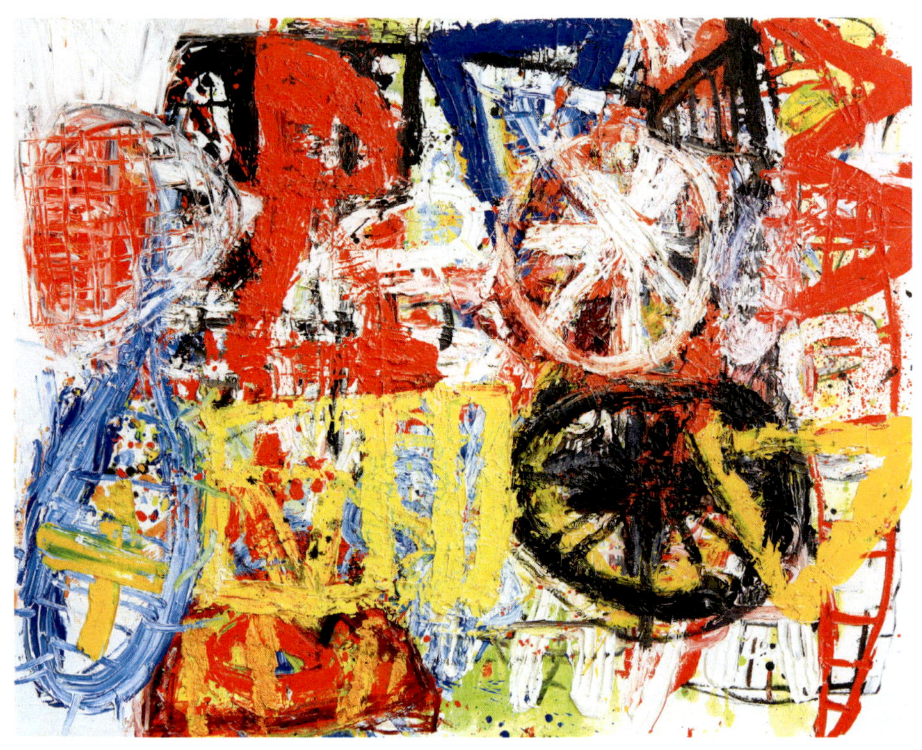

Gods of the North
2004
Oil on canvas, 122x152cm

Reproduced courtesy of the artist (photo Peter Garrett)

Silent Pictures that Speak for Themselves

IAIN ROBERTSON IS a quiet man who prefers to let his painting do the talking to whoever cares to take the time to look at, and listen to, his work.

Some people might find my mixing of the auricular with the optical rather odd and surprising. I would suggest, however, that to appreciate fully good painting, which is to be found in abundance with the work of Iain Robertson, you have to have a responsive ear as well as an inquisitive eye. The receptive and the active will of all of us must work in harmony with each other, whether in relation to art in particular, or life in general. This crucial combination applies, for instance, every time we engage in meaningful conversation with someone else. We instinctively use our eyes to check – through hand gesture, facial expression, body language etc – the validity and sincerity of what is being said to us. To be fully engaged with, Iain Robertson's paintings also require to be listened to as well as looked at. Their abundant complexities generate a synesthetic effect where emerging barely decipherable forms and suggestive sonorous colours resonate and mutually create a truly multi-sensory experience.

Some will say, of course, that these paintings might 'talk' but, for them, unfortunately, it is in a strange foreign language. Language of course, like art, is a complex business and is not just that stuff we all use to negotiate the demands of our everyday lives. In the quotidian world, we are merely dealing with the mundanely obvious but, unfortunately, this attitude can also spill over into the realm of the aesthetic as well. Thus, the popular attitude and response to art is sadly dictated not by what people like but merely by what they know and are used to. Whether in life or in art, the familiar and the predictable reassures but also seals off other kinds of potential possibilities and new types of pleasures.

Iain Robertson's paintings are richly redolent of these 'new types of pleasures' and other kinds of revelatory opportunities, which are openly laid out for us like 'gifts from the hand of God, the simple soul'. Such over abundant generosity of spirit as displayed here is sometimes difficult to accommodate. It requires a particular kind of attitude, possibly even a childlike state of grace where things are accepted and enjoyed for what they are, instead of what they might be. Such unmediated honesty as found in Robertson's paintings is often difficult to handle.

Unfortunately, western society, since the Renaissance at least, has preferred to go down the primrose path of practical reason (*logos*), rather follow the yellow brick road of spiritual enlightenment (*mythos*). If we apply this historic parting of the ways to the languages of communication in painting, then clearly the seductive allure of the mimetic – through technical devices such as linear and aerial perspective, chiaroscuro and illusionistic naturalism – has triumphed over the innately expressive, the purely decorative

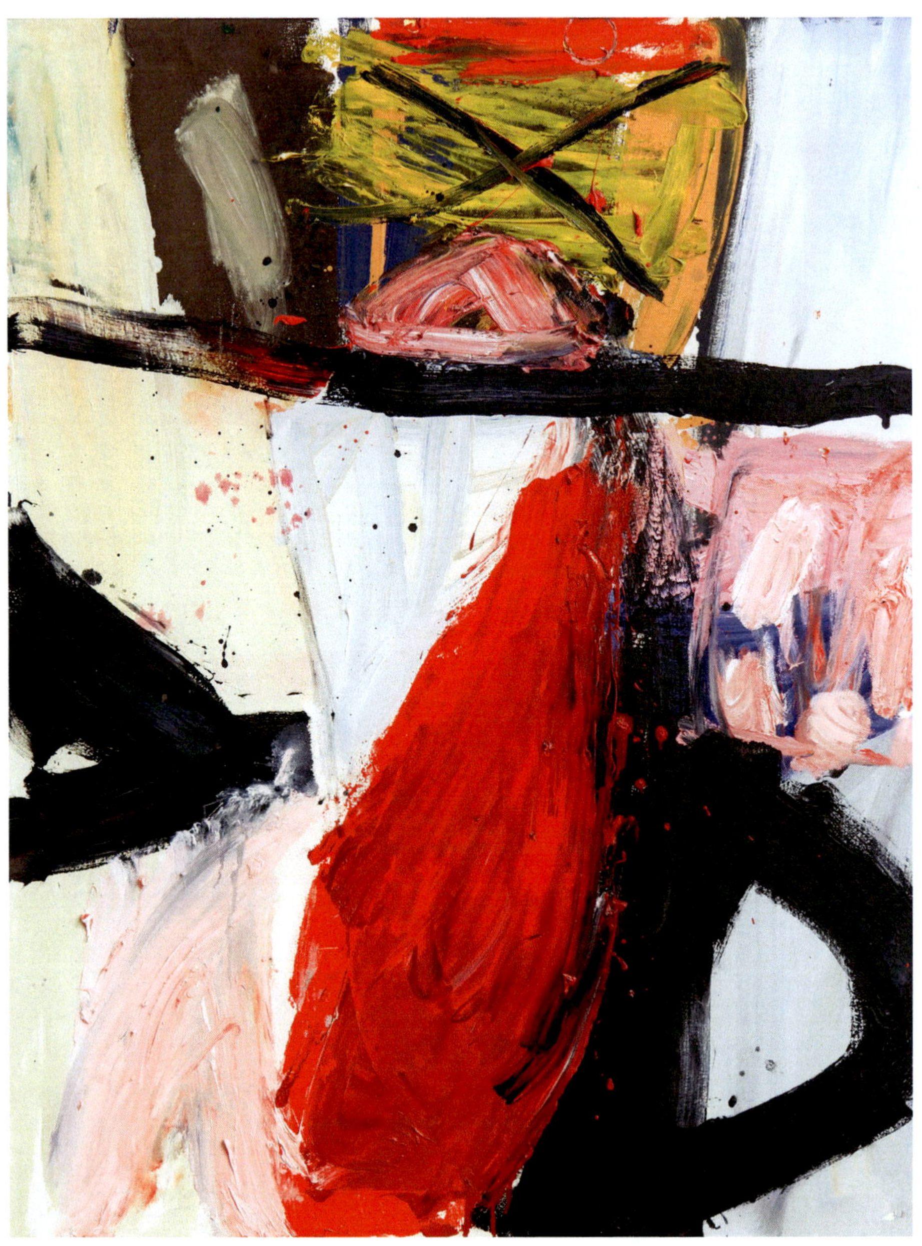

CW
1991
Oil on canvas, 122x91cm
Reproduced courtesy of the artist (photo Peter Garrett)

and the inherently symbolic. Western painting quickly became so ruthlessly subjected to the will of reason, by being forced to become the compliant agent in the tyranny of illusionism. Today, of course, the lure of illusionism has become so endemic and extreme that our world is no longer a 'window', in the terminology of the Rennaissance theorist Alberti, but has now become an electronic screen reflecting back our self-created hyper-reality.

Not surprisingly, in an age of rampant solipsism and visual sophistry, the straightforward honesty of Iain Robertson's work is challenging and truly subversive. These paintings are exceptional, for unlike most aspects of our advertising-saturated culture, they speak for themselves. Here, the medium of communication, the raw material of the tangible paint itself, is not a means to an end but, through the coaxing hand of the artist, is allowed to bring forth an authentic presence in its own right. Here painting is not forced to eradicate its essential self and disappear in order to make way for the entertaining theatricalities of the illustrative mimetic image. These paintings in all their glorious manifestation declare who they are through their own independent visual voices.

Some contend that abstract painting is all surface and no depth. All great painting, figurative or abstract, has pictorial depth as well as picture surface. Depth in painting is like conversation in human society – it is the elixir of life. Space frees up the essential dialogue between painting and people. The free-flowing sense of space allows the eye and the ear to map, re-construct and re-experience the sensation of the creative act of painting itself. In Robertson's case, we can all see afresh – as if at the immediate moment of their making – the gestural marks, the accidental drips, and intuitively respond to the emergence of the inchoate forms at the birth of their creation. This imaginative act – of making marks and trying to understand what they might be trying to say to us – is so fundamental to our basic creative human nature that it must be accessible to all of us.

These paintings of Iain Robertson are, of course, non-political yet, contradictorily, they are truly democratic. As with all healthy democratic communities, these paintings are responsive to direct dialogue and discussion about fundamental human sensory experience. They will commune with anyone that approaches them with a sensitive eye, a sympathetic ear, an imaginative mind and an open heart.

Iain Robertson's paintings may be abstract (whatever that might mean) but they do not speak in some rarefied universal language but in vernacular parlance. They communicate directly through the ubiquitous power of our collective spirit. These joyful paintings that could lighten the most leaden heart, talk – nae, sing – directly to us all in their own distinctive richly nuanced voices. They maybe look and sound a little different from the predictable, the artificial, but through their authentic nature they are all the more interesting, engaging and rewarding for that.

This essay was written by Bill Hare in 2006 and published by Lemon Street Gallery, Truro.

Section Five
Three Independent Artists

Craigie Aitchison (1926–2009)
Frances Walker (1930–)
Barbara Rae (1943–)

THESE THREE INDIVIDUAL artists are difficult to categorise and place within the broad development of British post-war modern art. They are, however, very notable because of the striking visual appeal of their work. They all have had very successful careers which have fostered a great many long-term and devoted admirers.

Craigie Aitchison came from a renowned Scottish legal family and initially studied law, until he decided to become a painter. He went to the Slade in the early 1950s, where he was taught by the distinguished art administrator and academic artist, William Coldstream, and his fellow students included such renowned figurative painters as Michael Andrews, Paula Rego and Euan Uglow. He quickly developed his own highly personal style of painting in which isolated figures, objects and landscape scenes are presented on vividly coloured backgrounds in a highly decorative manner. Throughout his career, he worked within certain pictorial genres with a relatively small array of subjects which he pictorially made his own. These included crucifixions, many with the accompanying presence of his beloved Bedlington terriers; still lifes usually involving vases of flowers, landscapes of Arran or Italy, both of which he regularly visited; and his strikingly colourful portraits of flamboyant sitters. Over his career, he built up a large popular and critical body of admirers for his distinctive paintings and prints, so that his reputation was so distinguished that he was commissioned to paint mural decorations for Truro and Liverpool Cathedrals and Kings College, Cambridge.

Frances Walker trained at Edinburgh College of Art just after the war (1947–53) and took up a teaching career, which eventually led to her being a long-serving, much admired lecturer in the drawing and painting department at Aberdeen's Gray's School of Art (1958–85). Through her dedicated career, Walker has established herself has a major Scottish landscapist. Walker takes a much more austere approach to her landscape subjects than most of her contemporaries, where her strongly graphic analysis concentrates much more on geological structures than on meteorological and atmospheric effects. Furthermore, even though she is concerned with the human history of her subjects there is rarely a figure in her remote scenes and she uses colour in a sparing but telling manner.

Barbara Rae was at Edinburgh College of Art in the first half of the

1960s, around the same time as Bellany and Moffat. Her time there was a very informative one for her, in which she received a sound academic training along with the facilities and encouragement to experiment with a wide range of practices in different mediums. After college, she taught secondary school art education and, in 1975, she moved to the drawing and painting department at Glasgow School of Art. In her painting, she was inclined to landscape subject matter, firstly relatively close at hand in Scotland but gradually to distant, remote parts of the world. However, she has never considered herself a conventional landscape artist, for her main objective is not to produce a topographical record of her subjects but, rather, to evolve a complex pictorial synthesis of both the human history within the landscape itself; and, at the same time, to find pictorial expression for her own physical, emotional, psychological and artistic experience of being there in that particular environment. She works in a very complex and experimental way to achieve the rich pictorial expression of her experiences both in the medium of painting and print-making. Her various projects and journeys have taken her all over the globe, most recently to the Canadian Arctic to follow in the footsteps of her famous explorer ancestor, John Rae.

I had always had tremendous admiration for Frances Walker's superb graphic and pictorial design skills and so it was a great privilege to be asked to write on her work for one of her exhibitions when I was at the Talbot Rice Gallery. I first came in contact with Frances Walker and Barbara Rae in the early 1980s when their work was included in an Edinburgh Festival exhibition, *About Landscape*, at the Talbot Rice Gallery. Since then, I have had the privilege to write on Barbara Rae's prolific artistic career for various catalogues, art journals and a monograph on her painting in 2008. I had the privilege to meet Craigie Aitchison and work with him on an Edinburgh Festival exhibition in 2010 at the Talbot Rice Gallery, *Craigie Aitchison: Paintings 1950–2007*. This was a memorable experience for me but, unfortunately, he was quite ill by then and sadly died before the opening of the exhibition.

Craigie Aitchison

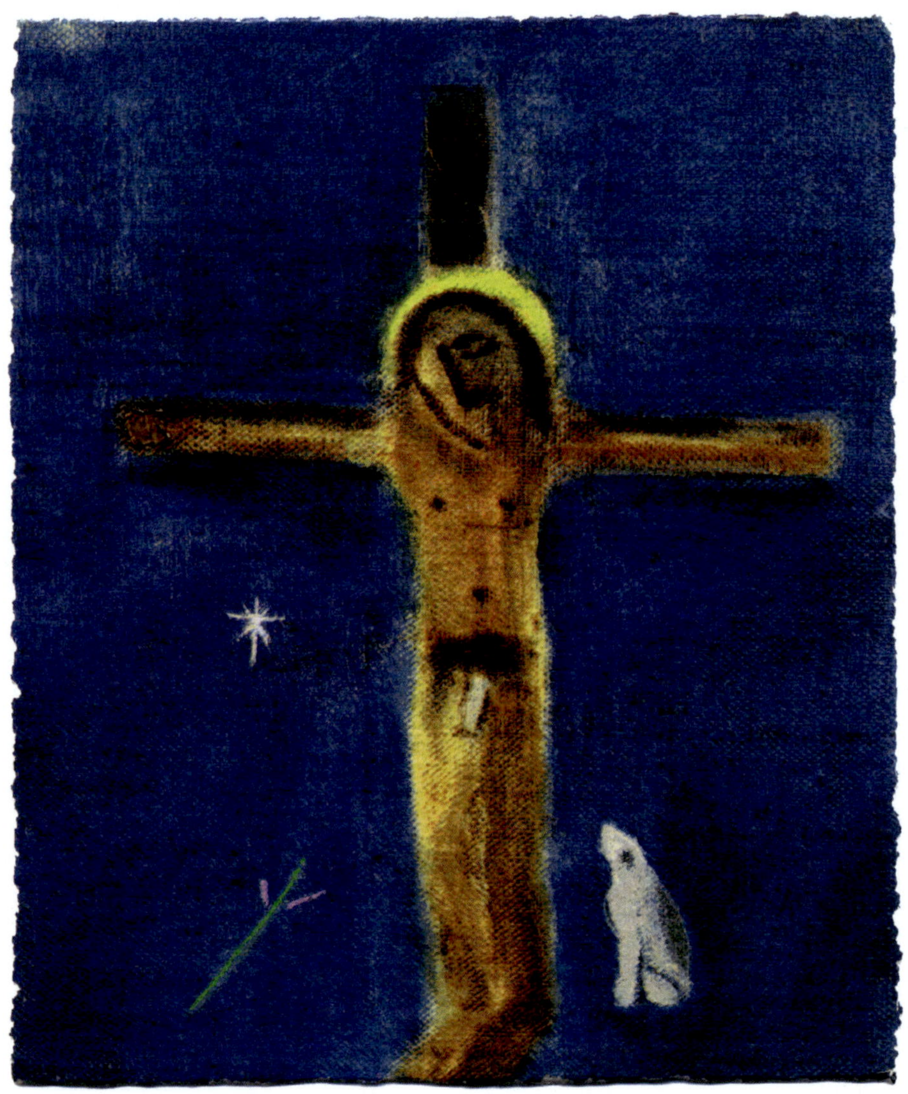

Crucifixion and Dog

2005

Screen-print, 15x13cm

Reproduced courtesy of the Craigie Aitchison estate and Advanced Graphics, London

Between Subject and Subjectivity

The Modernist Painting of Craigie Aitchison

It's got to be a shape, but an iris as well, the two things at once.
Interview with Aitchison, 1975

We work toward serenity through simplification of ideas and of form. The ensemble is our ideal.
Interview with Matisse, 1909

WITH THE DEATH of Craigie Aitchison in December last year [2009], the art scene in this country is undoubtedly now a less colourful place having lost of one of its most distinctive and attractive individuals. He was a much loved and admired figure in British modern painting and, with his life-long air of mischievous childlike innocence, he was affectionately regarded by many as the Peter Pan of the art world. His pictures of animals, especially his Bedlington terriers; his charming still lifes; his haunting landscapes; his arresting portraits; and especially his deeply moving crucifixions all seemed to reflect a truly authentic nature which was as simple as it was pure. Yet on serious consideration, can this really be the whole story? Could this seemingly uncomplicated approach in a major artist sustain such a long and successful career? As Oscar Wilde was quick to point out, the truth is rarely pure and never simple.

Unfortunately, in this country, there can often be found a critical attitude that it is improper, if not downright vulgar, to intellectualise about art. This is especially the case with a medium like painting which has such a direct impact on our immediate sensibilities. Such opinion holds with the connoisseur's view that, in matters of aesthetics, we should solely rely on our instincts and personal taste. Of course, no one who cares about painting would deny that these intuitive subjective reactions do matter and many artists, including Matisse himself, have been wary of too much over-analysis of their work. Craigie Aitchison also expressed a similar reticence when he protested that 'as soon as anyone asks questions the pictures get more complicated than I could ever have intended them to be.' On the other hand, however, we, as admiring and interested viewers, may also be required to utilise our mental faculties in order to further understand and more fully appreciate why the work of an artist such as Craigie Aitchison is of such a high and consistent aesthetic quality.

One of the recurring stumbling blocks to giving Aitchison's painting the serious critical attention it deserves is that his work has tended too readily to be placed solely within a British art context. This usually involves either a tenuous connection with the Scottish Colourists or, due to the English love of quaint eccentrics and artistic outsiders, Aitchison has been misplaced in the company of such 'mystical mavericks' as Blake,

Palmer and Spencer. There could, of course, be something in this. Yet an alternative European approach to the interpretation of Aitchison's art should lead to a richer and more rewarding appreciation of the work of this highly gifted and profoundly knowledgeable artist.

In her introduction to an exhibition of recent paintings at the Rutland Gallery in 1975, Helen Lessore perceptively wrote:

> Of all the artists now living and working in Britain there is none with such a Mediterranean soul as Craigie Aitchison.

Viewed from this wider international perspective, Aitchison can then be seen as one of the most dedicated modernist painters this country has produced. Within this alternative critical approach, it needs, however, to be immediately pointed out that modern art and modernism should not necessarily be taken as being synonymous. In fact, it could be argued that modernism grew out of a critical and creative reaction to orthodox modern art, especially if we regard impressionism as the foundation of modern painting. Matisse certainly felt this when he exclaimed:

> Impressionist painting – and I know, having come from there – teems with *contradictory sensations*, it is a state of agitation. We want something else.

As with Matisse, Craigie Aitchison's art also seeks to resolve these 'contradictory sensations' through a concentrated process of distillation, simplification and synthesis. This complex refining process involves, amongst other things, drawing on connections with a range of modernist practices. Thus, Aitchison's work can, in varying degrees, be seen in relationship with the expressionism of van Gogh, the semi-abstract decorative synthetism of Gauguin, the symbolism of Redon, the fauvism of Matisse and even the colour field painting of abstract expressionism. In addition, as with many other modernists, Aitchison also greatly admired earlier artists who, under different circumstances, appeared to pursue similar painterly aims, such as Giotto and Piero della Francesca, the latter being a particular inspiration for the artist. Certainly Aitchison could sympathise with Matisse's reaction when, looking past the merely illustrative to a much deeper insight, he observed:

> When I see the Giotto frescoes at Padua I do not trouble myself to recognise which scene of the life of Christ I have before me, but I immediately understand the feeling that emerges from it.

It is this concentrated pursuit and sensitive expression of underlying 'feeling' which is at the heart of the painting of Matisse and Aitchison. Both artists carefully select their subject matter and return to the same pictorial themes again and again. Yet in the words of Matisse it is not the

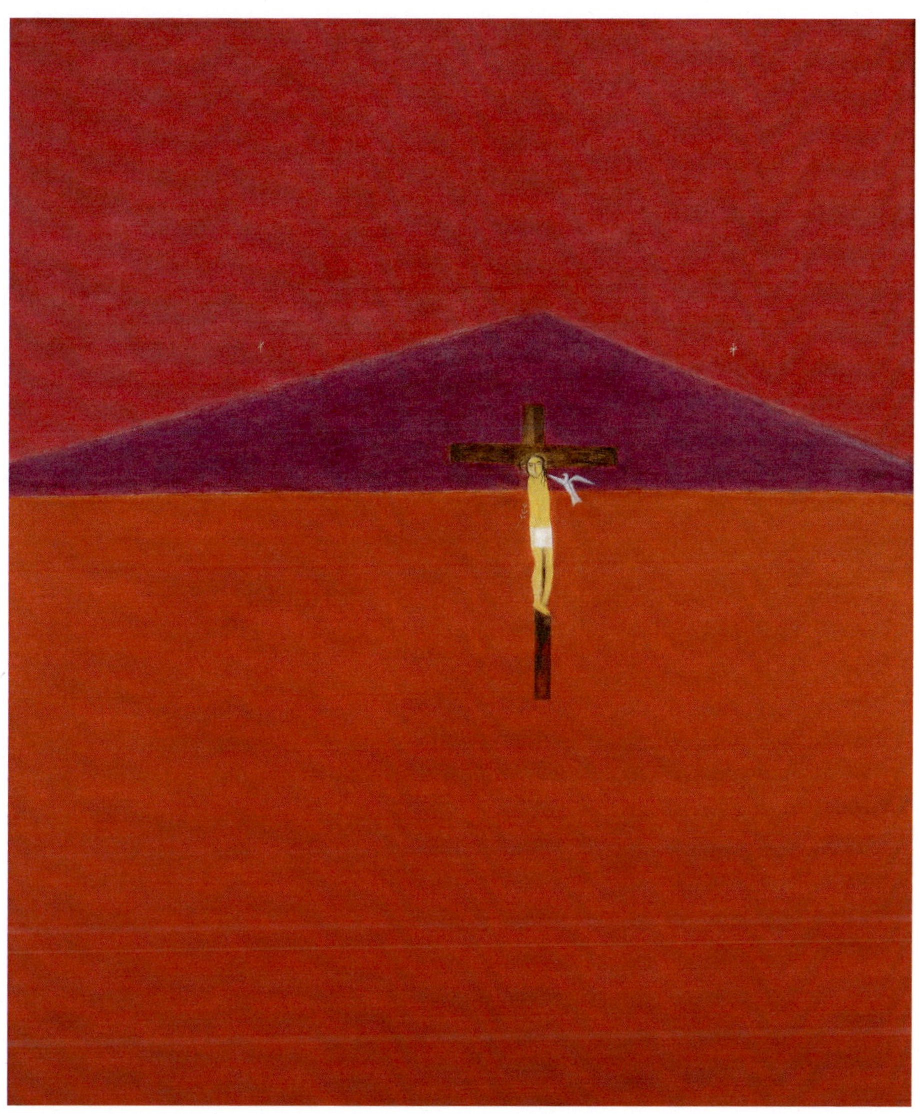

Crucifixion

1979

Oil on canvas, 173x145cm

Reproduced courtesy of the Craigie Aitchison estate,
Scottish National Gallery of Modern Art and Ingleby, Edinburgh

subject in itself that is the source of expression but 'the entire arrangement of the picture which is expressive' – or, as Aitchison argued, 'If the shape is right, the whole picture will have taken a life of its own'.

During their careers, Matisse and Aitchison were sometimes criticised for their seemingly simplistic approach to painting, yet nothing could be further from the truth. The apparent naivety in their art was in fact a result of their acutely perceptive and undistracted relationship to the richly sensual and ever-changing visual world around them. Yet they did not aim simply to record and re-present that observed world in an impressionistic manner. As Braque put it, true painting does not strive to 'reconstitute an anecdote' but rather to 'constitute a pictorial event'. Thus, both artists were constantly enriching their art by their empathetic understanding and personal response to the inherited language and tradition of painting through a wide range of artistic sources.

'I have never avoided the influences of others', Matisse admitted to Guillaume Apollinaire, while Aitchison in his typical tongue-in-cheek, naughty school-boyish manner confessed to Andrew Lambirth that he also readily 'cribbed' from other artists. Yet it is not the 'borrowings' in themselves which raise the aesthetic level of these artists' work – that would be mere eclecticism. Rather, it is the highly intelligent and subtly enriching manner by which they incorporate these shared influences that transforms them into their own stylistic vision. Interestingly, this mutual respect for the artistic achievements of the past may have resulted from the fact that both Matisse and Aitchison studied law before deciding to become painters. The practice of law, of course, is very much built on past precedents. Likewise, as Gombrich pointed out in *Art and Illusion*, the making of art has much more to do with the inherited traditions and examples of previous art than any other factor.

So what is the essential characteristic that distinguishes the modernist painting of Craigie Aitchison? To answer this, we have to return to Matisse's comments on impressionism. Modern art wished to represent visually the modern experience with all its fragmentary 'contradictory sensations' as directly and accurately as possible. On the other hand, modernist painting, while fully aware of the conflicting nature of modernity, sought not to ignore but to resolve the tensions resulting from these differences and create a vision 'of balance, of purity and serenity', as Matisse declared. This harmonising process at the heart of modernist painting is always ultimately based on formal decorative colour composition as Aitchison fully realised when he stated:

> In the end it's the shapes that, whatever anyone says, decide whether a picture is any good.

It has to be remembered, however, that for all the highly abstracted appearance of his paintings, Aitchison – as with Matisse – laid the foundation of his art on a solid academic training. He studied at the

Slade in the 1950s under the rigorous empirical teachings of William Coldstream, which he continued to practise throughout his career in his own modified way. Like Matisse, he always preferred to work directly from the motif: as he stated 'I paint what I see… to get a likeness'. Yet that 'likeness' could never be a mere mimetic facsimile. On the contrary, it needed to be a harmonious plastic one in which the empathic feelings of the artist for his subject emerge through the creative process of painting itself. Ultimately what a modernist artist such as Aitchison seeks is a single unified vision of the complex optical and psychological relationship he has developed with his source of inspiration. As with Matisse, the range of subject matter in Aitchison's art is relatively narrow and even conventional, for what really matters is not so much what he paints but how he is able to convey that inner bond between himself, his subject and the viewer. Through subtle and playfully suggested poetic themes and veiled compositional connections, the viewer is gently invited to speculate and meditate on the painter's intriguing, even mysterious relationship to his alluring multi-layered pictorial world.

Stylistically, Aitchison achieves this enthralling effect in his own unique manner. He eliminates all distracting inessentials – his saturated, decorative colour holds our attention by being suspended between factual description and sensual expression – while outline and shape give a formal identity and presence to all the interrelated compositional elements in a perfectly blended pictorial ensemble. Through the artist's highly refined skill and graceful elegance, the central dialectic of modern painting – delicately hovering between figuration and abstraction – achieves its perfect synthesis of the real and the ideal on the surface of Craigie Aitchison's painting.

This essay was written by Bill Hare in 2010 and published by the Talbot Rice Gallery at the Edinburgh Festival. It was also published in *Scottish Art News*, issue 14.

Frances Walker

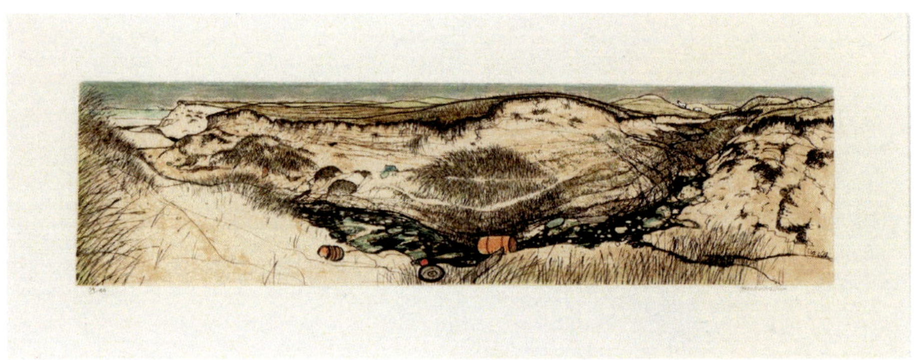

Shore Burn

1994

Hand-tinted collograph, 35x120cm

Reproduced courtesy of the artist

View from a Raised Beach

Scotland is the land of tradition and of poetry, every district has some scene in it of real or fictitious events, treasured with a sort of religious care in the minds of the inhabitants and giving dignity to places that in every other respect would, to the man of the world, be considered barren and unprofitable.
David Wilkie, 1817

ALTHOUGH THIS CENTURY still has a decade to run, the art of our age has been pronounced dead and thrown overboard. With every recent 'Art of the 20th Century' exhibition, modernism is being left high and dry on the shores of history, and its ideals of scientific progress, international cosmopolitanism and original individualism are being swept away by the oncoming waves of its successor. In Scotland, where it was rarely liked, let alone loved, the demise of modernism has been met with an enthusiasm throughout the art media and establishment which verges on the distasteful. Yet it is hardly surprising that the causes promoted by post-modernism, the decentralisation of cultural control and a subsequent revival of interest in national and regional divergence should strike a particular chord with the Scottish art scene, which was, until recently, severely marginalised. Now that it has again become perfectly acceptable to assert the distinctive aspects of your artistic culture through local history, indigenous landscape, and traditional community, Scottish art has been on a wave of public and critical acclaim that it has not experienced this century. Needless to say, the Scottish National Gallery of Modern Art, not wishing to miss out on this possibly shortlived jamboree, have got in on the act, most recently with their own *Scottish Art since 1900* exhibition.

Frances Walker, as with many of her fellow artists from the North East, did not feature in that survey of 20th-century Scottish art. The reasons for her omission are of little concern here, except that one of the aims of that exhibition seems to have been to devise, if not to define, a distinctive tradition for the art produced in Scotland this century. Unfortunately, the work of Frances Walker is not readily reconciled with the orthodox view of the decorative, *belle peinture* Colourist tradition of modern Scottish painting. Neither does her work take on the neo-Victorian earnestness and pseudo-symbolism which is so fashionable at present. Furthermore, despite her subject matter of the remote landscapes of northern and western Scotland, with their turbulent character and tragic histories, Frances Walker's work does not succumb to the kind of visual romantic melodrama or vapid expressionism which is a common trait of much recent Scottish neo-figurative painting. As Hugh MacDiarmid points out in 'On a Raised Beach', 'it is easy to find a spontaneity here'. Both poet and painter decline, preferring to delve beneath the immediate surface of shifting appearances for a more profound experience.

The dramatic coastlines of Scotland have, of course, been a favourite inspiration with artists since the Romantics but Frances Walker's work has little to do with the sublime treatments of Turner, McTaggart or Eardley. By contrast, Frances Walker's attitude to her subject is a restrained, even academic one, with the emphasis on considered line and structural form, rather than on bold gesture. This objective, analytical approach, which also has a long tradition in Scottish art – from Allan Ramsay to William Dyce through to James Cowie, and up to the early 20th-century Scottish printmakers – can most clearly be seen in a comparison of photographs of Frances Walker at work with those of Joan Eardley or William McTaggart. The latter two are seen with their large canvasses pegged to the shore, fiercely battling against the elements to put down in paint their immediate experience of the turbulent forces of nature; whereas, by contrast, Frances Walker is crouched up over her board, patiently building up her drawing of some rock formation she is intently studying. As Cézanne pointed out, artists 'cannot be too scrupulous, too sincere or too submissive to Nature'. This is especially so, if the artist, like the geologist, is as concerned as Frances Walker is to reveal the structure, anatomy and profound origins of the landscape or, as Hugh MacDiarmid succinctly put it, 'the Earth écorché thus'.

Yet Frances Walker's art would be a coldly objective view of nature, like the 'scientific' landscapes of minor Pre-Raphaelites such as Bett or Inchbold, if all she were solely concerned with were the structures and the fixed forms of her subjects. However, as she also writes:

> My work has a lot to do with people and their environment, also about me in my environment. In nearly all my work there is frequent evidence – often ancient and long-lasting – of man's changing influence on the environment by occupation of the landscape.

Admittedly, the human presence in her new *Tiree Works* is not too conspicuous. Yet the seeming emptiness of her landscapes should still draw our attention to the social community which once fully occupied these islands and still clings on in depleted numbers, despite continuing outside economic pressures. Amongst other things, *Tiree Works* can be seen as a metaphor for a way of life that has almost vanished, a once industrious island which used to be known as the 'granary of the isles'. Sadly, during the last century and a half, Tiree's culture and society have been eroded, first by aristocratic greed, 'incorporating the soil into capital' (Marx), then decimated by the exodus of able-bodied men to serve British military imperialism and finally denied the possibility of renewal by the understandable defection of the young for a seemingly more hopeful and rewarding life elsewhere. Nevertheless, it has to be pointed out that all these social and moral concerns are only implicit in Walker's *Tiree Works*, for those who wish to see these landscapes as serving also as history paintings.

I doubt whether the artist would wish to make too much of such ideas and associations in her work. She is first and foremost a visual artist whose duty according to John Ruskin is 'to see something and tell what

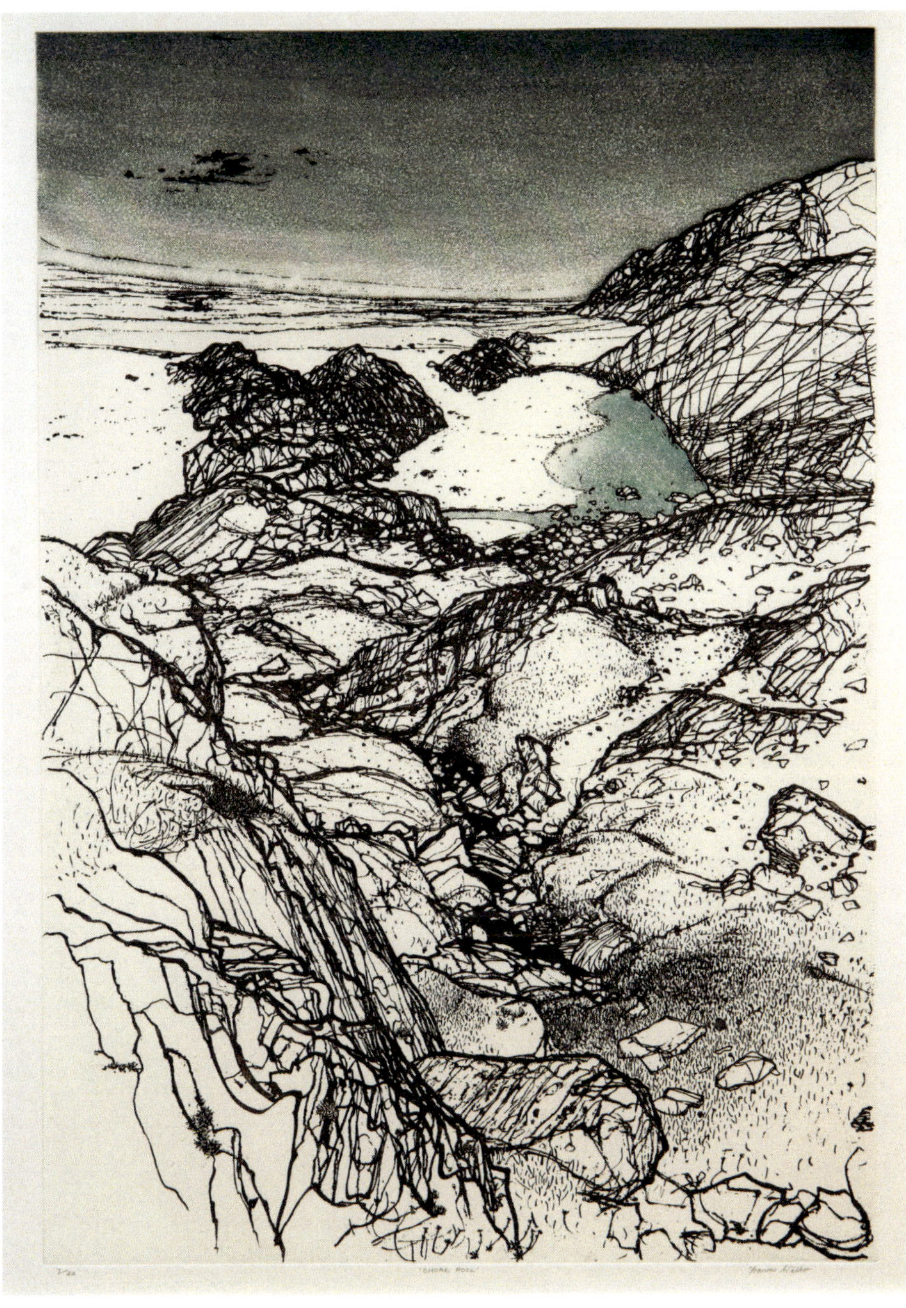

Shore Pool

1995

Hand-tinted collograph, 75x55cm

Reproduced courtesy of the artist

[she] saw in a plain way'. However, if that were all there was to it, Frances Walker's pictures would only be exceptionally good topographical views. The imaginative difference is that there is a prolonged process of subtle selection, rearrangement, meditation and distillation (and, in the case of the prints, of technical intervention), between the point of observation and the final rendering of the image. It is this process of artistic evolution, the search for the perfect balance between time and space, which creates the powerful sense of distance between the concerned response of the artist to her subject and the impassive presence of the rocky landscape – Hugh Miller's 'terrible muse' of geology. Yet although the artist is surely philosophically aware of the mortal implications of such a confrontation between human and geological time, which have haunted art since the beginning of the Christian era, her work is not to be seen as some kind of *memento mori*. In fact, she writes that although painting is an

> isolating occupation, you are also of course by painting making a very positive assertion that you do not want to die – yet. For painting is about life and living.

Still, as with all serious art, Frances Walker's mature work is concerned with the passage of time from geological, historical, human to individual, and thus suggests an awareness of the relationship and ultimate reconciliation between life and death. As MacDiarmid writes,

> I lift a stone; it is the meaning of life I clasp
> Which is death, for that is the meaning of death.

Finally, if I might be permitted to end on a personal note, I am a Lowland city person, born and bred. As such, I was brought up to regard Gaelic Scotland as something quaint and exotic, as if it were almost a foreign country. I have to say that not surprisingly my heart is not in the Highlands and the Cuillin are not pulling me away. I have never been to Tiree and, unless I develop a belated interest in windsurfing, I am unlikely ever to go there. Yet the fact that Frances Walker each year returns to her cottage on Tiree to work, quietly producing this intensely committed visual poetry, free from any of the usual clichés connected with such subjects, is strangely reassuring and comforting to me. As I study these *Tiree Works* of Frances Walker, I begin to feel, in a limited way, the sense of reconciliation and reassurance that MacDiarmid describes as he confronts the foundations of the Scottish landscape:

> These stones will reach us long before we reach them.
> Cold, undistracted, eternal and sublime.
> They will stem all the torrents of vicissitude forever...

This essay was written in 1990 and published by the Talbot Rice Gallery, Edinburgh.

Barbara Rae

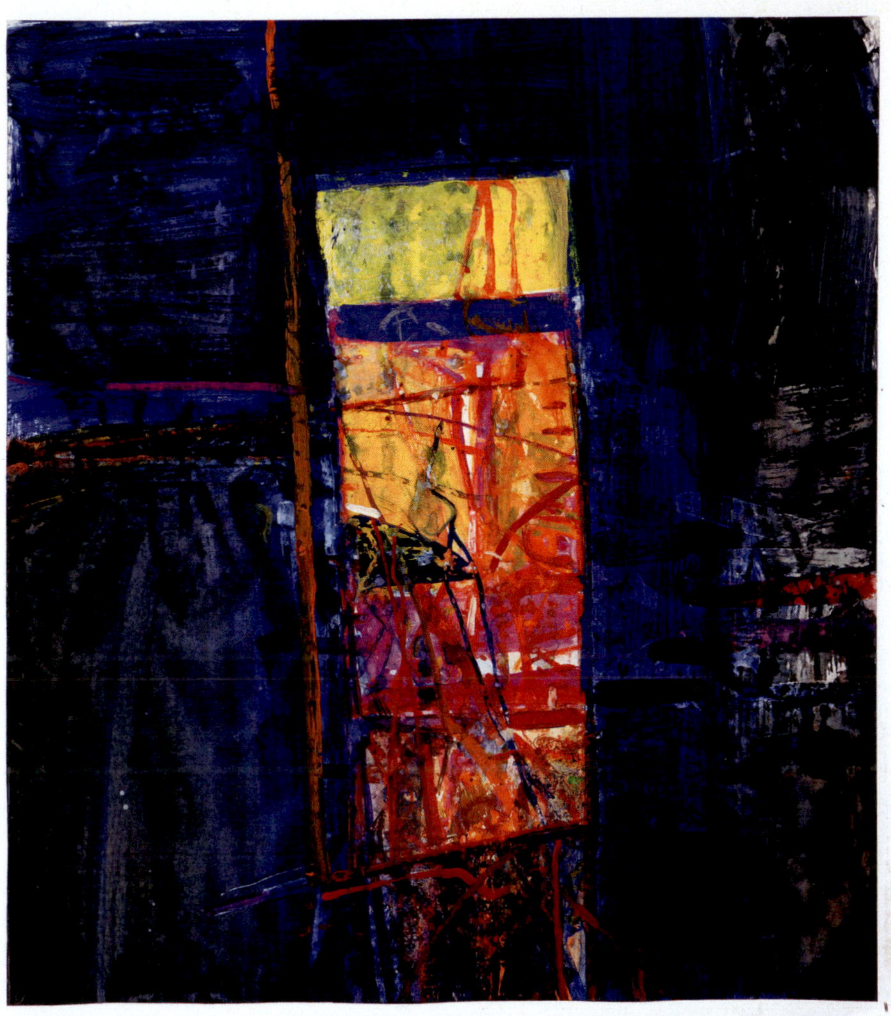

Doorway Trevelez
1991
Acrylic on canvas, 108x95cm
Reproduced courtesy of the artist

Barbara Rae Interview

I have always felt that if collage is at the heart of Eduardo Paolozzi's working practice, layering is central to your own creative practice, both in your painting and printmaking. Why is layering so important in the way you work?
I do not describe 'layering' as important or central to my practice. By its nature, printmaking involves the process of layering colours to create other colours and textures. This process influences the way I make paintings, whether using mixed media on canvas or working on paper.

Layering is an additive process; on the other hand, you also believe that removing – 'taking off'– is just as important in the making of your art. If that is so, how do you negotiate these two seemly contradictory practices?
'Taking off' involves obliterating that which has gone before and is no longer relevant to the composition in its evolving form.

On many occasions, you say you are constantly seeking pictorial simplification in your work, yet you appear to go through a very complex process trying to achieve this. How do you reconcile your aim of simplification with the multi-faceted complexities of your studio practice?
I work from studies completed in my chosen location. I begin with a deep knowledge of my subject matter and then start a process of reduction. I hope to capture an essence of the original study in as direct and as simple a way as possible but, in the studio, the painting dictates its own path.

You studied at Edinburgh College of Art in the 1960s when it was still dominantly traditional in its academic teaching. What did you learn there that has remained useful to you throughout you career and what did you feel you had to abandon?
We had long days studying the life model, clothed and nude, through both drawing and painting. The emphasis was on intense observation issuing from studying the human figure during anatomy lessons. Hours spent in life studios paid off when we were finally free during evening hours without supervision. We were encouraged to collect visual information to inform our compositions. I enjoyed working outside in industrial locations and in close observation studies in the Royal Scottish Museum. That has been my working method since. We also had study trips to London and Paris to see some of the great exhibitions: Goya and Bonnard were particularly inspiring.

Up to the mid-1980s you worked mainly in oils but you have said that you always had a problem with oil painting. What was that problem?
Oil is a joy to use in many ways and has many qualities that other paint mediums lack. I used it throughout my college career. During my later

college years, I used acrylic mediums with powder pigments to make
the mural sized works that we created with Jimmy Cummings as our
inspirational teacher. He was experimenting with acrylics so we were given
them free.

*You seem to have had a 'Road to Damascus' experience in 1985 when
you discovered acrylic paint for your own practice. Why, and how, did it
have such a transforming impact on your art?*
I had been using acrylics since third year at college in their earliest basic
form. In 1985, when working in New Mexico, I decided to abandon
the use of oil paint. I was using oil-based washes involving quantities of
turpentine. Besides being toxic, it resulted in the darkening of vibrant base
colours. Working in the dry climate of New Mexico meant that I could
exploit the fast drying of the acrylic.

*While you say you regularly need to travel all over the world to seek out
inspiring landscapes in order to 'recharge your batteries' you are hostile to
being classified as a landscape painter. Why this is so, and what do you do
in your art practice that is contrary to conventional landscape painting?*
I have little interest in plain topography – that is, fields, with trees and
fluffy clouds. I need a 'story' offering historical context, a space where
people have lived and left their mark. I am equally inspired by industrial
subjects such as the series that I did on Leith docks, principally because
they are places where people work.

*You always have an outside subject in your pictures. Your studio practice,
both in printmaking and painting, is much more steeped in the pictorial
language of abstraction than figuration. How has this come about and
have you ever considered becoming a fully abstract painter?*
I don't have any boundaries. The inside of an old farmer's cottage can
have the same attraction as dead sunflowers on a field's edge. I aim to
achieve abstraction through simplification.

*Your studio practice involves a great deal of spontaneous improvisation.
What strategic role does unforeseen accident play in how you work?*
The 'unforeseen accident', the dissonance, occurs through knowledge
of how the paint behaves in certain circumstances. Knowledge and
confidence allow me to take risks.

*What do you mean when you say 'I am trying to get the surface right, not
the structure'?*
I don't recall saying that. The structure of a painting is everything,
balance, the composition. If the composition is flawed then the painting
won't work. The surface of the work – the manipulation of the paint is
secondary.

Do you work on a number of related prints and paintings at the same time and play them off against each other?
I work in subject series, so if I am involved in a certain subject, I will create paintings of various scales and prints.

If accurate topographical description is not your aim, what are you measuring the success of a work against and how do you decide when you have achieved it?
I enjoy the process of creativity, whatever I'm involved in. I don't pause to measure success. Experience tells an artist when it is time to finish.

This interview was conducted in 2019 by Bill Hare for this book.
See also: Andrew Lambirth's interview with Barbara Rae in *Barbara Rae* (Lund Humphries, 2008).

The Worked Surface of Barbara Rae's Painting

'THE INNOCENT EYE' was the artistic delusion of 19th century positivism. With all the will in the world, no artist ever followed John Ruskin's urgings and went to nature accepting everything, rejecting nothing. Every artist who draws inspiration from the world around must make choices depending on cultural conditioning, personal sensibilities and particular skills. This is especially true in the great tradition of landscape painting, where the selection of subject and the ordering of expression is crucial to the intrinsic meaning of a picture. For instance, the Stour Valley may have 'made' Constable a painter but only carefully chosen aspects of its scenery were considered, according to Constable's own particular sensibilities, to be worthy for inclusion in his paintings.

Unfortunately, much of the critical writing on Barbara Rae's work has tended to concentrate on her choice of landscape subjects at the expense of how she actually responds to and particularly treats those subjects. Because those landscapes which she seeks out for inspiration and attention are usually fairly remote, or at least off the beaten track for most urban critics, her paintings are inclined to induce a romantic response, with much talk about 'poetic atmosphere' and 'evocative associations'. As a consequence, some people have questioned the 'authenticity' of her work. On the contrary, however, I would suggest that anyone who takes the time and attention to look seriously at her work will be able to appreciate that in the area of intellectual and emotional engagement, as well as technical facility, there is a strong controlling vigour which endows Rae's paintings with a powerful sense of intellectual conviction and material authenticity.

Barbara Rae's paintings, like the rugged landscapes she seeks out for her art, express a 'strong feeling of independence' and as such are to be admired more for their own intrinsic qualities rather than dependent ones. Her paintings are not, for instance, reliant on topographical detail nor sentimental associations. Rae is certainly not a picturesque landscape artist by any stretch of the imagination. Her choice of subjects hardly celebrates the conventional beauties of the countryside. She is more inclined to be drawn to amorphous shapes and patterning forms to elaborate upon, rather than record specific views of appealing pictorial beauty such as rusticated cottages or quaint fishing villages bobbing by the sea.

What gives her paintings such sustaining appeal is that they do not present the well-tried and predictable, but rather they present a fascinating and stimulating challenge to 'the beholder' both in the choice and the freely wrought treatment of subject. In the end, however, the artist's treatment of her subject is the controlling factor, rather than the other way round.

Although Barbara Rae's landscapes 'tend towards the abstract', they are never fully so. For her, as an initial spur to creativity, there always has to be an external subject, a point in the landscape, a connection with the world, a reference to another reality. Admittedly on first acquaintance one might be forgiven for regarding her paintings as being purely abstract compositions. Yet on closer investigation, their bond with the actual landscape begins to emerge. Elements from the fundamental language of landscape painting can be discerned – a high horizon, a foreground rock formation, the outline of the stern of a boat or the lop-sided angle of a fishing creel catch the eye and hold the attention. Thus, these paintings are as much indebted to the formal pictorial semantics of cubism as the free non-mimetic expressiveness of abstraction.

Barbara Rae's landscapes are never just single views or one-off moments in time. Her paintings are the outcome of an ongoing and complex creative struggle. Thus the link between the painter's final hard-wrought image and the original moment of inspiration in the landscape itself, may seem very remote and difficult for the beholder to grasp immediately. That makes her paintings all the more intriguing, for that connection is vital to a deeper appreciation of the final appearance of the work.

Over the last few years, Rae seems to have achieved a fuller maturity in her work. Her paintings (and prints) have emerged from a long and sustained period of artistic development. Much in her working method, however, is still due to her training at Edinburgh College of Art, where the teaching and example of the staff, especially William Gillies (one of Scotland's finest modern landscape painters), has been a lasting influence. Significantly, Gillies's work, with its 'wonderful sense of pattern in the landscape' appealed to her own instincts for decorative pictorial order. The art college training that Barbara Rae received from Gillies and his staff has continued to direct her basic working methods. As with all academically trained artists, she draws her initial response and ideas from her sketches of directly observed subjects, in order to capture and graphically articulate her immediate impressions. Yet this is only the first step in making these initial impressions into something much more lasting. Like Cézanne, she aims to make a 'Poussin out of Nature' – something more essential and permanent. As she explains it herself, 'I have to put the drawings behind and keep to a much more simple idea'. This search for 'a more simple idea', a more clear and definite statement (which makes her at least as much a classicist as a romantic) ironically involves constant changes and improvisation. This latter stage of the creative process in the studio involves all kinds of experiments with various picture dimensions, the free application of different types of painting materials, from acrylics to gold leaf, and the introduction of additional collage elements to build up elaborately wrought surface textures.

The richly coloured textured surfaces of Barbara Rae's paintings certainly give an abundance of sensual pleasure to the eye of the beholder but the pictures are also much more than 'an arena for the display of skill'

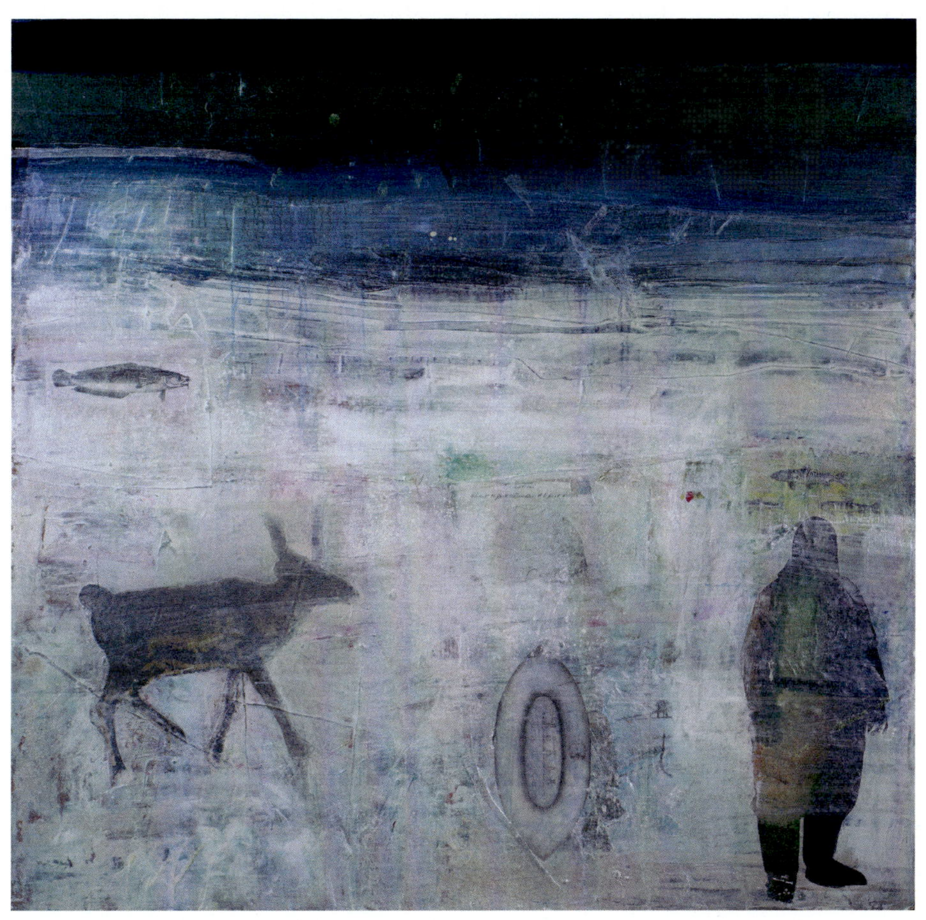

Ice Tracks
2017
Acrylic on canvas, 183x183cm

Reproduced courtesy of the artist

as one unsympathetic critic once put it. In addition to the power of the artist's highly developed sense of decorative expression, there is also to be found an underlying consistent thematic content. Not that there is any overtly ideological agenda to Rae's paintings but they do, amongst other things, express her sensitive awareness of the interconnection between the human and the natural world. She herself observes, 'my work always relates to what man has done to reconstruct the landscape'. This is the constant recurring connection between the paintings and the incidents of passing human presence in the landscape to which the artist is drawn. The patterns of lines and shapes in her paintings echo the marks left by previous generations working on the face of the Earth. While, at the same time, the heavily worked picture surfaces and the strata-like compositions in Rae's paintings suggest, through the power of pictorial allusion, the layers of human toil which lie just beneath the surface appearance of immediate observation.

This concern with the content of Barbara Rae's work is not to deny that ultimately it is the processes by which she works the surface of her paintings that is the crucial factor. It is through the elaboration of compositional presentation, and choice and deployment of colour, that her painting achieves such poetic power. The colour is especially vital. It is the selection of colour, sometimes dark and impenetrable, other times intense and inviolable, which reveals the artist's deepest feelings for her observed world and her creative art. While line and shapes appeal more to the discerning eye and intellect, colour, when treated so sensitively and intently, directly excites the imagination and stirs in the heart 'feelings too deep for tears'.

Yet for all the undeniable expressive power of Barbara Rae's paintings she is neither a romantic nor an expressionist. Rather she is a truly consummate decorative artist in the great modernist tradition of Gauguin and Matisse, where the painter must achieve a fine balance between subject and expression, content and form, through line and colour. In the best of her most recent work, Rae does just that, with such accomplishment you feel that she could equally claim with Matisse that

> Composition is the art of arranging in a decorative manner the diverse elements at the painter's command to express feeling and I am unable to distinguish between the feelings I have about life and my way of translating them.

It is here, on the worked surfaces of her paintings, that the authenticity of Barbara Rae's art expresses itself.

This essay was written by Bill Hare in 1993 and published by Highland Region Council. See also: *Between Two Worlds – Outer Perception and Inner Vision in the Art of Barbara Rae* by Bill Hare in *Barbara Rae* (Lund Humphries, 2008).

Section Six
Two Sculptors

Bill Scott (1935–2012)
Doug Cocker (1942–)

SCULPTURE IS MAYBE more difficult to define than painting. For instance, Boyle Family and Hamilton Finlay produce three-dimensional objects in their work but would they be termed sculptors in the same way as Paolozzi and Turnbull? The work of Bill Scott and Doug Cocker, however, would, I feel, be likely to be seen within the more conventional notion of the practice of modern sculpture. They both had a solid academic sculpture training at their respective Scottish art colleges, Edinburgh College of Art and Duncan of Jordanstone, Dundee, where craft and technical skill were high on the teaching agenda.

As with most sculptors in Scotland, Bill Scott went into teaching and rose to become Head of Sculpture at Edinburgh College of Art throughout the 1990s. Teaching always took up a great deal of his time and so he had relatively few solo shows or public commissions. His own sculptural practice maintained throughout his career a pronounced engagement with social concerns, whether dealing with the workplace, the domestic environment or the changing role of public monuments. He worked with a variety of materials which he subjected to carving or built up in a constructivist manner. Well respected within the Scottish art world, he was the first sculptor to become President of the Royal Scottish Academy in 2007 but sadly died suddenly while still in office in 2012. As an appropriate memorial, the Edinburgh Sculpture Workshop, which he did a great deal to set up, is named after him.

Doug Cocker, although he, too, was to become a sculpture lecturer in his early career, has always been determined to give as much of his creative energies as he could to producing his own sculptural work. Since leaving art college, he has regularly had solo exhibitions and, from the 1980s, has been awarded a number of major public commissions throughout Britain. Although Cocker works with relatively conventional materials, he is very open and experimental in his technical and creative approach to his sculptural practice and his work has covered a wide variety of different themes over the years.

I first came in contact with these two sculptors when I wrote for the catalogue of a Third Eye Centre group exhibition of Scottish sculptors, *Built in Scotland*, in 1983. I got to know Bill Scott well when he set up the Federation of Scottish Sculptors and asked me to be his assistant. I also worked with both when they each had solo exhibitions at the Talbot Rice Gallery in the mid-1990s. I have written on Cocker's work on a number of occasions.

Bill Scott

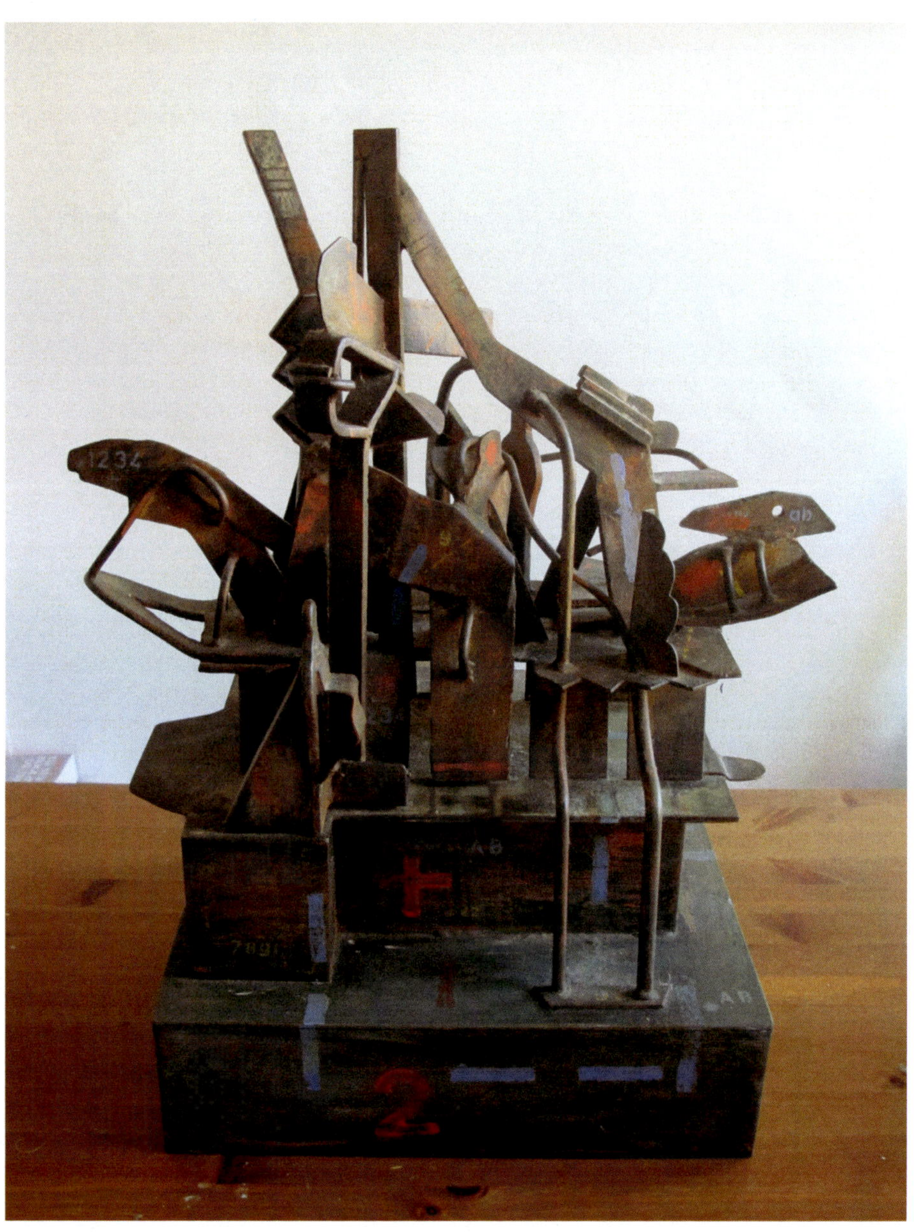

Rig and Platform
1978
Mild steel, 96x45x35cm

Reproduced courtesy of the artist's estate

The Sculpture of Bill Scott

IT IS APPROPRIATE that this display of Bill Scott's drawings and sculptures, his first showing since 1980, should take place at the invitation of Kirkcaldy Museum and Art Gallery. In this institution is housed, for public display, a comprehensive and inter-related range of objects with strong local associations. Many of the man-made items in the collection, whether they are functional, decorative or aesthetic, are of undoubted interest in their own right. They convey a sense of individual identity, as do the separate works of Scott. At the same time, the presentation of the Kirkcaldy collection allows the visitor to sense a strong feeling of community and tradition. These qualities and values are also deeply inherent in Bill Scott's work, even if they might be a little more difficult to readily appreciate for those not conversant with the language of modern sculpture. The fact that Kirkcaldy combines under the same roof its museum and art collection is a reminder that scientific and artistic investigations and achievements should not be separate and are, in fact, complementary to each other. This concept has particular relevance to the mythological origins of sculpture. The ancient Greeks gave the honour of making the first statues to Daedalus, who was also credited with many practical inventions.

This vital interconnection between artistic creativity and scientific/technological development is a recurring aspect in Bill Scott's work, evident here in some of his drawings and with sculptures such as *Rig Platform* and *Boatyard*. In these works, the sculptor clearly admires and identifies with the technical ingenuity of his counterparts in engineering design and industrial craftsmanship. Yet Scott's intricate constructions in wood and welded metal are not miniature versions of the real thing – like ships in a bottle. They certainly do portray aspects of the subject's appearance, through the use of appropriate materials and similar construction techniques but, more importantly, they convey in abstracted forms, the essential animating forces of their function and character.

As with a good museum curator, the sculptor is not merely involved with an objective interest in his subject and the works he puts on display. He is always concerned to express a human dimension. With the work of Bill Scott this can most readily be seen in the more obviously realistic works, which are directly inspired by his observation and experience of everyday life. Whether the sculptor is dealing with the workplace or, as in *Pad*, the more intimate area of domestic environment, a strong sense of humanity is conveyed. How this is achieved is open to speculation, but much of it may be due to the accessibility of scale and open framework composition, which allows us to sense the close bond we have with the objects we make and have at hand around us.

Bill Scott's more recent sculptures, the wood constructions and carvings under the generic titles *Monuments* and *Markers* may be a

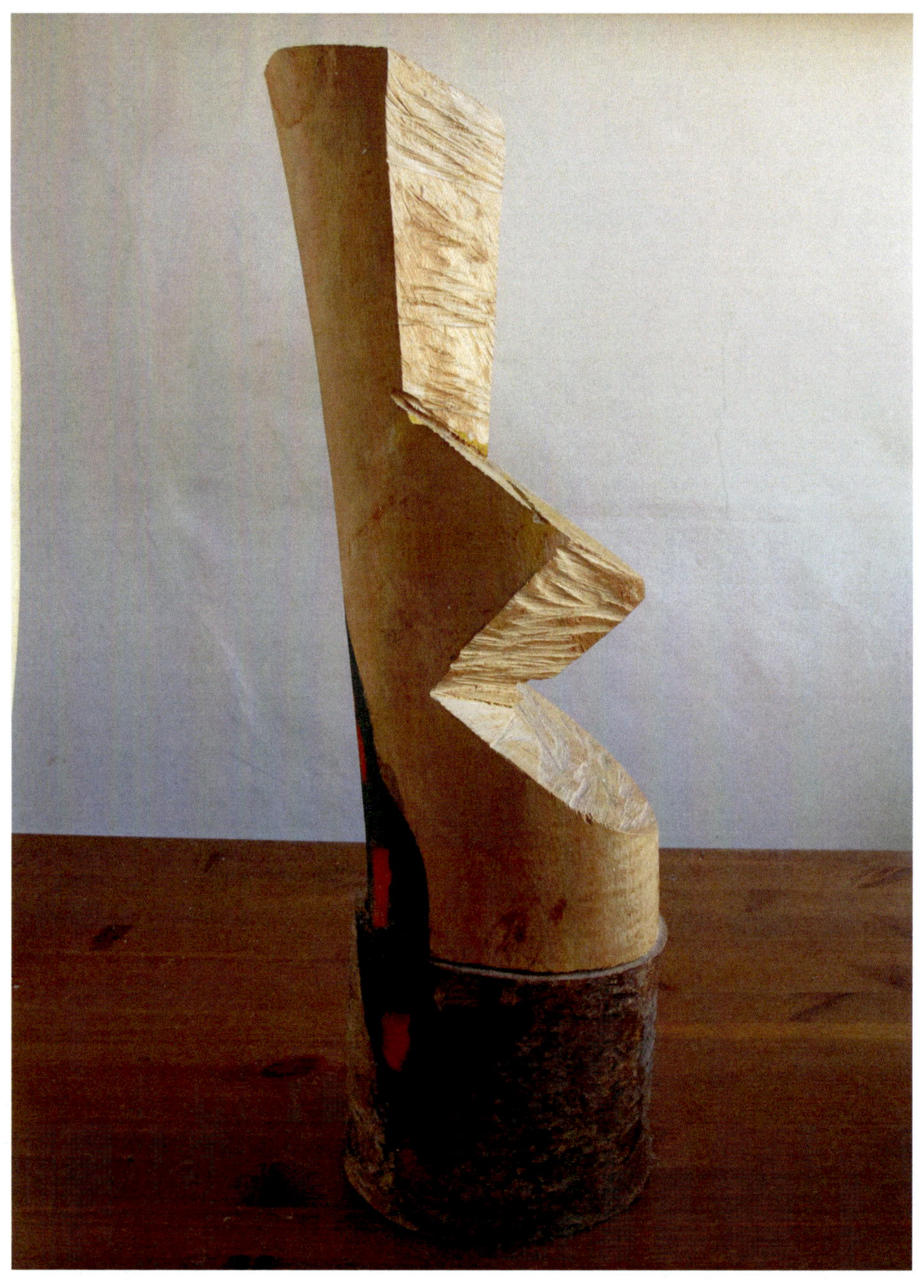

Marker
1985
Wood and paint, 60x18cm (base diameter)
Reproduced courtesy of the artist's estate

little more difficult to come to terms with than some of his earlier work. However, I feel they are no less concerned with human issues. Any museum or art gallery that does not wish to become merely a depository for obsolete fragments from the past must enliven that which is put on display with insights and speculations as to their functions and their origins in human society. A thoughtful and socially concerned artist, Scott also involves himself with such speculation. In the *Monuments* series, for example, the sculptor seems to be posing questions as to the past tradition and the future role of civic sculpture. These various pedestal-supported figures on a maquette scale, made up from various blocks of wood but further encrusted with additional paraphernalia and daubed with gaudy paint, seem to relate back to the beginnings of ceremonial monuments in religious and civic rituals. At the same time, they also reflect on their gradual disintegration since their ubiquitous heyday last century.

Ernst Fischer in his *The Necessity of Art* offers the profound proposition that 'man becomes man through tools' and that 'man takes possession of the natural world by transforming it'. With his *Markers* sculptures, Bill Scott seems to present similar notions, as he delves deep into the origins of human creativity. The will of the sculptor is imposed on the raw material, through the use of cutting, rearranging and colouring of the tree sections. An artist, or an inventor for that matter, stamps his authority on what he creates but also simultaneously brings into being something new, mysterious and independent. The *Markers* may appear crude, in comparison to some of the sculptor's earlier other work but, in fact, he is tentatively and speculatively searching for that elusive dividing line between conscious human control and intuitive natural freedom.

As with all Bill Scott's work, these various sculptures, whether they remain in the abstract or become suggestive of interrelated human, animal or plant forms, create their own appropriate environment and suggest their own distinctive origins. Kirkcaldy Museum and Art Gallery is a place where the full variety of local life and achievements can be examined and enjoyed. It concerns itself with all facets of the life of the area, be it industrial or rural. Bill Scott's work also expresses a similarly committed interest in many important aspects of the history and community life of this country.

This essay was written by Bill Hare in 1985 and published by Kirkcaldy Art Gallery.

Doug Cocker

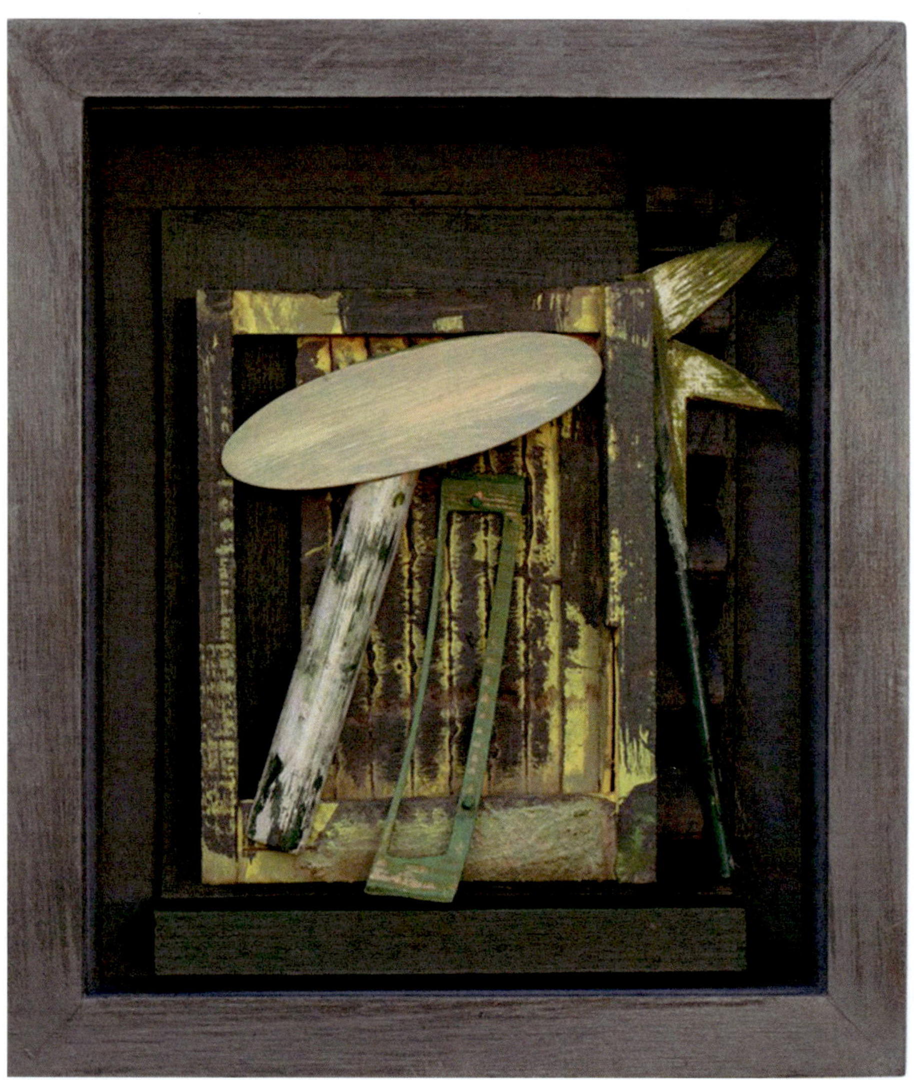

Gate

2012

Painted wood, 41x35x10 cm

Reproduced courtesy of the artist

Doug Cocker Interview

I first got to know your work back in 1983 when you were included in the Scottish contemporary sculpture group show, Built in Scotland, which was exhibited at the Third Eye Centre, Glasgow, and the Camden Arts Centre, London. In the accompanying catalogue the joint curator, Mike Tooby wrote: 'To some of the artists in this exhibition, "Scottishness" is an important question in its own right. To others, it is a question of little relevance to the understanding of the work.' I wonder where you stand on this 'question'. Could you say something about your Scottish background and what role it plays in your art?
I would be in the latter category. I was born, brought up and had my formal education in Scotland but my formative years as an artist were spent in England from 1972–82.

In terms of landscape, weather and imagery Scotland provides rich resource but overall the idea of 'Scottishness' has never been central to what I do… I always saw art as bigger and richer than national awareness, though it might be informed by it.

My first good size show, at the Fruitmarket Gallery in Edinburgh in '77, had, as its basis, an exploration and comparison of landscape through works made for and in landscape in both Scotland and the East Midlands of England. Much of the work I have made since then has had its genesis in aspects of Scottish rural landscape but this is principally because it's what's around me and provides a rich source for investigation. I've never seen myself as an unpaid agent for Visit Scotland.

In the Lemon Street Gallery exhibition, some of the work derives from a short RSA residency spent on the Isle of Lewis last year. Uppermost in my mind at that time was a wish to engage more fully with colour without making paintings. So what I was seeing daily on the tide mark is what prompted the constructed monoprints and collages that resulted. My engagement was with the distinctiveness of the colour and texture that I was witnessing rather than any geo/historical/socio-political baggage about the Western Isles.

You and I were born around the same time at the end of the war. By coincidence, we both also went to art college in the mid-'60s. I, as a failed painter, ended up an art historian! What do you think were the deciding factors in you becoming a successful sculptor?
I suppose everyone who was around at the time has variable memories of Scottish art schools in the '60s depending on where you studied and who was running the show. The sculpture department at DJCA in Dundee under Scott Sutherland was a tough regime. I was the only sculpture student in my year, with none in the two years above me. Figuration was the only language countenanced so my curiosity about sculptors like Sol LeWitt or Donald Judd had to be pursued clandestinely… On the other hand, a five-

year diet of life modelling (it was a five-year course then) certainly helps you to understand form.

I understood early the importance of looking beyond what you're taught and finding your own route. A Greenshields Foundation Scholarship took me to New York for a period after I graduated but it was a few years before I began to find my own language in making sculpture. As often happens, this was primed more by chance than by design. My first teaching job in an art school at Nene College, Northampton, was running the Sculpture area. This came with a well kitted-out wood workshop. Over subsequent years, I used this resource at every opportunity and gradually evolved a new way of working which was essentially construction as opposed to modelling or carving.

Sculpture, amongst other things, is an inherited language of communication with its own histories and particular character and concerns. Could you say something about how your practice relates to the work of other sculptors, past and present?
Yes, I feel affinity of approach with many sculptors in differing ways. Brâncuşi, the Russian Constructivists, Caro, Richard Deacon, Paolozzi to some degree. Not necessarily in design or configuration or imagery but more in the sense that a hands-on journey taken is evident in their work: a physical negotiation with the materials… without losing sight of the need for an unexpected dynamic. Obviously you could say that they all work differently. Brâncuşi was essentially a carver though assembling forms was a key part of his practice. The others, in their different ways, put materials together: they construct and they do it with an awareness that craft skills are necessary but not primary… Ben Nicholson, Antoni Tàpies, Isamu Noguchi, Eduardo Chillida, William Tucker, likewise, they exude authority in their engagement with materials. Doing magic with stuff.

Looking over your career to the present there seem to be broadly three distinct periods. Up to the mid-'80s, you were concerned with expressing your own experiences through the formal languages and practices of modern sculpture. This was followed by a time when much of your work had a decided socio-political dimension. More recently, as evidenced by this new exhibition, you seem to have returned to your earlier concerns, although treated in a more refined and sophisticated manner. If you agree with my assessment here, what brought about these changes?
That's partially true. These kinds of decisions are always contextual and mostly predicated on prosaic issues to do with personal economics or sometimes just chance. In the mid-'80s, during Thatcher's second term, I was as disillusioned as most Scots with her policies and their trickle-down effect on life in general. I had returned to Scotland in '82 and had the luxury of a teaching job at Gray's School of Art in Aberdeen. So having a salary meant that I didn't necessarily have to earn through my output. So I could address these issues through my work. I made a number of big,

freestanding sculptures at this time. They had a directed narrative but were still formalist in their structure: *State of a Nation* (1985); *One of Us* (1989); *Persian Whispers* (1989), referencing Rushdie's fatwa; *Boss* (1990) for the Barbican show; and *Flock* (1992), during the Essex Fine Art Fellowship.

In 1990, because I wanted to focus solely on making sculpture, I took a chance and quit my job at the art school. I had a family to provide for and got by through competing for public art commissions and fellowships or residencies. Apropos your question, it was one of these experiences which prompted a shift of focus in my work.

In 2001, I was invited to undertake a ten-week residency at Ballinglen Arts Foundation in County Mayo. The Foundation is geared principally for painters and the studios equipped accordingly. Away from the lure of timber and power tools, I made a series of about 20 small simply constructed works in card, responses to the landscape around me, using colour as a major component. This line of enquiry was a big departure for me at the time but the addressing of form and colour simultaneously has remained.

Like the *Mayo Suite, Geography* and *Wall Dances*, some of which are in this show, engage with surface and colour to a degree that was never present in my earliest work. So I haven't returned to earlier concerns. As I see it, it's just the usual moving on to new fields of enquiry.

I would now like to discuss more specific issues in your sculptural practice. Firstly, could we turn to the role of drawing in your work? Clearly from what you have previously said and written on this topic, drawing is not just a means to a sculptural end. This is also evidenced by the presence of your graphic skills in this exhibition with the Wedding Drawings and City and Moon red conté drawings, for example. Why is this part of your art so important?

Drawing, for me, is speculation. It's an activity that runs parallel to making but provides opportunity to express thoughts and feelings in a way that's impossible in the more measured procedures involved in making sculpture. Most of my drawings are made in a3 sketchbooks – test beds for ideas and techniques but also an indispensable memory store. They provide opportunity for fast, spontaneous and often undisciplined output, which is a welcome relief after hands-on making which can be slow, trying and sometimes even tedious.

Occasionally, a tested process offers enough promise to be taken to a more resolved state… for example, the yellow *Wedding Drawings* in this show, working fast into wet, pigment-soaked paper. Sometimes, though seldom, I will make a work directly from a drawing. *Wee White Pot* is one such. Risky business because any vitality usually stems from the uncertainty of outcome.

Sometimes I make drawings after a three-dimensional work is complete, applying Oldenburg's 'what if?' premise. Sometimes the drawing or the speculation is done in the making as with *Geography* and *Wall Dances*, works made directly with no specific, a priori blueprint. So the functions of drawing are manifold. It's an indispensable platform. To quote from the 2008 exhibition, *Drawn to Sculpture*:

> the drawing process is efficacious for me precisely because there are aspects integral to drawing sessions which play little part in the making of sculpture… spontaneity, irrationality, speed of production, self-indulgence, unconcern for 'accuracy', 'rightness' or notions of 'resolution'.

You seem to work in two dimensions a great deal for a sculptor. In this exhibition, for instance, you have included monoprints (Lewis Suite), collages (Lewis Still Lives) and then there are, of course, the box relief constructions, such as the October Suite. These, along with your powerful drawings, certainly show off your wide range of expertise in creating absorbing imagery but how do they relate to the sculptural work in the round?
This is not an issue I spend any time thinking about. I assume most artists are invariably interested in extending their practice. I was recently in a couple of shows, *Sculptors Drawings* at Pangolin London and 3 *Sculptors' Prints* with the American sculptors, Ed Smith and Bill Tucker, and there was nothing 'in the round' to be seen.

It's arguable, of course, whether the *Lewis and October Suites* are or are not sculptures. Both are three-dimensional so they are neither prints nor paintings but who actually cares? This kind of debate seldom reveals much that's worthwhile. I can only deal with the area of enquiry that engages me at any given time. The late Neil Cameron said of the *Mayo Suite*:

> Cocker succeeds in fusing the often oppositional languages of sculpture and painting, creating imagery which stands in the compelling middle ground between abstract form and poetic analogy.

I don't know about 'succeeds' but I do know that this is still what engages me at present.

Two of the other box structures in the show have very intriguing titles – Poor Butterfly and Where the Moon Goes. I have always thought that the titles you give your work is art in itself. How do you go about Naming of Parts?
When I was younger, I used to spend time on titles, trying to offer a way into the work. Now they have become simply a means of identification so I can remember which work I'm thinking about. They sometimes present themselves during making and sometimes after the work is completed. Often they are borrowed from music I'm listening to at the time (*Poor Butterfly, Where the Moon Goes*) so the work has an association. My memory is pretty clunky so *Gabby Hayes hits the Reeperbahn* and *The Mighty Handful* resonate with me more effectively than, say, 'Untitled No. 37' or 'that piece with the green diagonal bit that sticks out on the bottom right'.

Like me, Doug, you are a great modern jazz fan – I even named my dog after the great Dexter Gordon. I raise this musical topic because you seem to share the jazz performer's love of improvisation and experimentation in the way you work. Over the years, for instance, you have produced a number of wall pieces in which the composition and assembly is left open-ended, making each showing into a new performance. In this exhibition, Geography would be a good example of this feature of your sculpture. Could you say something about the roles of chance and order in your work?

This year, when James Castle and I were hanging the RSA show together, James observed, 'Doug, this is the kind of job that you know how to do only after you've done it'. It's much the same with the work. If you don't get comfortable with chance, you're not going to make many discoveries. And if you don't make discoveries for yourself there's little point in doing it.

Working on *Geography* was good for me in this respect. When I started, I had no idea about an outcome. But establishing a manageable scale and a consistent format left lots of room for me to speculate and take chances in much the same way as I do working in sketchbooks, except I was drawing with a blade. The excitement for me lay in potential for speed of execution (which is seldom on offer) and the way one initiative inevitably bred others. I suppose, looking back, the *Geography* pieces continued to hold interest for me over such an extended period because I had devised a consistent, disciplined format within which I could go haywire (high attrition rate but a hungry stove to hand). Order and chance, meat and pudding – Scottish antisyzygy, where opposites meet.

It is widely felt that you are master craftsman when it comes to the making of your sculptural pieces. As someone who could not even pass his elementary woodwork test, I am in awe of your good self who, in medieval Scotland, would have been honoured as a 'Makar'. Even though you are a modern sculptor, do you also see yourself within that kind of historical tradition?

Not really. Hand skills and knowledge of materials are obviously necessary but not paramount. Common sense suggests, however, that Keith Jarratt, say, or Brad Mehldau could never have produced such sublime music without a full grasp of the fundamentals of their craft.

To finish, Doug, could we go back to your 'artist statement' for that Built in Scotland exhibition I mentioned at the beginning of this interview? There you talked about the dialectic at the heart of your sculpture between 'poetry and pragmatism'. Do you feel that in your more recent work for this exhibition that the art and craft of your sculpture is becoming more resolved?

The dialogue between poetry and pragmatism still appertains. I always thought that this was the territory occupied by sculpture but no, nothing is resolved. I remain bewildered by the entire business.

This interview was conducted in 2013 and published by Lemon Street Gallery, Truro.

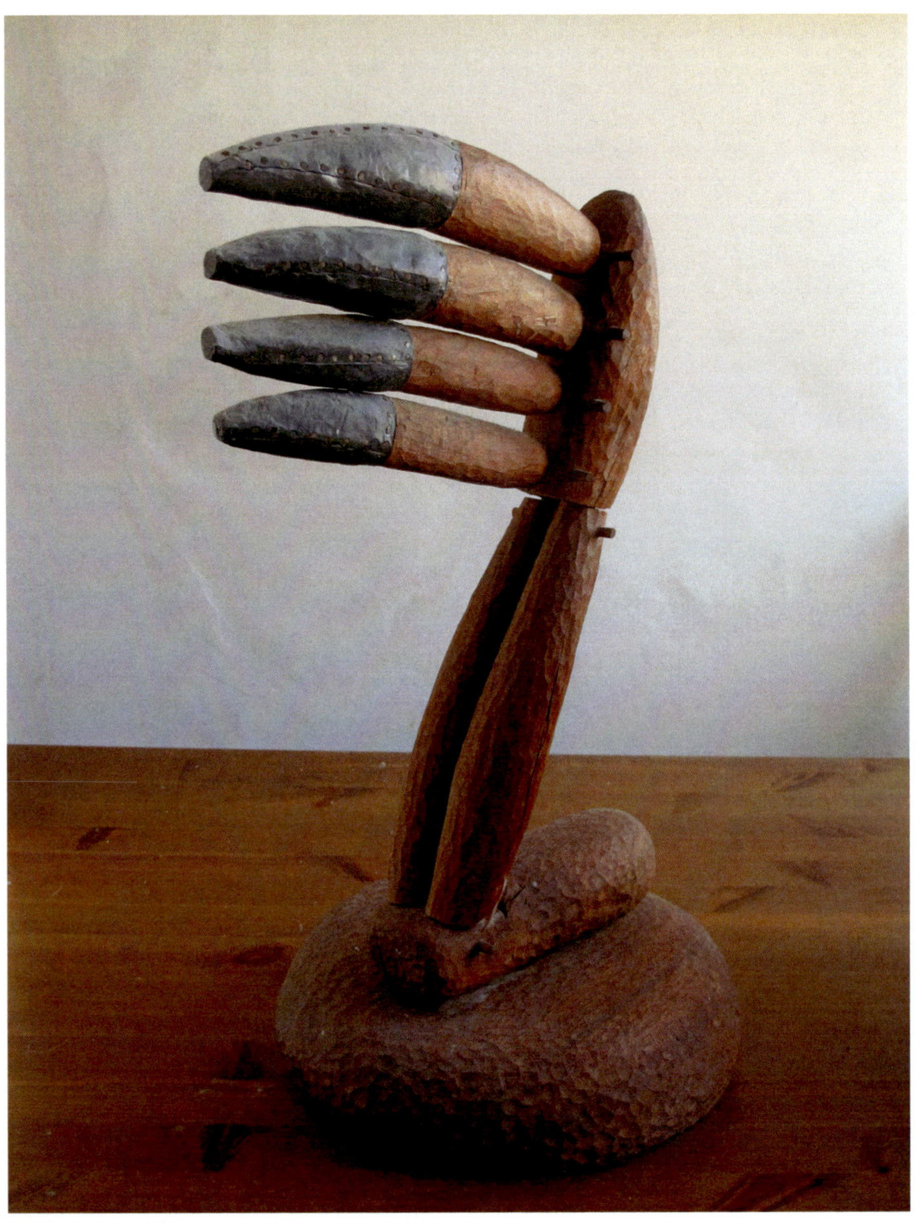

One of Us (maquette)
1987
Wood and metal, 55x26cm (base diameter)
Reproduced courtesy of the artist

Work that Opens Discussion

DOUG COCKER IS at the present time one of the few full-time sculptors working in Scotland. In 1990, he made the decision to leave his teaching job in Aberdeen, a brave – some might say foolhardy – decision for a Scottish sculptor to make, especially in the inhospitable economic climate of the 1990s. However, Cocker's choice was not made on impulse. It was taken by an artist, who, then in his mid-career, had built up a reputation based on a series of impressive exhibitions, major commissions and, as evidenced by an outstanding body of work, with a distinctive, recognisable style.

In the best of Cocker's sculpture, there is strong intent and ability to stimulate a socio-political awareness in the spectator. He has written:

> As receivers of global bad news on a bewildering scale, we are forced to respond or hide. Engagement with the implications of this informa-tion has been an integral part of my work since the early 1980s.

As with his English sculptural peers, Tony Cragg and Bill Woodrow, Doug Cocker's work is political in the broadest sense of the word. Such sculpture is not escapist, esoteric or purely aesthetic; it aims to draw attention to the underlying contradictions in late 20th-century capitalist society. For example, in one of his most provocative works, *Beneath the Screaming Eagle* (1985), the ultimate symbol of material status and security (the house) is encircled from above by an encroaching barrier that throws a protective but ominous shadow on all below. Here, Cocker echoes the dire warning of such social commentators as Noam Chomsky that we put our trust in false gods to protect us from our worst nightmares, only to find that they compound our sense of insecurity and heighten our fearful state, thus further imprisoning us.

Many of Doug Cocker's sculptures seem to allude to modern society's ongoing struggle with the aspirations of individual creative freedom and the deadening effect of institutionalised power and corporate consumer materialism. This takes on a particular personal significance in *Eyeless in Gaza* (1985). The allusion here is to the artist who is threatened by the blind philistinism found at all levels of public life, which places the pursuit of things material above those cultural and spiritual. For instance, within the practice of working for public or corporate sculptural commissions, the artist's room for personal creative expression almost inevitably closes down. Thus, the long process of translating the initial spark of inventive imagination to the finished product can turn out to be a disheartening one. What can become lost in the long bureaucratic and fabrication processes is the original authenticity which, for the artist, is to be found in the outpouring of ideas in his first sketches. Especially for Cocker, drawing is very close to the surrealist practice of automatism, where the

artist allows forms and images to body forth into being with little or
no rational restraint or control. These spontaneous outpourings are the
testing ground, where the sculptor rejects or further develops ideas for
possible three-dimensional work. Wherever appropriate, this exploratory
approach is continued through to the finished piece such as *Calvin's Tools*
(1995) or *Diaspora* (1995), where the gallery presentation is still very
open to improvisation and reassessment.

Doug Cocker's sculpture demands attention, inspires critical thinking,
opens discussion, and stimulates imaginative enquiry. Much of the
power of his work lies in an inner tension between formal concerns
and philosophical speculation. Such dialectical tension of oppositional
forces – between nature and culture, private and public, spontaneity
and manufacture, freedom and conformity, expression and silence – are
actively present in the body politic of Doug Cocker's sculpture.

This essay was written by Bill Hare in 1999 and published in *Contemporary Sculpture in Scotland*.

Section Seven
Three Expressionist Painters

Lys Hansen (1935–)
John Bellany (1942–2013)
Joyce Cairns (1947–)

JOAN EARDLEY WAS a much admired figurative painter working on the Scottish art scene when Lys Hansen went to Edinburgh College of Art in the second half of the 1950s. Hansen's career, however, took some time to take off because of her early teaching career and then family commitments and it was not until the 1980s that she could fully concentrate her creative energies on her painting. In a way, this was fortunate as, by that time, expressionistic figurative painting was beginning to dominate the Scottish and international art scenes. As would be the case with most of the other Scottish women painters, Hansen mainly focused on the depiction of the female body in her work which was usually bound into a tight claustrophobic framed space, forcing it to strike highly contorted poses and extremely anguished facial expressions. All this creates an immediate and powerful visual and psychological impact, but also ultimately forces the viewer to reflect on the position of women within an array of constricting pressures in wider society.

John Bellany went to Edinburgh College of Art (1960–5) where he soon made a reputation as a highly precocious and rebellious student. Along with his fellow student Alexander Moffat, he was committed to modern figurative painting, very much in the northern European expressionist tradition of van Gogh, Munch and the German expressionists. Throughout his career Bellany continually drew his inspirational subject matter from his own personal biography which was deeply rooted in his upbringing in the close-knit fishing communities along the Firth of Forth. After Edinburgh College of Art, he moved to London to further his studies at the Royal College of Art (1965–8) and remained there, quickly becoming a formidable presence on the London art scene with his powerful mode of epic expressionistic painting. Subsequently, he had a fractured personal and artistic life but continued to paint in his highly personal manner, all of which was brought together in his memorable retrospective exhibition at the Royal Scottish Academy in the last year of his life.

Joyce Cairns went to Gray's School of Art, Aberdeen, in the second half of the 1960s and then on to the Royal College of Art in London until the mid-1970s. Her work at that time was highly symbolic with overly mythic and religious themes. Then she returned to Aberdeen to take up a teaching position at her old art college and set up house in a small fishing community near Aberdeen harbour. This move subsequently proved to have a profound impact on her paintings, which began to focus on her own personal narratives and set them in the actual community and place she now inhabited. This grounding in the physical and social realities of her own life now gave her a platform to bring in all kinds of characters and incidents from her own personal memories and rich imagination.

I got to know Lys Hansen when she asked me to write an essay for the monograph on her work, *Passionate Paint – The Art of Lys Hansen* (1998) and was very pleased to include one of her powerful works, *Divided Self* (1985), in *The Scottish Endarkenment* exhibition in 2016. John Bellany had acquired an almost mythic aura when I got to work with him on a major exhibition of his work at the Talbot Rice Gallery in the early 1990s, I subsequently had the privilege to write on his work when he had his last great retrospective at the Royal Scottish Academy in 2013. I helped to curate and write the catalogue for Joyce Cairns's exhibition, *Ship to Shore*, in 1989 and later was asked to write an essay for the catalogue of her exhibition, *War Tourist – Paintings of Joyce Cairns* in 2006. Her work has featured in a number of group exhibitions I have curated. Joyce Cairns was appointed recently as the first woman President of the Royal Scottish Academy in 2019.

Lys Hansen

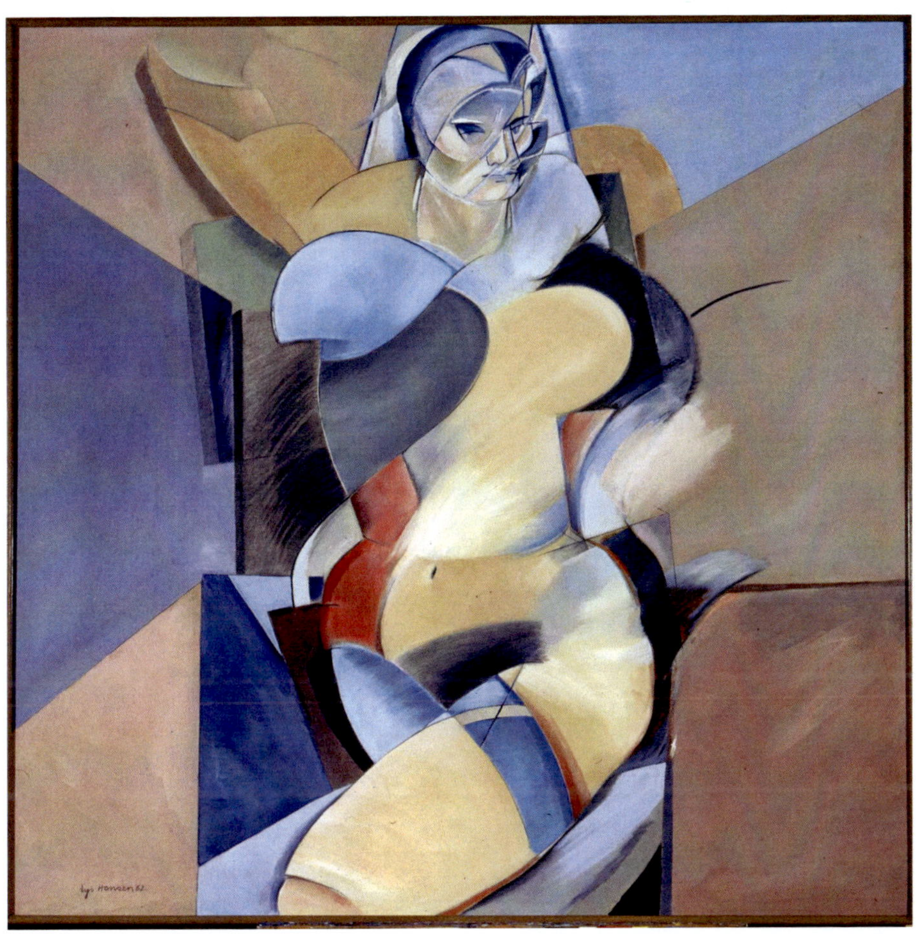

Athena

1982

Oil on canvas over board, 123x123cm

Reproduced courtesy of the artist

'painting is dead' has been the recurring verdict handed down from the courts of fashionable art criticism throughout this ultimate decade of our century. To be more accurate, it is specifically figurative painting which is now judged to have become completely obsolete and redundant. Scottish artists, however, seem not to have got the message and human subject matter is still the central focus of concern for many of our leading painters. The art of Lys Hansen is a notable example of this determined and continuing commitment to humanist values in contemporary Scottish art.

If one was asked to single out the most significant trend that has emerged on the Scottish art scene over the last 20 years, in which Lys Hansen has been a notable professional painter, this would have to be the spectacular rise in the number of women artists coming to prominence. What is also remarkable is that a high number of these artists have made the figure or, more specifically, the female body their primary subject. Lys Hansen, along with other women painters such as Gwen Hardie, Margaret Hunter, June Redfern, Helen Flockhart and Alison Watt are a loose but distinctive force in recent Scottish figurative art. Before focusing on the work and career of Lys Hansen, therefore, a brief discussion of the wider significance of this phenomenon is necessary.

In contrast to the history of art in most other countries, the depiction of the nude figure, male or female, is conspicuous by its almost total absence in Scottish painting. In the early 18th century, Richard Waitt exceptionally presented himself in a self-portrait, painting a rather naïve version of *Venus at her Toilet*. Needless to say, he did not find many takers amongst his prudish patrons for such a *risqué* subject. Even in the 19th century, when Scottish artists were granted a little more freedom in what they might be allowed to paint, the figure in the landscape was well and truly clothed against the cauld blast of conventional Caledonian morality. That great hedonist JD Fergusson apart, this cultural apartheid against the nude was still forcibly evident as late as the 1950s. When the hapless Joan Eardley, for instance, exhibited a picture of a sleeping male nude figure (now in the National Galleries of Scotland collection), she was ridiculed in the Scottish popular press with such juvenile headlines as 'Oh, he's got no clothes on'. Predictably, Eardley never repeated such a public exposure again!

In the late 1970s and early 1980s, when Lys Hansen returned to full-time painting after bringing up her young family, the art scene in Scotland was changing radically. After the predominance of conceptual art and minimalism in the previous decade, raw painting was back with a vengeance. And even though Lys Hansen was never part of any specific art movement, her style of painting could readily be linked with what later became known as Scottish neo-expressionism. There were strong affinities between her depictions of female figures in highly agitated and contorted poses and the dominant characteristics of much of the art of the younger Scottish painters of the 1980s. For instance, the male painters such as

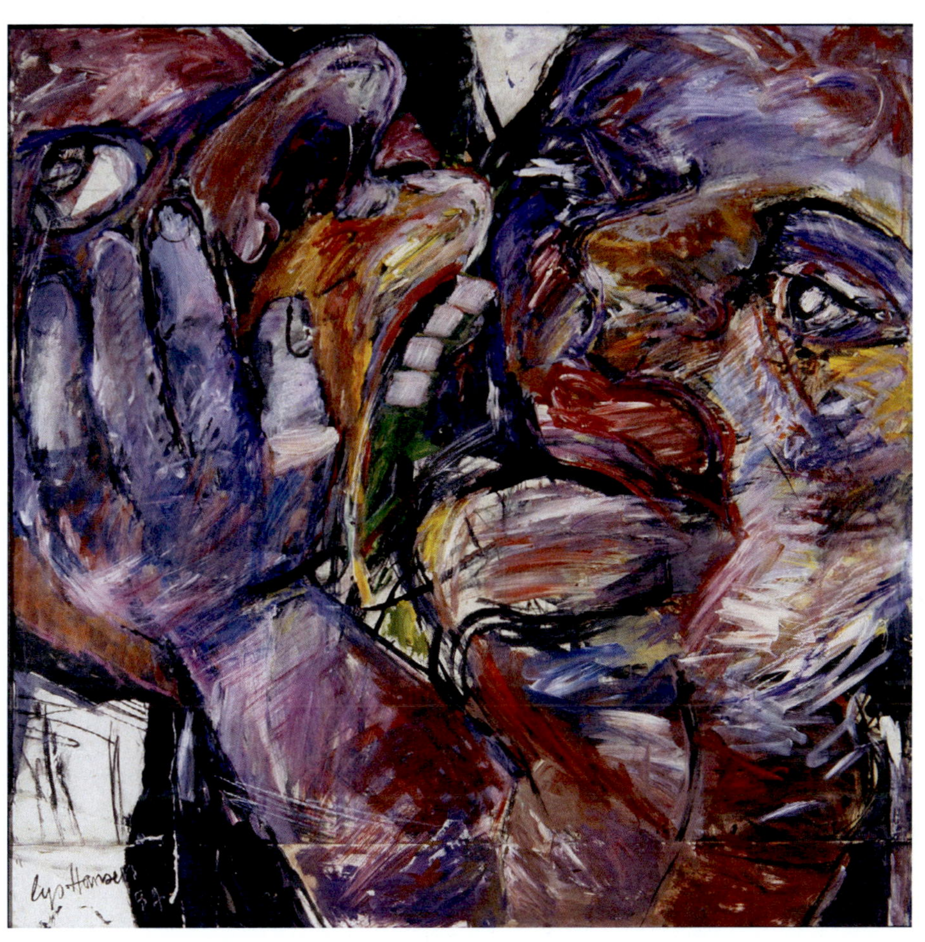

Licking and Biting
1984
Mixed media on board, 124x124cm
Reproduced courtesy of the artist

Ken Currie and Peter Howson, sometimes called the 'New Glasgow Boys', also concentrated on the human figure but usually in an overtly socio-economic or even political context. Hansen, on the other hand, as with a number of her fellow Scottish women artists, tended to disconnect her figures from any particular social or domestic environment and instead dealt with much more universal (and, at the same time, deeply subjective) themes. For these women artists, especially Lys Hansen, the female body became the scene for a whole range of disturbing discourses on our physical and emotional condition which the eminent Scots writer and psychologist RD Laing had earlier diagnosed as the 'Divided Self' in the 1960s.

Similar to the dominant characteristic in much figurative painting in the 1980s, Lys Hansen's early works also tended to have a mythic dimension. This can be found in her version of *Athena* (1980), for instance. Compared with her later free, expressionistic mode of painting, this rather pop art-style picture has a strong sense of graphic design in which the female anatomy is subjected to cubistic division and rearrangement in the fashion of, say, Richard Hamilton, for example. Yet, even in such a relatively academic piece of work, one senses that just underneath the surface powerful emotional forces could split apart this veneer of cool, controlled order.

This split immediately occurs in a subsequent work from this period, *One and the Other* (1980). It is almost as if the artist is now rewriting the mythical birth of Athena from a mother's point of view. In the ancient Greek version, the head of Zeus, Athena's father, is split open with an axe and the goddess is created fully formed as the original brain child. Clearly in such a story, the emphasis is on the male intellectual aspect of creativity. With *One and the Other*, however, Lys Hansen wishes to present a very different version of events.

Creativity and birth for an artist who is also a mother is a very potent topic. Lys Hansen's paintings continually return to different ways of expressing what this means and feels for her. The prevalent characteristic of her treatment of this theme is to emphasise the physical and emotional experiences involved. In *One and the Other*, therefore, it is not the male head, but the female body which is being split apart. The colour here is much more austere compared with the erotic *Athena*. The spinal area of the torso is torn wide open to reveal a dark chasm, while the rest of the body appears to shudder in great convulsions, breasts and buttocks quivering with seismic tremors of sensual pleasure and physical pain. That experience of cathartic ecstasy is most powerfully expressed in a work with the Whitmanesque title, *Electric Torso* (1980).

As images of convulsive sensual experiences, these paintings of the early 1980s are very compelling, yet they still tend to rely on a decidedly graphic mode of representation and so the intrinsically expressive potential of the painting medium itself is still not fully utilised. Throughout the mid-1980s, however, Hansen developed her own distinctive style of painting by concentrating on bridging the gap between form and expression in her work.

This begins in a relatively tentative manner, as can be seen in a picture like *Woman with Man* (1979–82). Here, colour is no longer restricted to being used in the flat and circumscribed manner of the earlier paintings but is much more freely applied, with the whole surface of the picture plane being worked over by aggressive brushstrokes. This gives more all-round organic unity to the work, although there is still a sense of a figure firmly placed in front of a fixed background. The figure itself is a commanding presence; like a not-too-distant cousin of one of Willem De Kooning's women, Lys Hansen's woman, however, represents a more primeval nature with her gigantic, overflowing breasts recalling the monumental sexuality of the *Venus of Willendorf*. Not surprisingly, the head of the male presence, perched precariously on the woman's chest, looks decidedly uneasy about his predicament. Yet powerful as this painting is, it still tends to have an over-reliance on drawing and graphic outline. In fact, the most resolved area in the picture is the massive right thigh, which is a *tour de force* in the use of colour to suggest form and yet, at the same time, to convey sensual energy.

From the mid-1980s onwards, that energisation of the painting medium becomes one of the outstanding features of Lys Hansen's work. The division between medium and message is successfully bridged by the animated manner with which she appears to activate the all-over surface of her canvases. This can be fully appreciated in a group of paintings that she produced around 1984–5, in which two human heads seem to be submerging themselves into each other in the manner of Brâncuşi's *Kiss*. Here, the highly charged tension, between tender attraction and brutal aggression is underlined in the pictures' titles such as *Licking and Biting*, *Love Bites* and *Agony in the First Garden*. In these works, the rapacious, devouring heads practically fill the whole canvas and so almost eliminate the foreground/background dichotomy which dogged some of her earlier works. Furthermore, there is now a real dramatic conflict involved which has an all-consuming focus of attention, as soft vulnerable tongues or fingers are lured into the gaping trap of the bared-teethed mouths of the ferocious lovers. In these highly charged paintings, mouths, teeth, tongues, fingers and lips are all sucked into a great vortex of sexual passion which recalls the 'battle of the sexes' work of Picasso and Giacometti in the early 1930s.

Lys Hansen is, in fact, one of the few Scottish artists who has been able to develop a meaningfully creative dialogue between her work and that of a modern master like Picasso, especially with his surrealist period of the late 1920s and early 1930s. The fruits of this scrutiny of Picasso can be seen further in the single-figure pictures that she was also producing in the mid-1980s, for example, *Allein (Alone)* or *Signals*, both from 1985. Such works recall the great *Bather* paintings by Picasso, especially *The Swimmer* of 1929. Yet, while Picasso's figures feel like giant puppets activated by the master's string-pulling control, Lys Hansen's women are clearly animated by their own disturbing internal emotional and psychic energy. In paintings like *Allein*, the figure appears to be trapped within the narrow confines of the picture frame. The space that the woman occupies seems less like a physical dimension and more like a psychological one, created by the mind of the protagonist herself. This results in any room for manoeuvre being reduced almost to the shallow surface of the picture plane, thus forcing the figure into a grotesque posture which powerfully suggests the turbulent mental condition of the woman herself. This figure generates a disturbing presence which, through contorted and displaced limbs, challenges and threatens the viewer's normal attitude to the representation of women within a whole range of artistic, sexual and social contexts.

Lys Hansen is truly a courageous artist, who is prepared to acknowledge and address the deep and troubling divisions which wrack, not only our own physical and mental life, but also the whole fabric of contemporary society. Yet Lys Hansen the artist, although disturbed and distressed, is not daunted by what she sees around her. The overall unity of her artistic vision, as evidenced by her major works, gives her the creative power to exorcise the demons which can terrorise our lives and haunt our imaginations. As with high tragedy, the paintings of Lys Hansen ultimately have a cathartic power, which is able to rejuvenate our senses and revitalise our spirit. Such painting is never dead.

The complete version of this essay was written by Bill Hare in 1998 and published in *Passionate Paint: The Art of Lys Hansen* (Mainstream, 1998).

John Bellany

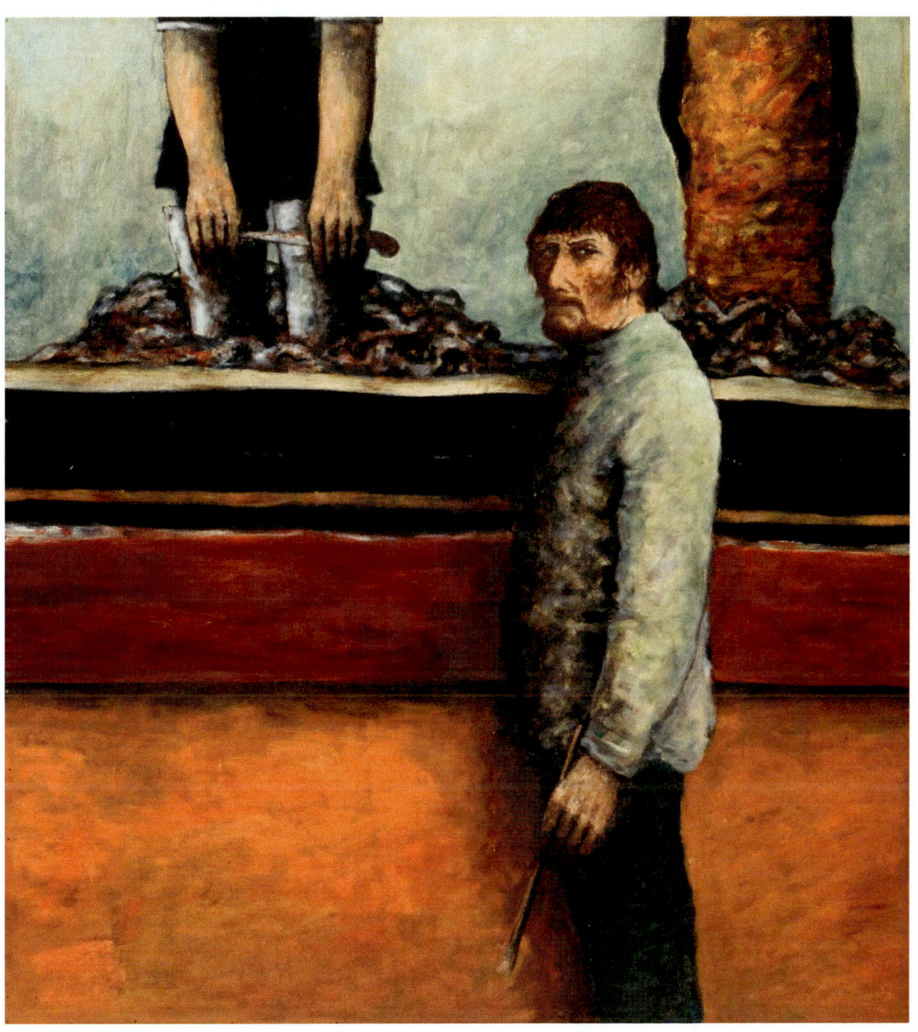

Self-Portrait
1966
Oil on board, 160x142cm

Reproduced courtesy of the artist's estate

John Bellany – Justified Painter

Painting or art generally, as such, with all its technicalities, difficulties and particular ends is nothing but a noble and expressive language.
John Ruskin, *Modern Painters*

FOR THOSE, LIKE me, who were privileged to be at the opening of the Scottish National Gallery's magnificent exhibition, *John Bellany: A Passion for Life*, marking the artist's 70th birthday, it was a special occasion to celebrate and remember. The most striking feature about the works that held their allotted place on the walls of the grand salons of the Royal Scottish Academy was their epic scale, both in physical size and imaginative vision. All could now see that Hugh MacDiarmid's rallying call in his essay, *Aesthetics in Scotland* (1950), for a new ambitious 'giantism' in Scottish art and culture had been fully achieved with these sublime grand paintings of John Bellany. In contrast, wheel-chaired under his towering achievement, the frail and storm-tossed figure of the artist clearly indicated that Bellany had, at great physical cost, drawn constantly on deep forces within himself in order to produce such an awesome and sustained body of art. If Bellany has had an undaunted 'passion for life', it has been equally matched by his unflinching commitment to his art, regardless of the destructive demands that have been involved for his own self and, unfortunately by consequence, those close to him. He has always fully realised and accepted this situation. As he defiantly stated in 1966, 'I believe that it's imperative that one is really excited and overwhelmed by the things one paints or writes about.'

Looking at Bellany's painting within a wider art historical context, which he expects of us as well, this unswerving dedication to art and life as a necessary interdependent relationship is one of the essential characteristics of a distinctive strand of modern art – that highly problematic artistic phenomenon termed expressionism. Despite the ongoing difficulties of a secure definition, Bellany must surely be regarded as a true expressionist and needs to be placed in the company of such giants of that modern movement as van Gogh and Munch. This being the case, the question has to be asked – what distinguishes these particular artists and their painting within the complex histories of modern art? It cannot just be the often disturbing, even violent, nature of their subject matter; for this is also the case with much of the avant-garde, from Dada to Damien Hirst. If, therefore, it is not subject matter which sets expressionism apart, is it to be found in the way these artists formulate their medium of expression, where the artist's immediate presence seems so keenly felt by the use of direct and spontaneous brushstrokes of raw jarring colour and distorted forms? Certainly, all such striking features might be expected to be found in expressionist art but most of these obvious tropes can be readily faked and cynically parodied, as manifested with the brief outbreak of neo-expressionism on the international art scene during the 1980s. Such dubious exercises in stylistic simulation and contrived 'immediacy' are convenient examples of what Hal Foster has called 'the expressionist fallacy'. I, however, would contend that Foster's blanket term should not necessarily be taken as a universal critical put-down of expressionism and that, by using a currently unfashionable biographical, rather than a theoretical semantic approach, one finds that there are a number of authentic expressionist painters who resist and challenge Foster's accusations. John Bellany is such an artist.

Needless to say, expressionism is not just another career choice for the aspiring artist but the inevitable outcome of a certain set of social and personal conditions which have inextricably imposed themselves on such an artist as Bellany. Thus, one of the central factors in the making of a genuine expressionist is the need for total integration of their life with their art – not some vague notion of art 'reflecting' life – but a state of mutual interdependence. Yet, paradoxically, this driving desire of the expressionist artist is invariably thwarted, as the merger of art and life cannot be successfully achieved because of the artist's own biographical circumstances and emotional personality. For instance, van Gogh's art is deeply motivated by utopian ideals for a return to a primitive harmonious community; yet sadly he himself was burdened in real life with a suspicious and even misanthropic nature. Munch's art is also driven by a profound longing for union – in his case, with the female presence – but he constantly found to his bitter cost that women from his own personal experience proved to be devious and destructive. Turning now to our third northern European expressionist, the 'catch 22' impasse which John Bellany had to confront was that, on the one hand, he was blessed by being born into the kind of caring and supportive community of fisher folk of which van Gogh could only dream; 'my childhood was idyllic', as Bellany himself put it. Yet, on the other hand, to fulfil the compulsive demands required to become a totally committed expressionist painter, he had to forsake, although certainly not to forget his former life, in order to follow his ordained artistic calling. Thus, constantly pulled between two irreconcilable attractions that cannot be mutually accommodated, Bellany summed up his position: 'I love to paint, whenever I am painting. At heart, however, I am a mariner.' Yet as Claude Lévi-Strauss has argued in his anthropological writings, it is out of such irresolvable social or personal dilemmas – what the ancient Greeks called 'aporia' – that myth emerges and there is undoubtedly a strong mythic dimension to the art of John Bellany.

The emotional and psychological tension created by the divided loyalties at the heart of Bellany's personal and professional situation is poignantly captured in one of his most moving family portraits. *My Father* (1966) is an unusual work within Bellany's oeuvre, in that, for once, the figure is not presented frontally and looking straight out towards the artist but has his head turned obliquely away to gaze searchingly into a mysterious space created within the picture itself. Yet, despite this lack of eye contact, there still seems to be an unspoken empathy and understanding between father and son. In this painting the father, who unselfishly chose to give up his inherited but highly dangerous life as a fisherman because of his wife's anxieties over his safety at sea, declares his superior devotion on his tattooed arm – 'True Love, Nancy'. Underneath the father's work-worn, weather-beaten hands, he holds a painting of two fishermen by his son, which reveals the son's love of art as the reason why he, too, like his father, cannot be a 'mariner'.

Another common trait of expressionist painting is the intense focus on visual analysis of the artist's life through the constant use of self-portraiture. This does not only require intense self-scrutiny by close and constant observation but usually also involves some form of self-dramatisation, with the artist creating an array of self-appointed roles and self-directed scenarios. For example, in an attempt to come to terms with his conflicting desires between wanting to be both mariner and artist, Bellany painted *Self Portrait* (1965). In his final year student work, he presents, in the manner of Courbet and van Gogh's painter/worker, an image of himself, dressed as a towering figure in full fisherman's gear, standing on the quay of a fishing port. Yet for all this pictorial posturing, Bellany also discreetly reveals to us that in the end his true vocation is to be an artist by showing in his hand the tools of his real trade, his paint brushes.

The other important commonality which binds Bellany to van Gogh and Munch is that they were all brought up in the Northern European Protestant faith of either Lutheranism or Calvinism. Although each reacted to this inheritance differently, they all drew deeply on their early religious experiences and readings of biblical literature to fire up the subject content and iconographical significance of their art. Bellany in particular in his richly referenced work continually draws on his scriptural knowledge and his creative relationship with the art of the past. For instance, his profound artistic and theological questioning come together in his harrowing painting entitled *Pourquoi?* (1967). Within this extremely disturbing work, he draws upon the iconography of Christ's Passion in religious painting, as well as the harrowing images of Goya's *Horrors of War*, in his resolute determination to confront universal evil in the form of the mutilated victims of the Holocaust. Furthermore, Bellany also uses his religious inheritance and the biblical beliefs he was brought up to follow in order to examine his own spiritual condition. This can be seen in another of his memorable family portraits, *The Bereaved One* (1968), in which Bellany's bedridden, widowed grandmother sternly stares out at the young artist with the same severe, judgemental gaze found in a Byzantine pantochrist icon. Lying before this figure of matriarchal spiritual authority is the family Bible spread out on the bed and significantly opened at the Gospel of St John, with its message of divine love and forgiveness for those who truly believe and repent their sins.

Punishment and redemption are recurring themes throughout Bellany's art and usually have a highly personal dimension to them. Up until his miraculous escape from the threatening deadly clutches of self-inflicted liver-damaged annihilation in the 1980s, Bellany constantly returned to the crucial issue of sin and salvation which stalked his life and haunted his imagination. Consequently, only epic paintings of high moral and spiritual integrity could do full service and justice to the all-pervasive themes of good and evil, sin and redemption, thus turning his paintings into great visual sermons. In such work the central tenets of the Christian

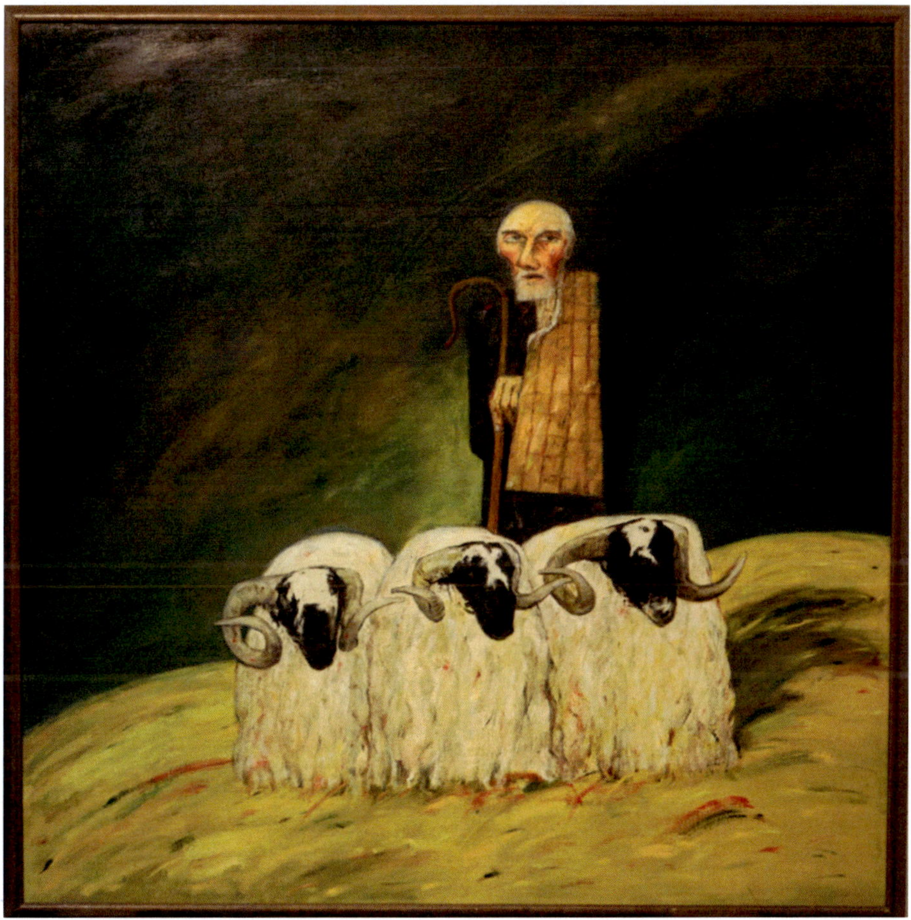

The Ettrick Shepherd

1967

Oil on canvas, 180x180cm

Reproduced courtesy of the artist's estate, the Fleming-Wyford Foundation and Dovecot Studios, Edinburgh (photograph: Stuart Armitt)

faith are addressed and transformed in a highly personal and symbolic manner, from the crucified fish triptych of *Allegory* (1964) through to the sacred ritual of the Sacraments obliquely implied in the grotesque fish-gutting of *Obsession* (1968). All these spiritual battles and personal doubts, which had long tormented this passionate Scottish artist, are brought together to confront each other in Bellany's supreme multi-layered masterpiece, the ironically entitled *Homage to John Knox* (1969). It is little wonder then that Bellany has consequently been enthralled by that seminal analysis of the Scottish psyche, James Hogg's *Confessions of a Justified Sinner*, in which the Calvinist themes of predestination and free will and the interdependence of sin and salvation are played out to their devastating conclusion. Significantly, Bellany pays homage to his literary predecessor in an imaginary portrait, where in biblical mode, but in this case wearing an appropriate tartan plaid, the good *Ettrick Shepard* (1967) is seen tending his flock but is also ominously being stalked by his doppelgänger's satanic *schatten*.

Scottish Calvinism is an extreme religion of Manichaean contrasts, especially when it comes to blessed rewards and eternal punishments. Yet interestingly, however, Bellany felt it necessary to turn to ancient Greek myth to devise an appropriate scenario of retribution for his fallen state. As a concurrent pictorial commentary on his relentless alcoholic assault on his liver, Bellany produced a series of paintings in the 1980s on the theme of the Olympian gods' vengeance inflicted on the original rebellious hero of humankind, the fire stealing Prometheus. Within Bellany's painting, however, it is the artist himself who is the victim of divine wrath and appropriately it is his own familiar Puffin who is the relentless agent of his pain and suffering. Yet there is still hope, through the Gospel promise, the manacles of punishment that bind the sinner to his sin can also be transformed into the unbreakable bond of faith. The great Victorian maritime hymn sung in the chapel of Bellany's 'idyllic' childhood asked the searching question, 'Will your anchor hold in the storms of life?'. Against all the odds, it seems so. Despite everything he himself and all the contingences of his turbulent life and art have thrown his way, John Bellany, up till now, still retains a tenacious grip on his own personal destiny and an unwavering faith in his artistic mission.

This essay was written by Bill Hare in 2013 and published in *Scottish Art News*, issue 20.

Joyce Cairns

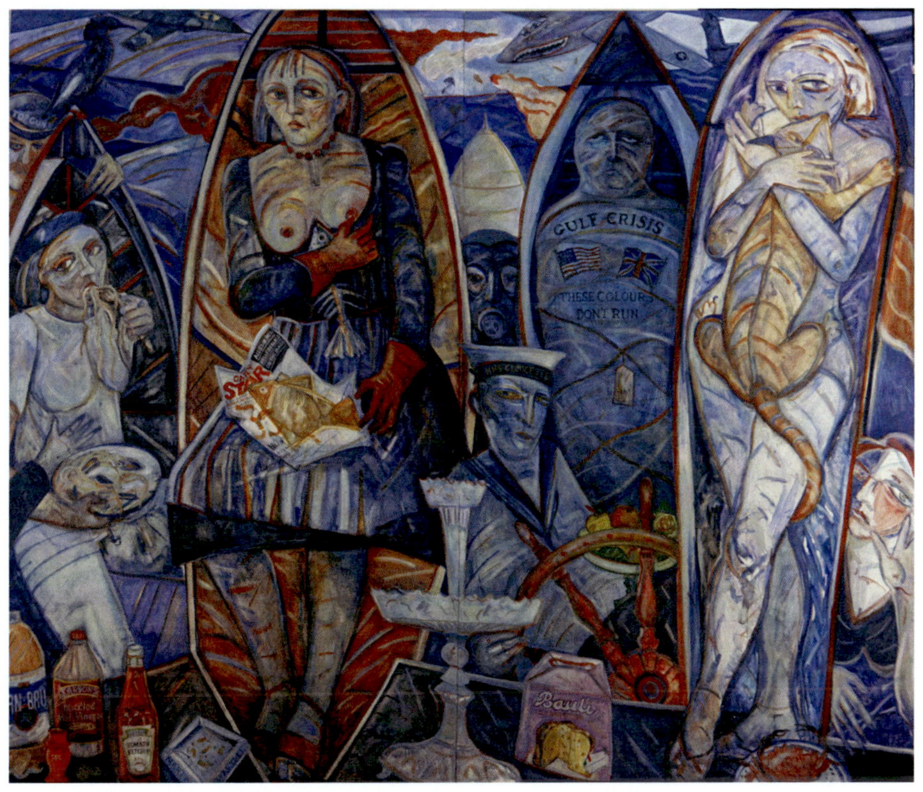

TV Dinners

1991

Oil on panel, 213x244cm

Reproduced courtesy of the artist and Glasgow City Council (Museums)

Joyce Cairns – Painting not Drowning

EVERYONE IN SCOTLAND has probably heard this story. It has now become part of Scottish folklore: how the local newspaper in the North-East, the *Press and Journal*, reported the sinking of the *Titanic* with the headline, 'Aberdeen Man Lost at Sea'.

What one finds funny about this tale is dependent, I suspect, on how well one is acquainted with Aberdeen and its citizens. To those who only know them by their reputation, this joke is mocking Aberdonians' supposed insularity. Of course, it is always dangerous to generalise from personal experience but after regularly visiting Aberdeen over the years, one almost begins to suspect that the cliché image of the mean and narrow-minded Aberdonian has, in fact, been perversely created by the locals against themselves. It certainly runs in the face of all my experience of the city and its community. One only has to stroll around the docks and harbour where Joyce Cairns lives and works to realise that this is an open city, with one of the few ports in Britain which still has thriving international connections. As with the far-travelled characters who frequent Joyce's paintings, the multi-national customers rubbing shoulders in the hotels and bars are flesh and blood evidence that the people of Aberdeen are far from isolated or insular and are in direct contact with all corners of the globe.

This openness to the world beyond and the consequent exchange of ideas and experience is also a conspicuous element in Joyce Cairns's work. Throughout the development of her career, she has sought out and responded positively to a wide range of artistic and social influences yet, at the same time, as with Aberdeen's own sense of civic pride, she has always jealously retained at the core of her art her own personal experiences and the firm conviction of her individual self. Over the last decade, the course of Cairns's work particularly bears this out. Cairns's most recent work is yet further confirmation that her paintings are now the product of a distinct personality. She has created a world of human affairs, both tragic and comic which, although drawn from the artist's own imagination and life history, opens up and touches deep feelings in the viewer as well.

Such is the inspiring attraction of Aberdeen that Edinburgh-born Cairns is only one of a number of artists who have gone and settled there. Her ties with the Granite City go back to the '60s, when she was a student at Gray's School of Art. There, she was trained in the long-standing Scottish academic tradition of sound pictorial skills through rigorously observed life drawing and painting. In retrospect, the artist, with such a strong figurative element in her work, acknowledges the invaluable benefit such a practical education has been for her in the technical aspects of picture making. After leaving Gray's, however, the need to develop her art and find appropriate subjects and themes in her search for a personal

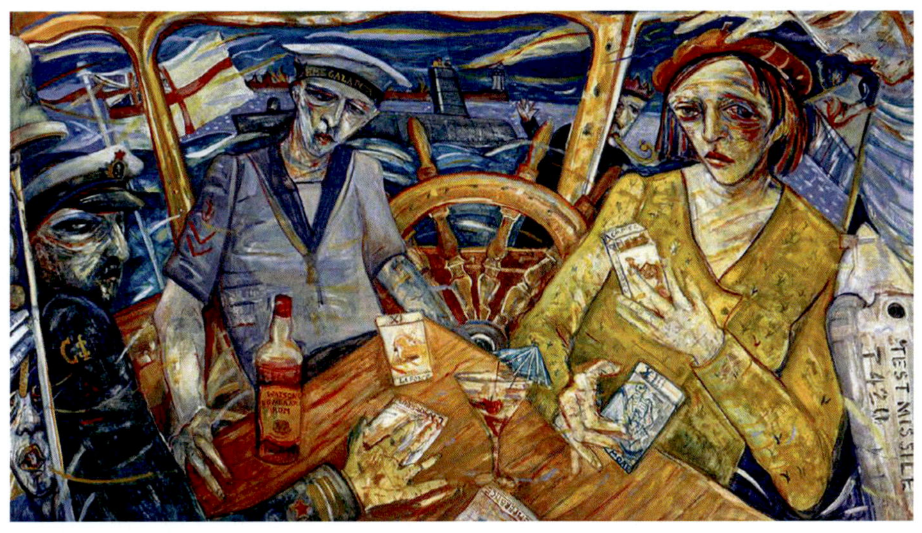

War Games

1981

Oil on panel, 120x213cm

Reproduced courtesy of the artist and Edinburgh City Council Collection

means of expression, took Cairns to further postgraduate studies at various colleges in London and the south of England.

In the great metropolis, the young Scottish artist began to follow up her interest in the evocative power of mythology and mystical iconography. At the same time, however, Cairns soon began to feel that, in London, she was losing touch with those other aspects of life that were meaningful to her. As such, her paintings from that period tended to be more the product of the enclosed world of her imagination rather than external social experience. Although of admirable technical quality, these London pictures lacked any distinctive edge. Stylistically, they were too dependent on second-hand iconographic influences from *fin-de-siècle* decorative mysticism to surrealist dream imagery. Unlike her later work, these London paintings convey little specific psychological reality. Rather, they are content with merely presenting grandiose religious themes such as *Requiem for a Soul* or *Ascendancy of the Soul*.

At this point in her career, Cairns must have felt all at sea. The need to jettison some of the recently acquired cultural baggage was urgent. Yet there were aspects of the works produced in London which were never abandoned and are still central to her artistic *oeuvre*. The dreamlike quality of her pictorial work remains but now there is more often an ominous nightmare atmosphere to her paintings. Also in the earlier work, there can be traced themes of imaginative and moral seriousness, as with pictures such as *Fallen Woman* (1969) or *Forces of Corruption* (1971). These concerns become more focused and as such are given greater conviction and authority in the later work. However, the pictures Cairns produced before her return and settlement in Footdee ('Fittie'), the village at the mouth of Aberdeen harbour, contained little of the vital dramatic power which infuses everything she was later to paint.

Back on course, Cairns returned north in 1976 to become a teacher at Gray's. Through a period of intense reassessment, she began to ditch the overt mysticism of her earlier paintings, some of which had even taken the shape of altar pieces. By the early 1980s, Cairns's paintings, while still retaining, if not intensifying, a strong autobiographical presence, began also to acquire a distinct sense of place. This now allowed a freer, more flexible framework for her picture compositions, so that the rather static theatrical posing of her earlier figures was replaced by much more dynamic arrangements. This new-found desire for an open approach to pictorial construction resulted from Cairns's renewed enthusiasm for the practice of directly working from things observed. Most significantly, she began to take a keen interest in the ever-changing patterns of shapes created by the maritime activities and climatic moods in the harbour around 'Fittie'. Along with this increasing emphasis on a sense of place came a growing awareness of the inspirational possibilities of her own experiences and personal life history.

The results of these insights began to have another direct effect on her painting in 1983, when Cairns's mother died. Then she began to discover, looking through family memorabilia and old photographs, how she could recreate and reinvent people and scenes from her family's past life, as found in such pictures as *They Said the War was Partly to Blame.* Through the power of her imaginative use of her filial memory and her skill as an artist recording the immediate world around her, Cairns realised that she could integrate aspects of her own past, especially her post-war childhood, with the present experience of living as part of the harbour community. Since the mid-'80s, past and present simultaneously work together, as the autobiographical nature of Cairns's paintings has developed.

The earlier work of her London period reflected Cairns's receptiveness to various stylistic influences. This she freely acknowledges. However, now that she has matured into an independent artistic personality, the relationship between her distinctive means of expression and the work of other artists is more complex. This can be seen in *Breton Produce*, for example, where there is a three-way exchange between the artist herself, van Gogh and Gauguin. Nearer to home, within the contemporary Scottish art world, her pictures have frequently been compared to the neo-expressionism practised by many of the younger Scottish painters. Any such links between Cairns's work and ideas, however, are mainly due to superficial similarities in style, originating probably from a shared Scottish art training, a common interest in modern expressionist art and a shared affinity to the northern European tradition of painting.

To grasp the importance of seeing yourself, as Cairns certainly does, as part of this great expressive tradition in European art, it has to be appreciated that the history of the painting developed in northern countries from the end of the medieval period onwards is not a sideshow to the celebrated classical tradition of Mediterranean art. It is the radical alternative. While Italian and French artists pursued the ideal of aesthetic and, later, scientific perfectibility, the painters in the north never lost their commitment to the search for spiritual and psychological truth. This quest for moral understanding is carried through in northern art, not by intellectual abstractions, but by the intense investigation of observed reality: a reality of natural and social experiences which the artist freely shares. Furthermore, because northern artists never wavered from this commonly shared commitment, theirs is an unbroken artistic lineage from before van Eyck to modern expressionist artists working in the late 20th century, including a few Scots like Cairns.

Working within this northern tradition then, Cairns can, without any post-modernist self-consciousness, incorporate and utilise for her own purposes modern expressionism's use of distortions and strident colour arrangements, along with the 15th-century Netherlandish practice of richly faceted, non-linear perspective. In fact, the special relationships between figures, objects and setting found in these recent paintings, where the scenes are tipped forward for our inspection, show some of the same psychological intensity and charged emotional atmosphere that one finds in the work of such earlier artists as Rogier van der Weyden or Hugo van der Goes. As with these great religious painters, Cairns's pictures are carefully built up and held together by the expressive use of directive lines and overlapping multi-layer narrative perspectives. Everything is balanced precariously between controlling order and emotional disruption.

One of the decisive factors which has given the more recent paintings such authority is Cairns's ability to handle large compositions. To execute works on such a grand scale, the artist is required to plan with great care, from the first flashes of inspiration to the fully worked-out pictorial arrangement. In the case of these large paintings, the bridge between initial conception and the final composition is the artist's long and patient deliberations on how to accommodate the formal with the narrative requirements for each picture. Narrative as applied to Cairns's paintings is, of course, far removed from the Victorian idea of an illustrated story. Her pictures are hardly chronological narratives but are more akin in literary terms to free-associative stream of consciousness. The paintings, although grounded in observation and direct study, are ultimately concerned with more than the mere depiction of appearances. As is found in much of the best of Scottish literature, Cairns's paintings delve beneath the surface to reveal the internal experiences of intense emotional and psychological drama, where the artist herself performs a cat-and-mouse game, both as witness and participant. Not for this artist the traditional couthy image of the little harbour village with boats bobbing by the sea. Cairns deliberately avoids any Scottish kailyard picturesqueness to expose a world of barely controlled human passions – sometimes a vortex of viciousness, at other times a crazy carnival of lust and lechery within a comic kaleidoscope of human fears and desires.

Throughout the history of this great seafaring city, many Aberdeen men have been mourned by their women folk after being lost at sea. Yet the one that everyone remembers but never knew is the mythical Aberdonian who went down with the *Titanic* in 1912. The significance of this modern-day legend relates in different ways to Cairns's 'Fittie' paintings. Ultimately, the *Press and Journal*'s story is not an extreme form of provincialism but rather exemplifies the need to reconcile the local with the universal, the human with the historical. All great art attempts something similar: Blake's universe in a grain of sand or when a Netherlandish artist paints the Annunciation taking place in the front room of a house in 15th-century Ghent. That profound human need to particularise, to give local and personal significance to human affairs and historical events, is found at the thematic heart of Cairns' art. She has made 'Fittie' the centre of her real and imaginative world. The village has given her art, after its rather rootless previous existence, a specific place to grow. Yet this settling into being a member of small historical community has not narrowed Cairns's horizons – quite the reverse. She only needs to look out of her studio window at the comings and goings out there on the sea to be constantly reminded of the wider world of international relationships and conflicts, which are continually alluded to in all kinds of obvious and veiled ways in her paintings. If 'Fittie' has given the artist a place from which to relate to the outside world, it has also granted her a place of retreat to uncover and rediscover many aspects of herself through her art for, at the core of all her work, the artist herself is to be found acting out different roles of lived and imaginary experience.

In Cairns's latest pictures, this adopting of various personae can range from the little gym-slipped schoolgirl reliving a family ritual drama, to the cat-suited siren luring wayward sailors by her sexual power; from the manic antics of a drunken good-time girl heedlessly courting danger, through to the dark depressive surrounded by images of her Calvinistic self-loathing and guilt. Cairns's paintings ring the changes. Seen all together, they could be likened to a game of musical chairs, played out on the lurching deck of that ship of fools, the *Titanic*: each picture petrifies the figures in a frozen moment of frantic activity, only to move on again to another stage in the dance of the living and the dead.

This essay was written by Bill Hare in 1991 and published by Peacock Printmakers. See also: 'Witnessing and Warning' in *War Tourist – Paintings of Joyce Cairns* (Aberdeen Gallery, 2006).

Section Eight
Two Socio-Political Artists

John Kirkwood (1947–)
Fred Crayk (1952–)

THE SOCIO-POLITICAL MOTIVATED work of these two artists was nurtured and formulated in the 1970s. This was mainly seen as a decade in British modern history of industrial strife and social disruption, and that alienated mood of dislocation, discontent and uncertainty that dominated much of that period found its powerful expression in the art of John Kirkwood and Fred Crayk. Although not exact contemporaries, they both attended Duncan of Jordanstone College of Art in Dundee where they received a solid academic education. Rebelliously, they then went on to use that training to attack the dominant picturesque conventions of Scottish modernism which still continued in the traditions of the Glasgow Boys' ruralism and the Scottish Colourists' *belle peinture* mode of picture-making.

John Kirkwood is a multi-medium artist working in relief sculpture, photomontage and graphic printmaking. All these different modes are linked to his concern in the way the potentially beneficial powers of technology and consumerism are, in fact, perverted and directed to create a profoundly alienating and highly threating effect on our contemporary world. His relief panels, under the generic title *Bulkheads*, ominously envisage a not too distant nuclear apocalyptic melt-down, while his photomontages, using a wide range of sources from grainy documentary to high gloss advertising imagery, play out a similar scenario in spectacular cinematic terms. Fred Crayk became a secondary school art teacher in the bleak post-industrial environment of West Lothian and used its severely blighted, and decidedly unromantic landscape of shale bings and dilapidated housing schemes for his critical and satirical riposte to the traditional conventions of Scottish scenic painting both in his choice of subject matter and in his raw, painterly technique. Needless to say, these two 'prophets of doom' have never been the darlings of the Scottish art world and never enjoyed the popular or critical success that I feel their work deserved.

I met with both Kirkwood and Crayk around 1980 and worked with them on their solo exhibitions at the Talbot Rice Gallery and was also involved when they were, amongst others, founding members of artists-run Collective Gallery in Edinburgh in the 1980s. Needless to say their work featured in *The Scottish Endarkenment* exhibition in 2016.

John Kirkwood

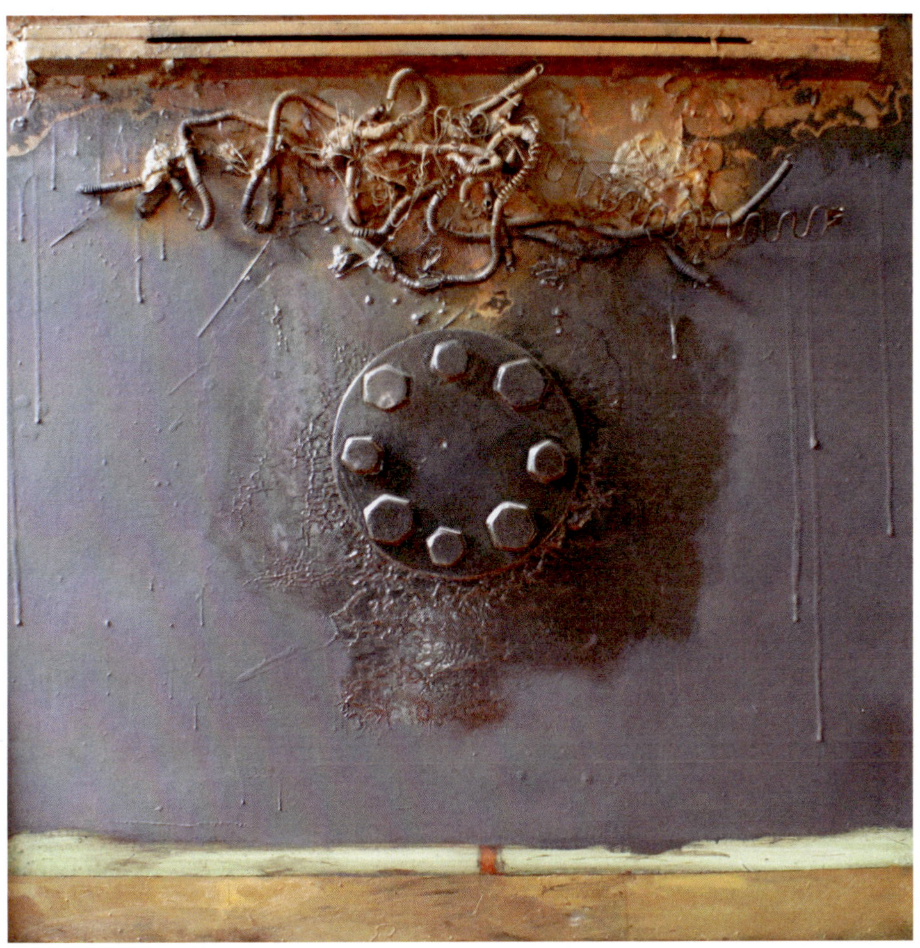

Medusa
1992
Mixed media on panel, 120x120cm
Reproduced courtesy of the artist

East of Eden

They looking back, all th'Eastern side beheld
Of paradise, so late their happy seat,
Waved over by that flaming brand, the gate
With dreadful faces thronged and fiery arms.
John Milton, *Paradise Lost,* Book XII

IF THERE IS one distinguishing characteristic that marks the best Scottish art since the war it would be a new found sense of urgency. This has come about through a strongly felt commitment to leave the hermetic safety of the studio which had been the refuge of most Scottish painting in the earlier 20th century and engage with the world outside. What these artists have found, however, as they survey our present times is usually dark and foreboding, where the human spirit is being threatened by all kinds of ominous forces. Hence the need for urgency, where personal liberty, social justice and the very survival of mankind are endangered. With the work of John Kirkwood, the situation is even more critical – our very survival is at stake.

It is in Kirkwood's photomontages and *Bulkhead* panels where this is immediately seen. It is here that we confront this urgency at its most extreme as the world seems to move inexorably towards its final state of catastrophic disaster. Our worst nightmares are being realised as our garden of technological delights appears to be blowing itself apart.

Many of course, would always prefer to be deluded by the false distractions of Metroland and Gogglebox. To those blind amongst the blind, Kirkwood's work is avoided or dismissed as mere sensationalism of shock and awe. Certainly, the violence and destruction in these explosive works of Kirkwood do of course make a strong impact. Kirkwood undoubtedly aims to assault our immediate sensibilities. Yet beneath the surface of these works is a complex struggle between interconnecting and contradictory forces attracting and repelling each other.

There are broadly four distinct but interlinked areas of concern. What holds them all together is Kirkwood's profound awareness of the historical process in human, social and political affairs. His photomontages and the *Bulkheads* both reveal what may happen when we selfishly gorge from the tree of knowledge and allow the fruits of technology to become our sole diet at the expense of moral and spiritual substance. While the photomontages speculate on the beginnings of the descent into the inferno of run-away nuclear chaos, in truly Miltonic terms, the *Bulkheads* seem to be the final set positions for the long-dreaded Battle of Armageddon, leading to the ultimate Last Judgement as announced in the Book of Revelation.

With such an apocalyptic vision, Kirkwood is unarguably a modern history painter in the grand epic tradition of Brueghel, Goya, Géricault,

Turner and Picasso. However, Kirkwood is also keenly aware that such a tradition runs in the face of the utopianism of much of 20th-century modernism. Undaunted, he has turned this to his own advantage, as did these earlier masters when they subverted the conventions of history painting to deal with contemporary events.

Academic authorities, ancient or modern – whether Sir Joshua Reynolds or Clement Greenberg – will always want art to deal with the general and the universal at the expense of the immediate and the particular. In the past it was appropriateness of subject and treatment that mattered, while with high modernism the critical concern has been with the essential nature of painting itself. Accordingly, the most authentic modern painting should be completely autonomous, untouched by the world, reflecting only its unique character which ultimately is the formal action of placing integrated marks on the picture surface.

As with Milton, Kirkwood is of the Devil's rebellious party. For him, the picture surface is not inviolate but becomes a battleground of

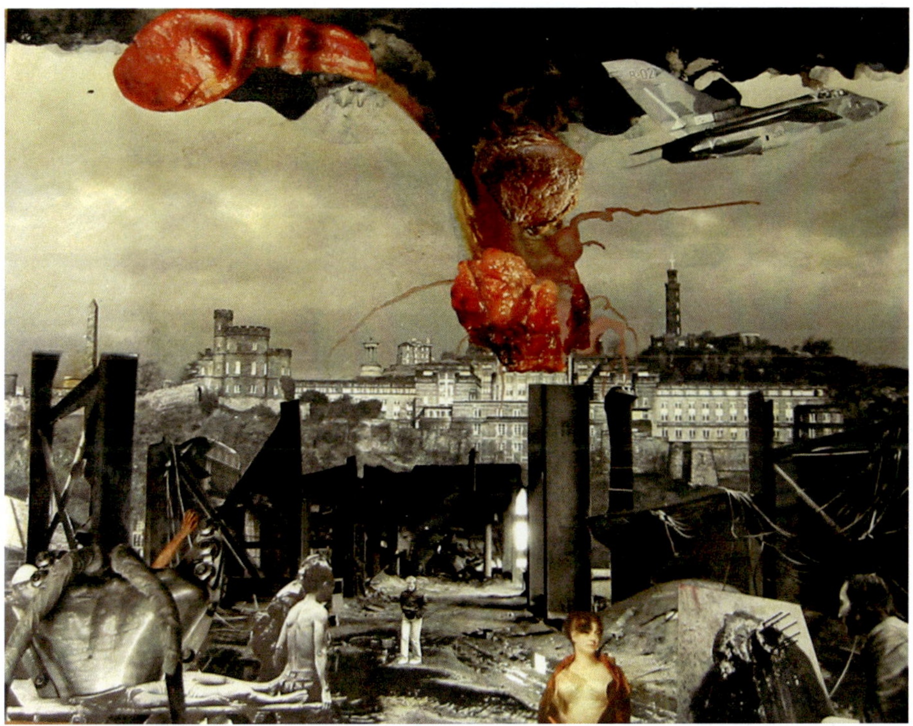

State of the Nation
1987
Photomontage, 40x50cm
Reproduced courtesy of the artist

contending forces which heretically fly in the face of the stern tenets of orthodox Greenbergian modernist dogma. In this case, the *Bulkheads* set out to challenge those rigid laws of modernism on all fronts by the deployment of such scorned devices as subject matter, narrative, illusionism, figuration, literary references, pictorial perspective and ultimately by the application of relief sculpture and actual objects from the real world itself. All this gives Kirkwood a freedom and flexibility to tackle his epic theme in the same way that Milton rejected 'the bondage of rhyming' for the expressive power of blank verse.

With such a variety of different techniques at his disposal, the artist can overlay his work with many levels of meaning. He can play off, for example, the real and the representational against the allegorical in a truly Carlylean sense of 'concealment and yet revelation' to give the 'double significance' of the 'symbolic as well as the real.'

Thus, the *Bulkheads* of John Kirkwood can possess the rhetorical power of that earlier Victorian prophet of doom, Thomas Carlyle, similarly dealing with the duality of modern experience. As Carlyle pointed out, that duality goes back to the Age of Enlightenment and the beginnings of the Industrial Revolution. In Scotland, we might even pinpoint this to the day Robert Burns tried to visit the armaments factory at Carron Iron Works near Falkirk and wrote the following verse when he was refused entry to that 'Satanic mill':

> We cam' na here to view your warks,
> In hopes to be mair wise,
> But only, lest we gang to hell,
> It may be nae surprise:
> But when we tirl'd at your door
> Your porter dought na hear us;
> Sae may, shou'd we to Hell's yetts come,
> Your billy Satan sair us!

Even in the late 18th century, Burns is already raising the questions which Thomas Carlyle and his subsequent followers will ask again and again: will progress make us 'mair wise' or leads us back 'to hell's yetts' at the East of Eden? John Kirkwood actually entitles one of his bulkheads *The Gates of Hell* which, along with the general deployment of destructive forces in much of his work, shows that he also takes a satanic view of our present critical situation. Certainly, there is no going back to a safer past as much Scottish art has tried to do. The immutable armour-plated sentinels of the *Bulkheads* stand guard over the war-torn landscape like the armed Cherubims posted to keep us from re-entering our former Paradise.

Yet the sheer creative energy and imaginative power of Kirkwood's work should dispel any sense of resignation. His art is catastrophic rather than terminally pessimistic. Destruction and mayhem may abound and overflow but what we witness is the general 'flux of things' between order and chaos. Ultimately the *Bulkheads* are the battlegrounds where our past choices and our future options confront themselves.

We now all live under the threat of imminent annihilation. At such times, it is the artist's duty, usually a thankless one, to remind us, as Faust did that 'This is hell, nor are we out of it'. At other troubled times in human history, other artists have done the same – Dante with *Inferno* and Milton with *Paradise Lost*, for example. John Kirkwood's *Bulkheads*, with their awesome sublimity, carry out a similar responsibility through the art of modern history painting.

As stated at the outset, urgency is the hallmark of the best post-war Scottish painting and, in the work of John Kirkwood, there is a strong feeling that time may be finally running out. As Edwin Muir writes in 'One Foot in Eden', 'The world's great day is growing late'. Yet if we look hard into our darkest nightmare, we might still find hope and see

Strange blessings never in Paradise
Fall from these beclouded skies.

This essay was written by Bill Hare in 1993 and published by the Talbot Rice Gallery, Edinburgh.

Fred Crayk

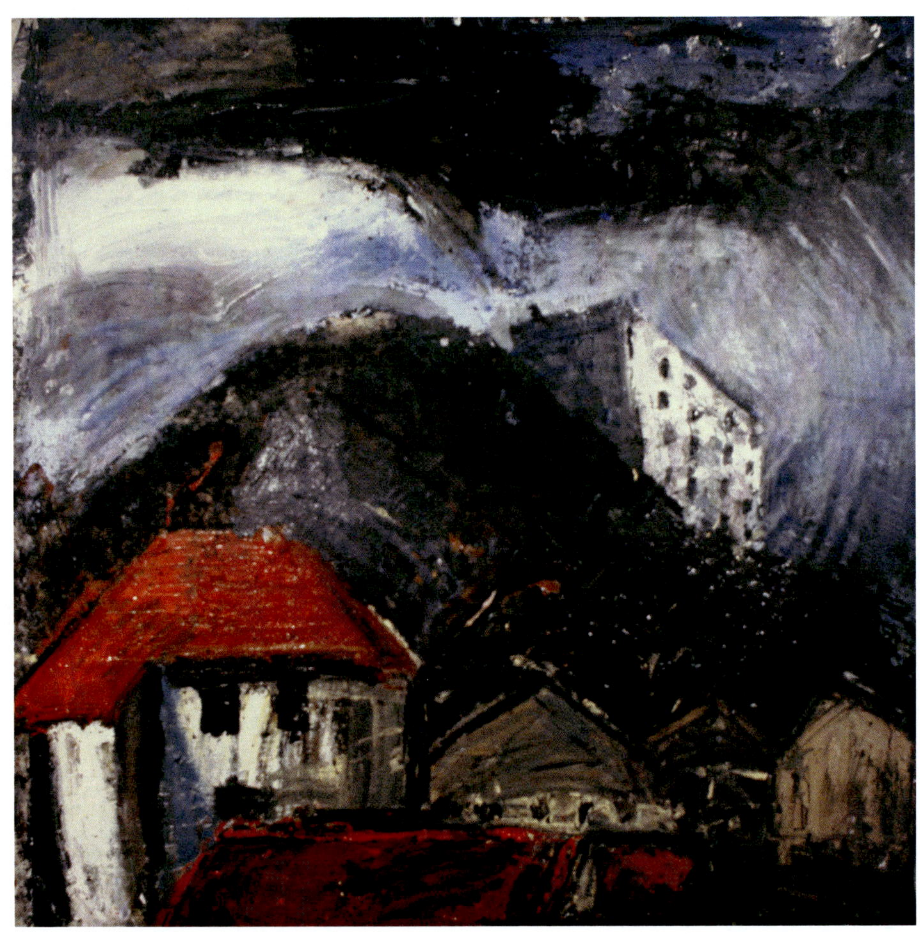

Parnassus

1990–1

Mixed media on paper laid on canvas, 226x216cm

Reproduced courtesy of the artist

Et in Arcadia Ego

The Other Side of the Coin

IF THE TRUE pastoral needs no heroes, Fred Crayk's exhibition *No Man's Land* takes no prisoners. Crayk's new paintings are the heavy artillery of political art in Scotland. They are not for the fainthearted, and many will probably find themselves shell-shocked by the onslaught on their sensibilities and wish to run for cover. As TS Eliot pointed out, most of us prefer to keep our heads well below the parapet when faced with raw reality.

Fred Crayk's choice of subject matter, by contrast, clearly underlies his commitment to identify his art with the 'raw reality' of the social and environmental disasters of one of the most deprived communities in Scotland – the West Lothian post-industrial wasteland. Yet for Crayk, a straightforward, concerned portrayal of life for the victims of economic and social injustice is not enough. Crayk takes a more oblique and challenging approach. He makes his attacks on injustice through his paintings themselves, by subverting the conventional notions of the role and character of the generic system of academic art. For example, his still-life paintings, with their ubiquitous empty tin cans and hammered nails, contradict the accepted image of still-life that is expected to celebrate 'the good things in life', from Dutch pictures of tables groaning under the weight of food and drink, to Andy Warhol's multi-images of endless supplies of Campbell's soup and Coca Cola. The still-life is at the bottom of the academic pile because it is meant only to deal with the merely physical/material aspects of living. As such, it is not expected to raise any awkward socio-political questions. The typical still-life should be as easy and pleasant to consume as the attractive food it presents. The usual public reaction to such paintings is, 'I feel I could reach out and pick up one of those succulent peaches and take a bite.' In contrast, it would be a foolhardy person who would want to do the same with one of Crayk's still-life pictures. They are hardly there to give sensual succulent pleasure. On the contrary, these are the still lifes of the 'have-nots'. They aim to lay bare the other side of the glossy face of consumer-led capitalism, as van Gogh wanted to show the other side of the extolled virtues of back-breaking toil with his painting of the worn-out muddy boots of the farm labourer.

With the landscape paintings, Crayk's approach is similarly oblique and disruptive. Yet here he works in a much larger dimension and more provocative manner. Within Scottish art terms, this is certainly true. This is the one area of painting in which the public does still take an interest and has firmly held beliefs as to what is acceptable, both in subject and appropriate style. On each of these counts, Crayk's landscapes would seem deliberately to fail – in a most perverse manner.

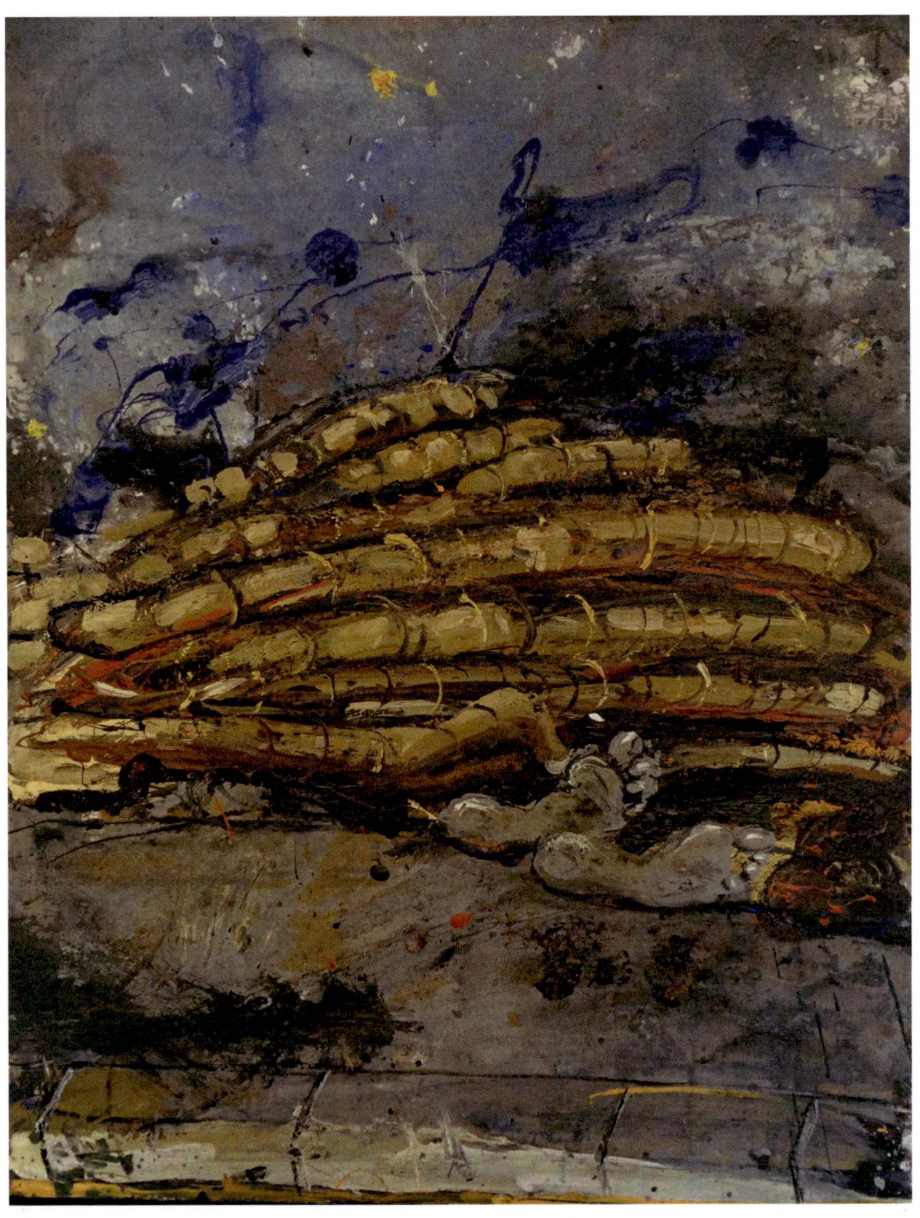

Duvet
1988
Oil on canvas, 140x110cm

Reproduced courtesy of the artist

Firstly, his choice of subject – the industrial urban wastelands of West Lothian (what Tom Nairn recently called 'the black hole between Glasgow and Edinburgh') – are hardly the stuff of Scottish landscape subject matter. As a recent catalogue, *Looking at Nature – Looking at Art* suggested:

> successful landscape artists are drawn to paint, the vivid nature of the Scottish terrain with [its] contrasts, between mountainous regions, lush farmlands and seaboard.

In other words, the picturesque postcard imagery of Scotland – and certainly not nasty shale bings and nightmare tower blocks! Therefore, despite the fact that over the last 200 years the majority of working people in this country have lived in an industrial/urban environment, there has hardly been a place in Scottish painting for such subject matter. Maybe a further thrust to the complex meaning of the recurring vast empty spaces in Crayk's landscape compositions is a reflection on this void in the history of our visual culture.

Secondly, the manner of expression Crayk employs merely compounds his crimes against the canons of good taste and only further runs in the face of the conventional appreciation of Scottish landscape painting. In these works, for example, you will not find the reassurance of the artist's skill in rendering detailed mimetic illusionism or find him indulging in the sensual pleasure of *belle peinture* bravura. It may be fine for Joan Eardley to press flowers into her paintings but shale gravel and coal dust is another matter altogether for Scottish pastoral sensibilities.

One might ask, however, are these new landscapes by Crayk so hostile that they are in danger of becoming inaccessible? Not at all, I would argue. There are different ways of stepping into a landscape painting. Admittedly, Crayk can make entry into his ruined post-industrial wastelands as uninviting as some of the scenery in West Lothian which inspired them. However, if the eye can be disturbed, the mind can also be stimulated. Again, I would suggest a familiarity with the great academic history of European landscape painting and particularly the pastoral tradition, as a way of 'getting into' these new works.

Within the history of art, the pastoral does not formulate itself into a distinctive sub-genre until the 17th-century. The two great artists most associated with the creation of this type of painting are, of course, those twin favourites of the European academies, Claude and Poussin. Their treatments of the classical landscape complemented each other perfectly and had a profound effect on European cultivated taste. Claude, the 'Raphael of Nature', as he was called in 18th-century England, presented in the most lyrical fashion the idealised beauties of our supposed arcadian origins. His landscapes are inhabited by idling shepherds and wandering poets – thus the ironic title of Crayk's *Parnassus* where, by contrast, refined poetic beauty is conspicuous by its absence. Poussin, on the other hand, expresses an elegiac sense of loss in his landscape paintings. His arcadian pictures suggest the waning of the Golden Age. They introduce the notion of decay and death, which hints at the undermining of the undisturbed harmony of man and nature, which was once, according to the ancient writers, our natural state of being. *Et in Arcadia Ego* is man's inevitable fate – even in Arcadia death will find us. The alienation between man and his environment which is so integral to Crayk's paintings is already born in Poussin's tragic landscape.

These new works by Crayk reveal him, I believe, to be a serious heir to the belief in this worthy role for art. His landscapes, although decidedly anti-pastoral in character, are just as much a battleground of intellectual and moral debate as the work of those 17th-century masters like Poussin. But where they presented a nostalgic backward view of the idyllic beginnings of human history, Crayk confronts us with the devastating effects, both on nature and society, of the long but relentless 'progress' from the Golden Age to the present one of steel and concrete. This is literally the case in one of Crayk's most successful works, *Laocoön*. Here again we are shown a wide expanse of blighted terrain with a sulphurous light on the horizon, which mocks Claude's dusky golden dawns. Dominating the foreground is a lump of broken-off reinforced concrete, with its twisted metal rods shooting upwards like some virulent triffid-like weed. The painting is full of satirical attacks. Under fire in *Laocoön* are both the cult of nostalgia associated with the sense of loss for the classical past (human civilisation in a 'handful of dust' syndrome) and, at the same time, the social planners' utopian vision of a future brave new world where everyone would live in ordered harmony within a concrete 'hell on earth'. The title, referring to the Trojan priest who was killed by the gods for trying to warn his countrymen against the Greeks' faked peaceful retreat, reminds us to be ever vigilant against those who would offer gifts of peace and progress to a new Golden Age.

With such a profoundly sceptical attitude, it is not surprising that Crayk's work reflects as much an anti-modernist stance as it does a critical academic one. For Crayk, both these institutionalised art movements have betrayed their original radical ideals and willingly succumb to identifying with the social establishment. If the academic system of genres sets the choice of subjects up for debate in Crayk's work, then the stylistic interpretation of these subjects is controlled by an assault on the formalistic ideals of high modernism. For instance, this can be seen by the awkward distortions and disjunctions Crayk perpetrates on the objects and overall compositions in his pictures, which parody the conventional language of clapped-out modernist painting. At the same time, the raw crudeness of the actual paint application mocks the expressionists' existential triumph of the individual gesture. In fact, if Crayk's new paintings could be classified stylistically, they are closer to minimalism than expressionism. But again he contradicts the cool platonic classicism of that movement, as he demonstrates, for example, in his picture of the modern urban nightmare entitled *Dwelling*. Yet in the end, like many of the great radical artists of the past, Crayk's paintings deliberately defy easy stylistic labelling.

This essay is written with the awareness that these powerful paintings by Fred Crayk do make strong demands on the viewer. However, as I have suggested, a thoughtful, open-minded approach can bring about a fuller appreciation of the high ambitions that the artist has for his painting. His new painting has thankfully shed its earlier rhetorical devices of printed texts and scenes from the history of political and artistic revolution. This now allows his pictures to speak more directly and authentically for themselves. Given considered attention, not only do these paintings stimulate intellectual and moral debate but, more importantly, they take on an awesome, sublime beauty – even if that beauty is of a 'terrible' nature.

This essay was written by Bill Hare IN 1991 and published by the Talbot Rice Gallery, Edinburgh.

Five Male Figurative Painters

Steven Campbell (1952–2007)
Henry Kondracki (1953–)
Ken Currie (1960–)
Peter Thomson (1962–)
Paul Reid (1975–)

FIGURATIVE PAINTING ALWAYS remained the dominant feature of art in Scotland right up to the end of the 1980s. This was mainly due to two factors: firstly, the Scottish art colleges continued to put figuration at the heart of their teaching, with strong emphasis on life drawing for example; secondly, the art-buying public in Scotland has always been relatively small in size and conservative in taste, preferring scenes with which they could identify. Therefore, painters who chose to remain in Scotland were on the whole obliged – through their art training and economic necessity – to work in some kind of figurative mode. By contrast, things were very different on the post-war international art scene where abstraction, minimalism and conceptualism had all at various times dominated. In the 1980s, however, with the rampant free market monetary policies of Reaganism and Thatcherism and the consequent rise of a new class of art-ignorant *nouveau riche* (but who had bags of money to spend on pictures they could 'understand'), figurative painting became the major phenomenon of the 1980s international art market.

With this 'return to figuration' Scottish painting was for once well placed to take advantage of the international situation. The art colleges now strove to produce a wave of young painters who could respond to and be part of what was fashionable on the international art scene. It was Glasgow School of Art, however, mainly under the direction of Sandy Moffat that made the most notable impact, especially with the work of Steven Campbell and Ken Currie.

After art college, Steven Campbell went to New York in the mid-1980s, where his large canvases of intriguing and witty pictorial narratives of lost hitchhikers on romantic Scottish hillsides were critically and commercially a great success. When he returned to Scotland in 1990, he was lauded as an inspiring example of what a contemporary Scottish artist could achieve internationally. Unfortunately, things did not turn out that well – the critical opinion and art market moved away from figure painting and the earlier enthusiastic support for Campbell's work quickly declined. He subsequently fell out of favour and sadly died far too soon.

Ken Currie probably had a clearer agenda for his art than Campbell, which in the 1980s was very much linked to his strong left-wing beliefs.

Initially the thematic subject matter of his work tapped into an area of socio-political life that had been almost completely ignored – the history and politics of the Scottish labour movement. He then turned attention to the tragic impact of the post-industrial decline on Scottish working class communities, while at the same time setting out to chronicle the violent fall out in Eastern Europe after the collapse of the Soviet empire. His paintings are now not so overtly political but he still uses the human figure as a powerful metaphor for the critical state of the body politic in contemporary society.

Peter Thomson, another graduate of Glasgow School of Art, initially worked broadly in the same areas of social concerns as Currie, using an almost Pre-Raphaelite attention to visual detail in his paintings. He subsequently moved away into much more psychologically orientated subject matter which owes more to surrealism than social realism.

Henry Kondracki is rather an outsider in this company. He is Edinburgh-born but went to London for his art education at the Slade in the mid-1980s. When he returned to Scotland, he quickly developed a distinctive style of painting where the exuberantly expressive nature of his painting technique matches his pictorial subject matter, which seems to body forth with all the delightful joy of a child's imagination. His pictures may appear childlike and even naïve in content but they are carefully considered and subtly sophisticated in their painterly execution.

Paul Reid, by contrast, paints his intriguing pictorial scenes of mythological figures in a very detailed and highly finished manner. By the time he went to Duncan of Jordanstone in Dundee in the mid-1990s, the academic approach to art student training was almost a thing of the past, so that Reid was deliberately and rebelliously going against the grain when he pursued what was generally regarded as a redundant tradition. What he did, however, was to breathe new life into conventional historical narrative painting by presenting his mythic figures in new and surprising settings and situations. Instead of just well-painted illustrations of mythical stories, Reid presents viewers with intriguing pictorial narratives full of tragic pathos and evocative mystery.

Steven Campbell

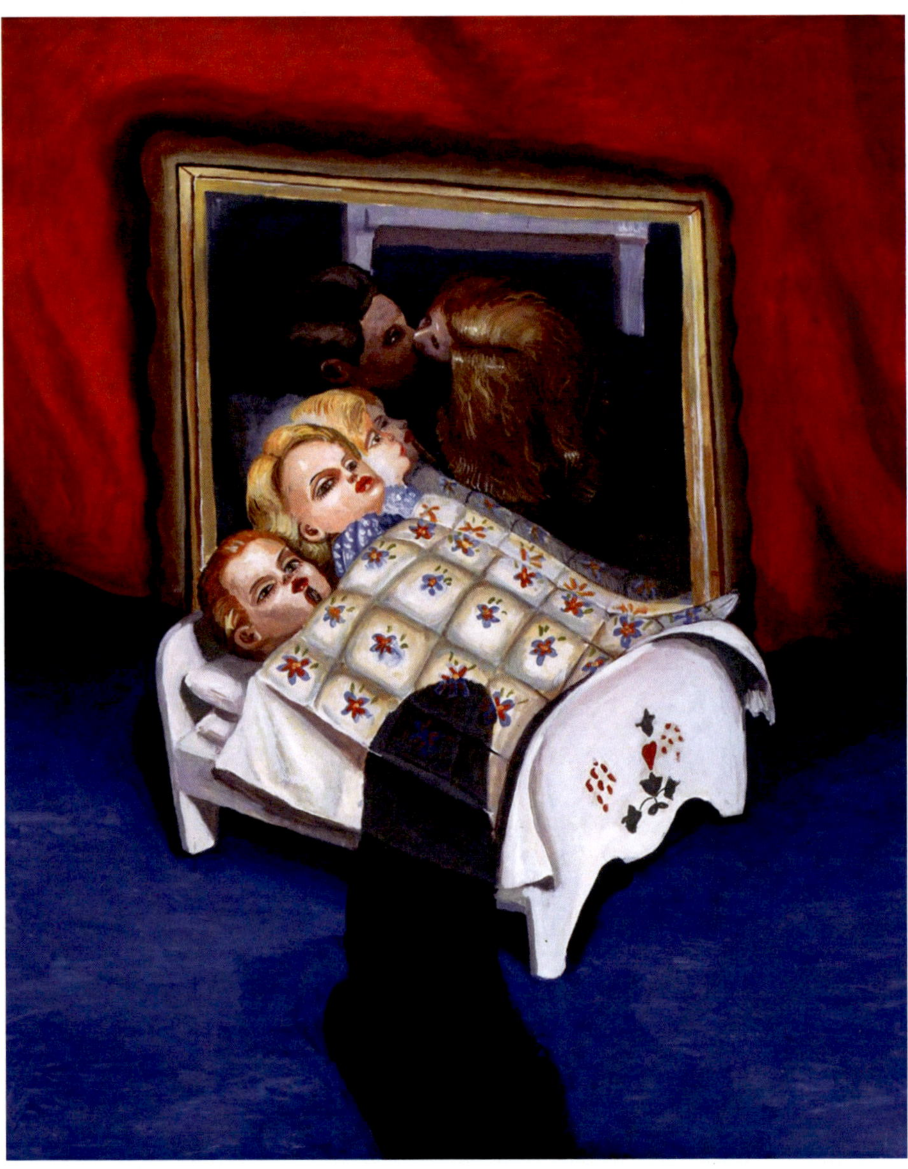

Dolls R Us

1992

Acrylic on paper, 183x144cm

Reproduced courtesy of the artist's estate

The Wit and Wisdom of Steven Campbell

STEVEN CAMPBELL IS that rare thing: a Scottish artist who has gained international recognition on his own terms. By that I mean he has not pandered to a stereotypical notion of what an artist from Scotland should paint but has always looked to tackle the important issues in contemporary art from his own distinctive and independent point of view.

There have been a few similar individuals in the history of Scottish art and undoubtedly Allan Ramsay was one of the first. Interestingly, there is an early self-portrait by Ramsay which focuses on one of the central concerns in Steven Campbell's work. In this portrait, we see Ramsay, splendidly dressed in his velvet morning jacket, not painting but pointing to a nearly bare canvas on which there is a very sketchy preliminary drawing of a figure, presumably the first outlines of a commissioned portrait. Interestingly, Campbell also includes this device of a bare canvas in a fairly recent painting called *Men in Pursuit of Simplicity* (1988). In this picture, which shows two men in a small dinghy battling against the swell of a turbulent sea, the sails of their boat have been left blank. The difference between these two paintings is striking. In the work of the 18th-century master, the artist is confident and assured. There seems no doubt in his mind that he can magically turn his blank canvas into the image of a living presence. What he paints is an image of what the painting is meant to represent – no argument about it. Campbell's stormy seascape, by contrast, is full of dangers and uncertainties but the central dilemma in the picture is the blank canvas – what to put there and what would the image mean anyway? This question of the appropriate language and purpose of pictorial representation has been a major issue in Campbell's work since he started painting in the early 1980s.

Campbell turned to painting in his last year at art school in Glasgow, when figurative painting was just beginning to enjoy the critical and popular success that was to become the phenomenon of the 1980s. However, Campbell, coming from a conceptual art background, where his interest had been in performance art, was acutely aware that representational painting was a very problematic concept. Unless you were very simple-minded (and that is the last thing you could accuse Campbell of being), there was no going back to the doubt-free confidence of Allan Ramsay, where there seemed to be a perfectly straightforward one-to-one relationship between image and what it pertains to represent. Campbell, more than any of the internationally acclaimed neo-figurative painters, was aware that modern art from cubism onwards had altered the rules and shifted the goal posts in the game of pictorial narrative. Furthermore, every serious-minded figurative painter therefore had to address the Magritte 'this is not a pipe' challenge. Throughout his career, Campbell has done so with superb wit and imagination.

When Campbell moved from performance to painting, he already had

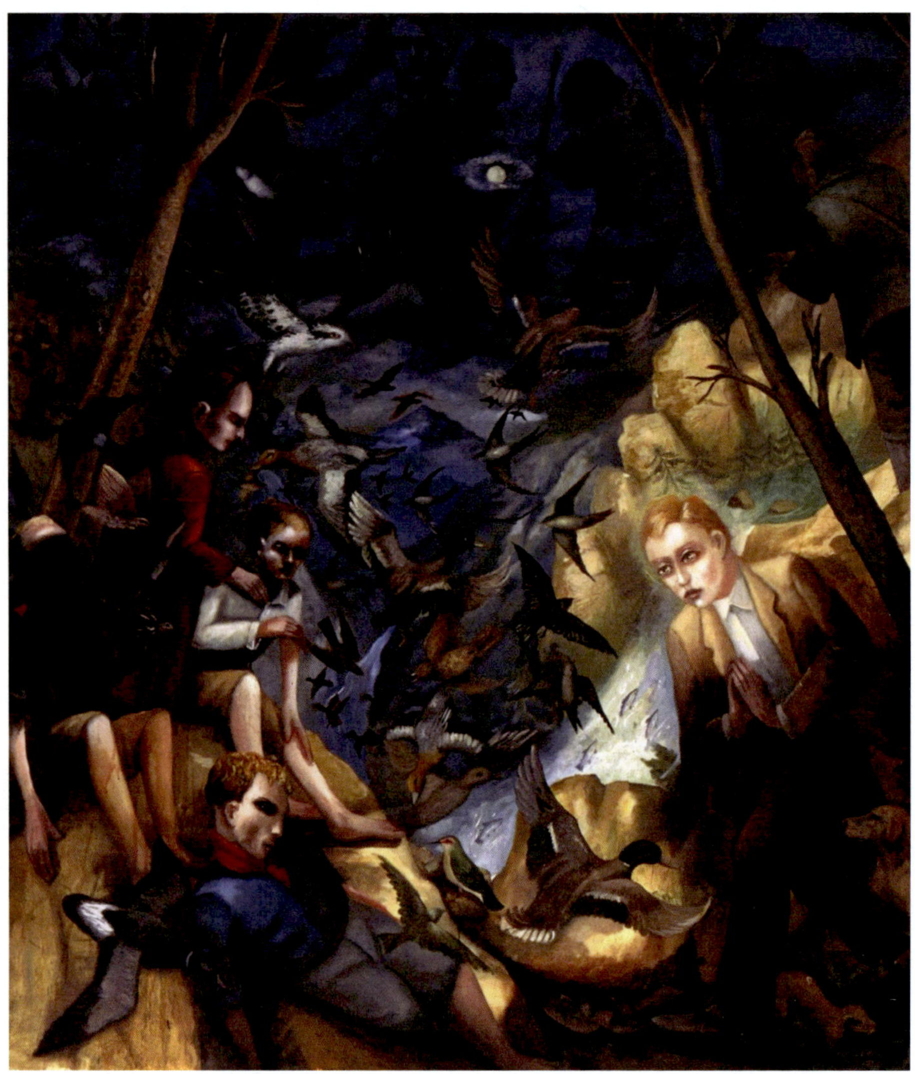

Painting in Defence of Migrants
1993
Oil on canvas, 272x256cm

Reproduced courtesy of the artist's estate

the basic strategy for breathing new life into figurative art. Certainly, like his contemporaries working in Germany, Italy and the States, Campbell could use the expressive power of raw painting to give his early work dynamic impact. But coming from performance art, where his main interest had been theatrical tableaux, Campbell realised more than most that the great strength of figurative art from Giotto onwards lay in its ability to present visual narrative.

From his study of the work of the great masters of narrative painting and his knowledge of the power of gesture and body language from performance, Campbell would set on a course of major paintings which was both challenging in its compositional inventiveness and intellectual wit. Broadly speaking, Campbell's paintings during the 1980s were developed in two consecutive stages and, although stylistically similar, each period had a different concern. The first stage, during his earlier time in New York, concentrated most particularly on the problems of pictorial narrative. In this case, how to paint pictures like the Old Masters, full of theatrical action and emotional drama but with a clear sense of distance and detachment. In his early 'Hiker' paintings, Campbell achieved this by the witty deployment of comic irony. Usually he would place his figures in some heroic romantic landscape but they would fail farcically to live up to their inspiring surroundings. For instead of being made of the stuff of ancient heroes, Campbell's figures were usually upper-class twits from the world of PG Wodehouse, who displayed to a comic degree all the basic failings and anxieties which we all tend to share. Added to this clash of comical contrasts, Campbell would also introduce the play-off of different pictorial languages so that in *Twas Once an Architect's Office in Wee Nook* (1984), for example, although we seem to be presented with a room drawn in traditional linear perspective, part of the interior is chaotically breaking up into a cubistic treatment of pictorial space. These early paintings of Campbell's are successful on many different levels and are extremely amusing examples of Freud's definition of humour, where there is a seemingly internal logic, but this begins to break down through the clash of irreconcilable forces.

In the later 1980s, when he had now become a master in the art of picture-making, Campbell turned his attention to another challenge. Now he began to address much more directly the complex aesthetic and philosophical issue of pictorial illusionism. The paintings of this period dealt openly with philosophical ideas of truth and image. In fact, the earlier 'hiking' characters in Campbell's paintings, such as Hunt and Van Helsing, were now supplemented by philosophers like the followers of David Hume and Michel Foucault. Art and philosophy directly confronted each other in such pictures as *Two Naturalist Philosophers Debating in a Garden* (1985) or *Bonjour M. Foucault* (1985). In these works, the potential chaos of the earlier pictures operates at a far deeper level of uncertainty. In the 'philosophical' paintings, much inspired by the ideas of Foucault, the language of communicating intellectual, moral and social ideas, the relationship between sign and signified, between knowledge and truth, is held up for scrutiny and found very much to be wanting. Yet this does not mean that these pictures are hopelessly pessimistic: on the contrary, the very flexibility and lack of a one-to-one relationship in contemporary representational painting allowed Campbell to produce works full of inventiveness and stimulating wit. Campbell could clearly see Foucault's point that, in a world where intellectual and moral certainties were a delusion, where two and two could be anything you want them to be, then art can, like everything else, be made to represent practically anything the artist wishes. As Picasso pointed out, it is the power of the artist to convince which really matters. So in the painted world, the seemingly most innocent thing – an abstract mark, for example – can take on all kinds of ominous significance within a specially created narrative context. Campbell demonstrates this in the painting *Portrait of Rorschach Testing Himself and Finding Himself Guilty* (1986), where the great scientific reader of signs is horrified to find a blood-stain on his own hand.

Eventually Campbell began to tire of these philosophical problem paintings and, by the end of the 1980s, he was looking for a way to bring his art back to dealing more directly with the intrinsic language and role of painting itself. He returned to Scotland and, in 1990, he began to put together his major one-man Scottish show, *On Form and Fiction* at the Third Eye Centre in Glasgow. This was an amazing multi-layered extravaganza, more a giant installation than a normal art exhibition. It consisted of 12 large paintings framed, labelled and spot-lighted in conventional museum fashion, while the rest of the gallery walls were covered with 150 small monochrome preparatory-type drawings. With such a presentation, this was not a straight painting exhibition but more an exhibition about the nature and status of painting itself. Two influential figures seemed to have been the inspiration for *On Form and Fiction*. On the one hand, there was Duchamp who pointed out the 'fiction' of art: that its cultural status lies not in how it relates to life and nature but how it relates to the institutionalised context in which you find it. On the other, there was Ruskin, who wished the 'form' that art took had 'some equivalent expression for the trouble and wrath of life'. This dialectical tension between the autonomous condition of modern art and its historical purpose to reflect on the 'trouble and wrath of life' has been the main motivating power behind Campbell's work in the 1990s. Unfortunately, many people who visited the Third Eye exhibition only saw the 'fiction' and judged it as another example of post-Duchampian neo-conceptual art. They missed the whole Ruskinian dimension, where Campbell was searching for a way back to an appropriate language for subject painting based on the great traditions in art, where universal ideas and emotions about human life and society within the natural order of things could be seriously addressed.

After *On Form and Fiction*, Campbell must have felt like his *Two Men in Search of Simplicity*. He needed to get back to basics. He temporarily put aside his brushes and began to make pictures out of what he regarded as the most common and unlikely material he could think of – string. Again, the twin spirits of Duchamp and Ruskin might be seen to be at work here. There was, on the one hand, the Duchampian belief that whatever object or material an artist chooses is by association turned into a work of art. On the Ruskinian side, because these string collages were so labour-intensive and so hand-crafted, the sheer process of making, the 'honest toil' involved, gave them artistic and moral authority. They certainly were not Whistleresque trifles!

Yet Campbell's string collages also challenge Ruskin's ideas on truth and beauty. This can be seen in one of the early works, appropriately entitled *Fake Ophelia* (1991). Campbell clearly had Millais's Pre-Raphaelite painting of the same subject in mind, a picture which Ruskin greatly admired for its 'truth to Nature'. Yet it is Millais's painting which is the real fake; in fact, it deals with a scene in *Hamlet* which the audience never sees. Furthermore, Millais paints with all the illusionistic mimetic tricks at his disposal. By contrast, Campbell's version of *Ophelia* with its string water, paper flowers and tapestry farmstead, presents the process of its making as openly as the nude figure displays herself across the picture. All art by its very nature is artifice but if the artist makes us aware of how the artifice works, then truth is respected and a different kind of beauty from that found in nature is created.

A contemporary artist like Campbell cannot draw his inspiration directly from nature as Ruskin urged artists to do in the 19th century. So where does Campbell look instead? Some answers are indicated in another of the string collages called *Artist's Chair* (1990–1). In this picture, we see a Francis Bacon-type room with a chair placed against a red-curtained background; all is very theatrical to emphasise the artificiality of the scene. As in van Gogh's painting of his chair, no one is physically present, emphasising the isolation the artist must endure during his periods of creativity. At such times, all the artist has for company are his intense feelings and creative thoughts as represented by the smoke rising genie-like from the bottle beside the chair and his own past achievements as seen in the painting propped up on the chair. Yet the artist is never completely alone, for he will always imaginatively keep company with his illustrious predecessors such as van Gogh, Bacon and Matisse whose presence is also felt through the *papier-collé* type flowers which pattern the floor.

Steven Campbell has always been a serious student of the history of art and, by the time of the Third Eye Centre exhibition, he was even more committed to the idea that his work should continue his investigation into the language of painting as found in the great tradition of academic and modern art. In his most recent paintings that followed on from the collages, this art historical awareness has continued to an even greater degree. These new pictures broadly follow the academic approach to painting. They were produced in two stages. Firstly, there are the smaller works on paper which are much more directly personal, dealing with the artist's thoughts and feelings about his own experience and reflections on things. Then, following on from these works are the large canvases, some of which are truly monumental in scale, which develop the various themes found in the smaller works but elevated onto a far grander, more universal scale of significance. These large canvases deal with the great themes in European art such as human desires, injustice, dispossession and death – the last of which is very much focused on the recurring figure of St Sebastian.

Fortunately because he is such a consummate picture-maker and the works are so passionately infused with Campbell's own distinctive way of looking at the world, these new paintings do not creak at the seams like some worn-out machine or appear to be yet another smart-ass piece of post-modern eclecticism. Nor has the humorous side of his imagination deserted him. This can be seen in *Two Women and an Otter* (1992). In this work, we view the interior of a room with the female nude – the arch trope of academic painting – as the dominant presence. One woman turns away from looking at herself in a triple mirror to acknowledge our voyeuristic interest; her body is fragmented in a cubist manner by the multi-mirror reflection. Another nude woman sits with her back to us but is aware of our presence from the mirror she gazes into. She is by contrast untouched by the surrounding mirrors and is painted as the classical ideal of passive female beauty. The male need to possess such beauty is present in the form of a young man who is trapped against a side wall. He is unable to reach the object of his desire because there is an obstructing tank of water in front of him containing a hungry otter. The otter, like the young man, is also frustrated because the fish it would like to devour is safely swimming in a separate tank below his one. Such a weird but inventive picture reveals Campbell's creative powers at their most assured. Not only does the painting demonstrate his supreme skill as a picture-maker and pictorial narrator but also his profound understanding of the work of earlier masters such as Van Eyck, Velázquez, Ingres, Picasso, Matisse, not to mention filmmakers like Hitchcock and Welles. He even has time to make a mocking comment on contemporary neo-conceptual artists like Damien Hirst.

The looking-glass world of such paintings as *Two Women and an Otter* fairly sparkles with pictorial inventiveness but it has to be said that the overall tenor of Campbell's new body of work tends towards a darker, more tragic view of things. In many of these new paintings, there are sinister, ominous forces at work threatening chaos and destruction. For instance, in the *Croatian Blouse after Matisse's Romanian Blouse* (1992), we see a naked man and woman in their seemingly safe domestic interior but, above them in the attic from where we view them, there are all kinds of dark presences which are beginning to seep onto the vulnerable couple below in the form of dripping blood stains. In another painting,

Murder Running through the Woods (1993), a similar theme of outside barbaric forces about to destroy civilised society is treated within the grand tradition of heroic landscape painting, which Campbell takes from such 16th- and 17th-century masters as Titian and Poussin. Yet balanced with these dark paintings, where violence and anarchy are about to take over, there is also the portrayal of the reconciliatory power of nature and the enduring human spirit to survive such destructive forces. This idea is celebrated in *Painting in Defence of Migrants*, where all those who have been driven from the love and protection of their homes and families, come together like the surrounding migrant birds to find a new spirit of human community amongst the protective world of nature high above the savagery from which they have fled. Some may say, of course, that such a work as *Painting in Defence of Migrants* (1993) is a false dream and that reality is very different. That is a point for debate. As far as Campbell is concerned, however, an artist must not only, in Ruskin's words, seek to find 'some equivalent expression for the trouble and wrath of life, for its sorrow' but also its 'mystery'. And the strength of the human spirit to endure is one such great mystery of life.

In his latest works, Steven Campbell shows himself as a painter who not only has great ambition for the continual development of his art, but also possesses the imagination and skill to fulfil these ambitions. Campbell has always shown himself to be a painter of supreme inventive wit. Now, with the more profoundly serious tone of these new works, he begins to reveal the concerned wisdom of his artistic vision.

This essay was written by Bill Hare in 1993 and published by *Contemporary Visual Art*, Volume 1, No. 4.

Henry Kondracki

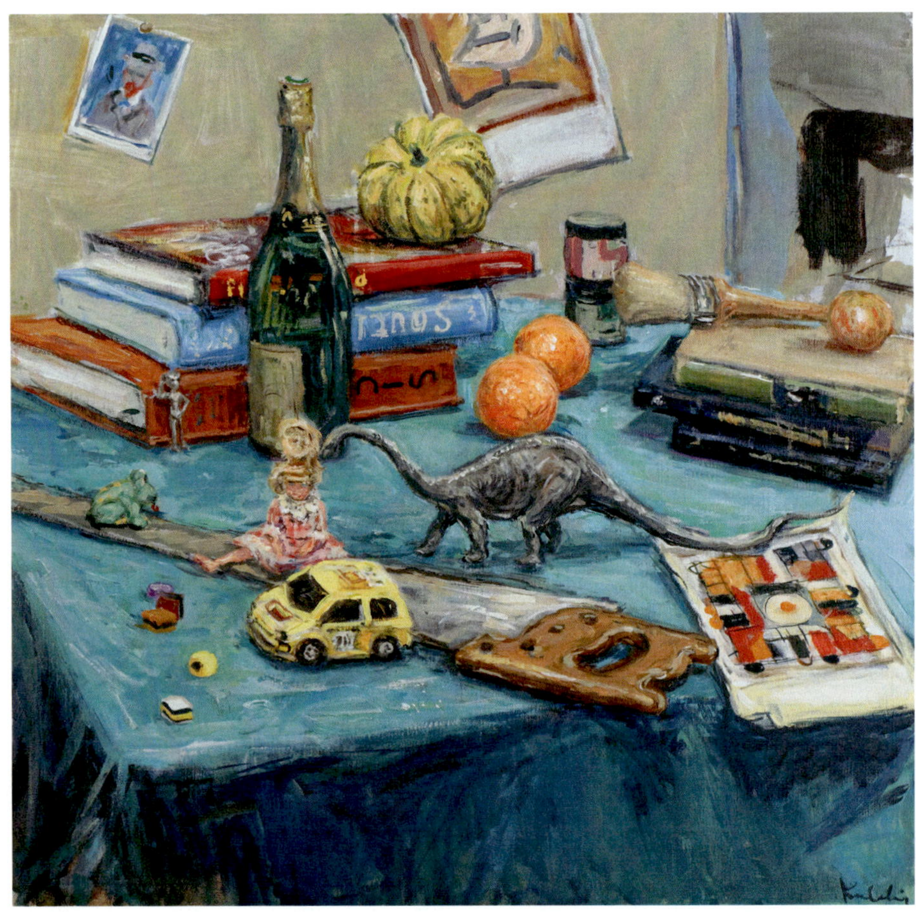

Still Life with Toys
2014
Oil on canvas, 28x28cm
Reproduced courtesy of the artist

Henry Kondracki – Magical Moments

HENRY KONDRACKI WAS trained in the 1980s at two of the leading
London art colleges – Byam Shaw and Slade School of Art – and was an
outstanding student and first-class graduate. The basis of the training
he received there has remained with him throughout his subsequent
career. Thus, with such an academic background, he always needs to
work from an observed subject which will initially be either sketched
and/or photographed. These preliminary studies will then be built up
and developed into their fully enlarged vision by traditional academic
procedures, with great care and attention given to sound foundational
pictorial structure through spatial composition and colour coordination.
Yet there is nothing dry or pedantic about Kondracki's art even if he has
to go through a prolonged struggle to gain the overall effect he desires.
Thus, although they are deeply considered and rigorously worked (and
reworked), Kondracki's paintings miraculously retain a spontaneous
vitality which makes such an immediate visual and emotional impact on
the delighted viewer.

While Kondracki's practice is founded on traditional technical studio
skills and values, the raw and sensual impact that his manner of painting
makes on our tactile and emotional sensitivities is the means by which
the 'primitive' operates within his art. It should readily be pointed out,
however, that the concept of the primitive here has nothing to do with the
usual tribal masks or prehistoric cave painting association, the likes of
which are normally found in art historical discourse on this topic. On the
contrary, the true nature of the primitive in modern art is not historical
or geographical but psychological – that constant quest for new ways
and means to tap into and realise original authentic 'feeling' through the
poetic powers of human creativity.

From the outset of the modern artistic period, avant-garde artists
realised – by their radical rejection of the previous conventional mimetic
role of picture-making and also through their innovative experimentation
in new techniques for depicting different kinds of subjects – that painting
could and should be an active means of expression and not merely a
passive medium for description. Kondracki continues to work within this
admirable modernist tradition. Through his long-developed knowledge
and instinctive understanding of the nature of modern painting,
Kondracki fully appreciates and relentlessly pursues this expressive
potential in painting. With such a rigorous approach to his art, this
enables him not only to depict his particular subjects with all their
distinctively appealing characteristics but also to delve beneath the surface
of visual appearances, in order to release deeper and more powerful
psychological truths about our own primitive emotional relationships
with our everyday lives and experiences.

It is one of the tragic misunderstandings of our present age that the primitive has become almost exclusively associated with the origins of human sexuality – restricted to the popular notion of the Freudian domain of the libidinous id in our subconscious. This is both a great disservice to Freud's ideas and a gross distortion of the true nature of the primitive, which is infinitely more concerned with the magical than the sexual. It is this magical aura of the primitive that permeates Henry Kondracki's art. Having a slightly different ethnic background and upbringing from the Scottish culture in which he lives, Kondracki retains the ambivalent position of being both an inside participant and outside observer of the social world he inhabits. As an artist, however, this fortuitously gives him the uncanny ability in his painting to transform the seemingly ordinary into the extraordinary, the familiar into the fabulous.

With such an open and flexible perspective, Henry Kondracki's art can also enable us to regain the power to see our world again through the fresh wide eyes of the child who is the collective unconscious source of the primitive in all of us. When gazing at Kondracki's pictures, we are granted that rare and precious opportunity to reconnect with our childhood innocence and wonderment. As such, we find in these paintings that the normal laws and effects of time and space appear to be suspended, and every detail of form, light and atmosphere is treated with equal excessive attentiveness and awe. Thus, with our innate visionary senses refreshed and our inner eyes restored, we are invited to shed our usual self-conscious relationship with the material and factual world and again become totally engrossed and lost in the magical world of our imagination and personal memories.

The last word, however, should go to Henry Kondracki himself, who made this artist's statement for my book, *Contemporary Painting in Scotland*, in 1992:

> I attempt to portray the beauty, ugliness and extraordinariness of everyday living. I build images that are a synthesis of thought, memory, emotion, fact and fiction.

This essay was written by Bill Hare in 2010 and published by The Scottish Gallery, Edinburgh.

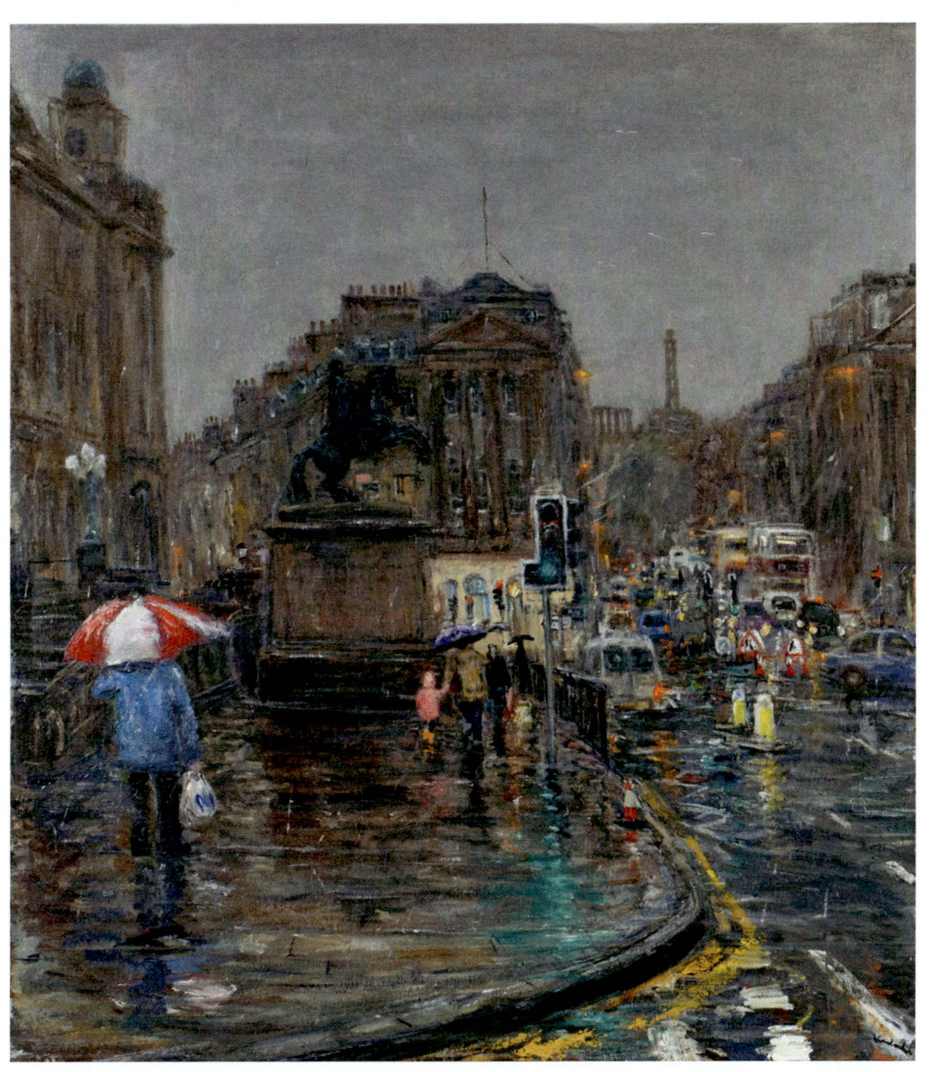

Wellington Statue
2009
Oil on jute, 150x133cm
Reproduced courtesy of the artist

Ken Currie

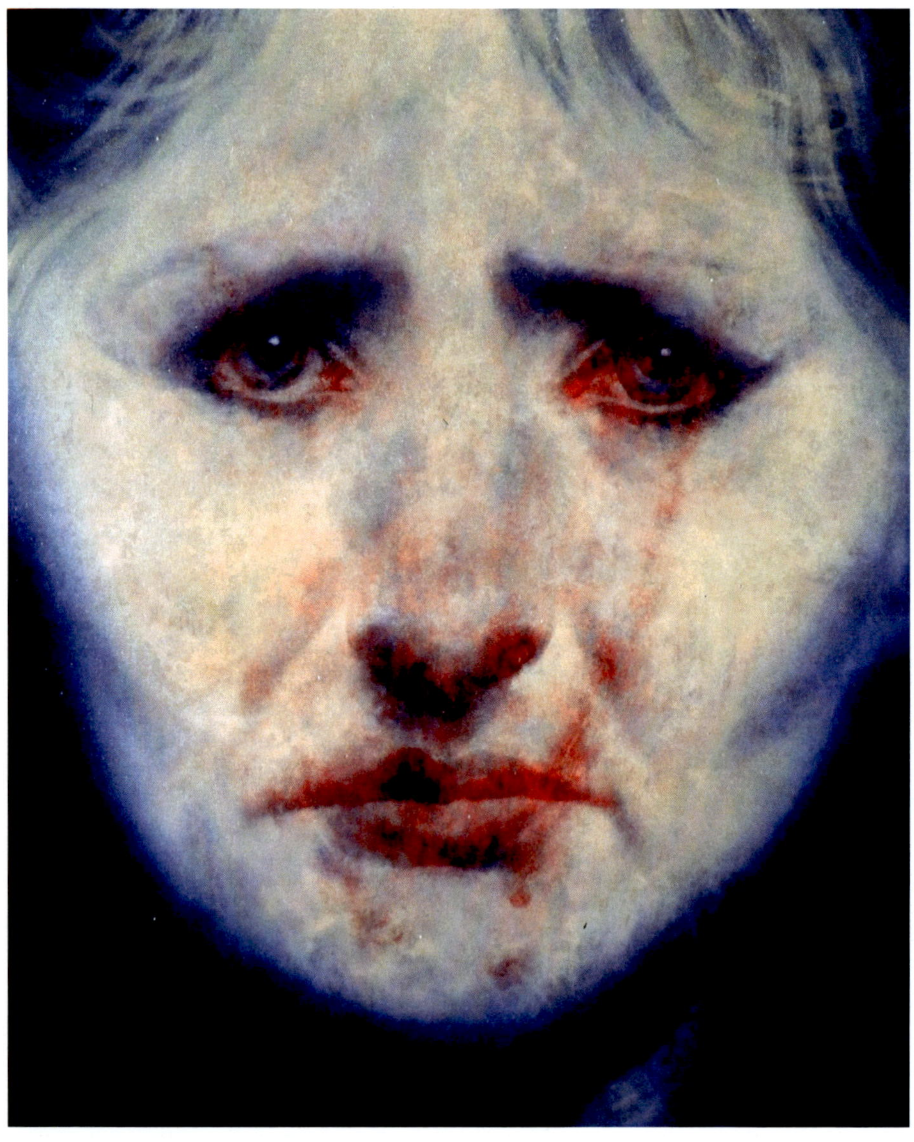

I Saw the World
2000
Oil on canvas, 183x152cm
Reproduced courtesy of the artist

Ken Currie Interview

*Ken, you have just had another successful London exhibition. Since the
1980s, you have regularly shown there and in Berlin but rarely in Scotland.
In fact, you have not had a Scottish exhibition for nearly ten years. Why?*
It's still impossible to maintain a full-time commitment to painting in
Scotland without representation in London. We continue to lack a large
enough gallery infrastructure to support independent artistic activity
without resorting to subsidised income from teaching and public awards.
So, in order to sustain my work as a painter I have to show regularly in
London and abroad and to some extent have neglected my responsibilities
to exhibit in my own country. However, I would argue that the neglect
is mutual. There have simply been no offers to exhibit in Scotland since
1992. In fact, I have not had a solo exhibition of new paintings in my
native city of Glasgow for 13 years – which is ironic when you consider
how closely my work is associated with the city. I think this is mostly to
do with the reaction against the new Glasgow figurative painting from
the end of the 1980s onwards and its eclipse by the Young British Artists
in London and their counterparts in Glasgow. Offers to exhibit in serious
galleries in Scotland have been non-existent.

*On the other hand, you still live and work as a full-time painter in
Scotland. Why, then, with so much international success have you
remained so attached to this particular place?*
I have travelled widely in Europe, a little bit in America. My feeling is that
life is pretty much the same in big cities in the developed world, especially
Europe. There are differences of scale, structure, custom and culture but,
in essence, things are pretty much the same. Glasgow is no exception. It is,
always has been and definitely always will be a seething, proletarian city
where a significant section of the population live life right on the edge.
Much has been made of Glasgow's cultural renaissance but the fact is
there are more heroin addicts in the city (around 10,000) than there are
artists. I find I cannot escape facts like that.

An unsponsored survey of the physical health of women found that the
worst place in the developed world for women's health was in the north of
Glasgow. This makes the city for me a kind of crucible of human activity,
a place to make significant observations about the human situation.
However, I am simultaneously repulsed and attracted to Glasgow. I loathe
Glaswegian populism, its stifling parochialism but love its profound
disregard for authority, its rebelliousness. I loathe its racist underbelly
but love its sense of solidarity, its ability to warmly embrace the 'other',
the outcast and the dispossessed. I loathe its almost pathological
egalitarianism which disallows discourse beyond populist assumptions but
love the Glaswegians' hostility to moral complacency and the passionate
belief in confrontational argument as a way of resolving contradiction.

For an artist like myself, Glasgow – like any other city – is about responding to the visibility of lives being lived in the flesh and blood here and now.

You came to early prominence during the mid-'8os with that whole trans-avant-garde phenomenon of the 'return to painting', 'neo-figuration', 'New Glasgow Boys' etc. Would you like to say anything about those times and make any comparison with the way you find the art scene today?
I think the most important point to underline here is the brevity of it all. As a group, the New Glasgow Painters' 'moment' was fleeting when compared to other more recent phenomena like the yba's who've gone on for years.

Looking back then, I would say there was much more of a feeling of energy, a 'buzz' if you like. Scottish art and culture generally was in the vanguard of the resistance to Thatcher in the '8os. Huge breakthroughs were being made by Scottish artists internationally and also, at long last, a modest infrastructure of new galleries began to emerge, all of which went on to benefit enormously from the recent generation of Glasgow based neo-conceptualists, whose success has now eclipsed anything ever achieved by the artists of the 1980s.

My work at that time was immature and unresolved. I always knew that painting was a very long game, a marathon as opposed to a sprint. I also knew that if your work became fashionable then it must, logically, become unfashionable and the real challenge was to find the resolve to continue working when no-one was interested in your work anymore.

I find the art world today dismal, an embarrassment. I agree fully with Donald Kuspit's recent observations – contemporary art is utterly decadent. Generally, we are witnessing a kind of moral and ideological collapse – a cultural malaise which has deepened since the end of Communism and pervades every fibre of life under capitalism. Art's crisis is terminal – the desperate strategies being deployed by artists now are merely part of an increasingly hysterical end-game. Art's radicalism has gone. It has surrendered, capitulated, become part of the spectacle. The artist meshes seamlessly with pop, advertising, celebrity, sensationalism, money, power, status. In Europe in the 1930s, to be an avant-garde artist usually meant that you were on a death list. Today in Britain, to be an avant-garde artist usually means that you're either on the short list or the guest list.

What do you think is meant by 'political artist' and do you still see yourself in those terms?
Politics, as I understand it, has ceased to exist as such since the fall of the Berlin Wall in 1989. Yet, paradoxically, 'political' artists are now the norm. In fact, it's impossible to be taken seriously by the establishment unless your work 'challenges assumptions', 'subverts traditional notions' and 'exposes underlying power structures'. This is a kind of Liberal Terror – any artist refusing to conform to the notion that the only thing art

should do is deal with 'issues' in an 'innovative' way is deemed unfit for public exposure. Yet art which is genuinely subversive and feral, genuinely politically radical is at best frowned upon, at worst, systematically ignored.

In my life, I have been both an artist and a political activist, often at the same time. I have been in the past involved with other artists whose idea of being a political artist is a cross between a social worker and a graphic designer. My experience now tells me that the whole idea of political art is futile. Political art is too readily absorbed and neutralised, too easily robbed of its momentary subversive power to have any actual political impact, which is surely its point. I feel there comes a decisive moment if engaged in political struggle where bodily you have to commit yourself. You, in the flesh, have to be there to exert physical and moral force in the environment in which your adversary operates. To do this, you have to give up art completely and never do it again. This is what I believe is necessary to become a political artist.

Having said that, I believe all great art is deeply political in that it has the power to induce a transcendent moment in the viewer – not, of course, in the mystical sense, more in terms of Marcuse's assertion that it has the power to present new horizons to the viewer and these can have profoundly political implications. This experience momentarily infuses the viewer with a deepened and heightened sensibility about the nature of the world, their place in it and how it might change.

Even by the end of the 1980s, a change in the development of your work was discernible, attachments to influential figures from earlier modern art – Léger and Rivera – being eclipsed by the likes of Giacometti and Bacon. What were the circumstances which brought about this marked shift in the direction of your work?
I had always been interested in Bacon and Giacometti, as early as 1980 in fact when I was still a student. They seemed to resonate with many of my literary, theatrical and cinematic interests at that time – Beckett, Sartre, Kafka, Tarkovsky. As I became more politically active as an art student my interests moved toward political art generally – in cinema, literature and painting and I began to absorb these influences. After moving on from a kind of realism, I gradually moved toward the more graphic work of Léger and Rivera, particularly their public works, and saw this as a kind of model for my own political concerns in the context of Scotland.

My work began to change after making several visits to Berlin in the late '80s, early '90s. These visits left a deep impression and altered the direction of my work, particularly after experiencing the contrast between seeing an exhibition of Léger's late work at the Whitechapel in London then seeing a huge Giacometti retrospective at the Neue Nationalgalerie in Berlin the next day. I exhibited in the city in 1988 and I remember being shaken by the contrast between the somewhat naïve, idealistic and romantic quality of my work and the chilling, historically loaded atmosphere of Berlin at the height of the Cold War. I think these brief encounters with such a great European city helped put my work and ideas into some kind of context, putting me in touch with much larger questions. The bold black outline disappeared and with it went a certain kind of political faith.

Frankly, the more I look at my work from the 1980s, the work that I became known for, and still am to this day, the more distance I gain from this period, the more I realise that all this work was a kind of detour from my instinctive concerns as a painter.

Who and what are now the major art historical influences on your painting?
I recently visited Oslo and saw both the Munch Museum as well as the National Gallery's collection of Munch's painting there. The rawness of the imagery unsettled me. They retain a psychological intensity way ahead of their time and confirm Munch's absolute radicalism as an artist.

A subsequent visit to Berlin to see the epic 'German Art in the 20th Century' exhibition at various galleries throughout the city confirmed my belief in the supremacy of 20th century German painting. It towers above everything else. In particular, the physical presence and aura of the works of Anselm Kiefer left me overwhelmed, not only in terms of their Pollock-like grandeur but also in terms of the historical scope of their subject matter. I also began to look seriously at Gerhard Richter for the first time, particularly his so-called photo-based works.

Last year, I visited the Prado and looked at Velázquez, Goya, Zurbarán, Ribera, El Greco, Brueghel and van der Weyden. I came to the conclusion that the Prado was quite simply the greatest painting museum in the world. I felt ashamed I had not been there when I was younger. Whilst in Madrid, I also saw *Guernica* in the Museo Reina Sofía. This is so obviously Picasso's greatest work, I really can't understand why so many people dismiss it. An immense painting, which has to be seen in the flesh to really be felt and understood – more than just a painting but, in fact, the National War Memorial for the defeated Republican cause. Seeing Goya, Velázquez, Picasso, together in the Spanish capital I suddenly realised that these artists constitute the most powerful national school in European painting.

The most recent influence was after a visit to the Tate Modern in London. Now, the Tate Modern is a curatorial disaster – you could call it London's GOMA – but in spite of that there's the Rothko room. The installation at the Tate is one of the most powerful artistic experiences available in Britain. I saw not decorative abstracts but images – gateways, sarcophagi, surrogate figures, shrouds. The word sublime is often carelessly bandied about these days but the Rothko room at the Tate Modern is a sublime experience, with its intimations of mortality, awe and terror – I could feel Aeschylus hovering somewhere.

Let us now turn to your most recent painting as shown in your London exhibition. I suppose the most striking thing about your new pictures is their content. In the past, your subject matter was drawn from socio-political history or your observations of social (or anti-social) community lived and fought out in the work place or on the streets. Now your paintings concentrate on isolated figures or even fragments of the human anatomy set against a dark void. Why this shift from the social and political to the individual and symbolic?

I can't offer a concise explanation in this context. However, I sense a subtext in your question, hinting at a suggestion of an abandonment of robustly held political positions in favour of hazy, liberal-bourgeois universalities. Bear in mind that many of the most recent works, although depicting lone individuals in decontextualised 'voids', are implicitly political in that they seek to represent aspects of the experience of those condemned to live on the margins. In that sense there is no shift from the social and political.

I have to say I feel your paintings have become much stronger because they have become much more 'visual'. Yet, conversely, they also are very challenging and difficult, if not painful, to look at. Is this a conscious move on your part and, if so, why?

I absolutely want to force a visual engagement with the viewer – but to hold their gaze, then mercilessly terrorise their complacency and unsettle them. Matisse, in his dotage, declared that art should be like a comfy armchair and certainly here in Scotland this myopic philosophy has been taken to extremes.

This is an intensely complex question for me. It goes right to the heart of what I'm trying to do as a painter. I want the viewer to be simultaneously attracted and repulsed by my work in the same glance. My aim is to provoke anxiety and discomfort in the act of looking.

By the way, I think my paintings have *always* been visual, how could they be anything else?

Your evocation of immense space and deep stillness in your paintings does profoundly disturb those who confront the pictures. The Romantic concept of the sublime immediately comes to mind and its fascination with terror. Is there an element of terrorisation in your approach to your art?

Edmund Burke listed qualities which embody the sublime, among them, vastness, emptiness, darkness, infinity. He believed that the corollary of experiencing these qualities was terror and awe. As you say, such ideas were at the heart of Romanticism, yet I've always felt that in the work of staunch classicists like David, one could also experience a feeling of awe and terror which could be described as sublime, for example, in *Death of Marat*. Although I don't see myself as a Romantic painter, I do want to overwhelm and terrorise the viewer but I want the feeling of terror to provoke a new way of seeing the world and to ultimately force the viewer to confront certain existential and ontological truths.

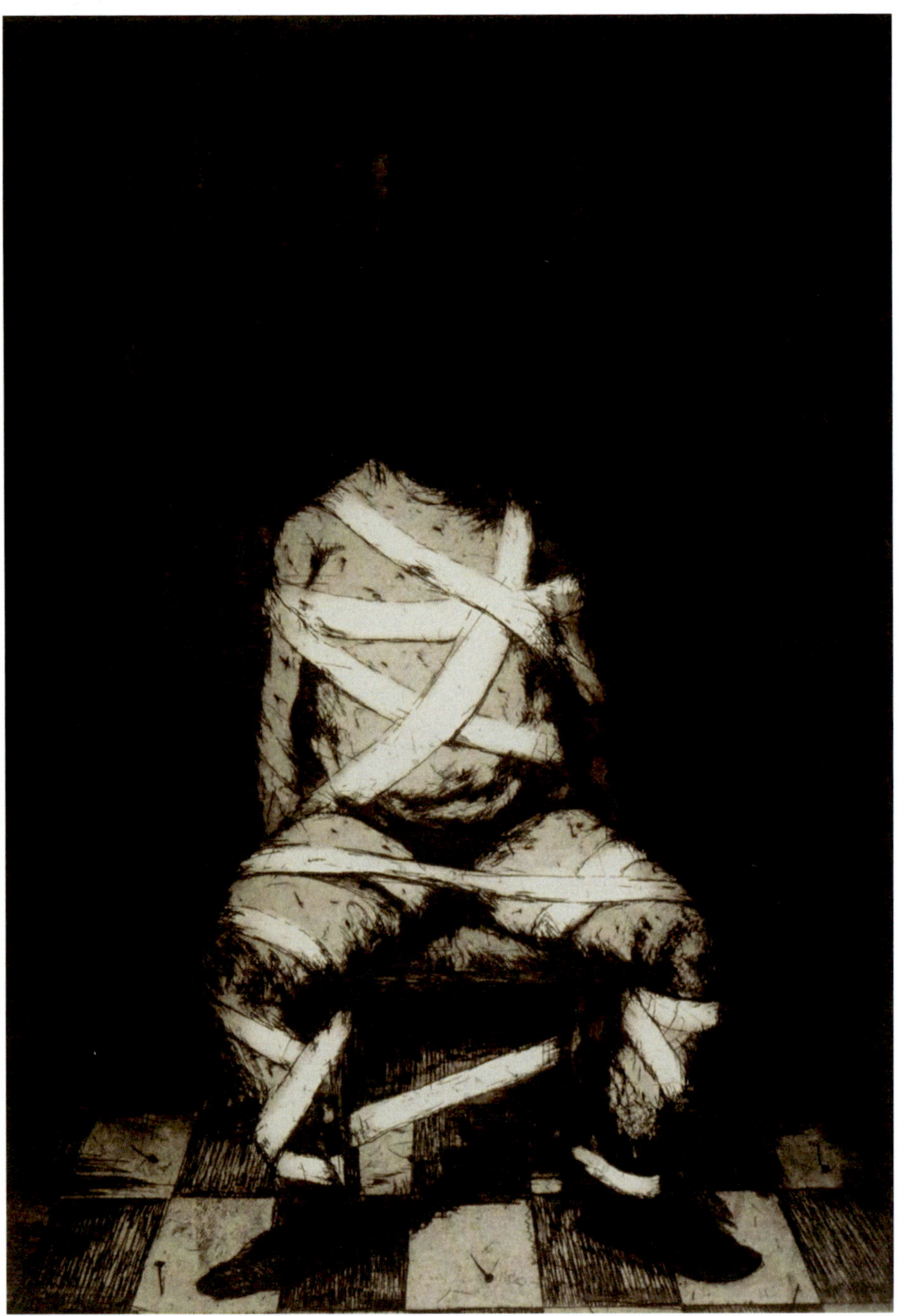

Knowledge is Power
1992
Etching, 30x21cm
Reproduced courtesy of the artist

Sometimes the sources for your subject matter and imagery are very obscure. How important is contextual knowledge to the appreciation of your painting?

I think my paintings work on different levels and communicate different things to different people. The cognoscenti may detect art historical or theoretical subtexts, the general art gallery-going public may miss this but respond more instinctively to the imagery in each individual subjective way. The capacity for misinterpretation is enormous although I like to keep the work as open as possible and not close it down with 'explanations'. All I really want is for the viewer to get the same rush of adrenaline in looking at the work as I got when the ideas first came to me. If that experience is enriched by a familiarity with the contextual references, then that's all to the good.

You are one of the most articulate artists I know and you have regularly written very lucidly on your own work in the past. I notice, however, that you did not write your recent catalogue essay. Is this an indication that you now have more confidence in your paintings to let them speak directly and individually to different people, that there is not a 'right and wrong' answer to their meaning? Furthermore, are you also allowing critics to have their say and earn their living?

I have never volunteered to write about my work and, in fact, I actually resent having to do so and probably never will again. But, for some reason, I have always been asked to provide statements, more so than any other artist I know in fact. Perhaps this has been to do with the contentious nature of my work and ideas – people demand explanations. I also feel that there is a growing mistrust of the work of art critics among the viewing public generally. I sympathise with this. The vast bulk of writing about art these days is dull, dense and esoteric and fails to connect with the public. They have busy lives and are often careworn. They want ideas presented lucidly and coherently with all traces of condescension removed. Sometimes they don't want to hear about what an artist is trying to do through a third party, they want to hear it from the artists themselves.

The fact that I have written about my work was never meant to detract from the aspect of purely visual communication. I have always had confidence in my paintings' ability to speak directly and individually to different people. I think in my most recent work I am looking for a response that is almost like a physical sensation – an 'assault directly on the nervous system' as Francis Bacon used to say. I am relying on the viewer's own intuition and intellect to explore their possible meanings and associations.

I have never disallowed critics to have their say with regard to my work and my paintings remain permanently open to critique.

This interview was conducted by Bill Hare in 2001 and published by *Cencrastus*, issue 70.

Peter Thomson

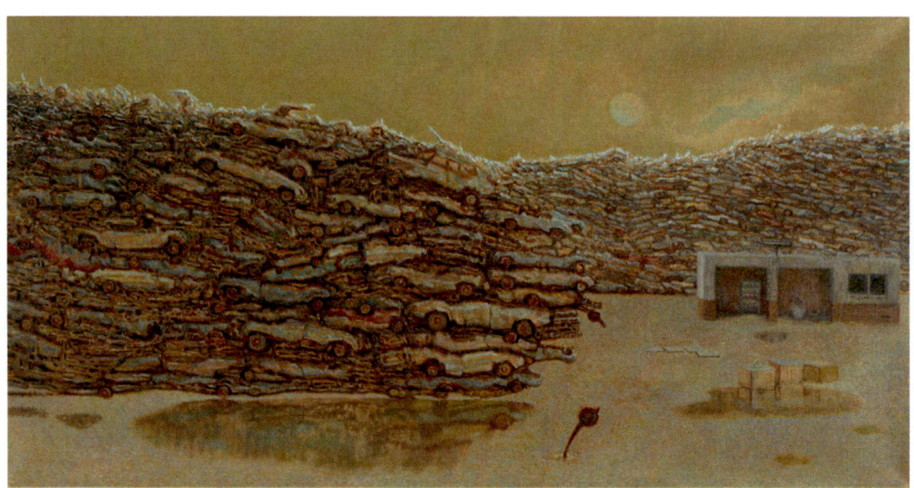

Scrapyard Full Moon

2015

Oil on linen, 45x100cm

Reproduced courtesy of the artist

Peter Thomson – Uncanny Scot

The uncanny is frightening precisely because it is not known and yet familiar.
Sigmund Freud, 'The Uncanny' (1919)

PAINTING'S ENDLESS APPEAL lies in the way it can satisfy a vast range
of desires in the human heart. Its most obvious attraction is painting's
seemingly miraculous ability to reproduce the visual reality of the world
through its highly mimetic descriptive powers. Yet over and above this,
painting can, by the abstract qualities of colour, shape and line, not only
describe but formally stimulate our intuitive response to the subject
painted. The sense and sensibility of painting empowers us to have
both an intellectual and emotional relationship with the things outside
and inside ourselves. Yet when these two sides – the objective and the
subjective – become blurred and overlaid, then a feeling of uncertainty
and anxiety begins to disturb our nervous system and our everyday
equilibrium. This unsettling experience, which all of us have encountered
in one way or another, falls under the domain and the sway of what Freud
termed the 'uncanny'.

This peculiar but commonly experienced sensation is a modern
phenomenon and is probably an offshoot of what both Marx and Jung
diagnosed in our contemporary society as social and psychic alienation. In
European literature, for example, we associate the uncanny with the writings
of Hoffman, Kafka and Beckett and, in the visual arts, there is also a shared
interest in similar themes – as found in the work of de Chirico, Magritte and
Bacon, which is further echoed in the cinema of Buñuel, Hitchcock and
Lynch. If we turn to Scottish culture, the uncanny is clearly a distinctive
feature in the writings of Hogg and Stevenson through to Muriel Spark
and Alasdair Gray. On the other hand, in the area of Scottish painting
the fascination with the uncanny is less readily discerned but there are,
however, a few distinguished predecessors to Peter Thomson, such as
James Cowie and Robert Colquhoun.

Freud's essay on the uncanny is still the most imaginative and
perceptive on the subject. In it, he distinguishes between the merely
sensational and the truly uncanny, where the latter is genuinely unsettling
because we are simultaneously experiencing both the unknown and the
familiar in a disorientating fashion. This is also the case with the subjects
and settings in Peter Thomson's sometimes socially satirical, but always
psychologically subversive paintings. Unlike the bizarre world of Salvador
Dalí for instance, Thomson's figures inhabit spaces that are imaginative
extensions of our own mundane environments, be they cinemas, bars and
cafés, hotel foyers, waiting rooms, football arenas, parks or seashores.
Yet what makes the presentation of these pictorial settings so disturbing
is the slight but crucial manipulation and disruption of our normal
expectations. For instance, one of the distinguishing features of the

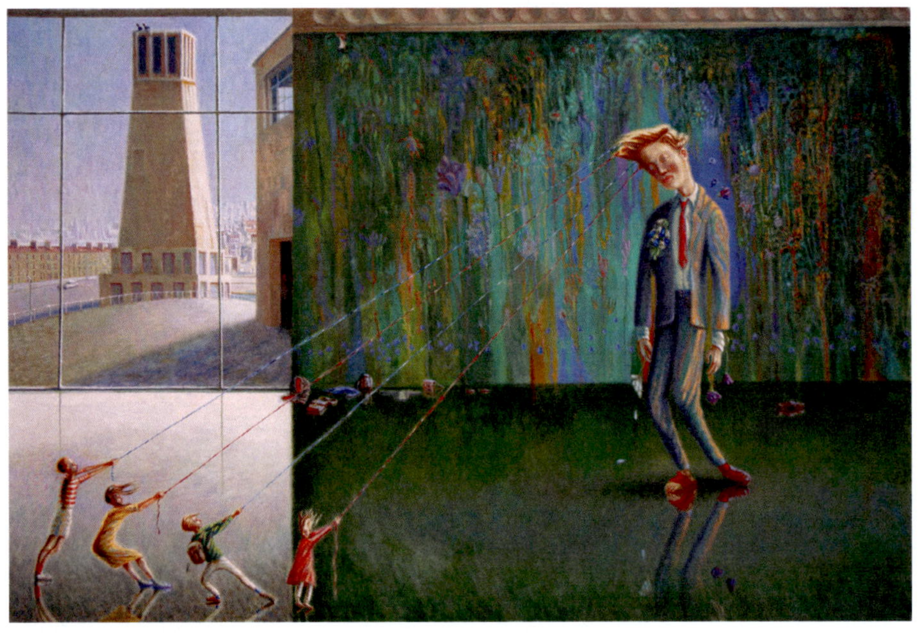

Nursery Games
2014
Oil on canvas, 35x50cm

Reproduced courtesy of the artist

uncanny is what Freud terms 'the compulsion to repeat'. This is clearly evidenced in Thomson's pictures, where it is not only the endless rows of uniformly dressed figures that express this all-pervasive sense of the repetitious but, more significantly, the actions of the figures themselves. Unlike conventional pictorial narrative in which the protagonists act out their preordained destinies, in the uncanny world of Thomson, actions seem to accomplish nothing and are required to be repeated – as with Sisyphus – endlessly. Furthermore, the striking use of perspective employed by Thomson is always slightly off-kilter and thus everything is made to feel unstable and in a permanent state of uncertainty. Added to this compositional disequilibrium is Thomson's subtle manipulation of scale which again fails to grant the viewer the usual reassurance – as, for instance, with Renaissance pictures – that everything is fixed and in its place. Look closely at Thomson's pictures and everywhere the spatial relationships between figures, objects and settings are full of ambiguity and uncertainty. What we are presented with is an obsessive image of another world which seems to have emerged from behind the mask of conventional appearances and is now beginning to take on a life of its own in which rational order no longer holds sway. According to Freud, and this certainly applies to the pictures of Peter Thomson, the uncanny is where the normal and the abnormal, the expected and the unexpected, the natural and the supernatural, the waking and the dream world collide and synthesise into a new kind of highly intensive visual reality.

As with the dreamscapes of de Chirico, which were painted around the same period as Freud's essay, the most striking quality of Thomson's images is not primarily the subject but the claustrophobic or agoraphobic spaces in which the action, if any, takes place. It is through these familiar, yet incongruous, settings that the eerie, but intriguing atmosphere of the artist's imagined world is poetically evoked. With his weird and wonderful use of vivid and arresting colour, the artist produces such strange lighting effects that we seem to be looking through a distorting tinted glass lens at another distantly remembered world. The painter draws us into this fascinating ambience by a mixture of immediate curiosity and profound empathy on our part. Yet the experience is an uneasy tension between desire and dread. Here we can never be certain of anything. Where are we? Who or what are these strange creatures? Are they human like ourselves or mechanical aliens merely dressed up to look like us? Finally, what are these seemingly dysfunctional figures doing and what does it all mean? With the uncanny, these questions and doubts race through the mind and higgledy-piggledy pile up on top of each other. Thomson's enigmatic pictures are, however, not there to be explained away but, on the contrary, to transform our normal rationality into an exhilarating mixture of sublime bewilderment and inexplicable longing. Surely this is the stuff that dreams are made of.

In the uncanny art of Peter Thomson, we are not served up the predictable quotidian reality we are all too familiar with but, rather, the one that is intriguingly unfamiliar and yet faintly recognisable at the same time. We are presented not with our material world but its metaphysical double, which only our dreams and the poetic genius of art have the power to conjure up. Such a parallel universe is to be found in the enigmatic and elusive paintings of Peter Thomson which can either terrify us witless like recurring nightmares and make us scurry back to our world of the safe and the predictable; or they can free our minds to all kinds of other possibilities, where the constricting divisions between reality and the imagination fade away.

This essay was written by Bill Hare in 2006 and published by Lemon Street Gallery, Truro.

Paul Reid

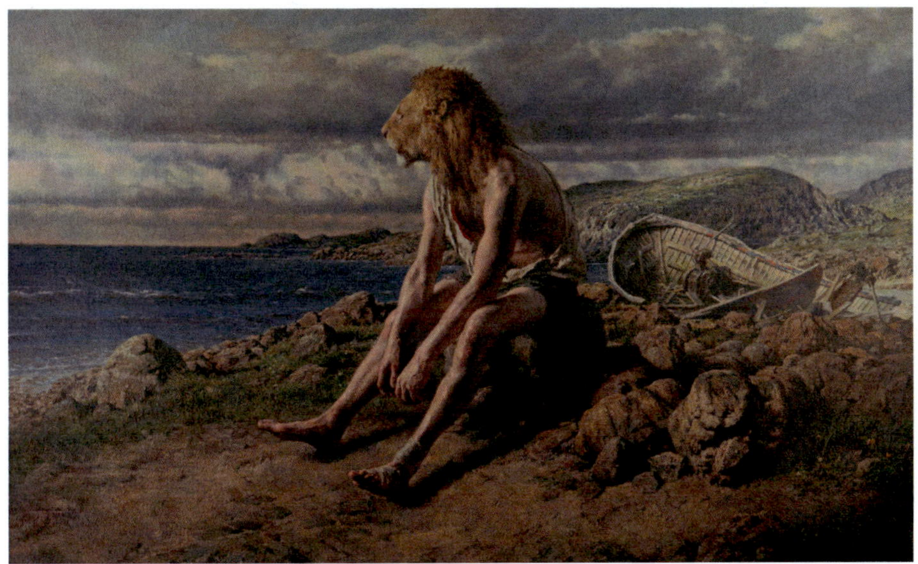

Stranded on the Island of Circe
2014
Oil on canvas, 65x105cm
Reproduced courtesy of the artist

Myth and the Art of Paul Reid

THE ART OF PAUL REID's mythological painting appears to have the miraculous power to transform poetic fancy into visual fact. This truly amazing effect is not, however, created by the painter through mimetic trickery but, rather, such transformation comes about as a result of the intense commitment and imaginative creativity which the artist bestows on every aspect of every picture he paints. He never aims merely to illustrate his carefully selected ancient mythic tales. On the contrary, it is through the long-evolved strategies of his art practice and the distinctive nature of his own interpretative approach to his subject that he is able to construct the appropriate schema for pictorially visualising the intriguing allure and the potent power of myth in such a visually poetic yet realistic manner.

The fascinating but enigmatic figures in Paul Reid's painted versions of the mythic tales even when they are captured in some freeze-frame action as if they were actors in an elaborately staged tableau – have a distanced, introspective feel to them. Removed from their familiar narrative context, they seem lost in their own private thoughts and appear to have turned away from us and our world. This alienated attitude may be their response to the fact that the myths have long lost most of their former significance and relevance to our modern age. Now they are mainly regarded as little more than sensational and spectacular stories, full of unbridled sex and violence, to be readily exploited for their entertainment and commercial value by Hollywood and the like. These dismissive and exploitative attitudes towards mythology are nothing new but have a long and recurring history. It was Plato who probably began this hostility towards the myths, accusing them of being dangerous, mendacious fabrications. Since then, every subsequent dominant ideology – whether philosophical, monotheistic, political or scientific – have all, in their different ways and for different reasons wished to discredit and undermine the power of mythology, regarding it as either a dangerous impediment, a subversive threat or, at the very least, an irrelevant distraction to the rational chronological course of human history.

One might then ask, with this long and sustained intellectual, religious and political hostility, why have the myths not been completely consigned to the dust bin of progressive history? How have they still managed to survive, even up to the present, as witnessed for instance by their very real presence in the work of Paul Reid? The main reason for this long-running saga of survival is that western society has been disingenuous in its attitude towards and treatment of its inherited mythic past. While espousing its cultural and moral distaste for the myths and the ancient and 'primitive' peoples who produced them, each historical era has been obliged, for a range of different reasons, to revisit and plunder the myths in order to bolster and enhance its own image of assumed superiority. For example, the Romans ruthlessly colonised Greek culture in general and the myths in particular for propagandist reasons, as seen, for example, by the innumerable statues of every tin-pot caesar and general posing as the heroic Hercules. Thus it has been with every subsequent military dictatorship. On the other hand, the theocratic powers of the Christian Church could use the promiscuous loves and nefarious cruelties of the all too human pagan gods to show the innate sinful nature of mankind, which constantly needed to be kept suppressed and controlled by the unflinching moral rectitude of the ever-vigilant, self-righteous clergy. Furthermore, the Age of Enlightenment pointed to myth as the product of the gross ignorance and enslaving superstition which had plagued the past but which would be at long last cast aside through the power of sceptical reason and intellectual liberty. All that being said, however, we find in the modern age of scientific rigor that, within the developing practice of disciplines such as comparative religious studies, anthropology and psychology, mythology has emerged as a phenomenon in its own right. Over the last century or so, myth has been seriously studied as a means to understanding a range of different aspect of human experience, from the structure of language, the formations of societies and the politics of gender relationships to the seemingly unfathomable psychological workings of the human mind.

Where, then, does Paul Reid's mythological painting fit into the complexities and contradictions of this long and ongoing branch of cultural history? To answer that, we firstly need to see his artwork within the tradition of academic history painting. Whilst this is a genre of painting rarely visited by Scottish artists, it has always been regarded as the supreme achievement of western art – with mythological subject matter as one of its main sources of inspiration. Like the great mythological painters of the past, from the superb Athenian masters of black/red-figure vase painting, to the sublime history painters of the 16th and 17th centuries such as Titian, Velázquez, Rubens, Poussin and Rembrandt, Reid, too, keenly seeks out inspiring subjects for his paintings from a wide range of ancient sources such as Hesiod, Homer, Apollodorus, Virgil and Ovid. From such literary research, he then skilfully fashions his distinctive pictorial world through the inventive power of his visually interpretive imagination. Furthermore, his creative approach to his carefully selected sources is in full accord with the intrinsic poetic nature of mythology. For mythmaking has always involved an ever-recurring ritual of re-working and re-presenting tales of universal fascination and profound significance in order to tell anew these wondrous stories to those with the receptive ears and enquiring eyes.

Paul Reid's technical practice in his role as a painter of myths is also very much in tune with the particular demands and aims of the academic tradition of history painting. He soon realised this even during the early stages of his developing career when mythic subject matter began to fire his visual imagination and stir his artistic ambitions. He could see that

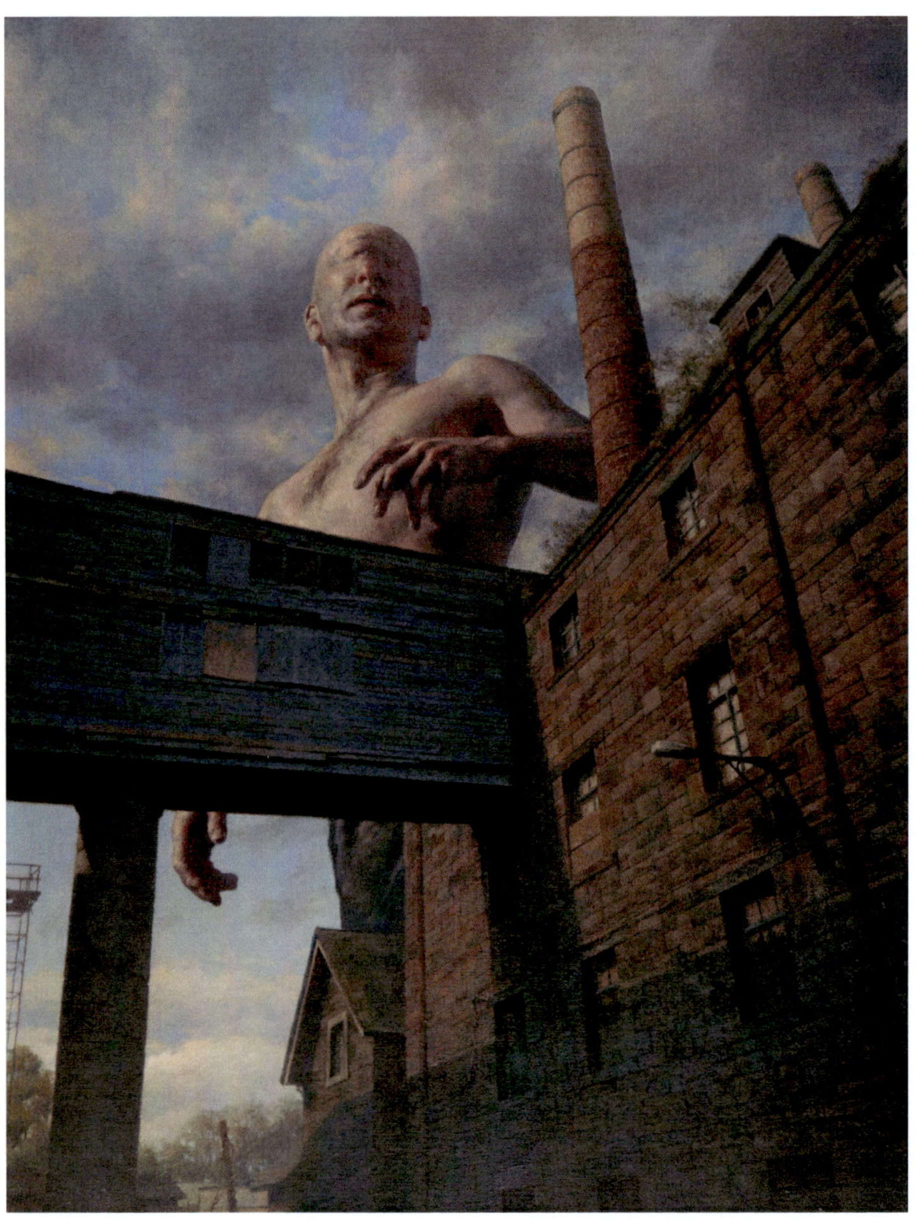

Cyclops
2012
Oil on canvas, 80x60cm
Reproduced courtesy of the artist

mythology was the ideal subject material for his personal interests and particularly suited his own technical accomplishments as a painter. In conspicuous contrast to most of his fellows in the contemporary art world, Reid has resolutely committed himself to a non-fashionable academic approach to his preferred medium and artistic practice. Thus, since his student days in the mid-1990s, he has been evolving an elaborate method of studio-based techniques involving closely observed drawings of highly detailed preparatory figure and still-life studies, carefully squared-up primed canvases, specially prepared oil pigments, supplemented with a range of tinted glazes and varnishes. As such, his pictures – of old master standard – are beautifully made objects in their own right. It is of little wonder, then, that Reid's larger works can take months to reach completion and satisfy the artist's demanding standards of technical and artistic excellence.

This long and elaborate studio practice of picture-making which the artist performs in order to body forth his mythological subjects also has wider significance in relationship to the essential nature and practice of mythmaking itself. One of the key features and necessary working components of all authentic mythmaking is the vital role of ritual, whether it takes place in the religious sanctuary or the artist's studio. In ancient times and within tribal societies, this ritualistic practice would of course have been an integral part of pantheistic worship. The central figure in these religious rituals would be the shaman/priest, who was also the designated vital source and productive medium for spiritual revelation which, in our secular age, has now become mainly associated with poetic and artistic creativity. In later times, art also became closely linked with the esoteric practices of alchemy (for instance, St Luke, the apothecary, became the patron saint of the guild of painters). Thus, it was through ritual in its various manifestations that the potent power of worship, magic and art became inextricably linked.

We now live in a highly secular and materialistic era where science and technology, not magic and religion, rule our relationship with the natural world. The semi-divine power of imaginative invention and metamorphic transformation, however, is still much associated with the role of art and the artist. This is certainly borne out with the highly convincing and disturbingly uncanny pictorial scenes and supernatural scenarios taking place in the paintings of Paul Reid. This fascinating, yet unsettling effect, in his work is achieved through a dialectic pictorial tension between content and form within Reid's images. Thus even though he is ostensibly dealing with subjects and stories drawn from the distant mythic past, these sources are visually rendered through such immediate and intense optical reality that they cause us to question our usual perspectival and chronological distinctions between far and near, past and present. In Reid's pictures, it seems as though the eternal now of the mythic universe has enfolded itself over the historic world of the Scottish landscape, turning it into a northern arcadia in which the Olympian gods and ancient heroes can still occasionally be found.

To appreciate fully the depth of associations that enriches the understanding and appreciation of Paul Reid's paintings, there is another important context – a scientific one – in which they need to be also placed. Contrary to what many may care to think, myths are not divinely gifted by the gods to us but, on the contrary, have always been man-made in an attempt to understand and somehow control the workings of the natural and human worlds. In his highly influential writings, the process and method of myth manufacture was termed 'bricolage', after a French slang word, by the great anthropologist/structuralist, Claude Lévi-Strauss. For Lévi-Strauss, the fundamental binary structure of myth – and ultimately language itself – involves a kind of do-it-yourself approach – ie 'bricolage'. The mythmaker scavenges from any appropriate source available, then composes fresh sets of binary relationships from the scavenged material in order to formulate further mythic narratives which will help explain and hopefully control the mysterious workings of the physical and spiritual worlds.

This concept of the bricolage mode of creativity can be readily applied to how Paul Reid also operates. In the constant search for new and stimulating source material for his painting, he will seek out and delve into a wide range of ancient mythic literature in his quest for some inspiring tale or fascinating incident, involving the gods, monsters and their human victims. Once this search has found a suitable and promising subject, the long and complex process of turning that initial inspirational spark of intention into a convincing full-scale pictorial composition begins. Right from the start, it is important that the artist remains as free, fluid and open as possible in his approach and attitude. He must avoid being dominated by preconceived notions as to how the finished painting will turn out for that would merely lead to artful illustration, which must be avoided at all costs. As with all true mythmakers, Reid will improvise and experiment by readily drawing on what he might need from the resources readily at hand. For example, he will, if required, use himself, his family or friends as handy models for his compositional purposes, dressing them up in concocted costumes. These may be less than historically and sartorially accurate but will satisfy the artist's own evolving vision of the mythic scene he is conjuring, as much from his fertile imagination as the literary text. The same also applies to supplementary pictorial details, such as the backdrop settings, props and drapes. These may come from intense detailed study of a discreet corner of some appropriate Scottish landscape that has caught his attention, a scene in an old Ray Harryhausen movie epic, a frame from a Hellboy comic strip or something copied from one of his kid's sf toys or computer games. In the true spirit of bricolage, anything in Reid's studio practice might be adapted to the mythmaker's purpose.

Paul Reid's paintings, like the myths themselves, are of a decidedly eclectic nature. As with all authentic mythmaking, the creative process

will bricolage together disparate bits and pieces. Yet, as we can see for
the stylistic consistency in Reid's work, it is the artist's own distinctive
vision and superb technical skills that holds everything together within
the alternative pictorial world which he presents to his viewer. In contrast
to the seemingly ubiquitous, all-pervasive distractions of multimedia
entertainment, Reid takes the art of mythmaking very seriously – and he is
correct to do so. For the myths are not just exotically delightful, if rather
quaint, entertaining stories, to be called upon when required to amuse us
and relieve the alienating routine and boredom of the modern world we
have created for ourselves. On the contrary, the myths are the universal
source and the abiding touchstone of our humanity in all its heroic
and tragic dimensions. With these paintings, the artist openly invites
us to enter his vision of this mythic world. After a period of enthralled
examination and personal reflection, we should gradually begin to realise
that Read's mythic world is not so strange after all. It is, in fact, a vital
visual manifestation of the human imagination which we all carry with us,
deep inside our multi-layered inherited memories and dreams.

This essay was written by Bill Hare in 2015 and published by The Scottish Gallery,
Edinburgh.

Section Ten
Three Female Figurative Painters

June Redfern (1951–)
Helen Flockhart (1963–)
Alison Watt (1965–)

ONE OF THE main answers that Linda Nochlin gave in response to her famous provocative question, 'Why have there been no great women artists?' was that, in the past, women had been denied access to study the nude model in the academy's life class. As with most countries, this was generally the case in Scotland right up to the end of the 19th century. Thereafter things gradually began to change and women artists had more opportunities to depict the human figure in their art but, more likely, they were still expected to be seen painting landscapes and still lifes. Even in the mid-1950s, when they dared to step out of line – as Joan Eardley did with her depiction of an undraped male figure in her *Sleeping Nude* – such actions could (and did) cause the Scottish eyebrow to be raised and the Caledonian finger to be wagged. Thus, in a Scottish context, the figurative paintings of Lys Hansen and Joyce Cairns from the 1970s were the first serious attempts by women painters to take on this potent subject. By the late 1980s and early 1990s, the situation had radically changed and a number of younger Scottish women painters were focusing their attentions on the figure as the central subject in their painting. Furthermore, there was now an international boom in figurative painting and these women artists were now also well acquainted with the latest developments in the feminist movement.

As with most of the other Scottish women artists of the 1990s, June Redfern, Alison Watt and Helen Flockhart focused their artistic and critical attentions on the depiction of the female body, which in some cases could be their own. Yet each treated their shared subject in their own particular fashion. For instance, Redfern's figures are usually set in a richly sensual and highly evocative timeless landscape where their action and poise merge in prefect harmony with an idyllic world. By contrast, Alison Watt has used her academic training at Glasgow School of Art to engage in a complex deconstructive dialogue with the male masters of figurative painting from the past. For instance, in her exhibition entitled *Fold* at Edinburgh's Fruitmarket Gallery in 1997, she produced a series of paintings that subtly and cunningly critiqued the work of the French neo-classical painter, Ingres. More recently, she has removed the depiction of the figure from her now highly abstract-looking paintings but the presence of the absent human body is still keenly felt, if not seen. Helen Flockhart was also a student of Glasgow School of Art but the stylistic character of her figure painting is again different. Her pictures are presented in a format that recalls Russian icons, yet rendered in a style that has a strong arts and crafts feel to it. In her recent work, pictorial narrative has become more prominent which can give Flockhart's highly detailed, densely painted pictures a disturbingly uncanny feel that sometimes verges on the downright sinister.

As none of these artists had a solo exhibition at the Talbot Rice Gallery while I was there, I never got to work with them in the same way as some of the other artists in this book. That was unfortunate for me as I greatly admire their painting and enjoy writing about their art. I did, however, include both Helen Flockhart and Alison Watt in *The Scottish Endarkenment* exhibition in 2016.

June Redfern

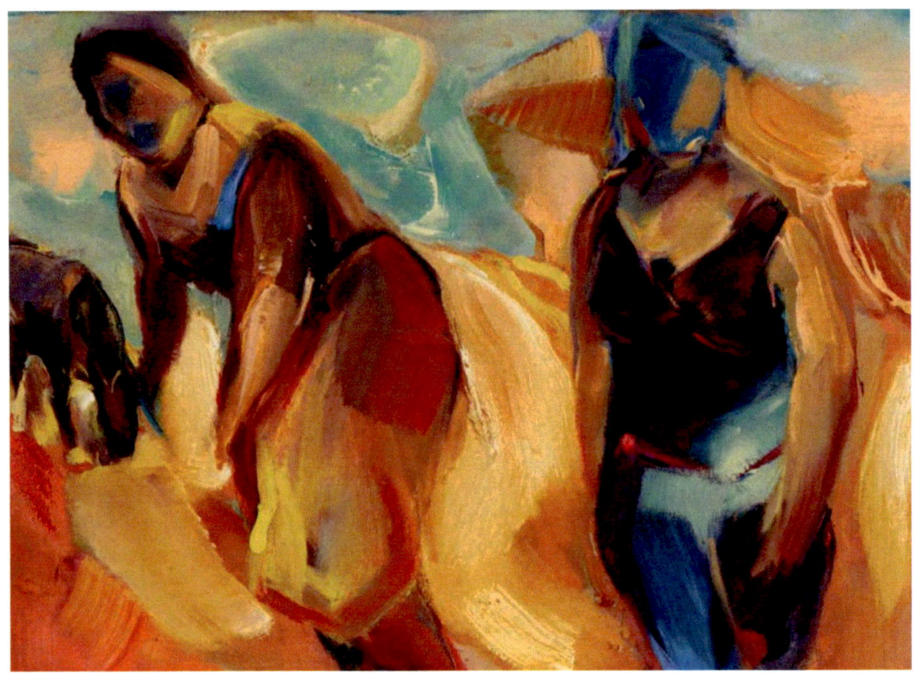

Figures in a Landscape
1992–3
Oil on canvas, 47x62cm
Reproduced courtesy of the artist

Figures in an Arcadian Landscape

JUNE REDFERN IS that rare being: a born painter with a deeply held personal view of human experience and a distinct way of expressing it. Through her own natural abilities and years of sustained practice as a fully committed painter, she has developed her art to such a level that it would not be an exaggeration to claim that she has gradually evolved through her painting a pictorial world of her own out of her creative imagination.

Entering again into Redfern's alluring realm of mysterious figures and evocative landscapes is always an exciting prospect for those who have journeyed through it on many previous occasions. Yet for people who are not acquainted with her work and maybe are coming across these visionary landscapes for the first time, access can initially be a little challenging. The figures may appear rather strange and alien and the landscape unknown and confusing. The artist herself is aware that some people do have problems in approaching her work, especially because of its semi-abstract nature. For instance, while she was artist-in-residence at the National Gallery in London, she found it disturbing and unsettling that some members of the public who visited her studio had certain difficulties because they could not find any specific meaning in her paintings. 'They seem to want to find "a story"' is how she put it.

Such a search for a literal meaning in Redfern's work would, I feel, be futile and against the whole spirit of her painting. While there are of course discernible figures set in her landscapes, these are not to be regarded as identifiable characters within some kind of pictorial narrative; for narrative involves the notion of chronology – that is, actions unfolding through an assumed timeline. Yet these paintings are untouched by that kind of temporal dimension. Here we are entering an imagined world beyond measurable time where the eternal and universal are the conditions of humankind's connectedness with nature. The figures in these landscapes are not characters or even anonymous types but essential aspects of basic human experience. Their existence comes from within themselves and their natural surroundings. Each figure is as much a spiritual presence with its own aura, caught and held in a pose which transcends the mere passing moment.

In her paintings, Redfern transports us to a world half-remembered, half-imagined, one which may have existed but probably only in the yearnings of human thought and desire. Yet we can all recognise its existence: it is a world deep within all of us, a long-lost memory to which we continually return in our profound longings and dreams. One of the great miracles of painting is its power to body forth such worlds of harmony and sensual delight. These pastoral idylls of Redfern continue within that exemplary tradition.

What is so exciting about Redfern's latest work is that she has infused

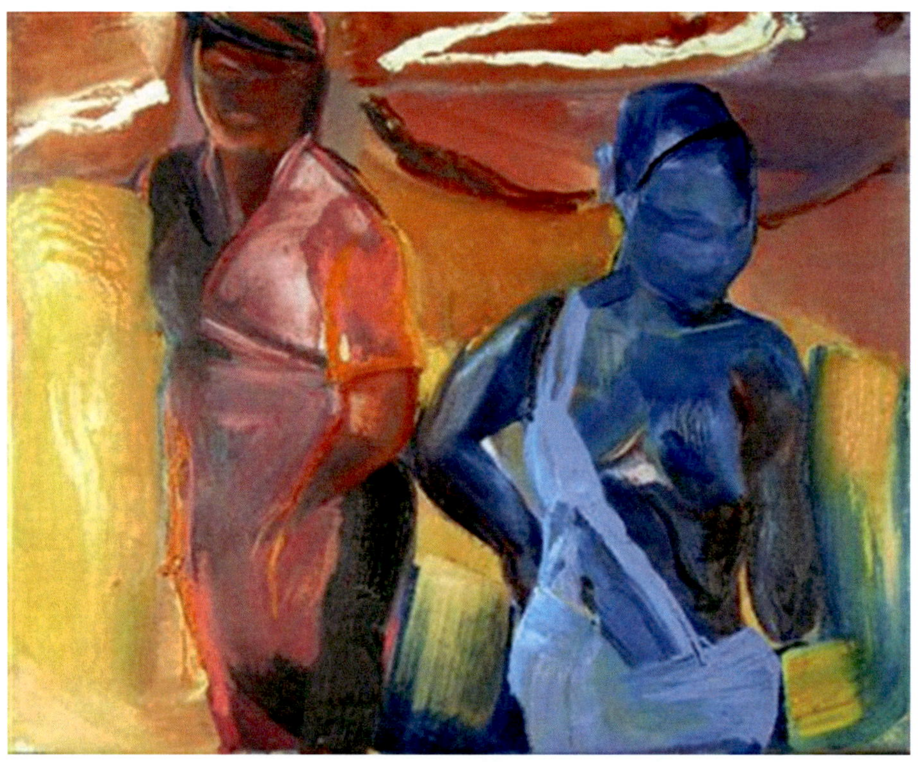

The Ferry Women
1993
Oil on canvas, 110x110cm

Reproduced courtesy of the artist

a new expressive power to this tradition of epic pastoral painting which began seriously in western painting with Claude in the 17th century. The common desire of this particular type of idealised landscape painting is to present nature in its most idyllic and sympathetic light. In such a world, the disillusionment and alienation that human beings feel about themselves and their own created environment is replaced by an imagined previous existence where the human presence is again at one with itself and its natural surroundings. Artists working within this pastoral tradition of painting have tended to use literary and classical allusions to recreate this feeling of poetic harmony between the figure and the landscape. Redfern, by contrast, takes us to a world before or beyond antiquity, even before the civilised. Here we are dealing with human community as it was before organised society.

To suggest the particular bond that existed between man and nature in such a world, the artist cannot turn to outside cultural props but has to rely on the indigenous expressive power of painting itself. How does Redfern achieve this? In her earlier work, while her technical skills in manipulating paint and co-ordinating colour were just as impressive, there was a great emphasis on movement and emotional agitation. These earlier paintings tended to be religious in theme and expression where there was an imminent sense of outside transcendental forces breaking through and creating moments of high emotion and baroque drama. In such vertically orientated paintings, with their very theatrical means of expression, the influence of El Greco, an artist much admired by Redfern, could clearly be felt.

These latest paintings by contrast, appear much more classical in mood – full of 'noble simplicity and calm grandeur'. They seem to have resolved the earlier tension between the physical and the spiritual, the human and the divine. As landscapes these new paintings tend towards the horizontal; furthermore, the horizon is usually placed quite high up in the composition, thus reducing the area of sky and excluding the sense of outside omnipotent forces. Now we are returned to earth in a world dominated by the human presence; a world before the creation of oppressive religion and the need for outside divine approval and punishment. This is a world with its own innate sense of grace, a land where the physical and the spiritual, the human and the natural are harmoniously and inseparably contained within each other.

This is powerfully conveyed through the act of painting itself. Each area of colour, each gestural brushstroke, holds its own, yet interrelates with the whole structure of the composition. The figures and the landscape are built up together, almost like modelled relief sculpture, emphasising the sheer material being of their natural existence. Each area in the painting is marked with the same degree of intense attention and feeling. Thus, the spatial relationships have little to do with conventional pictorial illusionism and are much more concerned with tactile and emotional ones. This integration and interpenetration of all the areas in the paintings, rendered in rich luxuriant pigments, creates landscapes of rich sensual beauty. The soft malleable quality of the thickly applied paint adds to the heavy atmosphere of sexuality and fecundity which seems to pervade the mood of the landscapes.

Ultimately what gives these works such classical authority is the predominant position of the human presence, and June Redfern is a supreme figure painter. After years of figure drawing and close study of the great masters of the human figure, from Piero della Francesca to Matisse, she can now produce from her memory a whole range of different human attitudes. In these paintings, the figures and poses are beautifully poised between the gravitational pull of their sustained attachment to the ground beneath them and their graceful movements through the space which permeates the world around their bodies.

This sense of movement pervades these landscapes which, although they seem timeless, are nevertheless also in a state of continual fluctuation. Painted in a seemingly intuitively expressive way, the artist's own manner of creating these pictures echoes the general feeling of ongoing shifting relationships found in the landscapes. Here the figures appear to have a nomadic existence, moving on, whether by land or water, with the alternating moods of the surrounding landscape. More than anything, it is the artist's highly sensitive use of colour and atmosphere which conveys this fluctuating physical and emotional harmonious relationship between the human presence and the diurnal natural world.

The paintings of June Redfern cannot be interrogated by direct questions. They will not yield answers to such an approach. Looking at her paintings, one must be prepared, like the figures in her landscapes, to embark on a long mysterious journey, an odyssey back into furthest reaches of human memory, an exploratory pilgrimage of self-discovery. Where the journey will take you depends on the strength of your sympathetic imagination, and the longer you travel, the less a final destination will matter. For, as another Scottish artist of high romance, Robert Louis Stevenson, once wrote, 'To travel hopefully is a better thing than to arrive.'

This essay was written by Bill Hare in 1993 and published by Oriel 31 (now Oriel Davies Gallery), Newtown, Wales.

Helen Flockhart

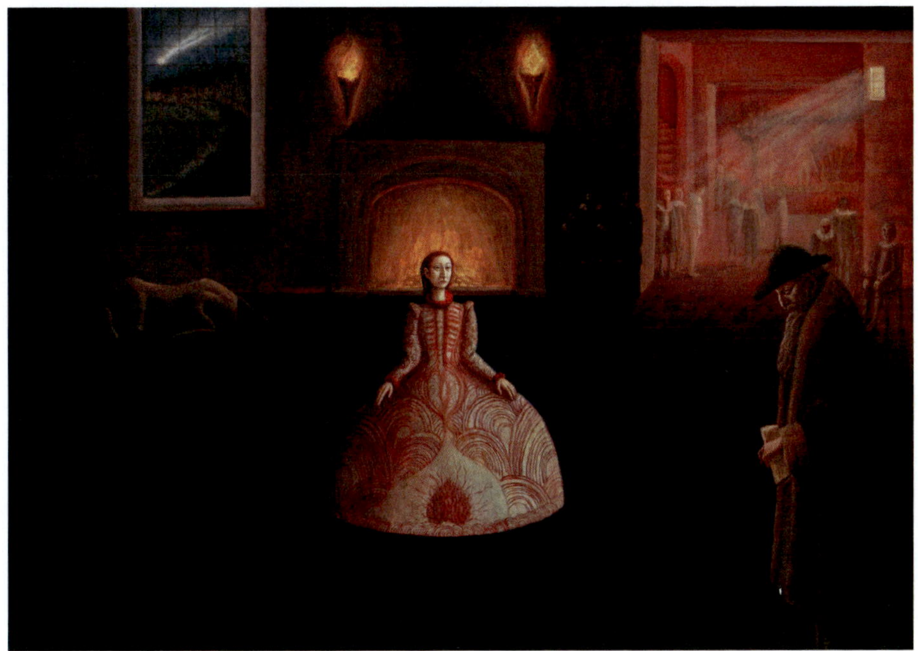

Suffer on Strike
2018
Oil on panel, 33x46cm
Reproduced courtesy of the artist

Helen Flockhart and Peter Thomson Interview

Where and when did you first meet?
We met in 1980 near the beginning of our first year at Glasgow School of Art, which back then was a general year, where we worked in separate studios. In our second year, we specialised in drawing and painting and found ourselves in the same studio, which is when our relationship began.

Did you both immediately have an empathy for each other's work?
No.

What was it like being a painting student at Glasgow School of Art in the 1980s?
It was an exciting time. There was a sense that painting was a valued practice. There was a lot of debate around it, and not just curricular; students were taking it upon themselves to organise their own things. There was a lot of political awareness and engagement among the student body.

We were lucky enough to work in the Mackintosh building and never took it for granted. We had space: physically we had a decent portion of a studio to work in with the massive Mackintosh north facing windows, and we had time and space to find our own voice. In our third year we had to choose a studio for our final two years. Helen chose Jimmy Robertson's studio which was typified by Scottish colourist, painterly, often landscape work, and Peter went to Sandy Moffat's studio which had a heavy slant towards figurative painting with a political and critical analysis.

There were weekly (or was it twice weekly?) life drawing classes which we had the option to partake in.

What was life like for you both after you left art school and were setting out to establish your reputations?
The few years after art school were different for both of us.

Peter left GSA after graduating in 1984, whereas Helen did a further postgraduate year there followed by a year at an art school in Poland, finishing in mid-'86.

For Helen there followed a couple of years working part-time, moving from flat to flat and trying to get to grips with producing artwork of any merit outwith an institution, but nevertheless exhibiting in some group shows. From 1986–7 we didn't see each other. A significant leap forward in finding a direction in painting came with a show in Transmission Gallery in 1989 when our first child was a few months old.

Peter spent a year as a mural painter for a London Health Authority. He found it a more disciplined environment than GSA and he noticed a real technical development in his painting. It was a more 'living in the real world' situation, where he decided to seriously try to make a living as a full-time painter.

Did you share a studio then, and do you continue to do so?
We didn't share a studio until 1992. However, we did not, and still don't, work in the studio at the same time, though we have our own allotted space within it. As we couldn't afford childcare, we would take turns to either look after our child (later children) or work on our painting. Even after our children left school we continued this system and still work shifts either in studio or in our own space at home.

How do you think you have contributed to the development of each other's art?
It is difficult to see that we have contributed to the development of each other's art, perhaps we are too close to see it. In a way our work has developed in parallel to each other's. We've always had our own quite separate influences. Occasionally imagery might converge but it's rare.

Unsolicited advice is not well received, we've learned to keep critical thoughts to ourselves. But of course we'll say if we think something is good. If it is, though, generally you know. And if it isn't, you know too.

In a way though, our circumstances (little money, little time, responsibilities) forced a discipline on our work lives. There was no time to waste when we DID get the opportunity to work. We learned to shut everything out, wherever we were, and immediately start working.

Has your working relationship changed over the years?
No.

How do you find the art scene in this country today, compared with the time when you were just beginning your careers?
We have different takes on this.
pt: Today there seems to be a received consensus among publicly funded galleries that painting is an archaic practice and that the real action lies in the kind of art loosely framed as conceptualism. While there's an inevitability of one orthodoxy replacing another, the most frustrating aspect of this is the often disingenuous marketing, still making claims of cutting edge, and ground breaking work, when it is simply another entrenched tradition. The ephemeral thrill of novelty soon passes.
hf: In the 1980s we had a meagre but crucial level of state support which allowed the embryonic careers of a generation of artists, musicians, writers and actors to persist long enough to eventually become self-supporting. Today young people have no such back up, unless their parents have the means to fill the gap. I wonder whether in the long run this will make for such a broad cultural output.

The art world is a crowded playing field these days. It's a massive industry and it can be daunting when you stand back and look at it. It's important to just focus on producing the best work possible. And, having absented ourselves from the scene for a lot of years when the kids were young, I value connecting with other artists.

What do you both hope the future holds for your careers?
To keep working and improve as an artist. Would hope that in the next 30 years (if we're lucky enough to make it) there would be less edge-of-the-seat anxiety regarding finance than the previous.

Finally, what would you say are the advantages and disadvantages of being a 'creative couple'?
Advantages are that we understand each other's position, the ebb and flow of successes and failures. Main disadvantage has been financial insecurity. For a long time we effectively worked a job share with two tiny, half incomes not even amounting to one, for a whole family. A disadvantage was that we could never afford childcare; paradoxically an advantage was that because we had no childcare, we got to look after our children ourselves, which we now look back on as having been very lucky. The other advantage is that because we were aware that the other was working so hard, it would have been a liberty not to do so too, so we developed a mutually reinforcing and beneficial work ethic.

This interview was conducted by Bill Hare in 2019 for this publication.

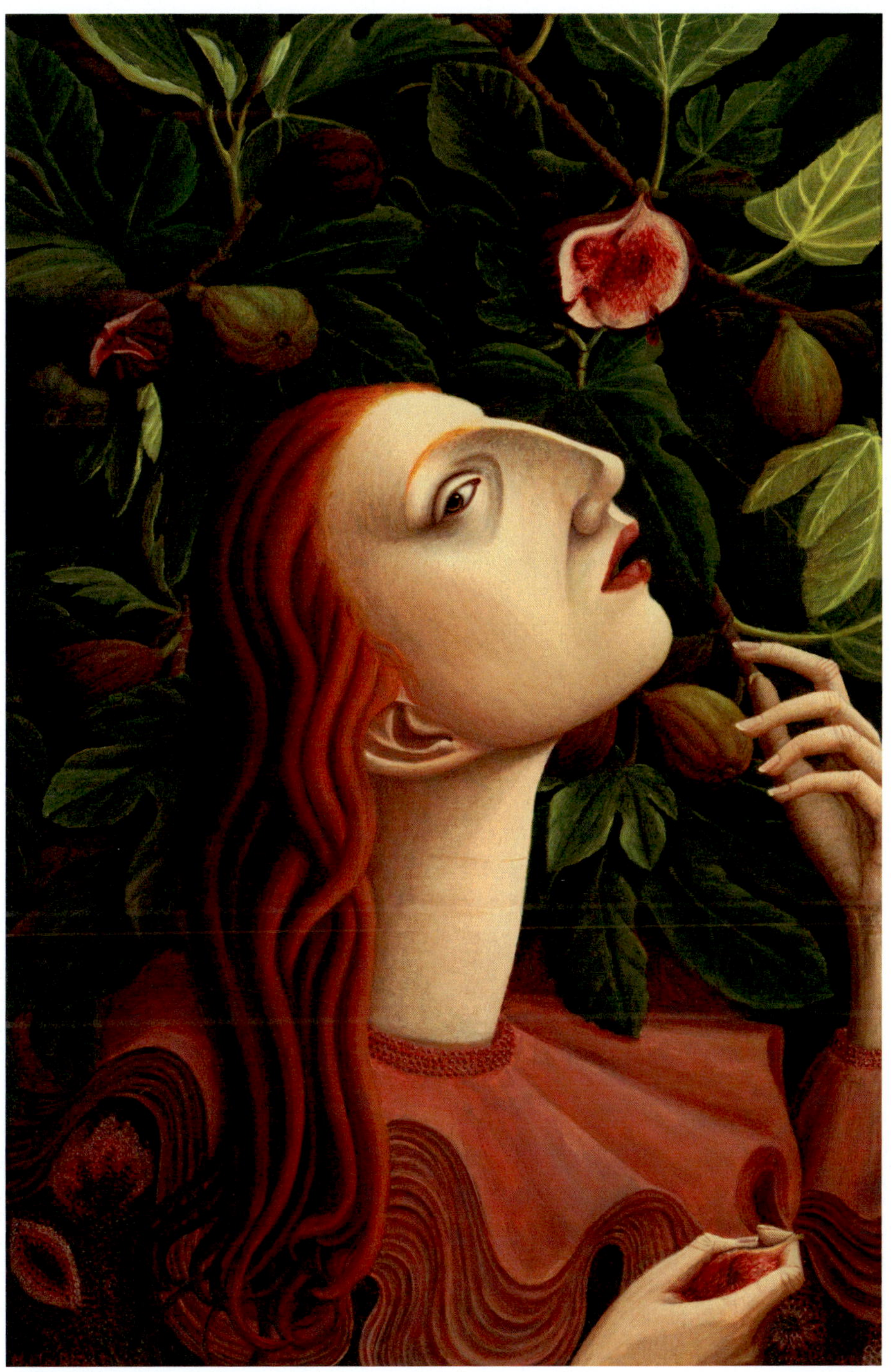

Crooked Rib
2018
Oil on panel, 40x26cm

Reproduced courtesy of the artist

The Paintings of Helen Flockhart

WITH AN UNWAVERING commitment to her own distinctive artistic vision, Helen Flockhart has now established herself as one of our leading figurative painters. Nobody paints like Helen Flockhart. In a contemporary art world where the egotistical and vacuous are everywhere, Helen Flockhart paints pictures which are deeply personal and unique and, at the same time, enthralling and universal. Through the transforming power of her vivid imagination, the poetic art of Helen Flockhart creates a fascinating visual world that is familiar and yet fantastic, one we have lost but also found again. As in our dreams, we both lose and simultaneously find ourselves in this magical realm of other existence. Here the mundane and the mythical are at one with each other. Yet there is no illusionism involved, nor is anything veiled or hidden from our intense gaze as we are openly invited to absorb and pore over the intricately painted patterns of decorative design and the scrupulously worked surfaces of minute descriptive detail. All this excessive display takes place within an enclosed domain where every action and expression is redolent with symbolic significance and emotional intensity. Helen Flockhart's paintings reveal a realm of alluring and strange beauty which for those of us who imaginatively enter can disturb, enthral and ultimately offer another world to the one of our distracted quotidian lives. For Flockhart's paintings are more concerned with the psychological than the socio-biological aspects of human experience. Her uncanny pictorial narratives, where the mundane and the mythical make uneasy bedfellows, are wrought with such excessive detail that the viewer is simultaneously enthralled and mesmerised. These densely ornate paintings transport us to another level of psychic reality where every tiny aspect of the scene appears to be redolent with symbolic significance and absorbing mystery, offering up a nether world of strange, but compelling beauty.

This essay is an amalgamation of two short pieces written by Bill Hare on Helen Flockhart in 2015 and 2019 and published in *Galleries* magazine.

Alison Watt

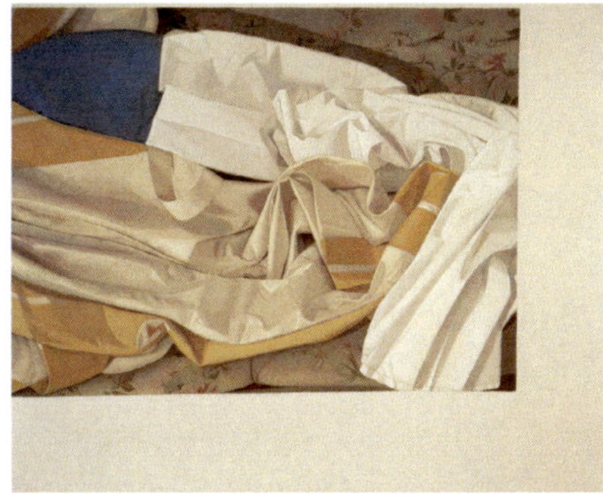 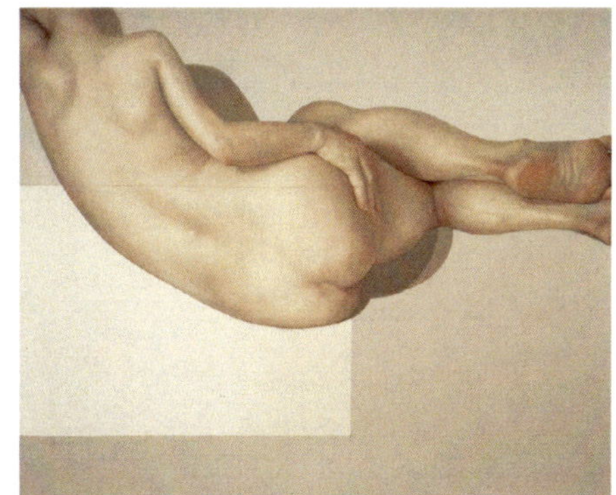

Odalisque/Fragment 1
1996
Oil on canvas (diptych), 152x183cm (each panel)
Reproduced courtesy of the artist and Ingleby, Edinburgh (photograph: Antonia Reeve)

Between the Sheet and Shroud

A NOTABLE CRITICAL and creative engagement with the depiction of the human body within Scottish art took place in 1980s and '90s. A number of Scottish women artists – including Alison Watt – took up the emerging challenges concerning the visual representation of the female figure which arose out of feminist debates on gender roles and identities. These Scottish women figurative artists in their different ways felt compelled to revisit, re-examine and re-present the female image within the inherited conventions of painting which were by that time under intense scrutiny and critical reassessment.

Alison Watt's first notable artistic contribution to these issues and debates on the representation of the female body in contemporary culture came with her memorable *Fold* exhibition shown at the Fruitmarket Gallery, Edinburgh, in 1997. Watt's painting at this time was very much involved in an intense love/hate analytical dialogue with the art of the 19th-century neo-classical master Jean-Dominique Ingres. This can be seen for instance in the way the pose that the nude female figure holds in Watt's *Fragment 111* recalls, but also subtly deviates from, Ingres's own famous *La Source* (1820). For example, there is a crucial differential factor between the approach of Watt and Ingres to this sexualised fertility theme. While the male painter is determined to produce an idealised image in which woman and nature conflate in perfect harmony, the young contemporary female painter by contrast, is equally set on decoupling the conventional enchainment of women to the natural world. Watt achieves this by removing and deconstructing the imprisoning glossy veneer of classical universalism with its subjection of the female form to its *a priori* code of predetermined ideal symbols. With striking difference Watt defiantly reveals the individual sexuality of the figure of the woman presented in her painting. Thus the symbolic eroticism of high class sophisticated academic eroticism is challenged and threatened by Watt's critical pictorial discourse – where idealism is subjected to realism and nudity to the naked truth of the body.

Like many other of Scotland's best artists in the post-war period Alison Watt started her career by going against the grain of the dominant and fashionable artistic ideologies and practices of her time. Independently-minded she defied and challenged the dominant pedagogical and critical opinion in the 1980s, by rejecting both conceptual art and neo-expressionism. As a student at Glasgow School of Art she preferred to work – with great determination and dedication – within the demanding rituals of the academic practice of the life class. Thus not surprisingly in her earlier work the human figure held a predominant position, with reference and quotation from the masters of the (neo)-classical tradition being incorporated into her paintings, as seen for example in *Marat and the Fishes* from 1990. It can be readily detected, however, from this work and by her other 'homage' pictures that Watt soon developed a complex and ambivalent attitude to the classical tradition within the history of western painting. Her approach to such sources, as expressed in these early highly referential works, appears to be a complex contrasting combination of admiring emulation and ironic deflation. Furthermore the recurring use of her own presence as a non-idealised model in these pictures only seems to add to the intriguing ambiguity.

Growing aware of the dangers of remaining too long on this course of eclectic pastiche, Alison Watt began to realise that she needed to be more seriously analytical and focused in her examination of her position and purpose as a contemporary woman artist working within the inherited male dominated history of art. As she observed in her essay for the *Fold* exhibition:

> As a woman who is an artist, the notion of contradiction is a poignant one. My status is a questionable one… I have chosen not to abandon certain conventions of painting but to use them to reassess our ideas and perceptions of the medium. It is vital that I be aware of the history and cultural traditions of painting in order to deal with them in contemporary practice: I am speaking in a particular language, yet at the same time seeking to challenge it.

In order to carry out this mission of re-examination of her position within the history of painting Watt felt it necessary to develop new strategies in order to challenge the symbiotic connectedness that classical masters like Ingres conspired to make in their academic pictures between the idealised female figure and the props that held that figure securely within the appreciative male gaze. Firstly, she found that the so-called classical Serpentine Line of beauty – with its hidden reference to female temptation and the Fall of Man – had 'been used as a controlling force on the female body.' It was this 'act of regulation' which had been used throughout the history of art in order to transform the 'female body into the female nude'. Watt, for her part, intended to paint pictures in which 'bodies resist such containment'. Secondly, she began to examine the complex role played by the still life accoutrements and frippery props in the pictorial figure compositions of Ingres. Through her deconstruction of this highly controlled stage-managed pictorial dialogue between 'fabric and flesh' with its 'emphasis on sensation' Watt came to the radical and challenging conclusion that in such academic paintings the 'eroticism lies within the folds of the fabric, not in the flesh'.

From these two insights Watt was to observe further that Ingres's 'women' are not objects for the viewer's contemplation of perfect symbols of female beauty; they are, in fact, 'aberrations.' As a result of her critical investigations Watt produced a series of paintings, mainly in the diptych format – with a truncated figure on one panel, and a drapery still life detail on the other – in which she could analytically examine and pictorially present 'the complex relationship between beauty and deformity'.

In her '*Fold*' paintings Alison Watt set out to disconnect and decouple the eternal erotic beauty of tactile drapery from the female presence of the less than perfect human body. In *Odalisque/Fragment* (1996) for instance, it is the rich fabrics that are granted the immortal erotic title while the self-enclosed fragmented female figure seems to act almost as a *memento mori* – a passing transitory presence. If the open sensual material delights of *Odalisque* attract and seduce by offering themselves up to visual and tactile intimacies, the truncated female figure in *Fragment* turns away and cuts us off from any such alluring contact. With the disruption and break-down of the conventional picture-viewing narrative in which the male spectator is invited to possess imaginatively the object of his desire, the viewer of Watt's figure painting finds that such erotic access is denied. As the artist claims:

> Resistance and restriction co-exist: when you confront these paintings you are immediately aware of surface: the material of the canvas is recognised. Distortions in scale disrupt normal spectator relations with the work: the result is a lack of conventional space between viewer and subject.

At this point in her artistic career Watt remained speculative as to the future development of her painting, but she could still say: 'Ultimately, my intention is to create images which suggest the contingency of the body in practice with significant social and historical dimensions.' Watt's wish to open up to 'contingency' in her practice led to her becoming 'intrigued by the imprint left when the model went… something beautiful was created by their leaving.' Consequently this unexpected revelation that 'absence' can have even more emotive and evocative power than 'presence' has now become one of the most potent and empathic features of Watt's art.

This radically transforming change in the content and execution of Alison Watt's painting appropriately took place at the turn of the new millennium as featured in her important exhibition *Shift* at the Scottish National Gallery of Modern Art. She returned to working on a single image yet on a greatly enlarged scale. With the removal of the visual representation of the figure, its place was now taken over by the monumental close-up of a carefully selected detail of 'cascading, pleated and ruched fabric.' It was not, however, until her next major exhibition *Phantom* at the National Gallery in London – where she was artist-in-residence for 2006 – that the true significance of the crucial changes in Watt's painting could be fully appreciated and critically assessed.

Through her time at the National Gallery, Watt gained access to its immense Old Masters collection and this allowed her an opportunity of close and sustained examination of the work of another, yet very different kind of artist from Ingres. If Ingres's painting had been associated with the erotic in Watt's earlier work, her growing enthrallment to the Catholic mysticism of the Spanish baroque painter, Francisco de Zurbarán, brought about a marked shift towards human morality in her art. In fact, this change in emphasis could already be detected in a 2004 commissioned work which the artist carried out for Old St Paul's Church in Edinburgh. Watt's Memorial Chapel altarpiece *Still* – with its highly evocative four, cross creating, panels of immaculate white drapery – was inspired by the way Zurbarán had painted the heavily drooping cassock in his much admired picture of the Scottish martyr *Saint Serapion* (1628). Significantly, Alan Spence, the poet, writing for the publication on *Still* perceptively described Watt's own painting as 'at once meditative and erotically charged.'

This pull between Eros and Thanatos is indicated by Alison Watt's shifting fascination between two specific paintings – Ingres's *Madame Moitessier* (1856) and Zurbarán's *Saint Francis in Meditation* (1635–9). In an interview for her National Gallery Residency Exhibition in 2008 she pondered on her changing attitude to the work of these two artists. She admitted:

> I've always liked Zurbarán paintings but I'd never once considered that that would be the picture that I would spend every day looking at. I thought it would be *Madame Moitessier* but it wasn't and I am still slightly confused as to why that happened.

The particular focus of Watt's analytical attention within both these works was what she called their 'points of entry'. For instance, she has described her fascination with the Ingres portrait in terms which evoke the erotic duality which Watt had seen in the French classicist's art between 'fabric and flesh':

> I think the most beautiful part of the painting, having known it for most of my life, is its darkest point. There is an exquisite shadow underneath Madame Moitessier's left arm, surrounded on three sides by fabric and on one side by skin. That's the part of the painting I want to enter into and it is fascinating to me that the very point of the picture that I'm most drawn to, is the point that's most concealed to me.

Furthermore, when Watt turned to discussing her obsession with the Spanish religious painting she again focused on an erogenous zone of the human body, but in a very different tone:

> I'm obsessed with the open mouth in the Zurbarán painting. I think the open mouth is the key to the picture and I've been having great debates with various curators here whether or not he's inhaling or exhaling and whether it's anguish or ecstasy that he's experiencing. It is probably both.

Finally another important art historical source which was an influential factor in Alison Watt's search for creating a somatic, erotic access to her now figureless paintings was a picture that, although notorious for its

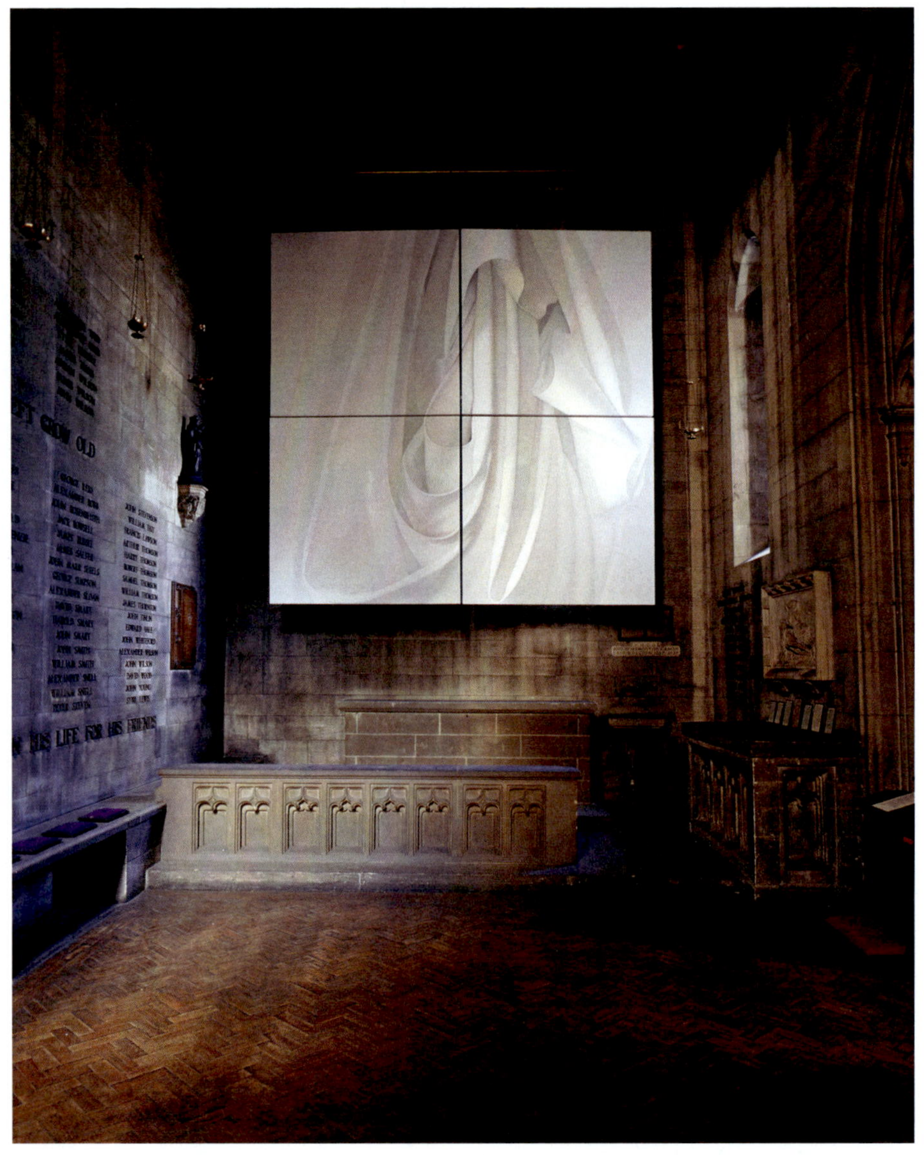

Still

2003–4

Oil on canvas, 368x368cm

Reproduced courtesy of the artist, Old St Paul's Episcopal Church, Edinburgh and Ingleby, Edinburgh (photograph: HK Innes)

open revelation of the female sex, has always been shrouded within a history of prudish concealment. For Watt, Courbet's *The Origin of the World* is 'one of the most extraordinary paintings ever made…You can't take your eye off it: it completely draws you in.' The impact of this highly erotic source can again be contrasted with a very different one to Watt's attitude towards Zurbarán's pictorial discourse on human mortality in his *St Francis in Meditation*. As she said:

> I suddenly realised that in the skull that he is holding, the shape of the eye socket was a shape that had appeared in one of my own very recent paintings. And so now, when I look at my painting in the studio, I don't see fabric, I don't see cloth; I see bone because I relate it to the skull in St Francis.

Thus with the mature paintings of Alison Watt we are presented with a contradictory display of visual ambiguity and alluring mystery. They seem to hover between being read, on the one hand, as a monumental still life of cascading pristine white fabric, and on the other, as great sweeping monochrome abstract compositions. Yet even if the abstract option is discarded these highly protean paintings still cannot be easily pinned down as they appear to oscillate and mutate in form and meaning, between fabric and flesh, cloth and bone, presence and absence, and ultimately between, sheet and shroud. Such paintings are an intense and profound meditation on our human mortality.

This previously unpublished essay was written by Bill Hare in 2016 for *The Scottish Endarkenment* exhibition, which Andrew Patrizio and Bill Hare curated at the Dovecot Studios for the Edinburgh Festival.

Section Eleven
Four Neo-Dadaist/Conceptual Artists

Robert Callender (1932–2011)
Matthew Inglis (1958–)
Douglas Gordon (1966–)
Kevin Harman (1982–)

AFTER THE RELATIVELY brief period in Scottish contemporary art when figurative painting was all the rage in the 1980s, a strong reaction set in against this traditional mode of artistic expression. Ironically, if not totally surprisingly, it was again in the Glasgow School of Art where this critical and artistic refutation was most noticeably found. The rebellious art students there turned away from the drawing and painting disciplines and the life class to take up multimedia courses, where it was the Dadaist and Neo-Dadaist work of Marcel Duchamp and Joseph Beuys which now inspired and set the creative agenda. This radical change in the direction of contemporary art from figurative neo-expressionist painting to neo-conceptualism was not, of course, confined to Glasgow and Scotland but was a nationwide phenomenon in Blairite Britain and was quickly given the blanket title, Young British Artists or YBAS.

Undoubtedly the most critically admired and successful young Scottish artist to emerge from this artistic sea of change in the early 1990s was Douglas Gordon, who went on to be the first of the Scottish artists to win the Turner Prize in 1996. Many of his celebrated works, including *Psycho 24 Hours*, were first shown at the artist-run Transmission Gallery or Tramway in Glasgow where installation, performance and video were the preferred mediums of expression.

Robert (Bob) Callender, a long-time lecturer at Edinburgh College of Art, had begun as a painter of beachscapes in a super-realist mode, but in the 1980s, he shifted to working in three dimensions. Still drawing his subject matter from maritime sources, he began converting his beachcombed, ready-made objects into highly mimetic painted cardboard facsimiles – from abandoned lobster pots and plastic containers to full-scale ship wreckage. Callender's work is never intended to be mystically romantic but rather engages with the Duchampian debates surrounding illusionism, the found and made object and its simulacrum.

Matthew Inglis also uses the found object in his work, using his favoured format, the box unit, to create miniature theatrical tableaux which have a fascinating surreal and absurd character about them. These doll-house scale scenarios are, however, not just there to visually entertain the viewer but also to raise questions and discussions regarding the cultural condition and moral values of our materialistic consumer society.

Finally turning to the youngest artist included in this book, Kevin Harman's artistic practice is very much within the Neo-Dadaist tradition. With its use of urban detritus, it is reminiscent of the early work of Robert Rauschenberg and Boyle Family from the 1960s. He also uses and experiments with a range of Neo-Dadaist, anti-aesthetic strategies, such as employing shock and even violent tactics in his highly variable and multi-layered work. Such strategies seek critically to engage directly and actively with both the contemporary art world and the everyday life on the streets. Harman likes to describe himself as 'a creator of situations'.

Robert Callender

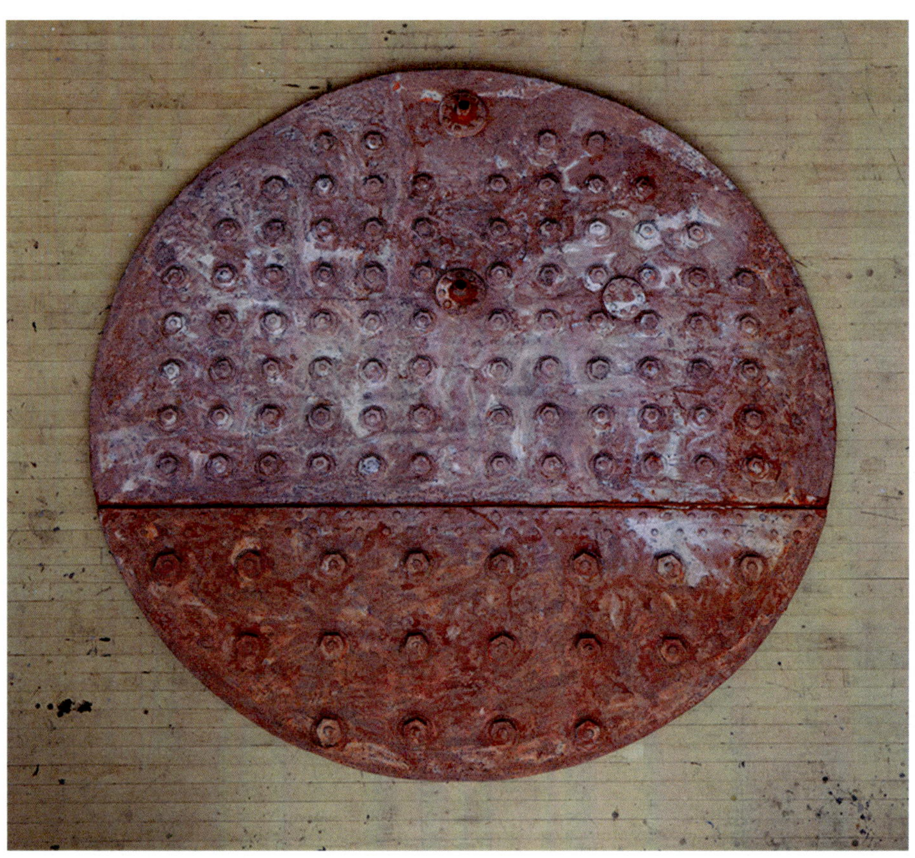

Boiler Lid
1988
Cardboard, paper, paint, 244cm (diameter)
Reproduced courtesy of the artist's estate

Robert Callender Interview

Could we start with a general question? The theme of the sea dominates your work – do you see yourself as a romantic artist?
The dictionary definition of the word 'romantic' in relation to the fine arts is: 'Emotional, remote from experience, preferring grandeur or picturesqueness, or passion and irregular beauty to finish and proportion'. I must deny that I am romantic; all my work as I perceive it is based on classical composition and structure – structure first, surface second.

In the catalogue for your last exhibition, Between Tides, you state that 'beachcombing for me is a way of life'. However, it is the seashore at Stoer Point in the remote north-west of Scotland where you constantly return to scour for material for your art. Why does it have to be that particular one – won't any other shoreline do as well?
With the discovery of the bothy at Stoer Point 20 years ago, I used to wonder if it could be a viable source of inspiration year after year. Now it isn't remotely a question anymore, the place has changed as I have changed and developed. Most of the time I am beachcombing endlessly or digging and searching. Also the place is an important sanctuary where ideas are born and writing can be worked at.

You are a 'beachcomber' but have no time for the objet trouvé approach to art. Could you briefly describe your working process, from seashore to gallery floor?
Found objects fire the imagination. I collect anything of interest that I can carry but they are not to be exhibited – they are the source from which a germ of an idea is born. That development takes place in the studio; converting scrap card into viable structures, is often a long and often hazardous process.

Is the actual physical construction of your sculptures, out of cardboard and recycled waste paper, vitally important to you? It must be very labour-intensive. Could you ever see yourself passing over the making side to other people as other sculptors do?
Basic materials are cheap and there is a real fascination in converting flat sheets of card and paper into solid free-standing objects. I take satisfaction from this activity which takes the product of trees and turns it back on occasion into objects that look like wood. On what I call a three-sweater day in the studio, at 4.30am when it's cold and wet and dark and the tasks for the day are daunting, the idea of assistants has an appeal and that's all. Making the work is at the heart of the creative act and I could not relinquish that to any other person – in any case, no one would be daft enough to do the job!

You are not a sculptor by training, but a painter. What developing relationship do you see between your previous highly realistic paintings and the later three-dimensional work?

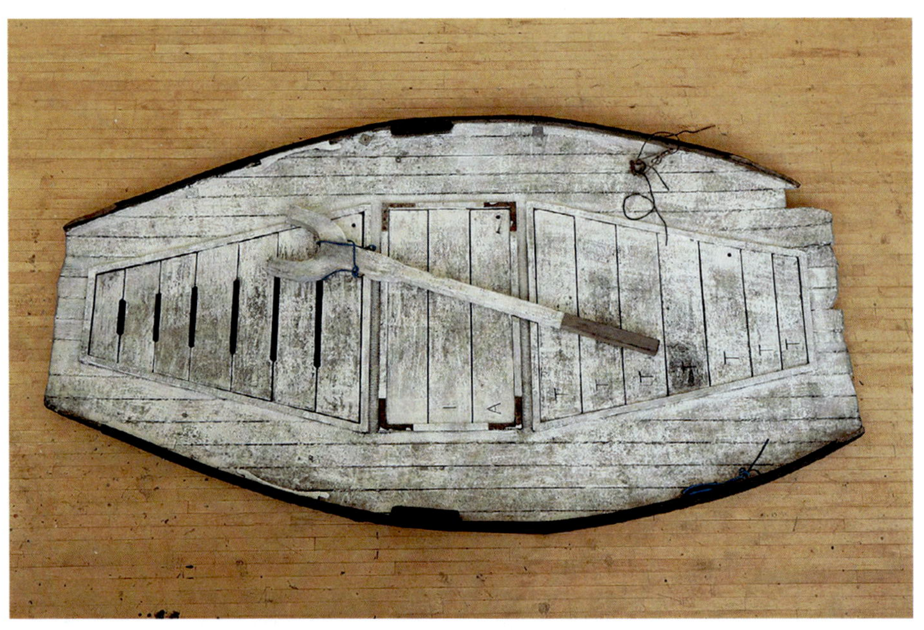

Gray Deck
1989
Cardboard, paper, paint, 218x456x9cm
Reproduced courtesy of the artist's estate

I see it all as painting. Previously my paintings were in no way as realistically painted as I wanted. It was a laborious and frustrating activity. Now I feel there is more realism. The work is still often tedious but I am excited rather than bored and no longer feel that I am destined to imitate myself for the rest of my life.

If I could remain with this question a little longer. Whether you like it or not, many people see both your paintings and sculpture within the photo-realist movement – in fact The Scotsman *critic described your last exhibition as 'the art of counterfeit'. How important, then, is illusionism in your art, particularly in relation to its effect on the spectator's response?*
I consider myself a realist, not a photo-realist – there is a huge difference. Of course, illusion is extremely important, as is technique, but not as a means to an end. I am curious as to how things are made. Hopefully the spectator is deceived, excited or even amused, tempted to touch, above all to have their eyes and minds opened and to become more aware of their environment.

What connections do you want to be made between the sculptures and the photographs in your work?
Black and white photography gives me great pleasure, it has texture, and a quiet stature – when it is enlarged and when used in sequence, it can portray the passage of time or movement.

What role do you see scale playing in your work?
Generally I like my work to have a human scale, for it to confront the spectator. *Sea Salvage* was specifically designed for the Talbot Rice Gallery – nearly a three-year project. It is a beautiful space, with height, light and a range of viewing positions. I have tried to complement that space.

In the early 1980s, Elizabeth Ogilvie and you had a very successful exhibition, Watermarks. *In the catalogue, Hugh Adams suggested that landscape was 'a metaphor to accord with the temper and prejudice of almost every period in history'. Do you see your recent work in any way as a metaphor for our present times?*
The work is about the past, the present and the future. I have matured a great deal since *Watermarks*. Above all, I feel the work is optimistic, where anything is possible. Living in a country with a massive industrial past and a land of spectacular natural beauty, where there is an immense natural resource of talented young artists. These are facts that I find stimulating. The country is on the move. There is more confidence despite EEC and government regulations regarding the fishing industry; wooden boats are still being built up and down the coast. In a country where more people visit galleries and museums than attend football matches, wouldn't it be marvellous if the usual three pages of sport were supplanted by a similar amount on the visual arts? What was the question again?

This interview was made in 1989 and published by the Talbot Rice Gallery, Edinburgh.

Matthew Inglis

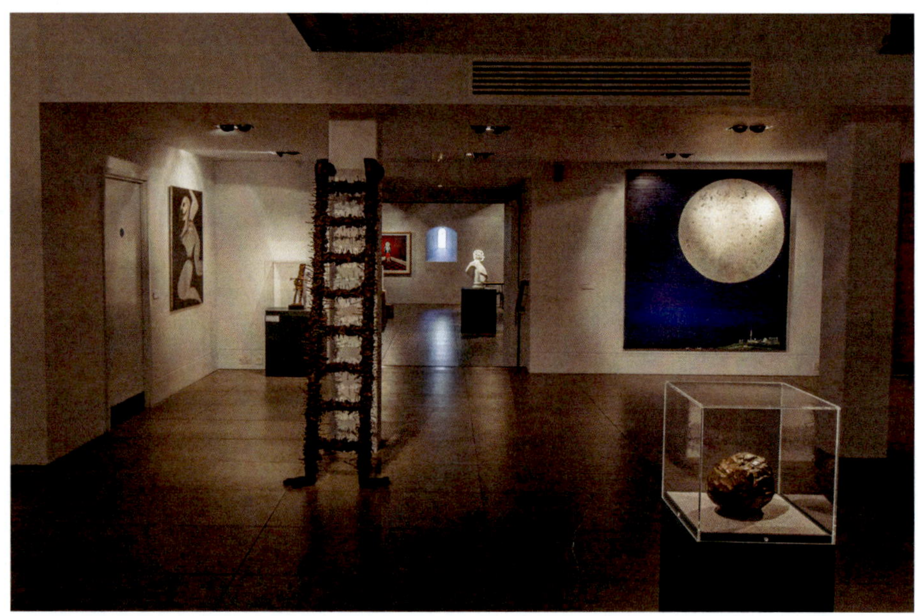

Success
1988
Ladder and mixed medium, 244x61x12cm (installation in *The Scottish Endark-enment* exhibition, 2016)

Reproduced courtesy of the artist and Dovecot Studios (photograph: Stuart Armitt)

Matthew Inglis Interview

Since leaving art college, you have participated in painting, sculpture and tapestry group shows. Was this a conscious decision to free your art from any easy pigeon-holing?
Not particularly. I trained within the tapestry department although I did little weaving. The main criterion then and now is basically to build a tradition of your own, not only realising your position within art but to try to understand and accept the influence of your time, your self-knowledge and your own economic and social history. Pigeon-holing may be other people's problem, it is not mine. I have more important issues to deal with, ie the problems of finding something to say, the content of my work and how I fulfil that in aesthetic terms. I have enough problems with that.

The traditional view of tapestry is that it is concerned with the art of making a finished object from raw materials. However, you seem to prefer to work with found objects which already have an identity before you get your hands on them. Why is this?
Using found objects is a tradition within art. I use them to make finished art objects. You still have to ask the same questions whether you use wool, sheet metal, paint or found objects. They enable me to build and compose other materials and act as a catalyst for ideas and trains of thought. They, of course, do have specific qualities which I hope to understand, the main one being the history within the object which I try not to supress and, at the same time, try to change by placing it within a new context of an artwork juxtaposed against other objects and mediums, hopefully enhancing its old identity by giving it a new one. One of the fundamentals of my work is the friction caused by the clash between social/political objectives, personal objectives and aesthetic objectives. The found object helps me to unite these elements by having strong ties to each.

Do you come across these 'found objects' by chance or do you go to certain sources because you know you will find what you are looking for?
Both. I am always looking for materials. Over the years, you find out where the skips, thrift shops and dumps are. One of the important things about the objects is that there may be an element of luck in finding them but there is no such element when I choose to use them within a piece.

The reason I asked the last question was to assess to what extent your work is motivated by a conscious political and social critique. Putting it crudely, do you see yourself closer to overtly political artists like John Heartfield and Conrad Atkinson or to the apolitical attitudes of Duchamp and the Neo-Dadaists like Johns and Rauschenberg?

I find Duchamp's work loaded with politics. I know he would deny any political intention was involved in recording specific political situations, choosing one side or the other. His work, however, is constantly involved with the right of the individual to challenge preconceptions. As I believe that art is part of the social/political/economic world and that the rights of the individual are one of the most important issues within that, Duchamp's work for me is political. Heartfield and Atkinson's work is obviously more publicly political, dealing with particular issues from their time, fighting propaganda with propaganda. Although I like Duchamp's work a great deal more, I do not see why I have to come down on one side or the other; there is room for both. The politics in my work are dictated by a desire to observe and record, to be a catalyst for discussion as opposed to trying to push my political opinions down people's throats. For when I do that, I diminish my work and patronise the viewer. It is what I choose to debate that reflects my position.

I realise this is a difficult question but, broadly speaking, what are the areas of 'debate' which you wish the viewer to consider and engage in when confronted with your work?
My major themes over the past few years have dealt with the effects and possible consequences that the consumer society and so-called affluence, including the nature of the media, have had on the freedoms and rights of the masses and the individual. Has the advance of communications and computers given more freedom of information or do they give more power to those who already have it? Can you go on strike or protest when you are up to your eyeballs in debt? The replacement of religion and its rituals by the pursuit of possessions (including art objects) or can you fill the vacuum created by the loss of belief in religion with toasters, two weeks in Benidorm or by the perceptions of the media? There has also been a series of one-off pieces influenced by specific events such as *Star Wars* and nuclear power that affect and worry me.

As a counter-balance to these, I have produced another body of work, an alternative which is about joy, hope and the possibility of what could be, revelling in the nature and beauty of the world – isn't Scotland stunning? – and of the human spirit and all its glories.

The third area is based on my own personal, intellectual and emotional experiences, often ritualistic, dealing with the necessities of life both physical and spiritual. Using myself as guinea pig, not to prove how individual I am, but hopefully to show how much human experience is shared.

These areas cross over, overlap and collide, providing different nuances and angles of debate, but all are reliant on my aesthetic ambitions and experience to be fulfilled.

There seems to me to be a strong narrative dimension to much of your art but of a fairy-tale quality – for example, walking tables or a giant boot coming through the clouds like a scene from Jack and the Beanstalk *in the*

piece titled Revenge. *What about, to quote St Paul, the 'childish things' in your work?*
My work recently is not so much influenced by children's art but by consumer goods made by adults for children. These include toys and cartoons. I owe Hanna-Barbera a lot. What I find interesting about these mediums is the imagination needed to create them and the way they seemingly communicate simply and with clarity. Yet like a lot of media, they are a form of undercover propaganda, perpetuating myths and stereotypes. Although I have an adult's idea of communication, the links with children enable me to take the stance of pretend innocent. Then I can look either at the world in wonderment or using the innocence by association against a political/personal theme to give my imagery/ideas more potency. The narrative dimension is strong at present because of this influence; however, I see it as just a part of my vocabulary, as are my more poetic, my matter-of-fact and my enigmatic pieces.

In a review of your recent Festival show, Territory, *one critic saw the exhibits as 'visual tragi-comedies'. Much of the creative energy of your work results from the tension of opposites. How important is this duality to your art?*
There are obvious links between opposites: humour comes from serious situations, fantasy can be an extension of realism, culture can be a luxury product and painting and sculpture are vocabularies within creativity. Nothing works in isolation but only in relation to other elements.

My work thrives on pulling out and using from all my observations and personal history, including humour, politics, emotions, intellect, aesthetics, experiences and opinions. I find that if I lean too much on one element of experience, say, politics, my work deteriorates. My art is the centre point where I try to understand and discuss the intricate and complex relations between all these factors. They are often not comfortable bedfellows; they have to be forced together. It is the battle to find a balance between contradictions that I find interesting, hopefully enhancing my subject and enabling me to provide something positive out of the milieu of contradictions.

The exhibition Territory was first shown at the Crawford Arts Centre, St Andrews, where you were artist-in-residence earlier this year. How important are such opportunities to a full-time practising artist like yourself, struggling to make a career in Scotland?
It was a great morale boost. It is good for anybody to have their work treated with respect. Publicly, it is important that people have contact with artists and vice-versa and, at the very least, I hope I managed to dispel the myth of the 'Artist' for some people. Within Scotland, there are many good young artists who are uncommercial or unfashionable, unsupported by dealers or power brokers, whose work deals with good old-fashioned artistic values, like personal integrity, quality and

risk – remember them? Residencies should have a policy of positive
discrimination in favour of these artists, as I believe the Crawford
has over the past three years. At the very least, the opportunity of the
platform, the morale boost, the support, should be seen to be available
to these artists, for it is very tough to work away without the hope of a
chance.

*One of my favourite satirical pieces by you, which is now in the Scottish
Arts Council collection, is entitled* Success. *It consists of a fetishist ladder
embedded with nails, doing a handstand against the wall. Is this how
success looks to you?*
It did then when I made it; it does today. There is danger in everything,
including lack of success – my next piece.

This interview, *Cultural Territory and Terrorism*, was conducted by Bill Hare in 1988
and published by *Alba*, issue 10.

Reflecting on the Box

The Art of Matthew Inglis

THE PAINTER WAS likened by Socrates to a man wandering around with a mirror desperately trying to capture the fleeting appearances of the world. Matthew Inglis is a very different calibre of artist than the Socratic one merely seeking mimetic illusionary effects in a naturalistic manner. The reality he is after is not something that is simply there and can be readily rendered into a convenient image but, on the contrary, has to be keenly sought, rigorously analysed and imaginatively constructed.

As with all creative disciplines, art grows out of its own particular history, within other contextual histories. There are also outside agencies – and their theoretical implications – which have played crucial roles in guiding and shaping the development of the history of art. Two of the most important are the 'mirror' and the 'box'. These highly influential instruments to which artists have regularly turned in their quest to give a more convincing representation of reality are nevertheless antithetical to each other. The mirror, on the one hand, with its apparently seamless ability to turn everything that falls within its sights into an arresting optical facsimile, misleads through its seductive illusionistic power which deceives as it distorts. By contrast, the box – the constructed space for pictorial and theatrical drama as exemplified by the work of Matthew Inglis – is not passively reflective but actively creative; presenting not fleeting glimpses of superficial experience, but rather, revealing reality's underlying psychological, economic, social and cultural workings, and how they relate and operate within and on each other.

Despite the range of serious issues facing the contemporary society that his art addresses, Matthew Inglis's 'diorama' boxes engage with his chosen topics of concern in a surprisingly playful way. He skilfully combines the thematic content of his art with the inventive and witty presentation of his intriguingly entertaining tableau scenarios. The particular feature of our contemporary consumer-orientated world, which seems to be the main source and inspiration for his art, is that of the ubiquitous cut-price store in which everything is forever in a transitory state of being desirable and expendable at one and the same time. He assiduously scans and sifts this raw material for the latest must-have attractions on offer in these plastic paradises. Perusing such stuff of other people's dreams, Matthew Inglis's encyclopaedic fascination with all that he casts his eye over is subsequently subjected to a highly complex process of selection. Those carefully chosen objects are removed and rearranged to take on fresh identities and different roles within a wide range of multi-layered mini-epic fables. Thus, all that normally would be dismissed as tawdry kitsch, lacking any artistic significance or cultural value, is transformed by a new investigative purpose, a radically different context and arresting presentation.

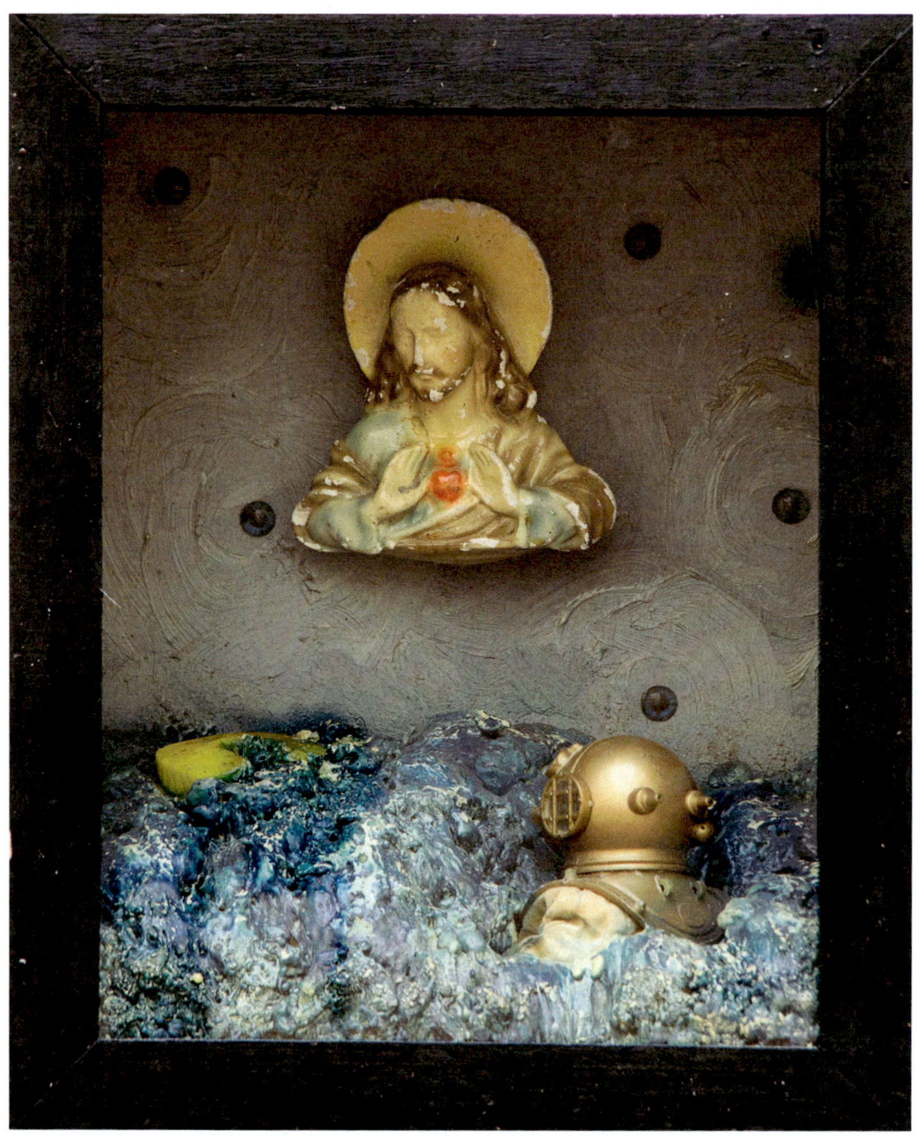

The Big C
2005
Mixed medium, 41x33x23cm

Reproduced courtesy of the artist

To return to the mirror, it can easily delude us with its judgmental reflection, which can ultimately pass an unforgiving verdict on our fractured failure to match up to the ideal image we have imposed on ourselves and others. With commitment and comedy, the art of Matthew Inglis is prepared to pick up the scattered and abandoned fragments of that tragic refracted reality and reconnect and reassemble them into a reconstituted vision of our lost childhood dreams, which not only enthrals and delights but can encourage resistance against the deceptions and delusional distractions of our fallen world.

This essay was written by Bill Hare in 2016 and published by Edinburgh College of Art.

Douglas Gordon

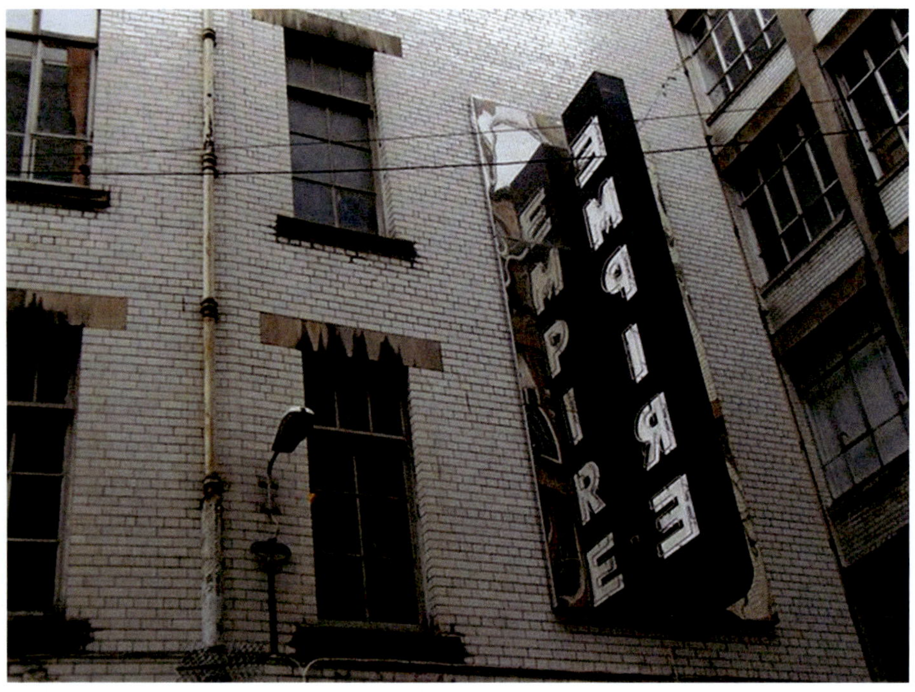

Empire Sign (day)
1997
Mixed media

Reproduced courtesy of the artist and Glasgow City Council

A Sign for our Times

Douglas Gordon's *Empire Sign*

THE TURNER PRIZE-WINNING and internationally acclaimed Scottish artist Douglas Gordon is forever on the move, travelling hopefully around the world from job to job like some itinerant medieval journeyman. Thus, as with many of his passing acquaintances, I have up until now, only met this artistic nomad on one occasion when, temporarily immobilised by a torn ligament football injury, I managed to catch him for an interview in his Glasgow flat, just round the corner from the School of Art. He graduated in 1988 and now occasionally teaches there. When we met in 1996, Gordon had been short-listed and was about to become the first Scottish artist to win the prestigious Turner Prize.

Needless to say, we never discussed art, but rather art-politics, football (Gordon is a Partick Thistle supporter for his sins), religion (we both come from an evangelical background) and his special passion, the cinema. On the latter topic, I don't recall we ever got round to the work of the avant-garde minimalist film-maker, Jean-Marie Straub. However, having seen Gordon's *Empire* installation in the narrow confines of Brunswick Street in Glasgow, I am reminded of Straub's film, *Leçons d'histoire*. In that piece of 1972, the French director simply placed the camera behind the anonymous driver of a car which seemed to wander aimlessly around the labyrinthine narrow alleys of Rome while, over the soundtrack, we hear random snippets of Roman imperial histories from the likes of Julius Caesar and Tacitus. Straub appeared to be implying that, no matter how far flung the Empire may stretch, it always has to return to its origins in the back streets of the City.

Straub's conceit of course raises one of the crucial obsessions of 'colonial discourse' – centre and periphery – but you can't tell a former native of Dumbarton like Douglas Gordon much about the peripheral. Originally hailing from that western outpost of civilisation, he prides himself in inheriting from his Dumbarton upbringing an ability to be 'underwhelmed' by most things that life and the art world care to throw at him. However, he did uncharacteristically allow his normal *sang-froid* to heat up during a recent interview for *Transcript* (volume 3, issue 3) when the question of Julian Spalding's Gallery of Modern Art (GOMA) was raised. Pulling no punches, Gordon angrily lashed out with:

> I despise anyone who claims to stand up and speak on behalf of Glaswegians and what they think Glaswegians are capable of understanding. How can he presume the taste of the city? How can he assume the intellectual inadequacies or attributes of a city?

Yet the Scots, and not just the Glaswegians, have a long and not very

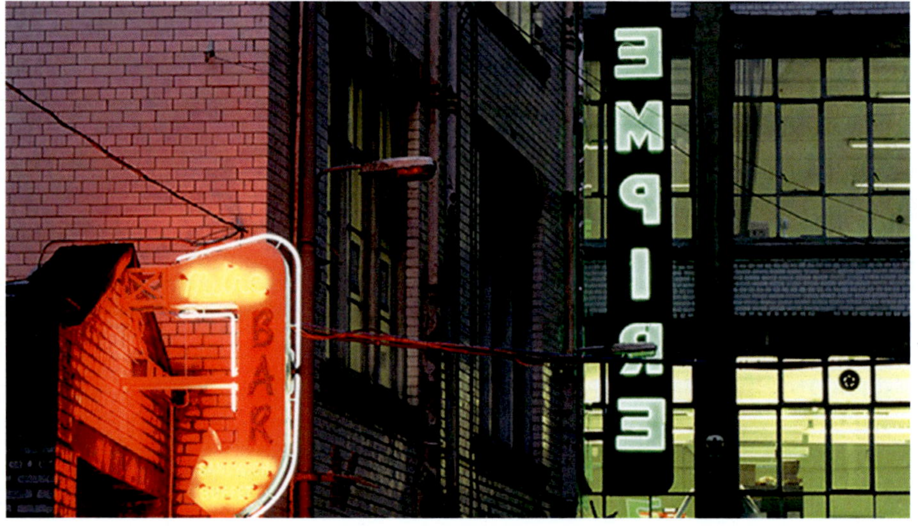

Empire Sign (night)
1997
Mixed media

Reproduced courtesy of the artist and Glasgow City Council

distinguished history of having their economic, political, social, cultural and aesthetic 'inadequacies', 'attributes', imposed upon them. You don't have to look far to find the most obvious and ubiquitous signs of this in the carefully chosen names given to the streets and squares in all our main towns and cities throughout Scotland. Leading with the example of the capital and its unequivocal subservient loyalty to its Hanoverian masters as expressed by the boulevards of the New Town, most of the major urban thoroughfares in Scotland read like a declaration of support for the British Union and its imperial and colonial ambitions. Clearly one can see this also in Glasgow with, for example, George Square (presided over by the effigy of that most loyal of loyalists, Walter Scott), Argyle Street, Brunswick Street and the likes of Jamaica Street in Merchant City, all going to prove that the 'Second City of the Empire' and 'the workshop of the world' was eager, whether in the slave trade or in heavy engineering, to live up to its given names.

As you battle against the mass of thronging shoppers in Argyle Street, you can easily pass by Brunswick Street almost without noticing it. Furthermore, as Gordon's *Empire* installation piece is placed fairly high up on a nondescript wall and also has to compete with a cluster of neon pub signs on the other side of the lane, you can readily be forgiven for missing it altogether. Yet this situation was carefully selected as the ideal one by the artist. As he stated, 'I always wanted to do something there, always loved the idea that it was almost a wee cinematic atmosphere in that lane'. So we are back in the world of films again and not surprisingly from the person who first gave us *24 Hour Psycho* at Tramway, Glasgow, in 1993, *Empire* has veiled Hitchcockian references and allusions, the most relevant being Hitchcock's celebrated masterpiece, *Vertigo* (1958). For it is in the *Empire* hotel of that film that the obsessive, megalomaniac detective, Scotty (James Stewart), relentlessly imposed his ruthless erotic fantasy onto his helpless victim, Judy (Kim Novak). Many, including the actress herself, have suggested that Hitchcock also might have been using the film to act out his own domineering impulses and desires. That being so or not, Hitchcock was nothing if not dictatorial – not only towards his somewhat unfortunate players, whom he once described as needing to be treated like 'cattle', but ultimately his ambition for absolute control also extended over the emotional response of his audience, whom he tended to treat as some kind of collective Pavlovian dog.

Hitchcock regarded the cinema as the 'Empire of the Senses', yet decidedly under his patriarchal sway. On the other hand, the antithesis of such an authoritarian approach is that of Andy Warhol, whose early film, again simply titled *Empire*, is a further allusion and reference embedded in Gordon's highly complex work. Warhol's ultra-documentary film is nothing more than an unbroken eight-hour static shot of New York's most celebrated landmark – the Empire State Building – as it lights up the Manhattan skyline throughout the night. Banal as it might seem, what Warhol innovatively brought to the cinema was the temporal freedom of the art gallery viewing experience. Having no plot to dictate to the audience, the viewer is free to look at Warhol's *Empire* as long, or as briefly as they wish, in the same way as they might engage with a painting or sculpture. Warhol is everything Hitchcock is not, and vice versa; and it is this central dialectical contrast between the two masters of narrative and non-narrative in cinema which lies at the heart of understanding and appreciating the art of Douglas Gordon. For it is here – where control and freedom face up to each other, and art and life collide – that *Empire* is to be found. As the artist himself explained about his hopes for his work, 'Maybe next time people see *Vertigo*, they might see something in the film that would remind them of real life'.

Such a speculative notion indicates Gordon's view of the highly complex and shifting relationship between the world we find ourselves in, and the reflective signs and iconic symbols we create for ourselves in order to understand and negotiate that world. For instance, *Empire* is an 'Alice through the Looking Glass' experience, where we are likely to misread the 'real' lettering as its mirror image, only to realise this when our mistake is pointed out to us in the reflecting plates attached to the wall beside the sign. This is only one of the many ambiguities and contradictions that are layered beneath the apparent simple surface appearance of *Empire*.

To attempt to unravel *Empire*'s multi-meanings we need to be 'active readers', not 'passive contemplators' as urged by Hal Foster. Being situated in the once foremost city of mass object production, we might firstly begin by asking the most obvious question – what kind of 'thing' might *Empire* be? Is it a bit of film memorabilia? Or a piece of monumental concrete poetry? Is it some public sculpture, in the same way as the stone and bronze statues raised to the illustrious corpses that populate George Square around the corner? Or is it merely more commercial signage, similar to those which grace the outside of the Mitre Bar across the way? *Empire* does not fit fully into any of these roles. Secondly, where exactly is it located? Is it at the centre of a great metropolis and former Imperial City? Up a blind alley? Or is it really only to be found in the random associations of the individual and collective memory? Furthermore, what of its changing appearance? Is this not another case of the metamorphosis of *Empire*'s protean condition? Stark, utilitarian white lettering during daylight, it transforms itself into a dream-like green-tinted aura once darkness begins to fold around the back streets of the city. Is it then that *Empire* really comes into its own and its true cinematic nature is allowed to body forth and display itself to those who can read its signs and fall under its spell?

Yet there is one particular area of concern which *Empire* encroaches upon that is less poetic and philosophical and more socio-political. It is also a discourse on Glasgow's, and Scotland's, function and role within British imperialism. We may think we are all now in a post-colonial era, but the legacy of imperialism is still very much with us, and 'its worst and most paradoxical gift' according to Edward Said 'was to allow the people to believe that they were only, mainly, exclusively white, or black or western or Oriental' (*Culture and Imperialism*). This colonial ideology of fixed and essential difference between us and the 'other' was created through the meta-narratives of imperialism. Again, Said points out:

> The power to narrate or to block other narratives from emerging is very important to culture and imperialism and constitutes one of the main connections between them

– in fact, 'nations themselves are narrations'. This is glaringly true of Scotland. We British Scots, as heirs to the mythic narratives of Ossian, Bonnie Prince Charlie, Rob Roy, Victorian Tartanry and Kailyard, Pontius Pilate's Bodyguard, Harry Lauder, King Billy, The Wembley Wizards, *The Sunday Post* and all kinds of latter-day celtic cultural and socio-political mythmaking, know all about this kind of narration to our sorry cost!

Douglas Gordon's *Empire* holds up a mirror to reflect, but also to reassess, the historical and contemporary reassuring assumptions we Scots have about ourselves. Employing a hidden array of subversive strategies, *Empire* deflects and challenges such all-embracing single fixed narrative meaning. Thus, for example, if *Empire* conjures up Loyalist red, white and blue, come nightfall Fenian emerald green then takes over. If you long to recall the glorious days of order and unity under the British Empire, where the sun never set, you also have to accommodate the allusion to the raucous anarchy of rowdy nights at the nearby Glasgow Empire music hall, that local bear-pit and graveyard of English entertainers. And after all that, when we Scots finally stare deeply into *Empire*'s mirror, who and what do we see there? Is it the helpless victim of English imperial oppression; or the eager, collaborative, acquisitive North British imperial racist? In the end *Empire* poses the crucial question, are we Scots the colonised or the colonisers?

This essay was written by Bill Hare in 2000 and published by *Cencrastus*, issue 65.

Kevin Harman

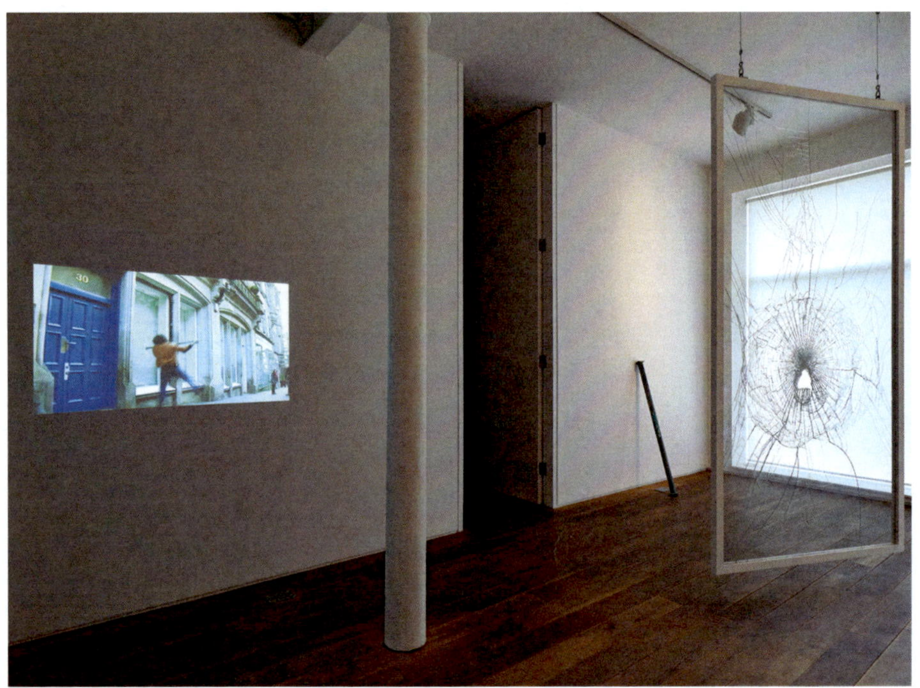

Brick
2009
Mixed media

Reproduced courtesy of the artist and Ingleby, Edinburgh (photograph: Finlay Pretsell)

Kevin Harman Interview

I know you have a brother who is also an artist – did you come from an artistic family?
I don't think they're artistic in an 'artist' sense but they were inventive and thrifty through necessity, wheeling and dealing if you like. My dad works as a butcher, he went from front of house in a butcher shop to a meat factory but was unemployed for large periods of time. Mum has been a stay-at-home mother for 99 per cent of the time I have known her. She's strong, determined and imaginative. My two older brothers and younger sister are creative with the eldest, Norrie being the first person in our whole family to go on to further education and get a degree in painting. So no, I'm not from an artistic family but imagination was our way out. It had to be when a holiday consisted of a bi-annual trip to the zoo!

When did you decide that you wanted to be an artist and needed to go to art college?
I didn't decide. Seems odd to me that people can choose to be artists. I remember going to see my older brother at art college. He showed me around the place, the materials, and the exotic people. I knew that it was the right place for me. The environment filled my lungs, to think I was doing a college course in digital design so I could use my talents to get a job! I quickly changed to a fine art foundation course which concentrated on portfolio building in preparation to art college – the rest is history.

Was Edinburgh College of Art what you expected? Did it give you the training and encouragement to develop your artistic ambitions in the way you wanted?
Edinburgh College of Art was a wonderful time in my life. Growing there among the building and everyone that was in it for six years was special. I got on with the work and maximised the opportunity. It exceeded my expectations.

You were an outstanding student and created quite a reaction and some notoriety with your post-graduate degree show (2010). Could you describe what was in the show and say something about your intentions behind the work you produced for it?
The work was titled *Brick* and it aimed to use a government-funded arts institution as the material. The project was designed to show that things aren't quite what they say on the tin – 'we celebrate and debate challenging work'. I neutered their control with a letter, broke a window and we stood back and watched it all unfold. I then displayed as much evidence as humanly possible to an audience in an exhibition and enjoyed a successful piece of institutional critique.

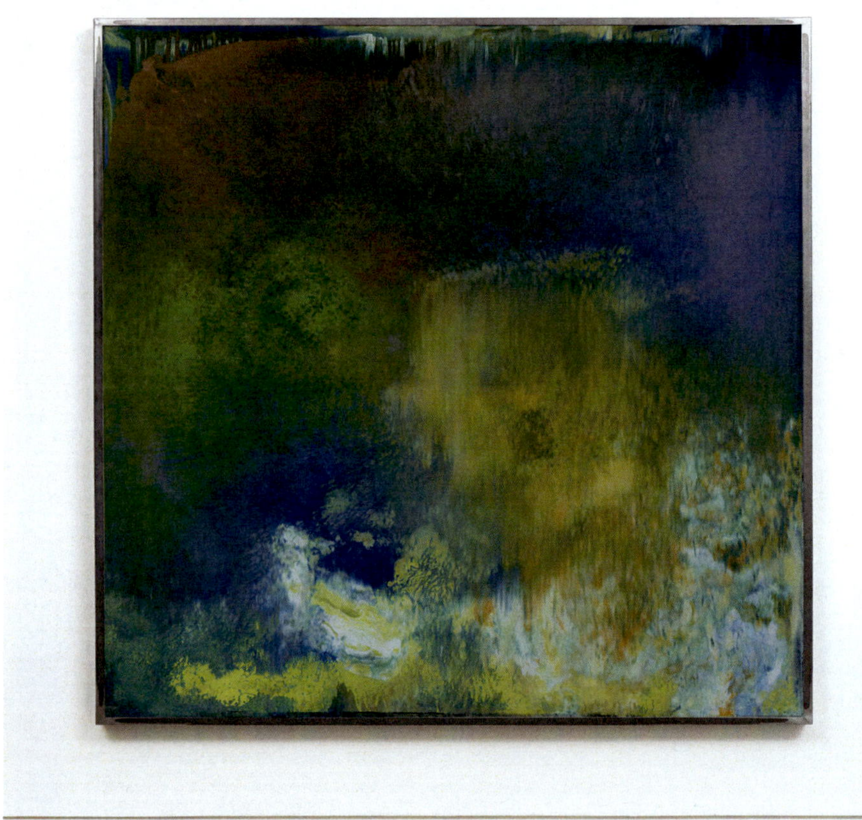

Carrier Frequency
2017
Household paint and double-glazing window unit, 201x201x6cm

Reproduced courtesy of the artist and Ingleby, Edinburgh (photograph: John McKenzie)

After leaving art college, you quickly made a reputation for yourself on the art scene. Do you see yourself as part of a 'generation' of young Scottish artists or as an outsider, doing his own thing?
I'm more of an outsider doing my own thing. I'm on the outside in an existential sense but physically too, probably because I keep doing projects that get me ousted. I'm constantly speculating and navigating from a distance, using myself in lots of the work as subject material. There are real risks and heightened emotions involved in the work so I don't blame anyone for turning a shoulder and not wanting to work with me. They might not like the projects or me but it doesn't matter – we still like them! We had a very strong group on the ECA Masters course and have continued to work as a collective, setting up project spaces in Glasgow, Edinburgh, Athens and London. We spur one another on through vigorous group critical debates and combatant quality assurance control. We are high achievers.

From where do you draw your inspiration and ideas for your highly varied work?
Hypocrisy, hierarchy, performance. People pretending to be fair and knowing full well it's not and will never be. Getting into the part of the mind that sits righteous and gaslighting it! I could write all day on my inspirations and it would only feel like the first sip of a large coffee with unlimited refills. Survival, people surviving, sadness…

As an art historian, I see traces in your art of Neo-Dadaism, performance, installation, social intervention and protest, yet, on the other hand, also high modern aesthetics as well. How do you reconcile such a variety of seemingly contradictory features?
I'm glad you are picking up on all these areas in the work as that's not by accident. I was heavily into embracing the Dadaists early on and took it to absurdity within my own practice. I feel a social responsibility to deliver a voice for people who haven't found theirs. I want less honest transparency and more dishonest transparency.

I would imagine that, financially, the highly successful double-glazed abstract paintings which you produce for your gallery are your main source of income. Do you see them as a means to finance the Neo-Dadaist side of your artistic operations or as an integral part of your overall work?
I was experimenting with the glassworks for years before the gallery began exhibiting them, since exhibiting them they have gone from strength to strength – I wish the same could be said for my back and knees! The thrill of making these delicious abstracts combine my influences with my passions and quite rightly have become the powerhouse of the practice. Most of my projects wouldn't get touched by government funding so I have to fund them myself. The gallery takes a

wide variety of my work and places it in good collections. I'm quite proud of not being a government-funded artist. I had my fill of free meals at school you see.

You have also been involved in putting on and curating exhibitions in your large studio and in various venues such as a warehouse depot in Leith Docks. Is this kind of curatorial activity something you want to continue to explore?
It's a great thing to be able to facilitate and discuss other people's visions, to work with other creatives whose work you want to get to know better. Putting together exhibitions is a great way to do this so, yes, I would like to keep building on that side of things.

You have moved to Glasgow. Do you find it a more exciting and challenging place than Edinburgh and a better place to be for your future career?
I moved to Glasgow for a couple of key reasons. I was having too much fun in Edinburgh – there was lots of good quality activity going on but too many distractions. I was drinking and partying like a fiend. Still nailing work though. My family and friends are in Edinburgh and they would come around the studio for a chat and a beer – it's not their fault but it was killing me. Few people understand the amount of work and how serious it is being on the forefront of the ideas to creation. So I moved to Glasgow to stop having such a good time and to get the head down. The community is really good here. As far as a career goes, it's not something I particularly engage with. I think the career is built by others and the momentum of the work. The stories around the work are what they are.

Finally, how would you describe the present art scene in Scotland at the end of the second decade in the 21st century?
No bad, Bill, no bad.

This interview was conducted by Bill Hare in 2019 for this book.

Timeline

1945   Hugh MacDiarmid opens New Scottish Group exhibition in Glasgow.
Society of Scottish Artists exhibit a major group show of contemporary French art.

1946   Paolozzi makes his first series of collages.
Arts Council of Great Britain formed.

1947   The first Edinburgh International Festival.
Royal Scottish Academy shows *Scottish Art from 1900*.
SSA exhibits *Modern Scottish Painting*.
Paolozzi's first exhibition at the Mayor Gallery, London.
Paolozzi moves to Paris.

1948   Turnbull moves to join Paolozzi in Paris.
Eardley elected SSA; travels to Italy.
Davie shows for the first time in Venice during the first post-war Biennale and meets Peggy Guggenheim.

1948–9   William Gear exhibits with cobra group in Amsterdam.
Paolozzi and Turnbull visit Giacometti and Brâncuși in their Paris studios.

1950   SSA exhibit a group German Expressionist show.
Paolozzi and Turnbull return to London.
Davie's first solo exhibit at Gimpels Fils in London.
Paolozzi and Turnbull show at the Hanover Gallery in London.

1951   Paolozzi designs a fountain sculpture for the Festival of Britain, the South Bank, London.
Gear controversially wins a prize for his abstract landscape in the Festival of Britain exhibition *Sixty Paintings for '51*.
Eardley visits Catterline for the first time.

1952   Paolozzi and Turnbull selected for Herbert Read's group exhibition *New Aspects of British Sculpture* shown at the British Pavilion in the Venice Biennale.
Paolozzi presents his *Bunk* slideshow at an Independent Group lecture at the ICA in London.

1953   Davie, Paolozzi and Turnbull hired to teach in various departments by William Johnstone, Principal of the Central School of Arts and Crafts in London.

The Independent Group, including Paolozzi and Turnbull, mount *Parallel of Life and Art* exhibition at the ICA in London.

1954   Eardley shows at the Parsons Gallery in London.
Davie creates a studio and house at Gamels, Hertfordshire and shows regularly at Gimpel Fils in London.

1955   Eardley shows her controversial *Sleeping Nude* at the Royal Glasgow Institute.

1956   Paolozzi and Turnbull contribute to the Independent Group's exhibition, *This is Tomorrow*, at the Whitechapel Art Gallery in London.
Paolozzi stars in Lorenza Mazzetti's film *Together*.
Tate Gallery shows the abstract expressionist exhibition *Modern Art in the United States*.
Davie awarded the Gregory Fellowship in Painting and has his first American exhibition at Catherine Viviano Gallery in New York where he meets Pollock, Rothko and de Kooning.

1957   Foundation of the artist-run 57 Gallery in Edinburgh.
Turnbull has his first major solo exhibition at the ICA in London.
Joan Hills and Mark Boyle meet in Harrogate.

1958   Davie has a work bought by the Tate Gallery and has his first retrospective exhibition at the Whitechapel Gallery in London.

1959   Scottish National Gallery of Modern Art at Inverleith House is given government approval.
Davie has a number of major exhibitions abroad and wins several awards.
Craigie Aitchison has his first solo exhibition at Beaux-Arts Gallery in London.
Jim Haynes opens Paperback Bookshop in Edinburgh and becomes a centre for avant-garde activity in the arts.

1960   The Scottish National Gallery of Modern Art is opened by Kenneth Clark.
Paolozzi moves to teach in Hamburg.

1961   Ian Hamilton Finlay and Jessie McGuffie found Wild Hawthorn Press.
Boyle and Hills make their first assemblages.

1962   Scottish National Gallery of Modern Art show *Contemporary British Sculpture*.
Paolozzi begins making screen prints at Kelpra Studios in London and works with CW Juby in Ipswich.

1963   Traverse Theatre Club, with the Richard Demarco Gallery, opens and shows the Boyles' junk reliefs in the restaurant.
The EIF's International Drama Conference in the McEwan Hall stages the Boyles' happening *In Memory of Big Ed*.

1964   *Joan Eardley* memorial exhibition.
Mark Boyle and Joan Hills make their first replication of a section of ground surface.
John Bellany and Alexander Moffat show their paintings on railings outside the RSA.

1965   Bellany and Moffat again show their paintings outside the RSA.
Boyle Family begin the resin earth studies with their *Shepherd Bush Series*.

1966   Ian and Sue Finlay settle at Stonypath, Lanarkshire, and start working on their neo-classical garden, later to be known as Little Sparta.
Demarco opens his gallery in Melville Crescent, Edinburgh.
Auto-Destructive Art event staged by Ivor Davies in Edinburgh.

1967   Scottish Arts Council established.
Edinburgh Printmakers set up.

1968   Compass Gallery in Glasgow opens.
The random selection of sites for Boyle Family's *World Series* held at the ICA in London.

1969   Bellany finishes at the Royal College of Art and takes a teaching post at Winchester School of Art.
Boyle Family launch their *World Series* with the object of replicating 1,000 sites around the globe.

1970   Demarco and Joseph Beuys organise *Strategy: Get Arts* at Edinburgh College of Art.
The Talbot Rice Art Centre is opened at the University of Edinburgh

1971   Eduardo Paolozzi's retrospective at the Tate Gallery in London.
Scottish Realism exhibition, including the work of John Bellany and Alexander Moffat, a Scottish Arts Council touring show.

1973   Collins Gallery, University of Strathclyde, opens.
Glasgow Printmakers Studio founded.
William Turnbull: Sculpture and Paintings, Retrospective, Tate
Gallery in London.
*A View of the Portrait: Portraits by Alexander Moffat 1968–
1973*, Scottish National Portrait Gallery

1974   Peacock Printmakers founded in Aberdeen.
Aspects of Abstract Painting in Britain 1910 1960 at the Talbot
Rice Art Centre in Edinburgh.
Joseph Beuys: Three Pots Action exhibition and Oil Conference,
Forrest Hill in Edinburgh.

1975   *Edinburgh Ten 30 Works of Ten Edinburgh Artists 1945–75*,
Scottish Arts Council exhibition.
Glenshee Sculpture Park founded.
Third Eye Centre in Glasgow founded.
Fruitmarket Gallery in Edinburgh founded and run by the
Scottish Arts Council.

1976   MacLaurin Art Gallery in Ayr opens.
Graeme Murray Gallery in Edinburgh founded.
Paolozzi touring ACGB touring exhibition.
Mark Boyle and Ian Hamilton Finlay feature in the group
exhibition *Inscape* at the Fruitmarket Gallery.
Paolozzi commissioned to design doors for the Hunterian Art
Gallery, University of Glasgow.

1977   Crawford Arts Centre founded at the University of St Andrews.
Workshop & Artists Studio Provision (wasps) founded in
Glasgow, Edinburgh, Aberdeen and Dundee.
Stills Scottish Photography Gallery founded in Edinburgh.
Four Abstract Artists, including the work of John McLean and
Fred Pollock shown at the Fruitmarket Gallery in Edinburgh.
Clement Greenberg writes the foreword in the catalogue.
Joan Eardley exhibition at the RSA.
Expressionism and Scottish Painting, Scottish Arts Council
Collection exhibition.

1978   369 Gallery founded in Edinburgh.
Scottish Sculpture Trust founded.
Boyle Family represent Britain at the Venice Biennale.
Painters in Parallel: 76 20th Century Scottish Artists, a Scottish
Arts Council exhibition at Edinburgh College of Art.
Scottish Arts Council Travelling Gallery established.

1979   The Pier Arts Centre, Stromness, Orkney opens.
Alan Davie: Magic Pictures shows at The Scottish Gallery in
Edinburgh.

1980   Scottish Sculpture Workshop opens at Lumsden, Grampian.
City Art Centre reopens in Edinburgh.
William Johnstone ACGB retrospective exhibition comes to the
Talbot Rice Gallery in Edinburgh.
Watermarks an exhibition of work by Robert Callender and
Elizabeth Ogilvie at the Fruitmarket Gallery in Edinburgh.
Paolozzi commissioned to design mosaics for Tottenham Court
Road Underground Station in London.

1981   *Contemporary Abstraction: Younger Scottish Artist,* New 57 Gallery
in Edinburgh.
Scottish Sculpture Open at Kildrummy Castle, Grampian.
Jock McFadyen appointed Artist in Residence at the National
Gallery, London.

1982   *Federation of Scottish Sculptors* founded. Bill Scott is Secretary.
Expressive Images (Group show including Steven Campbell) at
the New 57 Gallery in Edinburgh.
Scottish Art Now (Group show including John Kirkwood) at
the Fruitmarket Gallery in Edinburgh.
Steven Campbell moves to New York.
Steven Campbell, his first solo show at Barbara Toll Fine Arts in New York.

1983   Artist-run Transmission Gallery opens in Glasgow.
Ian Hamilton Finlay's First Battle of Little Sparta with
Strathclyde Regional Council.

1984   Scottish National Gallery of Modern Art moves to John
Watson's Building, Belford Road in Edinburgh

1985   June Redfern appointed artist-in-residence at National Gallery
in London.
New Image-Glasgow (Group show including Steven Campbell
and Ken Currie) at the Third Eye Centre in Glasgow.

1986   Paolozzi appointed Her Majesty's Sculptor in Ordinary in Scotland.
Ken Currie commissioned to paint murals for the People's
Palace in Glasgow.
Boyle Family have a retrospective exhibition at the Hayward
Gallery in London.
John Bellany exhibition at Scottish National Gallery of Modern
Art in Edinburgh.

1987   *The Vigorous Imagination: New Scottish Art* exhibition at SNGMA.

1988   *Ken Currie* exhibition at the Third Eye Centre in Glasgow.
Joan Eardley exhibition at the Talbot Rice Gallery in Edinburgh.

1989   *Contemporary Scottish Painting* at 369 Gallery in Edinburgh.
Scottish Art since 1900 opens at Scottish National Gallery of Modern Art in Edinburgh and goes on to Barbican Art Gallery in London.

1990   Glasgow is nominated European City of Culture.
Steven Campbell exhibits *On Form and Fiction* at the Third Eye Centre, Glasgow.

1992   *Alan Davie Works on Paper*, British Council International Touring Exhibition of Europe and South America.

1993   Douglas Gordon's 24 *Hour Psycho* shown for the first time at Tramway in Glasgow.

1996   Douglas Gordon is the first Scottish artist to win the Turner Prize.
Glasgow Museum of Modern Art (goma) opens.
William Turnbull: Sculpture and Paintings, retrospective exhibition at the Serpentine Gallery in London.

1997   Douglas Gordon represents Great Britain at the Venice Biennale.

1998   The Modern Institute opens in Glasgow.
Ingleby Gallery opens in Edinburgh.

1999   Dundee Contemporary Arts opens.

2000   *Alan Davie* retrospective exhibition at the Scottish National Gallery of Modern Art.

2001   Martin Creed wins Turner Prize with controversial *Work No. 227: The lights going on and off*.
Doggerfisher Gallery opens in Edinburgh.

2002   Callum Innes wins the Jerwood Painting Prize and later has major solo show at the Fruitmarket Gallery in Edinburgh.

2003   *Boyle Family*, retrospective exhibition at the Scottish National Gallery of Modern Art.

2004   The biannual Glasgow International Festival of Visual Art is launched.

2005   *William Turnbull. Retrospective 1946–2003* opens at the Yorkshire Sculpture Park.

2006   Douglas Gordon's *Zidane: A 21st Century Portrait* is premiered at the Cannes Film Festival.
Alison Watt appointed artist-in-residence at the National Gallery in London.

2007   Bill Scott becomes the first sculptor to be appointed President of the Royal Scottish Academy.

2008   Luke Fowler wins the inaugural Derek Jarman Award for experimental artist film.

2009   Martin Boyce represents Scotland at the Venice Biennale and wins the Turner Prize.

2010   Susan Philips is the first sound artist to win the Turner Prize.

2011   Martin Creed's multi-marble *Work No. 1059. Scotsman Steps* is opened in Edinburgh.

2012   David Shrigley's solo show *Brain Activity* opens at the Hayward Gallery in London.

2013   National Galleries of Scotland mount major John Bellany retrospective exhibition in the Royal Scottish Academy.

2014   *Generation: 25 Years of Contemporary Art in Scotland* opens in venues all over Scotland.

2015   Tramway in Glasgow hosts the Turner Prize.

2018   Rachel Maclean shows her film *The Lion and the Unicorn* at the National Gallery in London.

2019   Edinburgh Printmakers moves to a new venue at the Castle Mills Complex in Edinburgh.
Joyce Cairns is appointed the first woman President of the Royal Scottish Academy.

Select Bibliography

Essential publications on Scottish modern art

Gage, E, *The Eye in the Wind: Contemporary Scottish Painting since 1945* (London, 1977)

Hardie W, *Scottish Painting. 1937 to the Present* (Glasgow, 1990)

Hare, B, *Contemporary Painting in Scotland* (Sydney, 1993)

Hartley, K, *Scottish Art since 1900* (London, 1989)

Hartley, K et al., *The Vigorous Imagination: New Scottish Art* (Edinburgh, 1987)

Macmillan, D, *Scottish Art in the 20th Century* (Edinburgh, 2000)

Patrizio, A, *Contemporary Sculpture in Scotland* (Sydney, 1999)

Richardson, C, *Scottish Art since 1960: Historical Reflections and Contemporary Overviews* (London, 2011)

Strang, A, *A New Era: Scottish Modern Art 1900–1950* (Edinburgh, 2018)

General publications on Scottish modern art

Birrell, R and Finlay, A, *Justified Sinners: An Archaeology of Scottish Counter-culture (1960–2000)* (Edinburgh, 2002)

Campbell, M, *Line of Tradition: Watercolours, Drawings and Prints by Scottish Artists 1700–1990* (Edinburgh, 1993)

Cornish, S, *Stockwell Depot: 1967–79* (Greenwich, 2015)

DCA, *Here and Now. Scottish Art 2000–1* (Dundee, 2001)

Dewey, A, *New* (Edinburgh, 2002)

Edinburgh Review, New Scottish Painting (Edinburgh, 1986)

Edinburgh Review, Art and Scotland, Issue 91 (Edinburgh, 1994)

Finlay, I, *Art in Scotland* (Oxford, 1948)

Firth, J, *Scottish Watercolour Painting* (Edinburgh, 1979)

Fruitmarket Gallery, *Scottish Art Now* (Edinburgh, 1982)

Van Raaij, S, *Glasgow Gallery of Modern Art: The First Years* (Glasgow, 1996)

Harris, P and Halsby, J, *The Dictionary of Scottish Painters 1600–1960* (Edinburgh & Oxford, 1990)

Macdonald, M, *Scottish Art* (London, 2000)

Macmillan, D, *Scottish Art 1460–2000* (Edinburgh, 2000)

Normand, T, *The Modern Scot* (London, 2000)

Pearson, F et al., *Virtue and Vision: Sculpture in Scotland 1540–1990* (Edinburgh, 1991)

Scottish Arts Council, *Scottish Realism* (Edinburgh, 1971)

Elliot, P, ed, *The Concise Catalogue of the Scottish National Gallery of Modern Art* (Edinburgh, 1993)

Third Eye Centre, *Built in Scotland* (Glasgow, 1983)

Third Eye Centre, *New Image Glasgow* (Glasgow, 1985)

Third Eye Centre, *Scatter, New Scotland* (Glasgow, 1989)

White, N, ed, *New Art in Scotland* (Glasgow, 1994)

Wishart, A and Oliver, C, *The Society of Scottish Artists: The First 100 Years* (Edinburgh, 1991)

General publications on British post-war art

Buck, L, *Moving Targets: A User's Guide to British Art Now*, Vols 1 & 2 (London, 1997, 2001)

Garlake, M, *New Art/New World: British Art in Postwar Society* (Yale, 1998)

Harrison, M, *Transition: the London art scene in the Fifties* (London, 2002)

Hyman, J, *The Battle for Realism* (Yale, 2001)

Massey, A, *The Independent Group* (Manchester, 1995)

Morris, F, *Paris – Post War Art and Existentialism 1945–55* (London, 1994)

Royal Academy, *British Art in the 20th Century: The Modern Movement* (London, 1987)

Hughes, MM et al., *Blast to Freeze: British Art in the 20th Century* (Wolfburgh, 2002)

Selected publications on the individual Scottish artists featured in this book

ACGB, *Craigie Aitchison: Paintings 1953–1981* (London, 1981)

Haste, C, *Craigie Aitchison: A Life in Colour* (London, 2014)

McEwan, J, *John Bellany* (Edinburgh, 1994)

Hartley, K et al., *John Bellany* (Edinburgh, 2012)

Elliott, P & Hare, B, et al., *Boyle Family* (Edinburgh, 2003)

Hayward Gallery, *Beyond Image: Boyle Family* (London, 1986)

Locher, JL, *Mark Boyle's Journey to the Surface of the Earth* (Stuttgart, London, 1978)

Hare, B et al., *Joyce Cairns: War Tourist* (Aberdeen, 2006)

Macmillan, D, *The Paintings of Steven Campbell: The Story So Far* (Edinburgh, 1993)

Carrell, C, ed., Cocker, D., *Sculpture and Related Works* (Glasgow, 1986)

Normand, T, *Ken Currie: Details of a Journey* (London, 2002)

Hare, B, *Ken Currie: Age of Uncertainty* (Glasgow, 1992)

Bowness, A, *Alan Davie* (London, 1967)

Hare, B et al., *Alan Davie: Works on Paper* (London, 1992)

Hare, B, *Alan Davie: Channels of Communication* (Harrogate, 2006)

Hall, D et al., *Alan Davie* (London, 1992)

Elliott, P, *Alan Davie: Works in the Scottish National Gallery of Modern Art* (Edinburgh, 2000)

Elliott, P, *Joan Eardley: A Sense of Place* (Edinburgh, 2016)

Oliver, C, *Joan Eardley* (Edinburgh, 1988)

Andreae, C, *Joan Eardley* (London, 2013)

Pearson, F, *Joan Eardley* (Edinburgh, 2007)

Brown, K, *Douglas Gordon* (London, 2004)

Woods, A, *Douglas Gordon Transcript, Vol 3, Issue 3* (Dundee, 1999)

Hartley, K et al. *Douglas Gordon: Superhumanatural* (Edinburgh, 2006)

Abrioux, Y, *Ian Hamilton Finlay: A Visual Primer* (London, 1993)

Hendry, J, ed. Ian Hamilton Finlay issue in *Chapman No.78/9* (Edinburgh, 1994)

Sutherland, G et al., *Lys Hansen; Passionate Paint* (Edinburgh, 1998)

Macmillan, D, *Jock McFadyen* (Edinburgh, 2001)

Cohen, D, *Jock McFadyen: A Book about a Painter* (London, 2009)

Collins, I, *John McLean* (London, 2009)

Sykes, D ed., McLean, J, *Recent Work in Context* (St Andrews, 1998)

Hare, B, *Facing the Nation: The Portraiture of Alexander Moffat* (Edinburgh, 2018)

Ascherson, N, *Sandy Moffat: Seven Poets* (Glasgow, 1981)

Collins, J, *Eduardo Paolozzi* (London, 2014)

Pearson, F, *Eduardo Paolozzi* (Edinburgh, (1999)

Spencer, R, ed, *Eduardo Paolozzi: an anthology* (Oxford, 2001)

Thomson, A ed., Paolozzi, E. *Edinburgh Review No.104* (Edinburgh, 2000)

De Luca, C et al., *Paolozzi at Large in Edinburgh* (Edinburgh, 2018)

Wardell, G et al., *Barbara Rae* (London, 2008)

National Gallery, *June Redfern: Artist in Residence* (London, 1986)

Hare, B, *Paul Reid: The Art of Mythmaking* (Harrogate, 2014)

Elliott, P et al., *William Turnbull: Sculptures and Paintings* (London, 1995)

Davidson, AA, *William Turnbull: The Sculpture of William Turnbull* (London, 2005)

Fruitmarket Gallery, *Alison Watt: Fold (New Paintings 1996–97)* (Edinburgh, 1996)

Wiggins, C et al., *Alison Watt: Phantom* (London, 2008)

Abbot Hall Art Gallery, *Alison Watt A Shadow on the Blind,* (Kendal, 2018)

Acknowledgements

This book covers over 30 years of my writing on Scottish artists and my heartfelt thanks go to all those numerous people – in a range of different capacities – with whom I have had the pleasure to work over that time.

More specifically, for the publication of this book, I would first and foremost like to express my gratitude to the artists who agreed to be included, many of whom also took the trouble to supply images of their work.
I would further like to thank all the others – whether individuals, photographers (especially Ralph Hughes), galleries or institutions – for responding to my request for illustrations. Over the years I have been fortunate to be asked to write articles for a number of publications and this gives me an opportunity to thank all those exhibiting artists, gallery owners, exhibition curators, art magazine editors and publishers who have allowed me to express my critical opinions and aesthetic views in print. I must also thank the University of Edinburgh's History of Art department for providing me with all the facilities to compile and write this publication.

Finally I must thank all those who were involved in the production of this book: my good friend and long-time colleague Andrew Patrizio for writing the Foreword; the director of Luath Press, Gavin MacDougall, for agreeing to publish my writings, my editor Maia Gentle for all her useful advice and support and special thanks also to Duncan Thomson and Jennie Renton.

Luath Press Limited

committed to publishing well written books worth reading

LUATH PRESS takes its name from Robert Burns, whose little collie Luath (*Gael.*, swift or nimble) tripped up Jean Armour at a wedding and gave him the chance to speak to the woman who was to be his wife and the abiding love of his life. Burns called one of the 'Twa Dogs' Luath after Cuchullin's hunting dog in Ossian's *Fingal*. Luath Press was established in 1981 in the heart of Burns country, and is now based a few steps up the road from Burns' first lodgings on Edinburgh's Royal Mile. Luath offers you distinctive writing with a hint of unexpected pleasures.

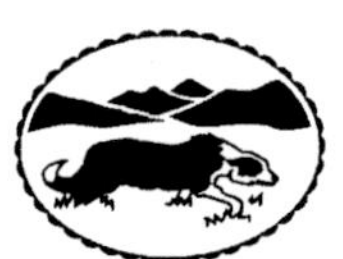

Most bookshops in the UK, the US, Canada, Australia, New Zealand and parts of Europe, either carry our books in stock or can order them for you. To order direct from us, please send a £sterling cheque, postal order, international money order or your credit card details (number, address of cardholder and expiry date) to us at the address below. Please add post and packing as follows: UK – £1.00 per delivery address; overseas surface mail – £2.50 per delivery address; overseas airmail – £3.50 for the first book to each delivery address, plus £1.00 for each additional book by airmail to the same address. If your order is a gift, we will happily enclose your card or message at no extra charge.

Luath Press Limited
543/2 Castlehill
The Royal Mile
Edinburgh EH1 2ND
Scotland
Telephone: 0131 225 4326 (24 hours)
Fax: 0131 225 4324
email: sales@luath.co.uk
Website: www.luath.co.uk